T0351070

# Federated Learning for Internet of Medical Things

The book intends to present emerging Federated Learning (FL)-based architectures, frameworks, and models in Internet of Medical Things (IoMT) applications. It intends to build on the basics of the healthcare industry, the current data sharing requirements, and security and privacy issues in medical data sharing. Once IoMT is presented, the book shifts towards the proposal of privacy-preservation in IoMT, and explains how FL presents a viable solution to these challenges. The claims are supported through lucid illustrations, tables, and examples that present effective and secured FL schemes, simulations, and practical discussion on use-case scenarios in a simple manner. The book intends to create opportunities for healthcare communities to build effective FL solutions around the presented themes, and to support work in related areas that will benefit from reading the book. It also intends to present breakthroughs and foster innovation in FL-based research, specifically in the IoMT domain. The emphasis of this book is on understanding the contributions of IoMT to healthcare analytics, and its aim is to provide insights including evolution, research directions, challenges, and the way to empower healthcare services through federated learning.

The book also intends to cover the issues of ethical and social issues around the recent advancements in the field of decentralized artificial intelligence. The book is mainly intended for undergraduates, post-graduates, researchers, and healthcare professionals who wish to learn FL-based solutions right from scratch and build practical FL solutions in different IoMT verticals.

# Federated Learning for Internet of Medical Things
## Concepts, Paradigms, and Solutions

Edited by
Pronaya Bhattacharya,
Ashwin Verma, and Sudeep Tanwar

CRC Press
Taylor & Francis Group
Boca Raton  London  New York

CRC Press is an imprint of the
Taylor & Francis Group, an **informa** business

First edition published 2023
by CRC Press
6000 Broken Sound Parkway NW, Suite 300, Boca Raton, FL 33487–2742

*CRC Press is an imprint of Taylor & Francis Group, LLC*

ISBN: 978-1-032-30076-4 (hbk)
ISBN: 978-1-032-30078-8 (pbk)
ISBN: 978-1-003-30337-4 (ebk)

DOI: 10.1201/9781003303374

Typeset in Times LT Std
by Apex CoVantage, LLC

# Contents

# Preface

This book discusses the introduction of Federated Learning (FL) integration in Internet of Medical Things (IoMT)-based ecosystems. With the rising concerns of privacy-preservation compliance worldwide, FL simplifies healthcare data privacy and allows local devices to collaboratively form shared prediction models, and thus ensures the privacy and anonymity of patient data. Thus, FL-based approaches are critical in assuring privacy laws and regulations that satisfy the outlook of the U.S. Healthcare Information Portability and Accountability Act (HIPAA), the European Union's General Data Protection Regulation, and other laws across the globe. The book forms a self-contained and paced roadmap that starts with the basics of fundamentals of IoMT and patient-centric healthcare management, and successively builds the importance of healthcare informatics in IoMT. The book presents the reference architectures, models, frameworks, and assisted case studies that establish the importance of FL in today's healthcare industry. The book discusses security-based and privacy-based FL solutions that assist and improve healthcare informatics and asserts the importance of decentralized learning over centralized models. The book also illustrates the applications of FL in edge/fog-based IoMT solutions that handle real-time streaming analytics. From a practical perspective, the book presents the practical simulation tools and platforms for the deployment of FL in IoMT. Finally, the book provides the importance of trusted FL, which mitigates adversarial attacks in IoMT ecosystems, and presents interesting use-cases and scenarios with practical FL deployments in IoMT ecosystems. Thus, the book covers the entire spectrum of FL-based solutions for IoMT from scratch and builds upon theoretical concepts, practical solutions, and security approaches. The book is presented in a simple and lucid writing style, is intended for both academia and healthcare industry professionals, and serves to address the issues of presenting FL in IoMT representing both implementation and security viewpoints. Readers of the book are expected to have a simple understanding of basic calculus, linear algebra, artificial intelligence (AI), and healthcare industry domain knowledge for an enriched reading experience. The purpose of this edited book is to propose the basics and introduction to FL in IoMT ecosystems. Through the book, we present effective and novel frameworks that can address security and privacy preservation concerns via FL models, and at the same time, ensure low-powered computational requirements. The book covers the tools, platforms, and case studies to integrate FL-based solutions for edge-fog ecosystems, and assisted IoMT in smart patient-centric healthcare. The book proposes novel architectures that drive economically viable healthcare businesses, and serves key research directions among academia, healthcare industry professionals, and researchers.

The book is organized into three sections. The first section is focused on the background and preliminaries, which includes four chapters. The second part illustrates the security use-cases of IoMT with four well-structured chapters. Finally, the last section focuses on FL-based IoMT with five chapters.

## SECTION 1 BACKGROUND AND PRELIMINARIES

The opening Chapter 1, "Potentials of Internet of Medical Things: Fundamentals and Challenges," presents insights of IoMT related to various factors to answer the basic curiosity of the reader, like how IoMT works, its framework, its technology front, its dependence on other sectors, etc. The chapter also discusses various initiatives taken by the government on IoMT fronts.

Chapter 2, "Artificial Intelligence Applications for IoMT," presents how IoMT devices can use AI and cloud computing and enhance the degree of diagnostic with pace and accuracy. IoMT has the ability to enhance early diagnoses, even as additionally bearing in mind statistics series for analytics, making it a win-win scenario for patients and people who take advantage of it.

Chapter 3, "Privacy and Security in Internet of Medical Things," brings an understanding of how IoMT is adopted in the medical field now and the various security challenges, along with technological solutions. The chapter also discusses the advanced technologies used in IoMT devices, different IoMT devices, all the possible threats and challenges, and the security requirement for IoMT devices. Solutions started incorporating federated learning to enhance the accuracy and security of the devices.

Chapter 4, "IoMT Implementation: Technological Overview for Healthcare Systems," discusses the role of federated learning in IoMT systems which provide security to end users. The study proposed consists of the architecture, benefits, and challenges of IoMT devices. With IoMT implementation in the healthcare domain, patients can control and manage their medical records in a better way. This technology has the potential to ensure better health facilities for everyone.

## SECTION 2 SECURITY USE-CASE OF IOMT

Chapter 5, "A New Method of 5G-Based Mobile Computing for Internet of Medical Things (IoMT) Applications," presents methods that encompass efficient resource allocation and greater ability to carry out computation, communication, strategy, and control on the network. The proposed scheme in this chapter supports a content-centric network (CCN)-based framework over 5G as the primary motivator for mobile health (m-health) applications. A practical example has been discussed in the proposed scheme for m-health services, which forms one of the emerging applications of 5G and IoMT networks. A medical image containing the electronic patient record is embedded in the speech signal. The proposed technique has several advantages like better management of resources, security, traffic unloading, and scalability

Chapter 6, "Trusted Federated Learning Solutions for Internet of Medical Things," provides the reader with an overview of federated learning systems, with a focus on trustworthy cloud computing factors, and discusses the broad solutions to federated learning's statistical challenges, system challenges, and privacy concerns, as well as the implications of implementing blockchain and other machine learning capabilities in the healthcare system.

Chapter 7, "Early Prediction of Prevalent Diseases Using Internet of Medical Things (IoMT)," presents cloud computing-based remote patient monitoring (RPM)

architecture, comprising a data collection module, a data preprocessing module, and a data analytics module, whereby stakeholders, doctors, patients, caregivers, and family members can access the analytics and prediction results computed by the model. Also, the recommendation module of the architecture will help patients with expert advice for the disease diagnosed.

Chapter 8, "Trusted Federated Learning for Internet of Medical Things: Solutions and Challenges," provides current state-of-the-art solutions, adoption challenges and future research directions, and a framework for trusted federated learning in healthcare applications. As artificial intelligence (AI) models require high-quality and large-scale training datasets collected from diverse sources to mitigate bias and better aid prediction accuracy on the unseen data. With secure and trusted federated learning, an organization's data can stay local and contribute to AI models' training for building better-trained models with improved accuracy and generalization. Thus, the trusted federated learning approaches facilitate sharing the trained AI models across different participating healthcare organizations by breaking down barriers, increasing trust, and preserving privacy for better disease predictions and diagnoses that can increase the deployment of AI models in clinical practice.

Chapter 9, "Security and Privacy Solutions for Healthcare Informatics," discusses the significance of protection and privacy in the healthcare system, possible cyber-attacks, and network security to avoid active attacks, and also presents a novel study on decentralized storage for healthcare and the implications of quantum-safe block-chain methodologies and their relevance to IoMT.

## SECTION 3 FEDERATED LEARNING–BASED IOMT

Chapter 10, "IoT-Based Life-Saving Devices Equipped with Ambu Bags for SARS-CoV-2 Patients" proposed a Internet of Things (IoT)-based healthcare system featuring an automatically operated Ambu bag (the proprietary name for a self-inflating resuscitation bag) that might be utilized to save patients' lives. The system can use a NodeMCU (node microcontroller unit, a low-cost open source IoT platform) to continually monitor the patient's oxygen saturation, pulse rate, and body temperature by using a DS18B20 temperature sensor at room temperature from any location in the world.

Chapter 11, "Security and Privacy in Federated Learning–Based Internet of Medical Things," discusses an FL-based healthcare system that secures and protects user privacy. The proposed framework uses the Paillier cryptosystem. It uses additive homomorphism for aggregating and training data in global data centers. Initially, the model collects the data specific to each organization and trains the model locally. Periodically, the data available in each data center is encrypted and sent to the global data center. At the global data center, the wearable resources and medical data are aggregated using the unique ID. Public key cryptography with additive homomor-phism is applied to ensure secure data aggregation and training in the global data center. A trusted party is involved in generating private and public keys for the local and global data centers.

Chapter 12, "Use-Cases and Scenarios for Federated Learning Adoption in IoMT," sheds light on the various divisions of federated learning in smart healthcare use-cases. These divisions comprise FL for electronic health record (EHR) management, remote health monitoring, medical imaging, and other exceptional use-cases. The chapter also browses through some of the recent use-cases of FL and shares deductions regarding FL's reliability based on relevant empirical findings. In order to recognize FL in real-world settings, a section on real-world implementation is also stated. To finalize things, the future scope for this reasonably new field of study and various findings based on FL's limitations is presented.

Chapter 13, "Blockchain for Internet of Medical Things," focuses on the usage of the blockchain framework, its challenges, and further research in the healthcare domain. As healthcare data is used often by all stakeholders, confidentiality and integrity of this data should be protected from unofficial access attempts within the network as well as from external attackers. Ensuring EHR security is an important but challenging task. Therefore, to maintain a definite trust during an exchange of EHR among all stakeholders and to secure data from misuse, blockchain technology is required.

**Dr. Pronaya Bhattacharya**
*Kolkata, India*

**Mr. Ashwin Verma**
*Ahmedabad, India*

**Dr. Sudeep Tanwar**
*Ahmedabad, India*

# About the Editors

**Pronaya Bhattacharya** is currently employed as an associate professor with the Department of Computer Science and Engineering, Research and Innovation Cell, Amity University, Kolkata, West Bengal, India. He received his Ph.D. degree in optical networks from Dr. A. P. J. Abdul Kalam Technical University, Lucknow, Uttar Pradesh, India, in 2021. He has more than eight years of teaching experience. He has authored or coauthored more than 100 research papers in leading SCI journals and top core IEEE COMSOC A\* conferences. Some of his top-notch findings are published in reputed SCI journals like *IEEE Journal of Biomedical and Health Informatics, IEEE Transactions on Vehicular Technology, IEEE Internet of Things Journal, IEEE Transactions on Network Science and Engineering, IEEE Access, Transactions on Emerging Telecommunications Technology* (Wiley), *Expert Systems* (Wiley), *Future Generation Computer Systems* (Elsevier), *Optical and Quantum Electronics* (Springer), *Wireless Personal Communications* (Springer), *ACM-MOBICOM, IEEE-INFOCOM, IEEE-ICC, IEEE-CITS, IEEE-ICIEM, IEEE-CCCI,* and *IEEE-ECAI.* His Google Scholar has 1472 citations to his credit with an H-index of 20, an i10-index of 36, and 873 citations in Scopus, with an H-index of 15. His research interests include healthcare analytics, optical switching and networking, federated learning, blockchain, and the IoT. He has been appointed as a technical committee member and session chair across the globe. He is a lifetime member of professional societies like ISTE and IAENG. He was awarded the seven best paper awards in *Springer ICRIC2019, IEEE-ICIEM 2021, IEEE-ECAI 2021, and Springer COMS2 2021.* He is a reviewer of 17 reputed SCI journals, like *IEEE Internet of Things Journal, IEEE Transactions on Industrial Informatics, IEEE Access, IEEE Network, ETT* (Wiley), *IJCS* (Wiley), *MTAP* (Springer), *OSN* (Elsevier), *WPC* (Springer), and others.

**Ashwin Verma** is currently employed as an assistant professor with the Department of Computer Science and Engineering, Institute of Technology, Nirma University. He received B.Tech. degree in IT from DAVV, Indore, and the M.Tech. degree in CSE from NIT, Jaipur, in 2013. He is currently pursuing a Ph.D. degree in CSE with Amity University, Jaipur, Rajasthan. He has seven years of teaching and academic experience. He has authored and coauthored more than six articles in leading SCI journals and IEEE conferences. Some of his top findings are published in *IEEE Journal of Biomedical and Health Informatics, IEEE Sensor Journal, Journal of Information Security and Applications* (Elsevier), *IEEE-ICIEM 2021,* and many more. His research interests include healthcare 4.0, federated learning, blockchain technology, and 5G and beyond communications. He was awarded the Best Research Paper Award in IEEE-ICIEM 2021, London, UK.

**Sudeep Tanwar** (Senior Member, IEEE) is working as a full professor at the Nirma University, India. He is also a Visiting Professor with Jan Wyzykowski University, Poland, and the University of Pitesti, Romania. He received B.Tech in 2002 from Kurukshetra University, India, M.Tech (Honors) in 2009 from Guru Gobind Singh

Indraprastha University, Delhi, India and his Ph.D. in 2016 with specialization in Wireless Sensor Networks. He has authored 4 books and edited 20 books and more than 300 technical articles, including top cited journals and conferences, such as *IEEE TNSE, IEEE TVT, IEEE TII, IEEE TGCN, IEEE TCSC, IEEE IoTJ, IEEE NETWORKS, IEEE WCM, ICC, IWCMC, GLOBECOM, CITS,* and *INFOCOM.* He initiated the research field of blockchain technology adoption in various verticals in the year 2017. His H-indices as per Google Scholar and Scopus are 61 and 49, respectively. His research interests include blockchain technology, wireless sensor networks, fog computing, smart grid, and the IoT. He is a member of the Technical Committee on Tactile Internet of IEEE Communication Society. Recently, he has been awarded a cash prize of Rs, 50,000 for publishing papers with 5+ Impact factor and publishing books with Springer, IET, and CRC under the scheme of "Faculty Awards and Incentives" of Nirma University for the year 2019–2020. He has been awarded the Best Research Paper Awards from *IEEE IWCMC-2021, IEEE ICCCA-2021, IEEE GLOBECOM 2018, IEEE ICC 2019,* and *Springer ICRIC-2019.* He has won the Dr. K.W. Wong Annual Best Paper Prize (with 750 USD) for 2021 sponsored by Elsevier (publishers of JISA). He has served many international conferences as a member of the Organizing Committee, such as the Publication Chair for FTNCT-2020, ICCIC 2020, and WiMob2019, and as General Chair for IC4S 2019, 2020, 2021, 2022, ICCSDF 2020, FTNCT 2021. He is also serving the editorial boards of for *COMCOM* (Elsevier), *IJCS* (Wiley), *Cyber Security and Applications* (Elsevier), *Frontiers of Blockchain, SPY,* Wiley, *IJMIS Journal of Inderscience, JCCE,* and *JSSS.* He is also leading the ST Research Laboratory, where group members are working on the latest cutting-edge technologies.

# Contributors

**Karthik Ajay**
Vellore Institute of
Technology
Vellore, Tamil Nadu, India

**Sakeena Akhtar**
Department of Electronics and I.T.
University of Kashmir
Srinagar, Jammu and Kashmir,
India

**Rehana Amin**
Govt Medical College
Srinagar, Jammu and Kashmir,
India

**Jonathan Atrey**
Vellore Institute of Technology
Vellore, Tamil Nadu, India

**Pronaya Bhattacharya**
Department of Computer Science and
Engineering
Research and Innovation Cell, Amity
University
Kolkata, West Bengal, India

**Madhuri Bhavsar**
Department of Computer Science and
Engineering
Institute of Technology, Nirma
University
Ahmedabad, Gujarat, India

**Jaimik Chauhan**
Department of Computer Science and
Engineering
Institute of Technology, Nirma
University
Ahmedabad, Gujarat, India

**Shivani Desai**
Department of Computer Science and
Engineering
Institute of Technology, Nirma
University
Ahmedabad, Gujarat, India

**Pranshav Gajjar**
Department of Computer Science and
Engineering
Institute of Technology, Nirma
University
Ahmedabad, Gujarat, India

**Prasad Gokhale**
Vishwakarma University
Pune, Maharashtra, India

**Bramah Hazela**
Amity School of Engineering and
Technology, Amity University
Jaipur, Rajasthan, India

**Md Ilyas**
Prestige Institute of Engineering,
Management and Research
Indore, Madhya Pradesh, India

**Ankit Jain**
Pranveer Singh Institute of
Technology
Kanpur, Uttar Pradesh, India

**Bivin Joseph**
Vellore Institute of Technology
Vellore, Tamil Nadu, India

**Pranalini Joshi**
Vishwakarma University
Pune, Maharashtra, India

**Rupal Kapdi**
Department of Computer Science and
Engineering
Institute of Technology, Nirma
University
Ahmedabad, Gujarat, India

**G.R. Karpagam**
Department of Computer Science and
Engineering
PSG College of Technology
Coimbatore, Tamil Nadu, India

**Sagar Lakhanotra**
Department of Computer Science and
Engineering
Institute of Technology, Nirma
University
Ahmedabad, Gujarat, India

**Abhishek S. Mattam**
Vellore Institute of Technology
Vellore, Tamil Nadu, India

**Tanisha Mishra**
Amity School of Engineering and
Technology, Amity University
Jaipur, Rajasthan, India

**Sajid Nazir**
Glasgow Caledonian University
Glasgow, Scotland, United Kingdom

**Jigna Patel**
Department of Computer Science and
Engineering
Institute of Technology, Nirma
University
Ahmedabad, Gujarat, India

**Jitali Patel**
Department of Computer Science and
Engineering
Institute of Technology, Nirma
University
Ahmedabad, Gujarat, India

**Shital Patel**
Department of Computer Science
and Engineering
Institute of Technology, Nirma
University
Ahmedabad, Gujarat, India

**Vivek Kumar Prasad**
Department of Computer Science
and Engineering
Institute of Technology, Nirma
University
Ahmedabad, Gujarat, India

**Sohan R.**
Vellore Institute of Technology
Vellore, Tamil Nadu, India

**Rajeev Raghuvanshi**
Prestige Institute of Engineering,
Management and Research
Indore, Madhya Pradesh, India

**Ramani Selvanambi**
Vellore Institute of Technology
Vellore, Tamil Nadu, India

**Pooja Shah**
Department of Computer Science
and Engineering
Institute of Technology, Nirma
University
Ahmedabad, Gujarat, India

**Neha Sharma**
Prestige Institute of
Engineering, Management
and Research
Indore, Madhya Pradesh, India

**Javaid A. Sheikh**
Department of Electronics
and I.T.
University of Kashmir
Srinagar, Jammu and Kashmir,
India

**Anita Shukla**
Pranveer Singh Institute of
  Technology
Kanpur, Uttar Pradesh, India
  Raghvendra Singh
  Department of Electronics and
  Communication Engineering
PSIT, Kanpur, Uttar Pradesh,
  India

**Shikha Singh**
Amity School of Engineering and
  Technology, Amity University
Jaipur, Rajasthan, India

**Jainil Solanki**
Department of Computer Science and
  Engineering
Institute of Technology, Nirma
  University
Ahmedabad, Gujarat, India

**Garima Srivastava**
Amity School of Engineering
  and Technology, Amity
  University
Jaipur, Rajasthan, India

**Swathi J.**
Department of Computer Science and
  Engineering
PSG College of Technology
Coimbatore, Tamil Nadu, India

**Hua Tianfield**
Glasgow Caledonian University
Glasgow, Scotland, United Kingdom

**Sadhana Tiwari**
Prestige Institute of Engineering,
  Management and Research
Indore, Madhya Pradesh, India

**Akash Vegada**
Department of Computer Science and
  Engineering
Institute of Technology, Nirma
  University
Ahmedabad, Gujarat, India

**Ashwin Verma**
Department of Computer Science and
  Engineering
Institute of Technology, Nirma
  University
Ahmedabad, Gujarat, India

**Tarjni Vyas**
Department of Computer Science and
  Engineering
Institute of Technology, Nirma
  University
Ahmedabad, Gujarat, India

**Yan Zhang**
Glasgow Caledonian University
  Glasgow, Scotland, United Kingdom

# 1 Potentials of Internet of Medical Things
## Fundamentals and Challenges

*Tanisha Mishra, Shikha Singh,*
*Bramah Hazela, and Garima Srivastava*

## CONTENTS

DOI: 10.1201/9781003303374-1

## 1.1  INTRODUCTION

Internet of Things, or IoT, is shaping up the world fast and branching into various sectors to ease human labour in an advanced and efficient way. One such sector is medical. The medical technology ('medtech') industry produces and develops a broad array of products, from pregnancy testing kits to surgical tools, prosthetic joints, and MRI scanners. Internet of Medical Things (IoMT) is a connected infrastructure of health systems and services that allows these gadgets to generate, gather, scrutinize, and transfer data [1]. IoMT is a linkage of Internet-connected medical equipment, hardware infrastructure, and software applications that connect healthcare IT [2]. The path to IoT began with some graduate students of the computer science department at Carnegie Mellon University connecting a modified Coke vending machine to the internet, back in 1982. This resulted in a smart device which would provide network status reports about inventory and temperature control.

The trend of wearable watches can be dated back to 1500 with Peter Henlein, a locksmith and clockmaker from Nuremberg, Germany, inventing small and watches to be worn as a necklace or attached to clothes. Today there is a wide market of watches with advanced escalation of technology which turns it into more than just a watch. Modern-day wearable technologies can connect to your smartphone and enable you to surf the internet, play music, make phone calls, text, and monitor heart rate, oxygen level, sleep, workout routines, calorie count, etc. [3]. Vaccine distribution with the help of drones and IoT devices helps to improve the proper vaccination in remote areas [4], and blockchain technology provides trust architecture in such scenarios [5]. IoT in the healthcare sector has transformed views of patient care and treatment in the field over recent decades. IoT in the healthcare system has been ingrained in current mechanisms, primarily in the context of real-time remote patient monitoring, health data collection and transfer, and end-to-end connectivity that aids in patient management automation at organizational units and facilitates interoperability, data flow, critical data analyzation and exchange, and machine communication. To maintain the trust in the sensitive medical records, we need cryptographic solutions [6] and if the volume of such medical records is high, it requires efficient access to that data [7]. In the context of health diagnostics, the IoT has aided in the transformation of routine clinical check-ups to become more patient and domestic rather than hospital centric. As a result, IoT in healthcare has helped to re-define monitoring, diagnostics, treatments, and therapies in traditional healthcare viewpoints, lowering costs and mistakes [8]. IoMT in healthcare sector enables the rise of smart hospitals equipped with smart automated and optimized medical technology based on ICT infrastructure, which enhances patient care techniques. IoMT is not just confined to patient care techniques; it also expands to various other areas, giving rise to a variety of services like telemedicine, telehealth, and remote robot surgery which may house smart hospitals. Providing patient treatment remotely is known as telemedicine, while providing non-clinical care remotely is known as telehealth. In remote robot surgery, medical robots perform surgery while being supervised by a surgeon who is in a different location.

Figure 1.1 depicts an illustration of a digital health system in which data from various sources is first gathered (for example, remotely or physically) and then sent to an EHR (electronic health records) system. Unstructured data may be used to describe

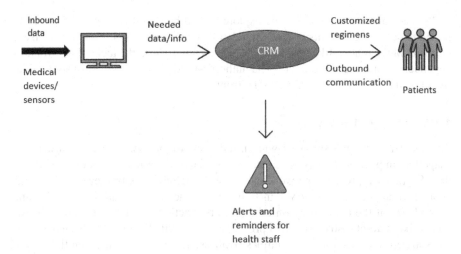

**FIGURE 1.1** Smart Healthcare System [9].

information that has been collected by professionals and written in hospital records. It is simpler to process data in other systems, such as CRM (customer relationship management) systems, when it is collected from sensors and devices in a structured manner using designated data fields that users must fill out. Utilizing tools to evaluate data and then assigning it to a predefined target within the network is made possible by the CRM. Patients and medical workers in the ecosystem receive additional inputs as a consequence of the processed data. Patients get outbound communication in the form of customized health regimens from physicians and healthcare specialists. The same CRM solution in the ecosystem notifies physicians and other therapeutic workers about reminders and other notifications [9].

### 1.1.1 Contribution

IoMT is a group of medical devices and applications that connect to healthcare information technology (IT) systems via online computer networks. Medical devices equipped with Wi-Fi–enabled machine-to-machine (M2M) communication, which is the basis of IoMT. Connecting to cloud platforms like Amazon Web Services (AWS) allows IoMT devices to store and process acquired data. IoMT is yet another name for healthcare IoT. IoMT is a part of IoT focused solely on solving healthcare and medical-related problems. The impact of IoMT on the healthcare sector market is hence undeniably positive and continues to reflect a bright scope. The IoMT market is made up of smart devices including smartwatches and medical/vital monitors that are only used for healthcare purposes on the body, at home, in surrounding communities, health centres, or hospital settings, as well as any related real-world environment, telehealth, and other services. This technology, if applied in healthcare, can bring changes to in-home, on-body, in the community and in-hospital healthcare services. IoMT has a myriad of advantages—and some challenges, too.

Its reach and ways are yet being explored—and here in this chapter, the authors intend to delve into insights of IoMT in relation to various factors to answer the basic curiosity of the reader, like how IoMT works, its framework, the technology front, its dependence on other sectors, etc. The authors would also discuss on various initiatives taken by government on the IoMT front.

### 1.1.2   CHAPTER LAYOUT

The chapter starts in Section 1.1 with introduction to the topic, covering how IoMT shaped its impact on society. The rest of this chapter is organized as explained further. Section 1.2 presents the working of IoMT, including its framework, and talks about current scenarios of IoMT in India and in the world's leading countries and dependence of the technology on other sectors. Section 1.3 covers economic viewpoints like market distribution and profit and loss, while Section 1.4 discusses various start-ups and Section 1.5 examines rivalries, awareness and trust on the part of public, and the impact of the COVID-19 pandemic on the same. Furthermore, a brief discussion on various pros and cons of IoMT is described in Section 1.6. Section 1.7 offers deep insight on the various challenges to IoMT, followed by covering government's initiative in this area in Section 1.8. The chapter is summed up in Section 1.9, where conclusions are drawn to support the entire contents of the chapter.

## 1.2   WORKING OF INTERNET OF MEDICAL THINGS

The framework of IoMT can be mainly classified into the following three layers (see Figure 1.2).

**Things Layer:** The things layer is composed of equipment for patient monitoring, sensor systems, actuators, health records, controls for pharmacies, as generator for feeding schedules, and other items. This layer is in direct touch with the ecosystem's users. At this layer, data from wearable tech, patient-health data, and distant healthcare data is gathered. To maintain the integrity of the data acquired, the devices utilized should be securely housed. The ecosystem's local routers are in charge of connecting these devices to the fog layer. The data is further analyzed at the fog and cloud layers to offer pertinent information. Furthermore, healthcare professionals may access patient data using this router to decrease delays [9, 10].

**Fog Layer:** This one lies in the midst of the things and clouds layers. This layer entails local servers and gateway devices for a thinly dispersed fog networking system. Local processing power is used by lower layer devices to give their users real-time responses. Additionally, the security and integrity of the system are monitored and maintained using these servers. Records from these servers must be routed through the gateway components of this tier toward the cloud layer for the further administration. Furthermore, healthcare professionals may access patient data using this router to decrease delays [9].

**Cloud Layer:** Data storage and computing resources are part of the cloud layer, which is used to analyze data and create judgement systems from it. Large healthcare and medical firms may simply manage their daily operations thanks to the cloud's extensive reach. The data produced by the healthcare system will be stored in this layer's cloud resources, where analytical work can be done as needs arise in the future [9, 11].

Many opportunities are opened up by the growth of IoT products specifically for the healthcare industry, and the massive amount of data generated by these connected devices has the potential to completely change the healthcare industry.

The four steps of IoT architecture can be thought of as steps in a process (See Figure 1.3). Each of the four phases is connected to the others in a way that allows information to be captured or interpreted at one level and thereafter transferred to another. By incorporating values into the process, new business opportunities are created and insights are produced [12].

**Step 1:** The initial phase is the deployment of interconnected devices, such as video systems, monitors, detectors, actuators, sensors, and actuators. These gadgets are what gather the data.
**Step 2:** Analogue information collected via sensors and other technologies must be converted into digital data in order to be processed further.
**Step 3:** The information is then pre-processed, standardized, and transmitted to a data centre or the cloud after being digitized and aggregated.
**Step 4:** The resulting data is processed and reviewed at the necessary level. Advanced analytics offers useful business insights for enhanced decision-making when implemented to this data.

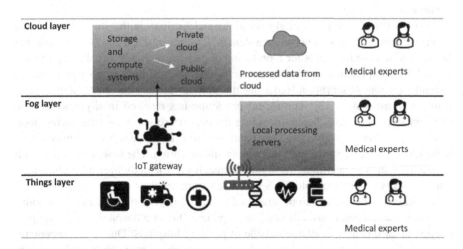

**FIGURE 1.2** Layers of IoMT [9].

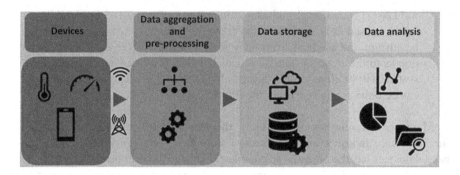

**FIGURE 1.3**  Architecture of IoMT [12].

By ensuring better care, optimal treatment results, and reducing rates for patients, as well as better processes and workflows, superior efficiency, and a quality therapeutic experience for healthcare professionals, IoT is revolutionizing the industry [12].

### 1.2.1  CURRENT SCENARIO OF IOMT IN INDIA

For a fast-developing country like India, healthcare is amongst the most crucial areas in requisites of need, economy, services, and revenue. The medical sector of India is supported by enhanced private investment and medical tourism. Medical tourism has two basic demands—excellent facilities and low costs. IoMT, as we discuss in the chapter, is just the way to achieve this. Government insists upon finding a promising solution that reaps profits and boosts economy of the country. IoMT can cut down healthcare expenses and provide effective and efficient treatment of the patients—not only to attract foreign patients, but the technology shall also help boost the facilities provided to the nation's public, hence lowering the need for people to fly elsewhere for treatment.

IoMT is transforming hospital operations and facilitating the shift of healthcare services from hospitals to private residences. The recent COVID-19 pandemic has heightened the requirements for monitoring of patients remotely and the deployment of IoMT in outpatient and residential care scenarios, resulting in a surge in online consultation and observation, reducing the number of hospital visits, and thereby limiting transmission [13]. The recent pandemic has resulted in skyrocketing use of technology in various fields, including the healthcare sector. As the saying goes, "there's opportunity in adversity"; the pandemic, too, has given way to enhanced technological advancements through innovation and invention. The new normal demands a paradigm shift to acclimate to digital outreach via telemedicine and e-pharmacy. On of the key changes unfolding is how healthcare services are not restricted only to hospitals anymore, but can be stretched to the comfort of the patient's own home. Although many operations still need an in-patient stay in a hospital, a growing proportion of care is now available outside of primary hospitals. Due to advancements in telemedicine, secondary and tertiary care set-ups now reasonably offer better care for fewer patient. One of the advantages served is that specialists who work solely for primary hospitals in major cities are no longer restricted to serving patients in person. Patients at secondary hospitals, tertiary institutions, and even remote clinics can be treated electronically. Patients and doctors may now monitor conditions at a previously unheard-of level thanks to smart gadgets. Applications for consumer devices like smartwatches and fitness bands deliver real-time data to patients and allow physicians to track data over time. Monitoring certain situations is achievable using medical-specific gadgets such as monitoring patches and heart rhythm monitors. Lower-level hospitals might transfer more information to experts at main facilities using services like DocBox, which captures and transmits up to three terabytes of structured data per patient every day. In India, IoMT innovation is already under way. Ansys and the Indian Institute of Technology Kanpur have formed a company to develop a modular, energy-efficient, and low-cost ventilator. The company Nocca Robotics Private Limited plans to create these ventilators with an IoMT functional design that will allow them to be controlled from a central place, allowing resources to be used more efficiently. In light of the COVID-19 pandemic, the need is evident, but the advantages of IoMT programmes in India will be considerably greater. If India's healthcare system is to improve significantly, a greater emphasis on preventative care is required. Improving general wellbeing relieves pressure on the medical system's resources, while also lowering patient care costs. In a country where only approximately 15% of people have insurance, lowering prices is a key aspect in increasing people's accessibility.

The improvements brought about by IoMT, artificial intelligence (AI), and other technology breakthroughs have the aptitude to completely overhaul India's healthcare system. Providers will be better able to offer more preventative care as access, monitoring, inventory dependability, and new research all improve, resulting in a lower demand for reactive therapies. The data supplied by IoMT is intelligent and quantifiable, allowing for speedier and more precise diagnosis and more efficient and successful therapy. IoMT allows for remote clinical monitoring, preventative treatment, chronic illness, and administration of medications, and it aids to those needing succour with routine tasks—such as the aged and disabled—to subsist more independently or therapies that are reactive [14].

## 1.2.2 PROGRESS IN IoMT IN THE WORLD'S LEADING COUNTRIES

### 1.2.2.1 France
France has been ranked among one of the world's best countries in the IT healthcare sector for 2022. Some of the reasons are listed as follows [15].

**Doubled Healthcare IT:** The 2012 Hospital Plan in France aims to increase expenditure on Hospital Information Systems (HIS) from 1.7% to 3%, putting the country towards the bottom of the EU league table. Modernizing HIS is one of the plan's overarching goals. The financial commitments are substantial. The Hospital Investment Plan 2012, according to the main French financial newspaper *Les Echos*, would require a €10 billion investment over five years.

**The ATIH:** The Technical Agency for Hospitalization Information (known by its French acronym ATIH) was established in France in 2000, and this decision's roots can be located there. The primary hospital information system for the nation is coordinated technically by the ATIH, a government institution. Its purpose was to replace laborious, expensive, and slow traditional data handling and transmission processes between hospitals and local healthcare establishments, as well as to meet the demand for more regular administrative data access in domains like pathology, patient care, and diagnosis.

**Smart Cards and Biometrics:** With a focus on smart cards, a technology in which France has long been a pioneer, ATIH joined forces with another top IT programme in France. The allegedly smart health card, initially presented in 1998, was primarily designed to computerize medical services, simplifying and expediting this process. The CPS smart card, which is designed to give healthcare workers access to the e-health infrastructure, now has around 600,000 users. In addition, the Carte Vitale—for patients— is used by about 60 million people. The year 2006 saw the new editioned Carte Vitale established (first in Brittany and the Pays de la Loire), with the goal of covering the whole population by 2010.

**Activity-Based Hospital Financing:** The development of new activity-based financing methods at hospitals in 2004 gave France's healthcare IT reform programme a boost. This has prompted them to improve IT systems to guarantee that clinical activity is correctly recorded in order to be reimbursed. In addition, increased awareness of variables such as return on investment (ROI) and quality of care measures is increasing want for healthcare IT.

**DMP:** In order to create an electronic medical record for every French citizen covered by health insurance, the dossier medical personnel (DMP), sometimes known as a 'personal medical file', was formed in 2004. Comparable to similar programmes elsewhere in Europe, the DMP intends to improve information exchange and synchronization between medical practitioners and medical centres during the consultation process, diagnostic testing, and treatment in order to increase healthcare competence and eminence. By enabling patient record access at any location and at any time, the DMP aims to boost treatments continuum and efficacy overall.

### 1.2.2.2   United Kingdom

**Government Support of Medtech:** The best National Health Service (NHS), in the UK, creates a centralized network that permits the easy and quick construction of a medical technology product [15]. Digital health and medical technology are strongly backed by the NHS. It has long collaborated with the commercial and non-profit sectors to give the British people access to effective and affordable technology. The National Institute for Health and Care Excellence (NICE) and the National Institute of Health Research (NIHR) are two examples of government institutions that operate centrally and make it simple and obvious for developers to manufacture medical technology products. State support has been essential for organizations like

Sky Medical Technology. The Department of International Trade provides funds for the Foreign Market Introduction Service, which helps businesses set up meetings with prospective foreign clients and prepare for trade shows. Because of this, Sky Medical Technology has been able to successfully distribute its OnPulse technology throughout the world. The common peroneal nerve, located just behind the knee, is stimulated by the OnPulse device, which is integrated into a geko, a little device that is wrapped around a patient's leg.

**Using Robotics to Enhance the Digital Health Sector:** This culture has contributed to the United Kingdom's position as a global leader in medical AI. Babylon Health, a mobile healthcare software that works in a similar way to Push Doctor and also has an AI chat bot that can diagnose patients, is one example. Similarly, Skin Analytics has been using a smartphone app to create digital records of patients' skin in order to enhance melanoma diagnosis, while Cambridge Cognition is using AI to better understand brain health. Another area where UK businesses are at the forefront is surgical robots. CMR Surgical is revolutionizing keyhole surgery with the Versius surgical robotics system. Versius, which will be available commercially later this year, claims to reduce the procedure's learning curve from two or three years to a few weeks. It also allows the surgeon to stay sitting, reducing physical strain, and—as an outcome—the likelihood of fatigue-related procedural mistakes.

### 1.2.2.3  South Korea

South Korea is a technological trendsetter, boasting some of the world's fastest internet connections, and the government hopes to make the country the third most technologically competitive in the world by 2030 [16]. Healthcare has been identified as a high-growth industry. The Healthcare Innovation Park (HIP) at Seoul National University Bundang Hospital (SNUBH) was established in 2016 to foster industry-academic collaborations in areas such as healthcare IT, medical genomics, and regenerative medicine. It was one of the first paperless hospitals when it opened in 2003.

**Current State of Digital Health:** BESTCare 2.0, a digital and all-encompassing healthcare system developed by SNUBH, is already utilized by around half of South Korea's digital hospitals. Nonetheless, the healthcare Big Data industry in South Korea is predicted to develop at a rate of over 17% per year, outperforming the worldwide market. Management of healthcare services are projected to be the rapidest expanding and largest segment in the congested Big Data market. This is reflected in HIP's research funding of US$53 million in 2019, an increase of nearly 18% over 2018.

**Reason Why SNUBH Is Flourishing in the Digital Health Sector:** Staff and faculty have embraced new technology quickly and collaborated to find innovative solutions to user needs. The task force teams and committees that examine and evaluate user proposals for advancement include the Clinical Pathway Task Force, the Terminology Standardization Committee, and the EMR Task Force, to name just a few. Since early 2000s, when the country's hospital information system was created, these feedback channels have been operational, and they have managed to keep the system current and user-friendly.

### 1.2.3 TECHNOLOGY AND OTHER SECTORS INVOLVED IN IOMT

**Technology of Blockchain:** Blockchain technology works as a type of distributed ledger that keeps track of all transactions made across network computer nodes [9]. Blockchain addresses many of the safety issues that have been raised regarding medical systems, and IoT has fuelled growth in the distributed computing industries. The blockchain consists of blocks or nodes connected by a network, and the data sent between them is recorded and may be used for cross-referencing. Since these blocks incorporate data from earlier blocks, this method makes it easier to identify the precise location of network criminals. Although the amount of data entering the healthcare environment is always increasing, adopting blockchain technology has an advantage that involves building trust. The increased demand for data transfers across the healthcare infrastructure may be satisfied by the blockchain. Worldwide clinical research using blockchain for EHR systems is currently being conducted in hospitals.

**Physically Unclonable Function (PUF) Devices:** For the vulnerable components of the IoMT ecosystem, PUF devices produce a distinct fingerprint. These unique fingerprints or signatures are the result of variances in how these devices are produced. These fingerprints can be employed to produce secret keys (cryptography keys) to protect end devices (sensors) in the IoMT environment, where they are susceptible to hardware tampering efforts. Figure 1.4 shows how PUF devices are mapped to the structure portrayed in the preceding section. In our mapping, the PUF devices are in the thing's layer. When it concerns to the identification of IoMT devices inside the network, these devices are critical. After the fog layer, as depicted in Figure 1.4, additional specialized corporate security solutions given by service suppliers in the framework (such as AI/ML-based) assure security.

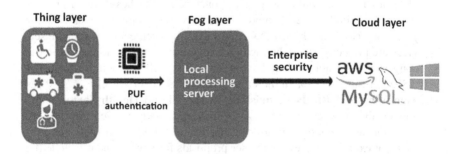

**FIGURE 1.4** Model of PUF devices [9].

**Artificial Intelligence:** On the basis of historical and real-time data, AI offers quick fixes for identifying fresh avenues for treating specific diseases. AI-based solutions have the potential to transform a number of elements of the healthcare industry. These will combine AI techniques for classifier construction, such as automating the collection of patient data, planning patient visits, choosing laboratory testing, treatment plans, medications, surgical therapies, and other activities. These classifiers could be enhanced and utilized as decision support tools. Natural language processing (NLP) approaches allow for extrication of information from such unorganized pieces of data in the system for the rest of classifiers that cannot be acquired digitally. Test results, clinical assessment notes, notes from operations, and other patient-related discharge data are examples of this. Additionally, machine learning forecasts future events using historical data. It makes use of reinforced, unreinforced, or supervised learning to predict future events. Figure 1.5 shows how AI can be implemented in IoMT.

**Software-Defined Networking (SDN):** In IoMT, the network consists of two components: the data plane and the control plane. The control plane performs the tasks that allow the data plane to perform the decisions that allow it to route traffic to its destination. SDN enables standard communication between the control plane and data plane. Among the popular SDN protocols, OpenFlow, Open vSwitch Database Management, and OpenFlow Configuration (OF-CONFIG) are only a few examples [17]. Since the interfaces between the data plane and control plane may be standardized using a standard SDN protocol, various data from the data plane may be obtained using the standard OpenFlow protocol from an external server (which might be in the cloud). Diverse e-healthcare applications may be developed on the cloud layer, allowing for the expansion of new e-healthcare applications.

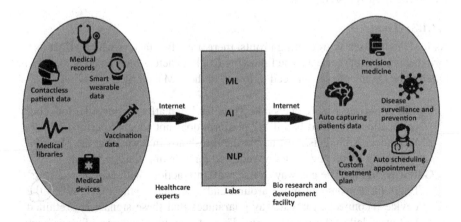

**FIGURE 1.5**    AI in IoMT [9].

## 1.3   ECONOMIC VIEWPOINT

### 1.3.1   MARKET DISTRIBUTION, PROFIT, AND LOSS

#### 1.3.1.1   Market Distribution

The IoMT market is tripartite, depending on the product range, such as the following.

- Wearable external medical devices
- Implanted medical devices
- Stationary medical devices

Again, depending on the relevance, the market can be divided into patient observation, treatment adherence, telemedicine, etc. The market is also divided into government agencies, patients, healthcare workers, etc., on the basis of end-users. In addition, the market is distributed across five primary geographical regions: Latin America, Europe, Asia-Pacific, North America, and the Middle East. The worldwide IoMT market is projected to escalate at a compound annual growth rate (CAGR) of 29.5% from 2016–2028, touching US$187.60 billion. The market is estimated to increase in response to rising IoT spending in healthcare and advances in healthcare IT. The market has benefited from the operation of the fourth-generation (4G) technology standard for broadband cellular networks. The telehealth industry is anticipated to grow and the market to be expanded by high-speed networking. The industry is likely to develop even faster in the future years as 5G networks become more widely used [18].

#### 1.3.1.2   Profits

In 2020, the worldwide IoMT market was valued at US$41.17 billion. COVID-19 has had a massive and unprecedented worldwide impact, with IoMT having a positive effect on demand across all areas throughout the pandemic [18]. According to research, the IoMT worldwide market will expand by 71.3% in 2020, compared with the average yearly rise from 2017–2019.

#### 1.3.1.3   Loss

As IoMT witnesses skyrocketing profits, there are a few factors which affect its performance in the market [19]. The following five key factors mentioned here, which if failed to be taken care of, can lead to losses in the IoMT market.

**Platform Sizing:** Sizing plays a key role for IoT platforms, just like for other applications. A cloud-based IoT platform does not equate to error-free performance. Architects must adjust the thresholds in a way that the platform can easily set up new nodes as required for a flexible design system.

**Gateway Sizing:** The gateway oversees all interactions with endpoint sensors. Endpoint sensors can move around and lose their connections. When the device reconnects, the gateway guarantees that these signals are retained and provided to the IoT platform. The gateway may manage a few or hundreds of devices, depending on the use-case. Because the gateway is the principal node for interacting with all endpoint devices, it must function well. Because these gateways are small and portable devices with restricted hardware, determining thresholds is essential for benchmarking the IoMT platform's performance.

**Open-Source Technology and Open Standards:** The cost of building IoMT-enabled medical devices can be seen as one of the downsides or losses of the sector. Implementing open-source technologies and standards for IoMT devices, like Apache Ignite and Kubernetes, has various advantages, including cost savings and simple access to corporate versions of required software. To teach devices, open-sourced AI including Google's TensorFlow can be employed. Open-source solutions are simple to use and scale, and they offer a cost-effective way to improve the performance of IoMT infrastructure. Moreover, customers, suppliers, and system integrators will be able to deploy compatibility across IoMT platforms if open standards are adopted.

**High Availability and Observability:** Because IoMT devices are components of a distributed network, they must be able to connect to a business network quickly. Monitoring IoT apps must have a low overhead and function within device limits (memory, computing resource, and network connectivity).

**Rules of Communication:** A thorough understanding of process will aid in the design of endpoint behaviour. Every few seconds, gateways and sensors provide data and receive commands to deliver new messages. There are no standard protocols for establishing communication between IoT applications and devices in an IoT network. HTTP, AllJoyn, MQTT, XMPP, DDS, COAP, IoTivity, AMQP, and other IoT protocols are among them. The communication protocol used is determined by the operational use-case and has an influence on an IoT platform's performance.

## 1.4 START-UPS

With the rising influence of IoT in the healthcare sector, new start-ups are welcomed at a fast pace. In what follows we have tried to throw some light on three of the more than 1,300 IoMT start-ups running across the globe [20]:

**Healthcare Originals:** This U.S.-based startup company deals with smart monitors. Smart monitors identify the signs of various illnesses' assaults (asthma, heart attack, epilepsy) prior to their development, allowing the wearer to control the situation before it becomes worse. When alarming changes are detected, smart monitors automatically send SMS messages and alerts to a registered caregiver.

**Elfi-Tech:** This company brought the idea of self-testing devices to the table. Patients may check their blood, urine, and other bodily fluids on demand with a surveillance system with self-testing options, which allows them to stay within the prescribed limits. The results of the test are instantly obtainable in the patient's app or on the gadget, which is linked to the tester. The mDLS device from Israeli company Elfi-Tech assesses cutaneous blood flow, blood velocity, coagulation, vascular health, and relative cardiac output (RCO) non-invasively in addition to conventional metrics like pulse and mobility.

**MedAngel:** This Netherlands-based company finds a solution to upper temperature limits. If any drug is harmed by being exposed to temperatures outside of its acceptable range, the consequences are severe. Smart sensors keep track of the temperature and the environment, alerting the user when something is about to go critically wrong or if the tablets are already damaged.

## 1.5 RIVALRY

The competitive face of IoMT market can be segmented into the following three tiers [21].

**Tier 1:** Players that are well-established corporations with a significant market share

**Tier 2:** Players with fast-growing enterprises

**Tier 3:** The inexperienced newbies

The rivalry depends on the level of the entrepreneur or businessperson. IoMT market distribution under various segments has been discussed in preceding sections. The more popular areas will have higher rates of competition. The trust of the public and the sceptical nature of the majority to experiment with companies also contribute to the difficulties faced by the lowest-tier players and disturbs the scale of fair opportunities. Some of the major tycoons in this business are the following.

- Boston Scientific Corp.
- Johnson & Johnson Services, Inc.
- Cisco
- General Electric Company
- Koniklijke Philips N.V.
- IBM
- Medtronic
- BIOTRONIK
- Siemens Healthineers AG
- Hill-Rom Holdings, Inc. (Welch Allyn)

### 1.5.1 COMPANIES AND PEOPLE CONTRIBUTING TO IoMT

Numerous people have made noticeable contributions to the medical technology sector, giving IoMT the shape it has today and planting the grounds for future advancements in the sector. These include the following.

**The Remote Monitoring System:** To create a remote monitoring system that might provide healthcare, Kaiser Foundation International and Lockheed Missiles and Space Company worked together in the 1970s. A distant location with few medical services was where the pilot programme was put into action [22].

**Patient Monitoring System**: With aid from his close friend Galileo, Santorio of Venice published directions for using a spirit thermometer to detect body temperature, as well as a pendulum to time pulse rate, back in 1625 [23].

**Telehealth:** Australia started one of the first radio communication–based telemedicine programmes in 1928. Using the telegraph, radio, and aircraft, Rev. John Flynn founded the Aerial Medical Service (AMS), which offered medical care to remote areas of the country [24].

**Telemedicine:** Teleradiology was the first type of telemedicine. Despite distance, telemedicine held the ability to provide rapid access to specialists. Any clinic may afford to set up a telemedicine site since it is so inexpensive to do so. Regardless of the mental disease, telepsychiatry is the suggested treatment [25].

**Smartwatch:** The first Linux wristwatch was created, developed, and manufactured by Steve Mann in 1998 [21]. Some of the best smartwatch brands include Mi, Fitbit, Samsung, HONOR, etc.

### 1.5.2 AWARENESS AND TRUST

IoMT has undoubtedly an enormous potential and a bright future. However, its growth can be hindered or slowed down by the way it is perceived by the public. According to a Deloitte survey, 71% of 237 respondents in the IoMT business say healthcare providers and doctors are not ready to use data provided by IoMT. Furthermore, Cisco (2017) stated that around 75% of IoT initiatives fail, accentuating that the 'human aspect' is the most vital component in project success or failure. As a result, our empirical research aims to uncover the key elements driving human factors' (healthcare providers') doubt and reluctance to IoMT implementation. IoT-related technologies are gaining traction as breakthrough developments in a variety of areas, including healthcare. However, IoMT's ultimate success is dependent on its acceptance by potential users [26, 27].

### 1.5.3 IMPACT OF THE PANDEMIC

The demand of IoMT-enabled medical devices skyrocketed during the global challenge of pandemic. COVID-19 witnessed the breakthrough of the emerging digitalization of the healthcare sector, forcing the authorities and public to switch up their perspective on IoMT.

The IoMT market has witnessed an upsurge in the investments and profits amidst the global pandemic. Onometra, in an article published in India, stated that 48% medical devices are IoMT enabled i.e., connected via IoT. Furthermore, this figure is estimated only to rise to 68% in the coming years. IoMT has gained quite a popularity in the past two years with its ability to track, test, and trace COVID-19 infections, hence proving to be extremely useful and akin to a boon in the dark times [24]. Researchers have worked in the field to predict the future of cases and requirement of beds in such pandemics [28], with some solutions using federated learning (FL)-based unmanned aerial vehicles (UAVs) to carefully observe the situation [29].

## 1.6 ADVANTAGES AND DISADVANTAGES OF USING IoMT

### 1.6.1 ADVANTAGES

**Early Intervention:** Key symptoms of a decline in health can be detected up early using linked medical devices and sensors that permit remote monitoring, allowing clinicians to administer treatment before patients seek hospitalization [30].

**Higher Accuracy of Diagnosis:** A vital tool for doctors is equipment that can continuously monitor crucial health markers in a way that is not possible during a few office visits. Data analysis, for example, can help doctors identify diseases and suggest much more effective methodology by recording such things as heart rate, blood pressure, and blood sugar measurements across many weeks.

**Better Treatment:** Smart tablets with nano sensors that activate when consumed are being utilized to monitor internal vitals, including core temperature and medicine efficacy. An article in *The Scientist* from 2019 [31] stated that the use of smart tablets in tracking the progress of cancer patients' therapy allowed clinicians to determine when patients missed a dose of an oral chemotherapy medicine or strived to follow it effectually. This enabled the experts to intervene and correct the treatment strategy before any serious consequences occurred.

**Cost-Effectiveness:** By enabling remote consultations and treatments, IoMT can help patients avoid in-person appointments, which are expensive for health institutions to arrange. Practitioners could use remote video monitoring to monitor patients after they have been released from the hospital, remind them to take their medications on schedule, and identify warning indications for readmission. Additionally, the prompt transmission of patient details to medical personnel enables quicker treatment and prognosis, which ultimately results in cost savings.

**Lowering the Financial Load on Healthcare Systems:** Remote patient monitoring (RPM) with IoMT sensors and gadgets can eliminate necessity of clinical visits and hospitalizations, potentially saving the global healthcare industry US$300 billion each year. However, the possibility of IoMT to free up space and resources is just as appealing. The adoption of RPM technology, via a one-year study of congenital heart diseases in Pennsylvania, resulted in a one-third reduction in hospitalized patients.

### 1.6.2 DISADVANTAGES

**Security and Privacy:** It gets harder to maintain the security of the data that IoT devices collect and transmit as they get better and find new applications [32]. IoT devices are not always a part of the plan, even if cybersecurity is a primary concern. Attacks on the hardware, network, software, and internet must all be prevented, as well as physical manipulation of devices.

**Technical Intricacy:** IoT devices may appear to be performing simple tasks, like adding up swipes at a secured door, but they actually contain a lot of complex technology. Furthermore, it is feasible that they will negatively affect everything connected to that process or system if they are providing essential data to it. It is not a major deal if you count the swipes incorrectly at the door, but it might be disastrous if another piece of equipment combines temperature readings with swipe data from the entrance—and fixing the problem is not always easy.

**Assembling:** Protocols and standards of IoT are not currently agreed upon, so devices from different manufacturers could be not in sync with current technologies. Deployment may be challenging because each one may need different hardware connections and configurations.

## 1.7   CHALLENGES TO IoMT

Any technology comes with some risk, some loose points which must be considered in order to achieve the best from that technology [33]. IoMT is no exceptions, following are the challenges with needs to be addressed:

**Security and Privacy:** In 2018, 82% of healthcare businesses faced serious security events, as per the 2019 HIMSS (Healthcare Information and Management Systems Society) Cybersecurity Survey. In spite of the abundance and dispersion of IoMT devices present in the network (usually 15–20 pieces of medical equipment per bed), healthcare facilities are particularly vulnerable because of their reliance on antiquated technologies. According to manufacturer General Electric, most MRI (magnetic resonance imaging) equipment in hospitals is utilized for at minimum 11 years, while some devices are used for over 22 years before being replaced. Furthermore, according to KLAS Research, a third of connected medical equipment cannot be patched, meaning that it is not updated to protect against new vulnerabilities because its original manufacturer no longer supports it [34].

While a security flaw in any company is significant, an assault on a healthcare facility has the capacity to affect equipment that saves lives. The U.S. Food and Drug Administration (FDA), for example, has recently ordered warnings for pacemakers and insulin pumps that have been linked to security concerns. If these vital devices are compromised, catastrophic injuries—if not fatalities—may result.

**Connectivity:** When the risks are as severe as they are in the medical industry, professionals, patients, and employees ought to be able to rely on 100% connection all the time. However, recent research under health IT infrastructures looked at medical/healthcare devices that are connected and discovered that 45% of connections fail from the start. Limited network bandwidth, insufficient IT employees, or physical obstructions obstructing

a wireless signal can all cause these connections to fail. Those probabilities
are unacceptable in the setting of a healthcare facility.

**Human Error Reduction:** Despite the fact that healthcare organizations are
more complex and digital than ever, healthcare IT expenditures and work-
forces are not rising at the same rate, and in some cases are diminishing.
The 30th annual U.S. Leadership and Workforce Survey from HIMSS finds
that only 28% of hospitals say they have an acceptable number of employees
working in health IT. According to the same study, only 37% of participants
anticipated an increase in IT staff in 2019. As a result, IT directors must
think about ways to streamline processes and systems while still improving
overall quality and dependability. Network automation appeals to a lot of
individuals [35].

## 1.8   GOVERNMENT INITIATIVES

Government has taken many steps and initiatives in order to promote these technologies for improvement of the healthcare sector of the country. A few are explained in
what follows [27].

**National Health Policy:** The Union Budget 2018 allotted INR 3073 crores
to the NITI Aayog to establish a digital economy using new technologies
including AI, IoT, blockchain, and 3D printing to assist these efforts. The
Ministry of Health and Family Welfare (MoHFW) is the nodal ministry in
charge of developing and enforcing health and health-tech policies and standards. In relation to medical equipment, the National Health Policy (NHP)
2017 favours local medical device manufacture in line with the "Make in
India" initiative. Medical device regulation should also be strengthened,
according to the public policy. Because medical equipment accounts for
more than 70% of all imports into India, the strategy emphasizes the need to
encourage domestic production. While the NHP 2017 outlines broad aims
for medical devices, the Medical Device Rules (MDR) 2017, which took
effect on January 1, 2018, establish medical device–specific laws in India.
The MDR controls equipment designed for internal or external diagnostic
use, treatment, mitigation, or prevention of sickness or disorders in humans,
and it is granted under the Drug and Cosmetics Act 1940. Meanwhile, the
United Nations praised the Ayushman Bharat initiative for establishing
excellent health IT infrastructure.

**Electronic Health Standards 2016:** The EHR Standards were announced in
2013 and amended in 2016 by the MoHFW in order to provide a consistent standardized system for the generation and management of medical
records by healthcare providers. The EHR standards' main goal is to assure
data semantic and syntactic interoperability across systems. The acceptance
of a vast array of International Standards Organization (ISO) standards is
referred to as the EHR standards. It also lays forth criteria for improving the
functionality, usefulness, and integrity of IT for health in India, as well as
promoting its wider adoption.

**Strategy to Implement AI:** The use of AI in healthcare can help increase access to healthcare, especially in rural regions. It is suggested that certain applications might help India, including AI-driven diagnostics, tailored therapy, and early detection of future pandemics. The focus, according to the strategy plan, is on the impact of AI paired with robots and IoMT to solve healthcare challenges through training and research, early detection, diagnosis, decision-making, and therapy.

In this regard, the NITI Aayog is undertaking an effort to create a 'Cancer Biobank'. This will be a pathology picture library with annotations and curation that will be utilized for cancer detection and therapy.

## 1.9  CONCLUSION

IoMT has been witnessing quite a positive response as the healthcare sector, and the public has started to be more accepting of it. IoMT has been transforming the conventional medical sector to provide a faster and more advanced perspective to the present healthcare sector. The continuous technological advancements and public belief has helped in the extensive use of IoMT services in the present-day world of the pandemic. It served as a boon for the doctors—as well as patients—as it gave way to crucial facilities like remote health monitoring systems.

Although IoMT can be perceived as all things good, it still has its disadvantages and challenges which are being continuously worked upon to pave the way for the bright and essential future of advancement in the medical sector via IoT. All around the globe, the governments of several developing and developed countries have been trying to provide better medical aid and keep up with the changing times. Hence, it becomes important to know about IoMT and understand its current scenario and future prospects to enhance the medical facilities of the country—and hence its economy and life expectancy.

## REFERENCES

[1] MedTech and Internet of Medical Things: How Connected Medical Devices Are Transforming Health Care by Deloitte. https://www2.deloitte.com/content/dam/Deloitte/global/Documents/Life-Sciences-Health-Care/gx-lshc-medtech-iomt-brochure.pdf.

[2] What Is IoMT: How Is IoMT Impacting Healthcare by Ordr. https://ordr.net/article/what-is-iomt/.

[3] Internet of Medical Things (IoMT). (30 August 2018). "Health IT Outcomes." *ICall, a Division of Amtelco.* https://www.healthitoutcomes.com/doc/the-internet-of-medical-things-iomt-0001.

[4] A. Verma, P. Bhattacharya, M. Zuhair, S. Tanwar, and N. Kumar. (2021). "Vacochain: Blockchain-Based 5G-Assisted UAV Vaccine Distribution Scheme for Future Pandemics." *IEEE Journal of Biomedical and Health Informatics*, vol. 26, no. 5, pp. 1997–2007.

[5] A. Verma, P. Bhattacharya, D. Saraswat, S. Tanwar, N. Kumar, and R. Sharma. (2023). "SanJeeVni: Secure UAV-Envisioned Massive Vaccine Distribution for COVID-19 Underlying 6G Network." *IEEE Sensors Journal,* vol. 23, no. 2, pp. 955–968. DOI: 10.1109/JSEN.2022.3188929.

[6] U. Bodkhe, S. Tanwar, P. Bhattacharya, and A. Verma. (2021). "Blockchain Adoption for Trusted Medical Records in Healthcare 4.0 Applications: A Survey." In *Proceedings of Second International Conference on Computing, Communications, and Cyber-Security* (pp. 759–774). Springer, Singapore.

[7] A. Verma, P. Bhattacharya, U. Bodkhe, A. Ladha, and S. Tanwar. (March 2020). "Dams: Dynamic Association for View Materialization Based on Rule Mining Scheme." In *The International Conference on Recent Innovations in Computing* (pp. 529–544). Springer, Singapore.

[8] Evolution of IoT in Healthcare by Guest Writer. (1 July 2019). https://www.iotforall.com/evolution-iot-healthcare.

[9] Sahshanu Razdan, and Sachin Sharma. (2021). "Internet of Medical Things (IoMT): Overview, Emerging Technologies, and Case Studies." *IETE Technical Review*. DOI: 10.1080/02564602.2021.1927863.

[10] P. Bhattacharya, P. Mehta, S. Tanwar, M.S. Obaidat, and K.F. Hsiao. (November 2020). "HeaL: A Blockchain-Envisioned Signcryption Scheme for Healthcare IoT Ecosystems." *2020 International Conference on Communications, Computing, Cybersecurity, and Informatics (CCCI)*, pp. 1–6.

[11] A. Verma, P. Bhattacharya, U. Bodkhe, D. Saraswat, S. Tanwar, and K. Dev. (2022). "FedRec: Trusted Rank-Based Recommender Scheme for Service Provisioning in Federated Cloud Environment." *Digital Communications and Networks*. DOI: 10.1016/j.dcan.2022.06.003.

[12] What Can IoT Do for Healthcare? By Dr. Rajashekhar Karjagi, Manish Jindal-Analytics Solutions, Wipro. https://www.wipro.com/business-process/what-can-iot-do-for-healthcare-/.

[13] Internet of Medical Things Augmenting India's Medical Industry by EH News Bureau. (2 March 2021). https://www.expresshealthcare.in/blogs/guest-blogs-healthcare/internet-of-medical-things-augmenting-indias-medical-industry/427629/.

[14] The Internet of Medical Things and Positive Disruption in the Healthcare Sector by Stanton Chase. (22 January 2021). https://www.ipa-india.org/wp-content/uploads/2021/02/The-Internet-Of-Medical-Things-And-Positive-Disruption-In-The-Healthcare-Sector.pdf.

[15] Healthcare IT in France, HealthManagement. www.healthmanagement.org.

[16] South Korea, the Perfect Environment for Digital Health. Produced by Nature Research Custom Media and Seoul National University Bundang Hospital. https://www.nature.com/articles/d42473-020-00347-x.

[17] Science at the Cutting Edge: Why Britain Is Great for Digital Health and Medical Technology Business by Pharmaceutical Technology in Association with Great Britain. (27 June 2019). https://www.pharmaceutical-technology.com/sponsored/uk-digital-health-2019/.

[18] IoMT Market Worth USD 187.60 Billion by 2028, with 29.5% CAGR | Market Projection by Technology, Major Key Players, Growth Factors, Revenue, CAGR, Regional Analysis, Industry Forecast To 2028, by Fortune Business Insights. (28 October 2021). https://www.globenewswire.com/en/news-release/2021/10/28/2322459/0/en/IoMT-Market-worth-USD-187-60-Billion-by-2028-with-29-5-CAGR-Market-Projection-By-Technology-Major-key-players-Growth-Factors-Revenue-CAGR-Regional-Analysis-Industry-Forecast-To-202.html.

[19] Top 5 Factors Affecting the Performance of IoMT Devices, by Amit Parihar, Sr. Manager, Citius Tech. (16 July 2021). https://www.citiustech.com/blog/top-5-factors-affecting-the-performance-of-iomt-devices.

[20] 5 Top Internet of Medical Things Startups out of 1.314, Research Blog by StartUs Insights. https://www.startus-insights.com/innovators-guide/5-top-internet-of-medical-things-startups-out-of-1314/.

[21] Market Research Report: Key Market Insights, by Fortune Business Insights. Report ID: FBI101844. https://www.fortunebusinessinsights.com/industry-reports/internet-of-medical-things-iomt-market-101844.

[22] Internet of Medical Things (IoMT) Market by Product, by Application, by End User and by Region: Industry Analysis, Market Share, Revenue Opportunity, Competitive Analysis and Forecast 2021–2028. Report Code: HC-U7068, by FutureWise. https://www.futurewiseresearch.com/healthcare-market-research/Internet-of-Medical/12468.

[23] The History of Patient Monitoring System, by e2aglen. (21 September 2017). https://www.glenmedsolutions.com/2017/09/21/history-patient-monitoring-systems/.

[24] The History of Telehealth: Telemedicine Through the Years by Sigmund Software. https://www.sigmundsoftware.com/blog/history-of-telehealth/.

[25] Quizlet Chapter 4 Flashcards by Starrangel08. https://quizlet.com/18945151/chapter-4-flash-cards/.

[26] Wikipedia Contributors. (17 June 2022). "Smartwatch." *Wikipedia, the Free Encyclopedia*. https://en.wikipedia.org/wiki/Smartwatch. Accessed 28 June 2022.

[27] What Is the Government Doing for Health-Tech in India? By Kasmin Fernandes. (11 June 2020). https://thecsrjournal.in/health-tech-policies-government-india/.

[28] V.K. Prasad, P. Bhattacharya, M. Bhavsar, A. Verma, S. Tanwar, G. Sharma, Pitshou N. Bokoro, and R. Sharma. (2022). "ABV-CoViD: An Ensemble Forecasting Model to Predict Availability of Beds and Ventilators for COVID-19 Like Pandemics." *IEEE Access*, vol. 10, pp. 74131–74151.

[29] D. Saraswat, A. Verma, P. Bhattacharya, S. Tanwar, G. Sharma, P.N. Bokoro, and R. Sharma. (2022). "Blockchain-Based Federated Learning in UAVs Beyond 5G Networks: A Solution Taxonomy and Future Directions." *IEEE Access*, vol. 10, pp. 33154–33182.

[30] The Game-Changing Benefits of the Internet of Medical Things (IoMT) for Healthcare by Olha Zhydik, Content Marketing Manager, ELEKS. (8 April 2021). https://eleks.com/blog/iomt-for-healthcare/. Accessed 4 January 2022.

[31] C.-Y. Hou. (2019). "Smart Pills Help Monitor Cancer Patients' Therapy." The Scientist: https://www.the-scientist.com/notebook/smart-pills-help-monitor-cancer-patients-therapy-66092.

[32] Top Advantages and Disadvantages of IoT in Business by Julia Borgini, Spacebarpress Media, IoT Agenda. (29 March 2022). https://www.techtarget.com/iotagenda/tip/Top-advantages-and-disadvantages-of-IoT-in-business.

[33] The Top 3 IoMT Challenges Keeping Healthcare IT Up at Night, by Extreme Marketing Team. (6 April 2021). https://www.extremenetworks.com/extreme-networks-blog/the-top-3-iomt-challenges-keeping-healthcare-it-up-at-night/.

[34] R. Gupta, Arpit Shukla, Parimal Mehta, Pronaya Bhattacharya, Sudeep Tanwar, Sudhanshu Tyagi, and Neeraj Kumar. (2020). "VAHAK: A Blockchain-Based Outdoor Delivery Scheme Using UAV for Healthcare 4.0 Services." *IEEE INFOCOM 2020 — IEEE Conference on Computer Communications Workshops (INFOCOM WKSHPS)*, pp. 255–260. DOI: 10.1109/INFOCOMWKSHPS50562.2020.9162738.

[35] Nastaran Hajiheydari, Mohammad Soltani Delgosha, and Hossein Olya. (2021). "Scepticism and Resistance to IoMT in Healthcare: Application of Behavioural Reasoning Theory with Configurational Perspective." *Technological Forecasting and Social Change*, vol. 169, p. 120807. DOI: 10.1016/j.techfore.2021.120807.

# 2 Artificial Intelligence Applications for IoMT

*Vivek Kumar Prasad, Jainil Solanki,*
*Pronaya Bhattacharya, Ashwin Verma,*
*and Madhuri Bhavsar*

## CONTENTS

## 2.1 INTRODUCTION

The new deadly spreading respiratory illness coronavirus 2019 (COVID-19) has posed the greatest worldwide danger to human health since the 1918 influenza pandemic. The use of wearable sensors and Internet of Medical Things (IoMT) in patient management during infectious disease epidemics has opened up a flood of possibilities. Until now, there has been a rapid increase in redirected research activities aimed at finding a long-term solution to this worldwide challenge [1]. In this digital technology era, smart healthcare based on edge computing and IoMT is gaining attraction. The growing popularity of wearable gadgets has opened up new possibilities for infectious disease prevention. Wearable and implanted body area network devices are thus particularly beneficial for continuous patient monitoring [2].

Both caregivers and patients have embraced remote patient monitoring, screening, and treatment via telemedicine, which is facilitated by IoMT. Smart gadgets based on the Internet of Things (IoT) are gaining traction at a breakneck speed, especially in the wake of the worldwide epidemic. However, given the large scope of the problem, healthcare is expected to be the most difficult sector for IoMT to address [3]. Remote

DOI: 10.1201/9781003303374-2

23

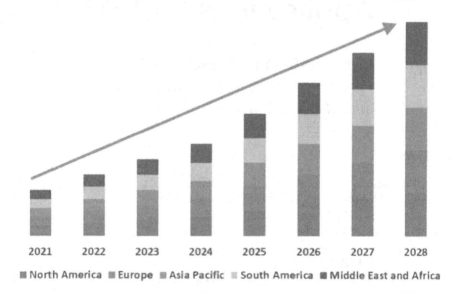

Global Internet of Medical Things (IoMT) Market is Expected to Account for USD 1,84,592.31 Million by 2028

■ North America ■ Europe ■ Asia Pacific ▨ South America ■ Middle East and Africa

**FIGURE 2.1**   Trends to be found in different regions for IoMT in the upcoming years.

or self-fitness tracking of various critical capabilities such as coronary heart rate, skin temperature, motion tracking, and tracking of contemporary fitness situations, vitamins, and rehabilitation of aged or infected patients is significantly going to lead to an increase in the average lifespan and a decrease in incidents and death. Within the forecast period of 2021–2028, The global market for IoMT is predicted to expand. According to Data Bridge Market Research, the market is predicted to grow at a compound annual growth rate (CAGR) of 23.0% from 2021–2028, with a total value of USD 1,84,592.31 million, the same also shown in the Figure 2.1. The rising demand for real-time healthcare solutions around the globe is driving IoMT software industry forward [3].

## 2.2   AI- AND IoMT-FUELLED HEALTHCARE INDUSTRY GROWTH

Smart sensors with built-in intelligence are speeding up the development of a connected ecosystem whereby data are collected and sent to centralised storage for further processing and necessary action, which could pave the way for distant or at-home healthcare to become a popular option [4]. Wearable and electronic skin sensors that spread all over the body area network somehow improve the management of chronic disease, with improvements in sensor sensitivity and communication capability that allows the system to monitor the patient's activity in real time. Such rising demand for remote monitoring of patient's health requires a smart ecosystem that contains smartphones, applications, wearable gadgets, and improved infrastructure that paves the foundation for connected smart healthcare facilities. AI, sensors, blockchain, and Big Data analytics are critical IoMT technologies since they benefit both consumers and establishments [5].

Personalised medication is possible with the help of connected IoMT infrastructure that allows medical staff or doctor to construct individualised treatments depending on the medical needs and conditions of each patient, as the IoMT-based system generally follows the loop-based feedback system to improve the medication based on the knowledge of past medication on same disease.

Different technologies playing vital roles in making smart connected hospitals a reality include the following (see Figure 2.2).

- **Big Data Analytics:** Smart hospitals can use analytics to gather actionable insights and apply digital prescriptive maintenance to keep medical equipment in good working order. Big Data analytics can be used to investigate electronic health records (EHRs) and hospital networks, as well as to regulate data keeping the privacy of the patients in the public domain for further research that will reduce the re-admissions of same patients [6].
- **Blockchain:** Current approaches for sharing medical records and patient health patterns in some specific populations can be developed using blockchain technology. A blockchain network allows exchange of medical records among multiple hospitals and insurance company seamlessly keeping privacy of the sensitive information with the help of InterPlanetary File System (IPFS) protocol [7, 8]. Blockchain can also be used to stored the vaccination details of the patients, along with their personal information to reduce the hoarding of vaccination [9, 10].

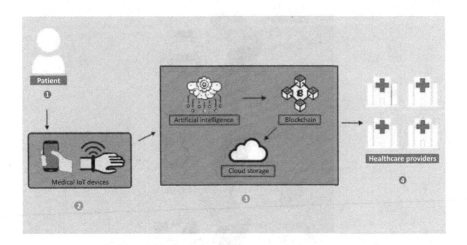

**FIGURE 2.2**   Blockchain and AI-based IoMT healthcare ecosystem.

The main aim that IoMT focuses on is to remove needless data from the medical system so that doctors may concentrate on what they do best, diagnosing as well as treating patients. Because it is a technological evolution, developers must give standardised testing standards to persuade medical establishments of its safety and efficacy, as well as to realise its vast potential.

- **Artificial Intelligence (AI):** This technology takes the huge statistics generated by IoT and analyses them using powerful algorithms to draw inferences and predict medical diagnoses. IoT and AI are integrated to provide smart healthcare facility [11].

## 2.3   KEY TYPES OF IoMT DEVICES

The World Health Organization reports that "There are an estimated 2 million different kinds of medical devices on the world market, divided into over 7000 generic device classes"; these devices exist in a range of shapes and sizes, ranging from house monitoring devices to pulse oximeters and insulin pumps [12]. The Figure 2.3 show the different categories apply to all of these solutions.

- **Point-of-Care Devices:** A wide range of diagnostic equipment, known as point-of-care devices, is designed to produce results without laboratory environment. They are frequently used by doctors or patients home to analyse the samples of biological fluids such as skin cells, blood and saliva.
- **Smart Pills:** Also known as intelligent drugs or electronic medications, smart pills are miniature electronic devices with ingestible sensors that are

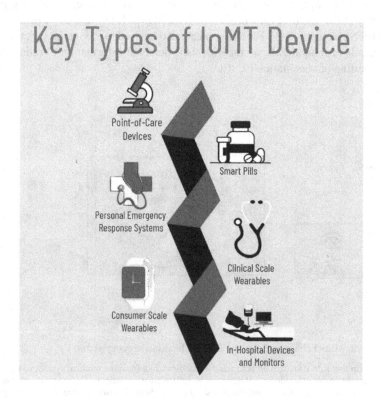

**FIGURE 2.3**   Types of IoMT devices.

placed in medical capsules. Smart tablets can, among other things, monitor vital health indicators such as temperature, blood pressure, etc. These smart pills are administered to a precise region for imaging for accurate gastrointestinal illnesses.

- **Personal Emergency Response Systems:** Personal emergency response systems (PERS) for individuals, often known as medical warning systems, are medical devices that use a help button to summon assistance in the event of an emergency. People who have restricted mobility and require emergency medical assistance, such as the elderly, can benefit from PERS.
- **Clinical-Scale Wearables:** Clinical wearables are IoT devices and platforms that have been verified for use of administrative and health bodies such as the U.S. Food and Drug Administration (FDA). This group of gadgets is commonly used at home or in clinics in response to a physician's prescription or suggestion. Their primary objective is to alleviate chronic illnesses and afflictions.
- **Consumer-Scale Wearables:** Consumer-scale wearables of several types are used to track key markers of personal health and body fitness. These have built-in sensors which collect and transmit data whenever a user engages in physical activity. Although such devices may be used for specialised health purposes in some cases, the majority of them are not authorised by medical officials.
- **In-Hospital Devices and Monitors:** Devices and monitors used in hospitals range from big instruments such as MRI or CT scanners to smart devices that help with monitoring patients, personnel and supply management, and more.

## 2.4 OVERVIEW OF HEALTHCARE INFORMATICS AND MANAGING EHRS IN HEALTH INFORMATICS

Health informatics is an interdisciplinary domain that focuses on use of technology to improve the healthcare facility, keeping the objective to develop standards and setup clinical guideline to enhance the management of EHRs among different entities. The ecosystem that works together is comprised of doctors, nurses, hospitals, and day care centres to provide better services. The information among the different stakeholders must be shared securely and smoothly. The connected knowledge among different stakeholders must be aggregated to provide better healthcare to each patient. Health analytics professionals ensure how efficiently this connected stakeholders communicate with other for better efficiency of the overall system [13].

The global healthcare informatics (HI) market was worth USD 18.6 billion in 2019 and is predicted to rise to USD 32.7 billion by the end of 2026, with a CAGR of 8.4% from 2020–2026 [14] (see Figure 2.4). An EHR is a collection of medical records created during clinical encounters and occurrences. With the proliferation of self-care and homecare devices and systems, valuable healthcare data is now created 24 hours a day, seven days a week, and has life-long clinical importance. These are designed to share data with other healthcare providers, such as laboratories and specialists, so they have data from all of the professionals involved in the patient's treatment.

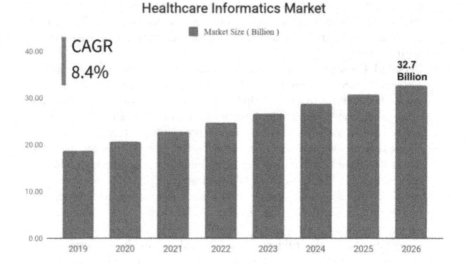

**FIGURE 2.4**   Trends to be found in different regions for HI in the upcoming years.

All members of the team have instant access to the most up-to-date information with fully functional EHRs, enabling more coordinated, patient-centred treatment. Benefits of EHRs include the following.

• Even if the patient is unconscious, the primary care physician's information alerts the emergency room doctor to the patient's life-threatening allergy, allowing care to be tailored accordingly.
• The lab results from last week are already in the record, so specialists can get the information they need without having to do further tests.
• Patients may access their own data and see a year's worth of lab results, which can inspire them to take their prescriptions and maintain the lifestyle adjustments that have improved their numbers.

Ways of managing EHRs include the following.

• At all times, guaranteeing U.S. Health Insurance Portability and Accountability Act (HIPAA) compliance.
• Developing a data governance plan.
• Leveraging technology to simplify EHR data collection.
• Transferring data to a centralised cloud repository.
• Investing in customer relationship management in healthcare.

## 2.5   IMPROVING EHRS WITH AI

While AI is most commonly utilised in healthcare operations to enhance data search and retrieval, as well as to adapt treatment suggestions, it has the potential to make EHRs more user-friendly, as well. Because EHRs are complex as well as difficult to use, and are commonly blamed for leading to physician fatigue, this is an important goal. At the moment, customising EHRs to make them easier for doctors is mostly a manual effort, and the systems' rigidity is a huge roadblock to progression. Machine learning (ML), in particular, has the potential to enable EHR systems adjust according to users' desires in real time, resulting in better health-care results and a better quality of life for doctors [15]. Figure 2.5 shows the growth of AI in recent year.

EHR AI capabilities are now limited, but we should expect them to dramatically increase in the future. They include the following.

- **Human "Abstractors":** These can supply us with health review provider notes and extract structured data, using AI to assist them recognise areas of focus and discover new information, allowing them to work more efficiently.
- **Algorithms for Diagnosis and/or Prediction:** These are working along with network delivery models to develop Big Data prediction algorithms to alert clinicians about high-risk illnesses like sepsis and heart failure. To give decision help, each of these might be integrated into EHRs.
- **Data Entry and Clinical Documentation:** Natural language processing (NLP) captures clinical notes, allowing physicians to concentrate on their patients rather than keyboards and displays.
- **Clinical Decision-Making Assistance:** Previously, decision support was universal and rule-based, suggesting treatment alternatives. ML systems that learn from new data are being released by vendors today, allowing for more personalised care.

To make their systems easier to use, mainstream EHR manufacturers have started incorporating the AI, ML, and NLP capabilities for better clinical decision, interaction with telemedicine and image analysis are all being used by businesses. The result will be integrated interfaces, access to data stored in the systems, and a variety of possible advantages.

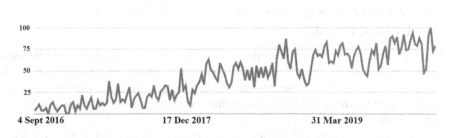

**FIGURE 2.5**   Growth of AI in healthcare in recent years.

## 2.6 MACHINE LEARNING USE-CASES AND APPLICATIONS IN HEALTHCARE

In healthcare informatics, ML provides powerful analytical capabilities. As a result, the quality of the electronic information offered to clinicians is improving dramatically. Doctors can readily obtain parameters such as the risk of a heart attack, renal failure, and hardening of the arteries. Patients' indicators are derived from a range of blood pressure readings, ethnicity, family history, and the findings of their most recent medical examinations. Following that, crucial clinical insights are collected that helps doctors and care takes to formulate a care-plan to provide better healthcare facilities. Possible outcomes assist patients in estimating the cost of the surgery, making therapy more reasonable [16].

Patients' health results are unquestionably improved when patients are more involved. ML can provide automated message warnings as well as appropriate targeted information that prompts action at critical times. In general, ML can personalise and improve the therapy process in a number of ways.

Following are some of the aspects where ML can be most useful.

- **Diagnosis and Disease Identification:** This is a wonderful place to start because ML is excellent at diagnosis. Many cancers and hereditary disorders are difficult to identify, but ML could help in the early stages of many of them.
- **Improvement in Health Records:** Vector machines and ML-based optical character recognition (OCR) approaches could be used to classify records.
- **Identifying the Most Effective Treatments:** ML is also useful in the early stages of drug development for patients. Companies now are using AI-based technology to try to develop personalised drug combinations to cure acute myeloid leukaemia (AML).
- **Making Diagnoses via Analysis of Medical Images:** With its InnerEye project, Microsoft is transforming healthcare data analysis. This firm analyses the images to process medical pictures in order to establish a diagnosis. ML will become more efficient in the near future, allowing for the analysis of even more data points in order to establish an automatic diagnosis.
- **Surgery with AI:** This is likely the most important use of ML, and it is expected to become more widespread in the near future.

## 2.7 DEEP LEARNING USE-CASES AND APPLICATIONS IN HEALTHCARE

Deep learning models' computer power has enabled fast, accurate, and efficient healthcare operations. Deep learning networks are revolutionising patient care, and they play a critical role in clinical practise for health systems. The most often utilised deep learning techniques in healthcare include computer vision, NLP, and reinforcement learning.

Medical practitioners and researchers are using deep learning to uncover hidden opportunities in data and better serve the healthcare business. Deep learning in healthcare enables clinicians to precisely analyse any ailment and effectively treat it, resulting in improved medical judgements [17].

Some of the aspects where deep learning can be most useful:

- **Healthcare Data Analytics:** Deep learning models can assess structured and unstructured data in EHRs—such as clinical notes, laboratory test results, diagnoses, and prescriptions—at lightning speed and with the highest level of accuracy. Smartphones and wearable devices also provide vital lifestyle information. They have the ability to convert data by monitoring medical risk variables for deep learning models utilising mobile apps.
- **Personalised Medical Treatments:** By evaluating patients' medical histories, symptoms, and tests, deep learning systems enable healthcare companies to provide individualised patient care. NLP extracts useful information from free-text medical data for the most common medical treatments.
- **Auditing Prescriptions:** Deep learning models can audit prescriptions against patient health information to discover and fix probable diagnostic errors or prescription errors.
- **Fraud Detection:** Deep learning systems also detect medical insurance fraud claims by examining fraudulent behaviours and health data from a variety of sources, including claims history, hospital related data, and patient characteristics.
- **Genomics Analysis:** Deep learning models improve the interpretability of biological data and provide a better understanding of it. Deep learning models' complex data analysis capabilities aid scientists in their research into genetic variation interpretation and genome-based medicinal development. Convolutional neural networks (CNNs) are widely used and allow scientists to extract properties from DNA sequence windows of a defined size.
- **Mental Health Research:** Researchers are using deep learning models to improve clinical practise in mental health. In continuing academic studies, deep neural networks, for example, are being utilised to understand better the effects of schizophrenia and other ailments on the brain. The researchers claim that trained deep learning models outperform ordinary ML models in a variety of areas. Deep learning algorithms, for example, can be taught to recognise important brain biomarkers.1.8. Challenges in IoMT.

Before widespread adoption of IoMT, various challenges and implications must be addressed, including confidentiality of information, information management, scaling and upgrading, law, compatibility, and cost effectiveness.

Some of these challenges are the following (see Figure 2.6).

- **Privacy and Security of Data:** One of the main issues and concerns in IoMT applications is ensuring adequate internet security within clinical monitoring devices. The huge volume of sensitive patient health data shared across systems poses a security challenge that has yet to be overcome.

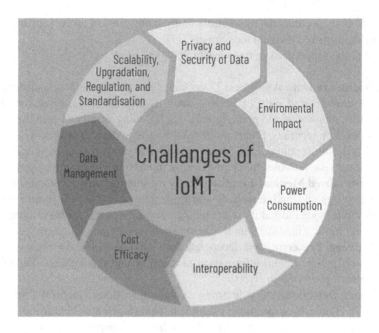

**FIGURE 2.6** Challenges in IoMT.

- **Data Management:** Data management is the ability to acquire, combine, regulate, and maintain the data flow of information. Data filtering techniques such as data anonymisation, data integration, and data synchronisation are employed to provide only the information required by the application while concealing the rest.
- **Scalability, Upgradation, Regulations, and Standardisation:** Scalability refers to a medical device's ability to respond to changes in the climate. As a result, a flexible and scalable system is one that can maintain consistency among connected devices while performing efficiently and quickly using available resources. A highly scalable system is more usable now and in the future. As IoMT technology develops and evolves, the need for regular updating of older devices has grown. This is still a struggle in today's fast-paced world. EMR recording IoMT devices must also be validated. To accomplish this, researchers, organisations, and standardising bodies can collaborate.
- **Interoperability:** Different sectors have different criteria for supporting their apps. The variability of devices and data derived from various sources, largely owing to interoperator variance, also limits the scale of utilisation. Data exchange across several IoMT systems with varying features makes interoperability difficult. As a result, consistent interfaces are essential, particularly in programmes that allow cross-organisational cross-systems. The exchange of a wide range of data generates a vast volume of data in the IoMT world, and the procedures involved in handling that data, as well as

controlling networked devices in an interoperable manner while considering energy constraints, remain major concerns.

- **Cost Efficacy:** In COVID-19 times, financial stress has increased to reach many individuals, enterprises, and even organisations, limiting widespread adoption of IoMT. As a result, cost efficacy becomes a major hurdle that demands careful consideration. The cost of the IoMT system's creation, installation, and use must be reasonable.

- **Power Consumption:** Another stumbling block to widespread use of IoMT devices is their high power consumption. The majority of IoMT devices are powered by batteries, and once a sensor is mounted, it is necessary to replace the batteries on a regular basis or utilise a high-power battery. To help address the global energy issue, the current focus should be on developing sustainable healthcare equipment that can generate their own electricity or merging the IoMT system with renewable energy systems.

- **Environmental Impact:** To fulfil functions, the IoMT systems include a variety of incorporated biological sensors. These are created by combining multiple semiconductors that contain earth metals and other harmful substances that could harm the environment. As a result, regulatory agencies oversee and regulate the sensor manufacturing process. More research into the design and manufacture of sensors made of biodegradable materials is needed.

## 2.8 CHALLENGES IN THE INTEGRATION OF TECHNOLOGIES WITH IoMT

The integration of technologies with IoMT—even with advancements—is still a challenge in today's times. Some result in the increase of cost beyond the expected scale; others are not yet suitable enough for scaling IoMT at a large pace [18, 19].

The challenges faced by each technology during the integration with IoMT are as follows.

### Blockchain Challenges

Blockchain technology is used to provide security to the data for the IoMT domain. However, because to the opposing requirements of these two technologies, combining them is difficult and creates a number of obstacles, including the following.

- **Processing:** Blockchain mining require intensive computing and high energy usage, which resource-constrained IoMT devices cannot afford.

- **Storage:** In little time, IoMT devices generate a huge amount of data. This data must be analysed and stored in a secure manner on blockchain to maintain their integrity. The cost of storing the data on blockchain is very high. This huge data from IoMT devices create unnecessary costly ecosystem, which is not feasible.

- **Mobility:** Blockchain was designed to have stable network topology. Medical equipment devices that are implanted or worn, on the other hand, are continually moving and modifying the topology.

- **Real Time:** In general, IoMT applications are mission-critical and require real-time updates and quick reaction. Creation of blocks, on the other hand, takes time. Every ten minutes, a 1-MB block is created in Bitcoin. It is difficult to group these data streams into blocks while maintaining real-time requirements.
- **Traffic Overhead:** The constant communication between blockchain nodes is a substantial source of overhead traffic. IoMT devices with limited bandwidth cannot afford this.

## Big Data Challenges

The challenges existing between Big Data and IoMT include the following [20].

- **Storage of Data and Its Management:** The data generated rapidly from IoMT devices is rapidly expanding. As the amount of data is generated is unlimited, it becomes expensive in terms of time to access the data. Managing such data and allowing stakeholders to update on time becomes critical.
- **Data Visualisation:** Systems receive data from heterogenous sources, and it is important to analyse this structured and semi-structured data which is in multiple formats. It is very difficult to find out facts by visualising data in the form of graphs and charts directly, so in order to take precise measurements and make real-time decisions, we require better data visualisation techniques to enhance the efficiency of the system.
- **Confidentiality and Privacy:** Data generated from different IoMT devices requires complete privacy, as it contains sensitive information about the patients and their diagnosis reports. We therefore cannot store data in plan format and share the same without security.
- **Integrity:** IoMT devices and other sensors in the ecosystem which receive data share it with other IoMT devices and should guarantee no data loss. Sometimes the data is analysed and then forwarded to other edge computing devices, so devices must work in cooperation and ensure integrity of the data; i.e., it should not change in between communication.
- **Power Requirements:** The continuous sensing, receiving, and sending of data from one node to another requires processing which requires sufficient hardware and uninterrupted power supply. As they are small in size, IoMT devices require efficient mechanisms and power supplies to perform such heavy tasks.
- **Device Security:** Storing the sensitive information of patients requires measures to protect that information during processing and transmission. Devices require a mechanism to defend against harmful and unauthorised use.

## AI with IoMT: Key Challenges

The challenges existing between AI and IoMT include the following.

- **Provability:** AI-enabled organisations are unable to demonstrate plainly why and what they do. It's no surprise that AI is a "black box." People are sceptical about it since they do not understand how it makes decisions.

- **Information Security and Protection:** To learn and make intelligent decisions, most AI systems rely on massive amounts of data. In order to learn and improve, AI frameworks consume data which is frequently sensitive and personal in nature. This renders it helpless in the face of complex concerns such as data loss and fraud.
- **Genetic Susceptibility Calculation:** An inherent problem with AI frameworks is that they are only as good—or as bad—as the data they are based on. Bad news is typically associated with racial, sex, or ethnic prejudices. Special computations are used to determine who is required to meet with a prospective employee, who has been granted bail, or whose advance has been approved. Such predispositions will most likely be emphasised more in the future, and a large number of AI frameworks will continue to be prepared to use bad data. As a result, it is critical to prepare these frameworks with unprejudiced data and to produce calculations that can be successfully understood.
- **Information Shortage:** The facts show that associations currently have access to more information than they have in the past. In any case, datasets that are critical for AI applications to learn from are rare. The most powerful AI machines are those that have been programmed to learn in a controlled manner. This preparation necessitates tagged data, which is data that has been sorted to make it ingestible by computers. Information with a unique identifier is not accessible. In the not-too-distant future, the computerised manufacturing of increasingly complex computations, which is mostly driven by profound learning, will only aggravate the problem.
- **Algorithm Transparency:** Transparent algorithms are essential not simply to comply with tight laws associated to drug development, and people also need to understand how algorithms create findings in general.
- **Electronic Records Optimisation:** There is still a lot of unstructured data scattered across many databases that has to be organised. When the scenario improves, personal treatment solutions will improve, as well.

## 2.9 EXPLAINABLE AI: ONE STEP AHEAD OF AI

AI is now omnipresent, with product and movie suggestions on Netflix and Amazon, as well as friend recommendations on Facebook and tailored advertisements on search result sites, and we have grown accustomed to AI making decisions for us in our daily lives. However, when making life-altering decisions like an illness diagnosis, it is crucial to understand why you are making that decision. The importance of describing AI outputs should be feasible and explainable at this point [21]. Figure 2.7 trends of XAI in recent and upcoming years.

However, despite their apparent effectiveness in terms of results and forecasts, AI algorithms—particularly ML algorithms—suffer from transparency, making it challenging to get clarity into their underlying mechanisms of operation. This complicates the dilemma, because putting important decisions in the hands of a system that is unable to explain itself carries clear risks.

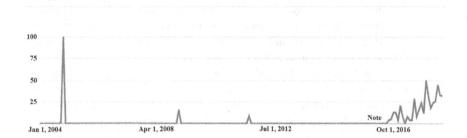

**FIGURE 2.7**   Trends to be found in different regions for XAI in recent and upcoming years.

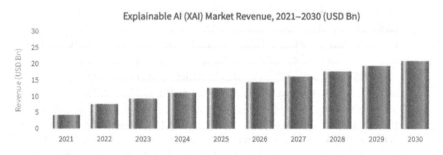

**FIGURE 2.8**   Market Revenue of XAI in recent and upcoming years.

The global explainable AI (XAI) market is expected to grow at a CAGR of 18.4% from 2022–2030, from USD 4.4 billion in 2021 to USD 21.0 billion in 2030 (see Figure 2.8).

XAI has a number of advantages, including improved client retention and inventory management. Understanding a model's flaws is crucial to maximising its performance. It is easier to improve models when you have a better grasp of why they failed. XAI is a useful tool for detecting system problems and removing biases in data, resulting in enhanced consumer trust. XAI aids in the verification of predictions so that models may be fine-tuned and new insights can be gained to solve the situation at hand.

## 2.10   APPLICATIONS OF XAI

The potential benefit of choosing an AI-based healthcare system is always better, keeping in consideration that selecting untrustworthy AI is even more dangerous. To improve machine-based decisions, you need to know how and on what basis the decision was made; i.e., to improve the performance and develop more trust in AI which needs decisions to be explainable, as actions taken based on those decisions may severely affect patients. It will be more beneficial if AI makes prediction with proper explanation to the conclusion always help to verify and check the accuracy of those decisions [22]. Based on ML algorithms, we predict the requirement of critical care unit such as bed and ventilators [23].

Major areas where XAI can be used in healthcare include the following.

- Allergy diagnosis
- Lung cancer diagnosis
- Traumatic brain injury (TBI) diagnosis
- Colorectal cancer diagnosis
- Chronic wound diagnosis
- Clinical diagnosis

Other areas where XAI can be employed include the following.

- **Banking and Finance:** Banking regulators like to examine overall business volumes as well as the number of questionable actions recorded. Any ratio that deviates from the industry standard will be investigated by regulators. In such circumstances, XAI can assist in the reduction of false positives. However, data misuse is reduced due awareness in many countries by introducing data policies and enforcing it as regulation, which includes Article 22 of the European Union's General Data Protection Regulation (GDPR) on restrictions on fully automated decision making and Articles 13–15 on the right to seek explanations for decisions made (though not explicitly stated). XAI systems [24] that are capable of producing excellent results and delivering clear explanations will gain adequate trust and satisfy regulatory standards, resulting in increased use of AI solutions in the sector. Cancellation of loans, increasing premium costs for healthcare insurance, and stock market predictions all have large financial risks. Therefore, XAI will solve the problem by providing explanation to the decisions made.
- **Defence:** XAI becomes significant in military activities because lethal autonomous weapon systems (LAWS) can inflict less damage if they can distinguish between a civilian and a combatant.
- **Automobiles:** Autonomous driving has been a developing subject and is the automotive industry's future. Self-driving autos or driverless cars are exciting as long as no mistakes are made [25]. In this high-stakes AI application, one wrong action will cost one or more lives. Explainability is important to understand and analyse a system's limits and capabilities before moving to development phase [26]. Understanding the weaknesses of driverless vehicle technology in the field when utilised by customers is critical in order to assess, explain, and rectify the issues as quickly as possible. To some extent, parking assistance is an important feature and voice assistants are relatively low-risk, whereas brake assistance and self-driving become critical—so in such cases, XAI will identify and correct the biasness in the system.
- **Systems of Justice:** In developed countries, AI- and ML-based systems are increasingly being used in decision-making process of any legal matter. ProPublica, a non-profitable and independent newsroom that produces investigative journalism, recently documented bias towards a single community by

reliving serial offender on payroll on repeat and multiple offence that create an unpleasant effect on society as well as reduces trust in higher authority; that is why fairness is required to protect individual rights [27].

## 2.11 CONCLUSION

In this chapter, the healthcare framework utilities and their applications were implemented using AI techniques. Various AI-based techniques were discussed and utilised for the framework of the healthcare system. The case studies of the healthcare-based scenarios were undertaken and have been solved using ML techniques. The real-time healthcare operations and patient monitoring with necessary actions were automated using the ML and deep learning techniques. The chapter concluded with the utility of XAI for the IoMT-based healthcare system. The detailed illustration of the case studies and their learning were discussed briefly. For future work, the detailed analysis with Quality of Service (QoS) in IoMT has to be used and identified using the advanced AI techniques for the healthcare systems. Also, the targets have to be achieved for fog computing and edge computing challenges with respect to medical IoMT healthcare systems.

## REFERENCES

[1] P. Manickam, S.A. Mariappan, S.M. Murugesan, S. Hansda, A. Kaushik, R. Shinde, and S.P. Thipperudraswamy. (2022). "Artificial Intelligence (AI) and Internet of Medical Things (IoMT) Assisted Biomedical Systems for Intelligent Healthcare." *Biosensors*, vol. 12, no. 8, p. 562.

[2] Huda Ghassan Hameed Abdulmajeed, Esraa Ahmed Ghafil, Mahmood Hameed Majeed, Wafaa Mohammed Attaf Mustafa Al-Attar, and Shallal Murad Hussein. (2022). "Remote Cardiac Patients Monitoring System Using Internet of Medical Things (IoMT) Devices." *Central Asian Journal of Theoretical & Applied Sciences*, vol. 3, no. 5, pp. 531–536.

[3] Fortune Business Insights. www.fortunebusinessinsights.com/industry-reports/internet-of-medical-things-iomt-market-101844. Accessed 8 January 2022.

[4] A. Verma, P. Bhattacharya, Y. Patel, K. Shah, S. Tanwar, and B. Khan. (2022). "Data Localization and Privacy-Preserving Healthcare for Big Data Applications: Architecture and Future Directions." In *Emerging Technologies for Computing, Communication and Smart Cities* (pp. 233–244). Springer, Singapore.

[5] Muhammad Adil, Muhammad Khurram Khan, Muhammad Mohsin Jadoon, Muhammad Attique, Houbing Song, and Ahmed Farouk. (2022). "An AI-Enabled Hybrid Lightweight Authentication Scheme for Intelligent IoMT Based Cyber-Physical Systems." *IEEE Transactions on Network Science and Engineering*. https://ieeexplore.ieee.org/document/9737386.

[6] Jalel Ktari, Tarek Frikha, Nader Ben Amor, Leila Louraidh, Hela Elmannai, and Monia Hamdi. (2022). "IoMT-Based Platform for E-Health Monitoring Based on the Blockchain." *Electronics*, vol. 11, no. 15, p. 2314.

[7] Mohammad Khalid Imam Rahmani, Mohammed Shuaib, Shadab Alam, Shams Tabrez Siddiqui, Sadaf Ahmad, Surbhi Bhatia, and Arwa Mashat. (2022). "Blockchain-Based Trust Management Framework for Cloud Computing-Based Internet of Medical Things (IoMT): A Systematic Review." *Computational Intelligence and Neuroscience*, pp. 1687–5265. DOI: 10.1155/2022/9766844.

[8] M. Zuhair, F. Patel, D. Navapara, P. Bhattacharya, and D. Saraswat. (April 2021). "BloCoV6: A Blockchain-Based 6G-Assisted UAV Contact Tracing Scheme for COVID-19 Pandemic." *2021 2nd International Conference on Intelligent Engineering and Management (ICIEM)*, pp. 271–276.

[9] A. Verma, P. Bhattacharya, D. Saraswat, S. Tanwar, N. Kumar, and R. Sharma. (2023). "SanJeeVni: Secure UAV-Envisioned Massive Vaccine Distribution for COVID-19 Underlying 6G Network." *IEEE Sensors Journal*, vol. 23, no. 2, pp. 955–968. DOI: 10.1109/JSEN.2022.3188929.

[10] A. Verma, P. Bhattacharya, M. Zuhair, S. Tanwar, and N. Kumar. (2021). "Vacochain: Blockchain-Based 5G-Assisted UAV Vaccine Distribution Scheme for Future Pandemics." *IEEE Journal of Biomedical and Health Informatics*, vol. 26, no. 5, pp. 1997–2007.

[11] Mohammad Wazid, Jaskaran Singh, Ashok Kumar Das, Sachin Shetty, Muhammad Khurram Khan, and Joel J.P.C. Rodrigues. (2022). "ASCP-IoMT: AI-Enabled Lightweight Secure Communication Protocol for Internet of Medical Things." *IEEE Access*, vol. 10, pp. 57990–58004. DOI: 10.1109/ACCESS.2022.3179418.

[12] Sandi Rahmadika, Philip Virgil Astillo, Gaurav Choudhary, Daniel Gerbi Duguma, Vishal Sharma, and Ilsun You. (2023). "Blockchain-Based Privacy Preservation Scheme for Misbehavior Detection in Lightweight IoMT Devices." *IEEE Journal of Biomedical and Health Informatics*, vol. 27, no. 2, pp. 710–721. DOI: 10.1109/JBHI.2022.3187037.

[13] Baneen A. Alhmoud, Daniel Melley, Nadeem Khan, Timothy Bonicci, Riyaz Patel, and Amitava Banerjee. (2022). "Evaluating a Novel, Integrative Dashboard for Health Professionals Performance in Managing Deteriorating Patients: Quality Improvement Project." *BMJ Open Quality*, vol. 11, no. 2.

[14] Businesswire. www.businesswire.com/news/home/20220801005349/en/Global-Medi cal-Imaging-Informatics-Markets-2021-2028-Rising-Demand-for-AI-and-Cloud-Based-Platforms-Technological-Advancements-in-Medical-Imaging-InformaticsRese archAndMarkets.com. Accessed 8 January 2022.

[15] Joseph Bamidele Awotunde, Sakinat Oluwabukonla Folorunso, Sunday Adeola Ajagbe, Jatinder Garg, and Gbemisola Janet Ajamu. (2022). "AiIoMT: IoMT-Based System-Enabled Artificial Intelligence for Enhanced Smart Healthcare Systems." *Machine Learning for Critical Internet of Medical Things*, pp. 229–254.

[16] Ventsislav Trifonov, Ivaylo Atanasov, and Evelina Pencheva. (2022). "Artificial Intelligence in Open Radio Access Network: Use Case of Internet of Medical Things." *2021 International Conference on Biomedical Innovations and Applications (BIA)*, vol. 1, pp. 5–8.

[17] Tianle Zhang, Ali Hassan Sodhro, Zongwei Luo, Noman Zahid, Muhammad Wasim Nawaz, Sandeep Pirbhulal, and Muhammad Muzammal. (2020). "A Joint Deep Learning and Internet of Medical Things Driven Framework for Elderly Patients." *IEEE Access*, vol. 8, pp. 75822–75832.

[18] Mohammad Wazid, Ashok Kumar Das, Joel J.P.C. Rodrigues, Sachin Shetty, and Youngho Park. (2019). "IoMT Malware Detection Approaches: Analysis and Research Challenges." *IEEE Access*, vol. 7, pp. 182459–182476.

[19] Anirban Mitra, Utpal Roy, and B.K. Tripathy. (2022). "IoMT in Healthcare Industry—Concepts and Applications." *Next Generation Healthcare Informatics*, pp. 121–146.

[20] Ajay Kumar, Kumar Abhishek, Pranav Nerurkar, Mohammad R. Khosravi, Muhammad Rukunuddin Ghalib, and Achyut Shankar. (2021). "Big Data Analytics to Identify Illegal Activities on Bitcoin Blockchain for IoMT." *Personal and Ubiquitous Computing*, pp. 1–12.

[21] Hammad Raza. (2022). "An IoMT Enabled Smart Healthcare Model to Monitor Elderly People Using Explainable Artificial Intelligence (EAI)." *Journal of NCBAE*, vol. 1, no. 2, pp. 16–22.

[22] D. Saraswat, P. Bhattacharya, A. Verma, V.K. Prasad, S. Tanwar, G. Sharma, P.N. Bokoro, and R. Sharma. (2022). "Explainable AI for Healthcare 5.0: Opportunities and Challenges." *IEEE Access*, vol. 10, pp. 84486–84517. DOI: 10.1109/ACCESS. 2022.3197671.

[23] V.K. Prasad, P. Bhattacharya, M. Bhavsar, A. Verma, S. Tanwar, G. Sharma, Pitshou N. Bokoro, and R. Sharma. (2022). "ABV-CoViD: An Ensemble Forecasting Model to Predict Availability of Beds and Ventilators for COVID-19 Like Pandemics." *IEEE Access*, vol. 10, pp. 74131–74151.

[24] H. Mankodiya, M.S. Obaidat, R. Gupta, and S. Tanwar. (2021). "XAI-AV: Explainable Artificial Intelligence for Trust Management in Autonomous Vehicles." *2021 International Conference on Communications, Computing, Cybersecurity, and Informatics (CCCI)*, pp. 1–5. DOI: 10.1109/CCCI52664.2021.9583190.

[25] R. Gupta, A. Kumari, and S. Tanwar. (2021). "A Taxonomy of Blockchain Envisioned Edge-as-a-Connected Autonomous Vehicles." *Transactions on Emerging Telecommunications Technologies*, vol. 32, p. e4009. DOI: 10.1002/ett.4009.

[26] H. Mankodiya, D. Jadav, R. Gupta, S. Tanwar, W.-C. Hong, and R. Sharma. (2022). "OD-XAI: Explainable AI-Based Semantic Object Detection for Autonomous Vehicles." *Applied Sciences*, vol. 12, p. 5310. DOI: 10.3390/app12115310.

[27] M. Obayya, N. Nemri, M.K. Nour, M. Al Duhayyim, H. Mohsen, M. Rizwanullah, A. Sarwar Zamani, and A. Motwakel. (2022). "Explainable Artificial Intelligence Enabled TeleOphthalmology for Diabetic Retinopathy Grading and Classification." *Applied Sciences*, vol. 12, no. 17, p. 8749.

# 3 Privacy and Security in Internet of Medical Things

*Karthik Ajay, Abhishek S. Mattam,*
*Bivin Joseph, Sohan R., and Ramani Selvanambi*

## CONTENTS

DOI: 10.1201/9781003303374-3

## 3.1 INTRODUCTION

In recent years, portable medical devices and e-health–based applications have received huge popularity mainly due to the facts that they are inexpensive and adequately available, and because they produce quality data for their pricing [1]. Such trends are due to high modification and developments seen in health-based devices of Internet of Medical Things (IoMT). Even though such devices have evolved to show great performance at such a small scale and compact bodies, wearables like smartwatches have attracted much more attention due to their simplicity, rapidly evolving efficiency, and portability. In the recent past, people used to only use external devices for checking their sugar levels, blood pressure, etc. Such devices were not connected to any internet services in any manner, nor did not they have to store any data—their purpose ended after displaying the data to the user, and when data become huge we need systematic way to access those records [2, 3]. Fast forward to today's time, and we have reached a phase when all the above mentioned devices and applications can do much more than a single task and they are connected to the internet for storage, exchange, and monitoring of data without the intervention of humans. Due to such developments, IoMT-based devices are prone to attacks, such as attacks on databases which can result in loss of data, attacks on the cloud server which can delay the processing of information and much more, direct attacks on the device such as denial of service (DoS) attacks which can even result in inaccessibility. Such vulnerabilities can cause major problems, as medical data are confidential and need to be protected which are vital for a person's well-being. Apart from devices, there are plenty of IoMT-based applications (standalone applications or applications that enable connection of IoMT devices to mobile phones) [4]. One such platform is Ubiquitous Monitoring Environment for Wearable and Implantable Sensors, also known as UbiMon, which is an online platform which monitors, processes, analyzes, and stores data from implanted sensors in the body of the patient using cloud services. Another such platform that utilizes cloud services is Biokin, where processing is done using the information from different sensor nodes implanted in different parts of the body [5]. Security issues are faced by these healthcare devices are not only from hackers, but also corporations that sell such devices. This is where federated learning plays a major role which we will discuss in the later sections [6, 7]. Table 3.1 presents the comparative analysis of existing state-of-the art approaches in the field of IoMT and its related privacy and security issues. Major technologies used in IoMT are the following.

1. Wi-Fi
2. Cloud computing
3. Zigbee
4. Bluetooth
5. Radio frequency identification (RFID)

6. Wireless sensor networks
7. Global positioning systems

We will be discussing the previously mentioned technology later. The following are a few areas where such IoMT devices causes great concern.

1. **Data Integrity Issues:** The accuracy of data throughout its life cycle. Data quality can be another term coined for data integrity.
2. **Data Storage Issues:** Issues regarding safety considering the database that stores the medical/other personal records.
3. **Processing Power Issues:** Accuracy and efficiency of computing power— can be the size of the cache or the time cycles that affect them.
4. **Privacy Challenges:** Data vulnerability is high, which is of great concern as these are confidential data.
5. **Security:** Due to lack of security for IoMT devices, they are still vulnerable to many attacks.

## TABLE 3.1
## Comparative Analysis of Existing State-of-The Art Approach

| References | Paper Title | Methodology Used | Limitation |
|---|---|---|---|
| [10] | *IoMT Security: SHA3-512, AES-256, RSA and LSB Steganography* | SHA-512 algorithm AES-256 algorithm RSA algorithm LSB steganography algorithm | Not implementable on all IoMT devices with varying specifications |
| [9] | *Ubiquitous Monitoring Environment for Wearable and Implantable Sensors* | Wireless communication Time division Multiple access | Less secure Less stability in biosensor materials More effort is required for network and spectrum planning for TDMA |
| [20] | *Research and Analysis of Denial of Service Performance based on Service-Oriented Architecture* | Extensible markup language Service-oriented architecture Simple Object Access Protocol DoS Attack | DoS attack based on web service depletes the system's resources |
| [11] | *Analysis of Security and Privacy Challenges in Internet of Things* | Advanced Encryption Standard (AES) Secure Hash Algorithm 256 (SHA 256) Redundancy algorithm | Complex software required for AES implementation; algebraic structure is simple |
| [8] | *Cloud Enabled Solution for Privacy Concerns in Internet of Medical Things* | Cloud-enabled framework AES algorithm ABE algorithm PDP algorithm | To encrypt data, the data owner must utilize the public keys of all authorized users for attribute-based encryption |

*(Continued)*

**TABLE 3.1** *(Continued)*

**Comparative Analysis of Existing State-of-The Art Approach**

| References | Paper Title | Methodology Used | Limitation |
| --- | --- | --- | --- |
| [3] | *Considerations Towards Security and Privacy in Internet of Things Based E-Health Applications* | Multi-agent architecture, Scala programming language, Jena Framework, Fuseki Database Server | Limited predictability, understandability, and control in multi-agent architecture |
| [12] | *Security and Privacy for IoMT-Enabled Healthcare Systems: A Survey* | Elliptic curve cryptography, proxy-based protection, IoMT security assessment framework | The ECC algorithm is more sophisticated and difficult to implement than RSA, so there is a higher risk of implementation mistakes. Proxy-based protection not compatible with all networks |
| [27] | *Towards Federated Learning at scale: System Design* | Cloud-based distributed service, pace steering, actor programming model | Actors only process a single message at a time and sequential order is not carried out. Federated learning faces few security threats (poisonal or adversarial attacks) |
| [30] | *Privacy-Preserving Federated Learning for Internet of Medical Things under Edge Computing* | FL-based system Edge computing Pseudo-random number generation, Diffie–Hellman key exchange | Federated learning faces few security threats (poisonal or adversarial attacks) Additional cost for data storage in edge devices Security risk is present in local devices in edge computing |

## 3.2 ADVANCED TECHNOLOGIES USED IN IoMT DEVICES

Let us discuss a few other advanced technologies that come under IoMT to get a clearer idea of the working and the overall structure.

### 3.2.1 UBIMON (UBIQUITOUS MONITORING ENVIRONMENT FOR WEARABLE AND IMPLANTABLE SENSORS)

WSN is an innovation that can be applied in sizable variety of sectors in the technologies used in IoMT devices. This wireless network was created for the purpose of detecting, locating, localizing, observing, or tracking users. The aim of having this wireless technology for sensors that are embedded in the wearable health devices is for monitoring the users health levels at a fairly standard (normal) health stage so that any malformation that may occur in the future can be easily detected [17]. They can be mainly used for post-surgical care of minimal access surgery.

The proposed wireless (distributed) system consists of mainly of the following five elements (see Figure 3.1).

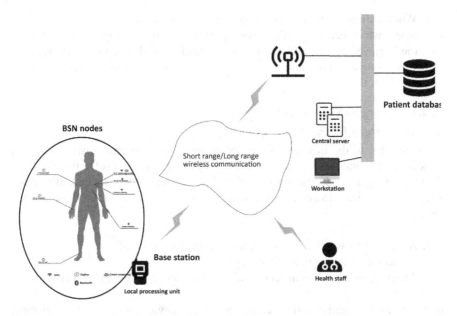

**FIGURE 3.1** UbiMon system diagram.

- BSN node
- Local processing unit
- Central server
- Patient database
- Workstation

1. **BSN Node:** BSN node is a mini wireless intelligent module to monitor the patients. Each node is equipped with a embedded biosensor, such as ECG, oxygen saturation, or temperature indicator.
2. **Local Processing Unit:** The main purpose of the local processing unit (LPU) is to accumulate all the data that is collected by the BSN node and transmit it. LPUs can also detect irregularities and give warnings to the users. They can be any portable device and the units also provide routing functionalities between the previously mentioned nodes and the central server through a Bluetooth connection or other methods (such as a wireless local area network [LAN]), depending on the range of transmission.
3. **Central Server:** The purpose of the central server is to transfer all the data collected in the local processing unit and to load them into the user database so that the system can run an analysis in the trend of the health level of the user. Through this analysis, the server is able to detect any irregularity in an earlier stage itself.
4. **Patient Database:** The patient database is for the storage of data which will be fed continuously.

5. **Workstation:** These are the end devices such as wearables or desktop computers which enable health workers to run an analysis on the patient using the retrieved records. The workstations achieve both live health tracking, which provides the current health status, as well as the long-term health record of the patient.

### 3.2.1.1   Emergency Response Systems

#### 3.2.1.1.1 Personal Emergency Response System

Nowadays, due to the increase in the population, access to immediate emergency services has become very difficult and challenging. In order to solve this problem, personal emergency response system (PERS) has been introduced which allows one to have timely access to emergency services. This system consists of the following parts:

1. A transmitter which acts as a personal help button (PHB)
2. A console which is linked to your phone
3. An emergency monitoring center which analyzes data from different sensors

Help buttons are feather-light electromechanical devices which are much more comfortable and handy than a phone. During the time of emergency, you can simply use the help button which is present on the console or the transmitter. As soon as you press the help button, it immediately directs you to the emergency monitoring system. The system will ask you how you are and you need to respond with what kind of help you need. Even if it is a false alarm, the monitoring center will make sure you get or you are provided with the service you need. It is the same case when you are not able to respond to the monitoring center after pressing the help button.

### 3.2.1.2   Benefits of PERS
- It is easy to use because one just has to simply press the help button during the need of emergency service
- It is relatively cheap and it is affordable to the general public
- It does not require any kind of charging because these are battery-powered devices
- It works effectively within a good amount of range
- It ensures your safety when you are living alone in your home

### 3.2.1.3   Limitations of PERS
- The monitoring fee is charged each month
- It is limited to a fixed range

### 3.2.2   MPERS (Mobile Personal Emergency Response System)

These are medical alert gadgets that allow people to be monitored about their health remotely. They are two-way communication devices which provide protection with the touch of a simple button. This is an ideal device for people becoming aged and

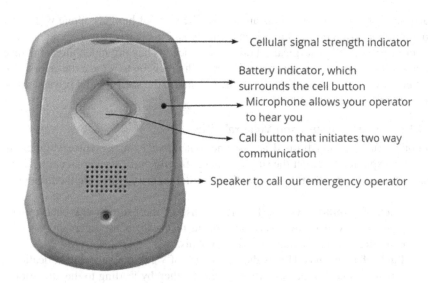

Cellular signal strength indicator

Battery indicator, which surrounds the cell button

Microphone allows your operator to hear you

Call button that initiates two way communication

Speaker to call our emergency operator

**FIGURE 3.2**   Mobile PERS device.

Source: www.towne.services/towne-monitoring/mpers-device/

for those living alone in their homes independently, and for people traveling around the world.

MPERS was created to the number of people visiting hospitals and also helps in promoting health at home with a simple button press (see Figure 3.2).

### 3.2.2.1   Benefits of MPERS

- It is water resistant
- It has a GPS which enables location tracking
- This device ensures one's safety when living alone in one's home.
- It is a two-way communication service
- It provides a peace of mind
- It is wireless

### 3.2.2.2   Limitations of MPERS

- It requires charging every two or three days
- Battery life is low
- There are instances when the GPS do not show the accurate location of the wearer

## 3.3   IoMT DEVICES

### 3.3.1   Surgical Robots

Advancements in technology have resulted in the integration of robots that are designed precisely using high-end technology into the field of medical science. The purpose of such enhanced robots are to ease the work of humans, along with detection of minor errors that go unnoticed by humans. This is where a special domain or sector of robots called surgical robots is introduced. They are much more enhanced in providing services and are created using such precision to reduce the errors. Even though they are very helpful in the medical domain, the security and privacy threats they pose is challenging.

### 3.3.1.1 Security Issues and Vulnerabilities

Robotic issues are not limited to just one, but rather to many vulnerabilities that could be exploited to target the surgical robots by which the hacker can either cause damage or take control of the robots. Some of the security issues are the following.

- **Lack of Confidentiality:** This is because of the use of weak encryption algorithms which can easily be broken, resulting in the interception and exposure of sensitive data and design plans.
- **Lack of Integrity:** This is due to the use of weak message authentication protocols that can be compromised easily, thereby leading to the alteration of sensitive data.
- **Lack of Verification:** This does not include any kind of biometric features to prevent unauthorized access.
- **Lack of Secure Networking:** This renders the communication between robots and the doctors/medical staff insecure and prone to different kinds of attacks.
- **Lack of Proper Authentication:** This leads to unauthorized access using common usernames and passwords which can easily be exploited by any attacker/hacker.
- **Lack of Security Patches:** If there are no proper security patches, the chance of attacks such as data theft and remote access will be very high.

Surgical robotic systems are prone to vulnerabilities that can affect their performance. Some of the vulnerabilities that are challenging are the following.

- **Network Vulnerability:** If there are no basic security measures to ensure network security, the system will be vulnerable to various attacks such as man in the middle, eavesdropping, sniffing, etc.
- **Security Vulnerability:** The adoption of new security measures without thorough testing can affect the performance of the surgical robotic system.
- **Platform Vulnerability:** The lack of regular software updates and firmware patches are included in the platform vulnerability.
- **Application Vulnerability:** The lack of testing and evaluation of applications can affect the system's performance. Hence, further testing is required.

### 3.3.2 CONNECTED INHALERS

According to a certain group of researchers, two in every three deaths due to asthma could be avoided or prevented by taking appropriate measures and proper medical treatment.

Connected inhalers (refer Figure 3.3), help patients suffering from asthma and any other respiratory diseases. IoT-connected inhalers help to reduce the risk of attacks and ensure patient safety. This device also helps in collecting and storing the data from the environment which guides the doctor or health sector workers to know the reason behind the attack. The collected data can be pushed to some secure blockchain-based immutable storage to provide trust in the patient data [18, 19]. This helps the doctors or the healthcare workers to choose an optimal treatment plan for his/her patient.

Following are some of the benefits for the people using a connected inhaler.

1. It collects and stores data
2. It provides education about the health condition
3. It provides tips on how to maintain hygiene and improve lifestyle
4. It helps in monitoring any kind of symptoms the person may have, and it provides valuable feedback
5. It alerts patients when they have left the inhaler at home
6. It helps with understanding the reason or cause of an attack

These smart inhalers help reduce the time which is required for diagnosis. They are linked to the patient's phone via a Bluetooth connection, which makes it handy. The data—such as time, date, and location—are recorded using a sensor technology which is inbuilt in the devices [20].

The connected inhalers transfer the data to an app which is installed on the patient's mobile phone. The app also shows all the alert messages and other details

**FIGURE 3.3**  Connected inhaler and smartphone app.

about the health condition of the patient. These alert messages pop up when the patient has left the connected inhaler at home. The app also sends reminder messages to ensure that the patient takes their medicine on time.

## 3.4   SECURITY AND PRIVACY CHALLENGES IN IoT

IoT has made significant contributions in a variety of fields, including business infrastructure and industrial control systems, in which an entire factory may be connected to the internet and operated through a smartphone, which is handy. IoT has also played a significant role in the healthcare industry. Regardless of all of the previously mentioned accomplishments, IoT's security and privacy remain a significant concern. But why are security and privacy so challenging to attain? The following are the answers to the question. Many IoT systems are vulnerable to both hardware and software flaws that have yet to be addressed. There will be zero-day attacks if a hacker takes advantage of those flaws. This might be disastrous for the entire company, as it will be difficult to counteract the attacks because the producers were unaware of the flaws. IoT has a bigger attack surface [21]. Because devices are connected to one another, multiple attacks are not only possible to a single device but to the whole network. Consumers have a very little understanding of IoT; they love it, but few grasp how it works, and they are unconcerned about security concerns.

## 3.5   CHALLENGES FOR IoMT TECHNOLOGY

An exponential increase in the threats to IoMT devices is witnessed in the trend as technology advances. This means that, despite improving standards of living, such medical devices with embedded technology are at great threat due to rising cyber threats. Due to the quick boost in the mobile industry, the electronics market is now filled with RFID (radio frequency identification) devices, smartwatches, health devices, and many other wireless connected devices. These devices make use of open networks for retrieving and transmitting data, which serves as a great threat as they become highly prone to different types of cyber-attacks. As most of the devices are getting introduced into IoT day by day, potential threats are also increasing. Thus, it has become one of the major requirements that networks are to be kept secure in today's world. Privacy and the protection of sensitive data such as medical data is vital in such devices. Such data transmission through networks should undergo a standardized form of end-to-end encryption from both senders and receivers. In cases such as the use of poor encryption standards or in the absence of any encryption standard, the medical records stored in a database or that are transmitted across networks may be leaked or modified, which can be catastrophic for the patient. Patient information is further processed to predict the future pattern of patients with the help of artificial intelligence [22, 23].

The information that is collected by IoMT nodes and devices is large and requires greater power for processing the record. Another challenge is providing adequate storage for the medical data. Storage of data in the cloud network is mostly preferred over other methods, mainly because of the high security they provide. Another challenge

**TABLE 3.2**
**Technology Comparison [10]**

| Technology | Wi-Fi | Zigbee | Bluetooth | BLE | RFID |
|---|---|---|---|---|---|
| State | | ✔ | | ✔ | |
| Range | 32 | 100 | 10–100 | 15–30 | 1 |
| Current Rate | M | – | M | - | Y |
| Bandwidth | 11 | 0.25 | 0.8 | 1 | 1–11 |
| Data | ✔ | | ✔ | | – |
| Audio | ✔ | | ✔ | | – |
| Video | ✔ | | | | – |
| Voice | Voip | | | | – |

is data integrity. Due to critical data that may be utilized for further research and are widely distributed, it is necessary to create effective and efficient platforms that maintain data integrity.

The use of different technologies used by wearable's and sensors are represented in Figure 3.4.

Wi-Fi is mainly used for mobile X-ray technology and glucose meters in hospitals, whereas Bluetooth technology is used in short-range communication such as phone-based glucose meters and pulse oximeters. Capturing systems and pulse oximeters make use of Zigbee technology. The detailed comparison of the technology mentioned in Table 3.2. The previously mentioned technologies face few challenges regarding the following.

- Safety
- Processing power
- Privacy
- Storage
- Data integrity

As the quantity and diversity of IoMT devices increases, there is an increase in the risk they face. Different types of cyber-attacks that might affect IoMT devices are hacking, intruding, Trojan horses, malware, and data theft. The protection of devices that store medical data from these kinds of cyber-attacks is of vital importance. Data transmission in wireless networks should be encrypted end to end. If there is no proper encryption over the wireless networks, sensitive medical data can be exposed to the public.

## 3.6 POSSIBLE CYBER-ATTACKS AGAINST IoMT

### 3.6.1 ROGUE ACCESS POINT

There are several nodes or points in the network that are not to be accessed by unauthorized personnel. A hacker can make use of the security vulnerabilities to access

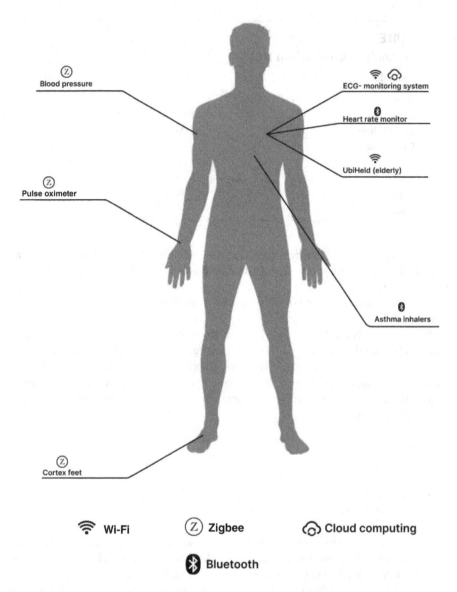

**FIGURE 3.4** Technologies used for IoMT devices.

such points that are connected to an IoMT device, through which the hacker may get full access to the data and information of the IoMT device that is present at that particular point. The attacker will be able to steal data or perhaps even control various IoMT devices that are interconnected within the network. Figure 3.5 represents the IoT with rogue access point.

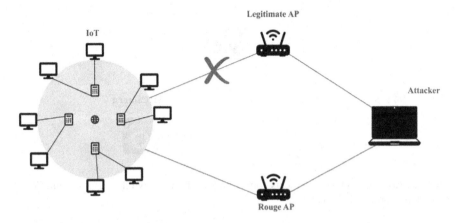

**FIGURE 3.5**    IoT network with installed rogue access point (AP).

### 3.6.2 MAN-IN-THE-MIDDLE ATTACK

Any user can track the whereabouts of their home using devices such as an internet protocol camera. When the user installs such devices at their home, they can see what is happening at their home from any point in the world, as such cameras are connected to a network and they keep sending the data packets across the network [24]. As the device is connected to a network, it is prone to network attacks; a hacker can use several tools to intercept the data and modify or just view it from their side. The hacker does this by controlling the data packets that is transmitted from the device. Such incidents are caused due to poor encryption standards used in securing the network through which the data packets are transmitted and received. Such a situation when a criminal inserts himself into a communication between a user and an application, either to eavesdrop or to mimic one of the parties, making it look as though a legitimate information exchange is taking place is called man in the middle attack [11].

Figure 3.6 shows a man-in-the-middle attack being performed on a network.

### 3.6.3 DENIAL OF SERVICE (DOS)

Another method of cyber-attack is denial of service (DoS), which consists of increasing/flooding the network between hosts and which can result in either a delay in packet arrival (which can result in huge loss) or the packet being destroyed. This type of attack is very dangerous in the case of IoMT devices because medical records require integrity confidentiality and there should not be any delay or loss of packet in inter-host or host–server communication. In DoS, the bandwidth of the receiving end (host) is overloaded with requests sent from the attacker's device. The random access memory (RAM) of the server is also exhausted as the attackers concentrate on the software vulnerability to infiltrate. However, DoS attacks can easily be stopped as

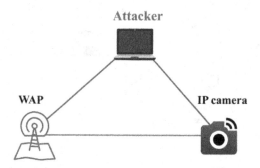

**FIGURE 3.6**   An attacker intercepts communication between wireless access point (WAP) and internet protocol (IP) camera.

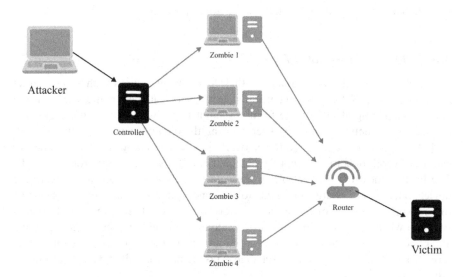

**FIGURE 3.7**   An attacker floods the network with multiple zombie hosts, using up the server time and random access memory (RAM).

the process takes place from a single IP address. Figure 3.7 shows the basic structure of the attack.

## 3.7   REQUIREMENT OF SECURITY FOR IoMT DEVICES

IoMT devices come in the category of devices that require the most attention in security matters due to the sensitive nature that their data must possess, the confidentiality that requires, and the accuracy that is expected. If the data packets undergo any delay due to increased network traffic due to DoS attacks or if the data packets are modified—i.e., the medical record of the patient is altered—results could be catastrophic to the patient. Medical personnel may take the wrong precautions or suggest incorrect treatment due to such an incident. Thus, it is very important for such devices to ensure their security and the security of the network via which they are transmitting and receiving the data packets. IoMT devices require different levels of security for the data that is being transmitted and the sensors which produce the data.

### 3.7.1   SECURITY FOR DATA

#### 3.7.1.1   Data Confidentiality

Transmission, collection, and storage of medical data through such devices should be strictly under the guidelines of legal regulations that have been set up by the government, ensuring that the data will not be misused in the hands of unauthorized personnel. These data must not be overlooked, since once stolen by cyber thieves, they may be sold on the black market or the illegal dark web, which affects not only on the patient's privacy but also financial and reputational harm. Personal data should be removed after it has been processed and is no longer necessary, with exceptions for archiving, scientific, historical, or statistical reasons, as stated in the European Union's General Data Protection Regulation, Article 5(e) (Article 89).

#### 3.7.1.2   Data Integrity

The major goal of data integrity in IoMT and healthcare systems is to ensure that the data arriving at the destination has not been tampered with in any manner during the wireless transmission. If attackers gain access to the data, they can alter it by exploiting the wireless network's broadcast feature, which might put patients' lives in peril. The ability to detect suspected illegal or malicious data alterations is crucial for ensuring that the data has not been compromised. As a result, we must take proper measures to protect data from harmful assaults. Furthermore, the data integrity saved on medical servers must be ensured, which means that the data cannot be tampered with. Attacks on the data packets such as DoS will affect the accessibility and availability of the data, which is of major concern [12].

### 3.7.2   SECURITY FOR SENSORS IN IoMT DEVICES

Because the computing capabilities and power constraints of the medical devices and services are restricted, the most challenging aspects of the three-tier IoMT healthcare system are security and privacy at the sensor level. The majority of calculations are now done at the personal server level, and security solutions at the sensor level must be lightweight and have low communication overheads, according to a new method in sensor level security research.

#### 3.7.2.1   Tamper Resistance

Sensors that detect the amount of light (photo-detection), pressure, or temperature around a component in IoMT devices are physically easy to steal, and they carry security information that might be revealed to an attacker. Reprogramming the environmental sensors is simple, and it might lead to unnoticed listening to conversations. In IoMT healthcare systems, this physical theft issue should be addressed.

The medical devices must include tamper-resistant integrated circuits, which prevent codes put on the devices from being read by a third party after they have been deployed.

### 3.7.2.2 Data Localization

On-body sensor position and placement in the environment are the two basic forms of sensor localization. The previous sensor localization systems were meant to determine whether the sensors are at the desired body positions. For applications like activity recognition, these forms of on-body sensor location identification are critical. The sensor localization for the Location of Things (LoT) is meant to find the sensor in the room or the patients wearing the sensor in a certain building. Because IoMT healthcare systems and medical devices are structured in such a way that they let devices to move in and out of the network coverage area often, real-time intrusion detection mechanisms are necessary. Figure 3.8 shows the location based interactive model of IoT.

### 3.7.2.3 Self-Healing

IoMT systems have integrated a technology that focuses on autonomous healing which was first proposed in autonomic computing, which is critical since IoMT devices must restart operations after network assaults. An IoMT system should be able to identify and diagnose assaults and apply appropriate security procedures with little human interaction in order to accomplish self-healing. In terms of network

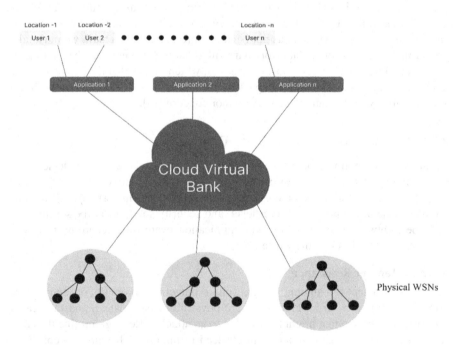

**FIGURE 3.8**   Location-based interactive model of IoT.

communication overhead and processing complexity for medical and healthcare equipment, the methods used in self-healing should be simple. The administrators must determine the sort of autonomous security strategies to deploy in the network, as different forms of network assaults necessitate different detection and recovery approaches.

### 3.7.2.4   Over-the-Air Programming

This method is of vital importance due to the fact that most IoMT devices are connected to a network and will require constant updates to keep them running smoothly with minimal or no errors. Over-the-air programming is a way to update the system, the configuration settings, and the software without the refusal of the device. This technique is also preferred due to its secure nature, and can be used to update the encryption standards used in securing the device information. It are widely used in the mobile phone industry for updates that cannot be avoided or refused. Another advantage for this mechanism is that data need not be backed up before updating of the software. The con to this mechanism is that since it is an autoupgrade to the device, if the new software or configuration is not compatible with the current version of the device, there are possibilities that the device may face trouble upgrading or processing the data. This may be of vital concerns since the devices are for medical purposes. Figure 3.9 shows over-the-air programming.

### 3.7.2.5   Forward and Backward Compatibility

In real-time healthcare applications, malfunctioning medical sensors should be replaced on a regular basis. As a result, backward and forward compatibility is essential. The forward compatibility characteristic is that future messages cannot be read by medical sensors if they are sent after the sensor has left the network. Similarly, backward compatibility means that messages sent before cannot be read

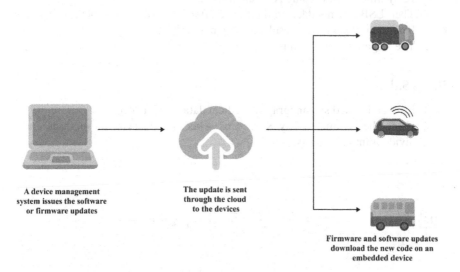

A device management
system issues the software
or firmware updates

The update is sent
through the cloud
to the devices

Firmware and software updates
download the new code on an
embedded device

**FIGURE 3.9**   Over-the-air programming.

by the sensor that has joined the network [12, 23, 25]. Compatibility concerns can be resolved by using over-the-air programming to distribute the most recent software update as soon as possible.

## 3.8   SECURITY ALGORITHMS USED IN IoMT

We can use cryptographic algorithms such as symmetric and asymmetric cryptography to ensure the security of IoMT devices. The algorithms that we focus on under symmetric cryptography are advanced encryption standards (AES-256), and the ones that come under asymmetric are Rivest–Shamir–Adelman (RSA) [8]. Least significant bit steganography is another security measure implemented. Finally, the hash algorithm is also used for keeping the data safe; SHA-512 is predominantly used.

IoMT devices will have constant data transmission with all available nodes. We will be applying the AES-256, RSA, LSB steganography and the SHA3–512 algorithm in the security scheme [26]. (Note: SHA3–512 is a very secure hashing algorithm and forms the confidentiality–integrity–availability triad, along with RSA and SHA-256.)

The implementation of the algorithm is described in the following steps. Let Alice be the sender and Bob be the receiver. The same is represented with the Figure 3.10.

### Alice's Side

1. Using the SHA3–512 hashing algorithm, we hash the confidential medical data.
2. The encryption using hash is applied to the result of the previous step using RSA algorithm with the help of the private key of Alice (PRa).
3. Output in step 2, i.e., the encrypted message undergoes concatenation with K (symmetric key) using AES algorithm.
4. Then LSB is embedded in the image after converting this encryption into bitstream; this process results in steganography
5. The steganography data is transmitted.

### Bob's Side

1. LSB-embedded steganography medical data is extricated.
2. Using the symmetric key K used by Alice, we decrypt the message and divide it into two parts.

**FIGURE 3.10**   Flowchart of the security measure.

3. One of the parts is again hashed using the same hashing algorithm (SHA3–256).
4. The latter undergoes decryption using the public key belonging to Alice.
5. A comparison is conducted to authenticate the data.

## 3.9 FEDERATED LEARNING

The confidentiality and integrity of data that is being processed in devices that come under the domain of IoMT are at risk from corporations, too. The companies that provide these devices use machine learning techniques to make their devices smarter and keep updating to improve the accuracy of the device. Traditionally, intelligence is implemented by collecting the user data and compiling them into a centralized server, where the data is assessed analyzed and later used to train the system to improve or upgrade itself [28, 15, 27]. Although the technology gets more advanced with help of this technique, such methods take place at the cost of the confidentiality of user data, and the back-and-forth client server communication can also affect user experience.

This is where federated learning comes into play. The main idea of federated learning is decentralized machine learning, whereby the user data is never sent to a centralized server; instead, the central server creates a model and sends them to suitable clients with enough data that could be used for learning. The model is deployed within suitable devices, and these devices train the model locally with their local data and create a new model, which is sent to the server. The server will collect models from multiple local devices and create a new master model which will function with greater accuracy than the previous model. The new model will then go through the same process over and over again, becoming more intelligent at the end of each round. Figure 3.11 shows the simple FL learning.

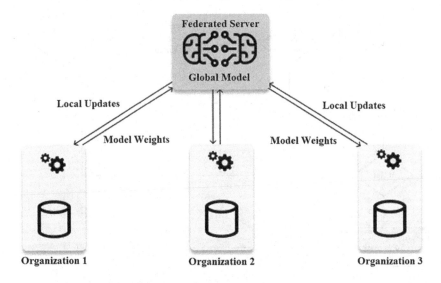

**FIGURE 3.11** Simple model of federated learning.

### 3.9.1 Federated Learning in IoMT

When it comes to IoMT devices, the speed with which data is transmitted and the storage of data are among the most important concerns. The conventional method of cloud computing will not serve the purpose of faster data transfer. This is where technologies like edge computing are of use. Edge computing will allow a faster rate of data transfer and storage by reducing the gap between the server and the storage. Still the main question remains: What about the privacy of such technologies? The privacy of user data needs to be guaranteed before, during, and after the transmission of data [29–31].

A combination of federated learning and edge computing is a privacy-preserving solution. The form of decentralized learning is preferred by the companies due to the ease with which their software can be upgraded, along with the security which it provides for the data by allocating local servers. This is more secure, since a person's medical information is particularly sensitive and will not leave their domain. Although this combination of federated learning and edge computing has the pros of distributed learning, better performance, faster data flow and storage, they also have some cons to their side [32]. If one of the clients which is found suitable for the federated learning model is of a malevolent characteristic, then they can tend to decrease the quality of the model by providing false or irrelevant data. Another issue is with the encryption mechanism used, whereby a major portion of the computing resources is being used up for encrypting the data that is being distributed [14, 33]. Figure 3.12 shows the protection algorithm.

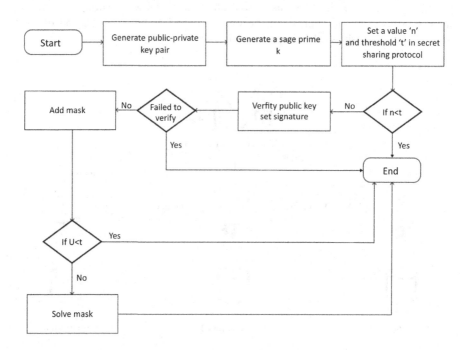

**FIGURE 3.12**   Protection algorithm.

## 3.10 CONCLUSION

In the past few years, there has been a rapid rise in the number of IoMT devices in the healthcare sector, which has greatly helped many doctors and health service workers. There is a wide range of devices, including smartwatches, smart thermometers, connected/smart inhalers, glucose level indicators, pulsometers, remote patient monitoring, mental health indicators, ingestible sensors, interconnected contact lenses, robotic surgery, insulin pumps, and many more. These smart devices have played a very important role in transforming and advancing health services and help a lot of patients residing in any corner of the world. Even though these devices are known for their substantially simplified monitoring and control due to a great network connectivity, at the same time, it invariably introduces high risks to these devices. IoMT devices, like other IoT devices and systems, may be vulnerable to security risks and assaults. Due to the sensitivity and confidentiality of the data processed by IoMT devices, they are more prone to cyber-attacks. Much of the data loss due to cyber-attacks takes place due to negligence in providing ample security measures to the devices or the networks through which such sensitive information is shared. The incorporation of machine learning in the form of a decentralized way—i.e., federated learning, along with the help of edge computing—brings a much more efficient, accurate, faster, and secure way to transmit and store data. They are the best for the task in IoMT devices, as their pros outweigh their cons.

## REFERENCES

[1] A. Verma, P. Bhattacharya, Y. Patel, K. Shah, S. Tanwar, and B. Khan. (2022). "Data Localization and Privacy-Preserving Healthcare for Big Data Applications: Architecture and Future Directions." In *Emerging Technologies for Computing, Communication and Smart Cities* (pp. 233–244). Springer, Singapore.

[2] A. Verma, P. Bhattacharya, U. Bodkhe, A. Ladha, and S. Tanwar. (March 2020). "Dams: Dynamic Association for View Materialization Based on Rule Mining Scheme." In *The International Conference on Recent Innovations in Computing* (pp. 529–544). Springer, Singapore.

[3] Todor Ivascu, Marc Frincu, and Viorel Negru. (2016). "Considerations Towards Security and Privacy in Internet of Things Based eHealth Applications." *IEEE 14th International Symposium on Intelligent Systems and Informatics*, pp. 275–280.

[4] N. Ellouze, M. Allouche, H.B. Ahmed, S. Rekhis, and N. Boudriga. (2019). "Security of Implantable Medical Devices: Limits, Requirements, and Proposals." *Proceedings of the 2 nd SysML Conference*, vol. 7, no. 12.

[5] Yingnan Sun, Charence Wong, Guang-Zhong Yang, and Benny Lo. (2017). "Secure Key Generation Using Gait Features for Body Sensor Networks." *2017 IEEE 14th International Conference on Wearable and Implantable Body Sensor Networks (BSN)*, pp. 206–209.

[6] A. Verma, P. Bhattacharya, Y. Patel, K., Shah, S. Tanwar, and B. Khan. (2022). "Data Localization and Privacy-Preserving Healthcare for Big Data Applications: Architecture and Future Directions." *Lecture Notes in Electrical Engineering*, vol. 875.

[7] D. Saraswat, A. Verma, P. Bhattacharya, S. Tanwar, G. Sharma, P.N. Bokoro, and R. Sharma. (2022). "Blockchain-Based Federated Learning in UAVs Beyond 5G Networks: A Solution Taxonomy and Future Directions." *IEEE Access*, vol. 10, pp. 33154–33182.

[8] R.M.P.H.K. Rathnayake, M. Sajeewani Karunarathne, Nazmus Shaker Nafi, and Mark A. Gregory. (2018). "Cloud Enabled Solution for Privacy Concerns in Internet of Medical Things." *2018 28th International Telecommunication Networks and Applications Conference (ITNAC)*, pp. 1–3.

[9] W.P. Jason, P.L. Benny, Oliver Wells, Morris Sloman, Nick Peters, Ara Darzi, Chris Toumazou, and Guang-Zhong Yang. (2004). "Ubiquitous Monitoring Environment for Wearable and Implantable Sensors (UbiMon)." *International Conference on Ubiquitous Computing.* https://cgi.csc.liv.ac.uk/~coopes/comp319/2016/papers/Ubiquitous ComputingMonitoring-Ng2004.pdf.

[10] Wassim Alexan, Ahmed Ashraf, Eyad Mamdouh, Sarah Mohamed, and Mohamed Moustafa. (2021). "IoMT Security: SHA3–512, AES-256, RSA and LSB Steganography." *8th NAFOSTED Conference on Information and Computer Science (NICS)*, pp. 177–181.

[11] Jean Pierre Nzabahimana. (2018). "Analysis of Security and Privacy Challenges in Internet of Things." *2018 IEEE 9th International Conference on Dependable Systems, Services and Technologies (DESSERT)*, pp. 175–178.

[12] Yingnan Sun, Frank P.-W. Lo, and Benny Lo. (2019). "Security and Privacy for the Internet of Medical Things Enabled Healthcare Systems: A Survey." *IEEE Access*, vol. 7, pp. 183339–183345.

[13] Rathin Chandra Shit, Suraj Sharma, Deepak Puthal, and Albert Zomaya. (2018). "Location of Things (LoT): A Review and Taxonomy of Sensors Localization in IoT Infrastructure." *IEEE Communications Surveys & Tutorials*, vol. 20, no. 3, third quarter, pp. 2028–2061.

[14] M. Armbrust, A. Fox, R. Griffith, A.D. Joseph, R.H. Katz, A. Konwinski, G. Lee, D.A. Patterson, A. Rabkin, I. Stoica, and M. Zaharia. (2009). "Above the Clouds: A Berkeley View of Cloud Computing." *Electrical Engineering and Computer Sciences University of California at Berkeley Technical Report*, vol. 800, p. 48.

[15] Anjie Zhu, Xiaokang Qi, Tenglong Fan, Zhitao Gu, Qinyi Lv, Dexin Ye, Jiangtao Huangfu, Yongzhi Sun, Weiqiang Zhu, and Lixin Ran. (2018). "Indoor Localization for Passive Moving Objects Based on a Redundant SIMO Radar Sensor." *IEEE Journal on Emerging and Selected Topics in Circuits and Systems*, vol. 8, no. 2, pp. 271–279.

[16] A. Verma, P. Bhattacharya, D. Saraswat, S. Tanwar, N. Kumar, and R. Sharma. (2023). "SanJeeVni: Secure UAV-Envisioned Massive Vaccine Distribution for COVID-19 Underlying 6G Network." *IEEE Sensors Journal*, vol. 23, no. 2, pp. 955–968. DOI: 10.1109/JSEN.2022.3188929.

[17] S.D. Bao, Z.K. He, R. Jin, and P. An. (2013). "A Compensation Method to Improve the Performance of IPI-Based Entity Recognition System in Body Sensor Networks." *35th Annual International Conference of the IEEE Engineering in Medicine and Biology Society (EMBC)*, pp. 1250–1253.

[18] A. Verma, P. Bhattacharya, M. Zuhair, S. Tanwar, and N. Kumar. (2021). "Vacochain: Blockchain-Based 5G-Assisted UAV Vaccine Distribution Scheme for Future Pandemics." *IEEE Journal of Biomedical and Health Informatics*, vol. 26, no. 5, pp. 1997–2007.

[19] U. Bodkhe, S. Tanwar, P. Bhattacharya, and A. Verma. (2021). "Blockchain Adoption for Trusted Medical Records in Healthcare 4.0 Applications: A Survey." In *Proceedings of Second International Conference on Computing, Communications, and Cyber-Security* (pp. 759–774). Springer, Singapore.

[20] Zhao Yuntao, Meng Yizhou, Huang Yingchun, Dai Yue, and Yang Jian. (2014). "Research and Analysis of Denial of Service Performance Based on Service-Oriented Architecture." *The 26th Chinese Control and Decision Conference*, pp. 5065–5069.

[21] Jean-Paul A. Yaacoub, Hassan N. Noura, Ola Salman, and Ali Chehab. (2021). "Robotics Cyber Security: Vulnerabilities Attacks, Countermeasures, and Recommendations." *International Journal of Information Security*, vol. 21, no. 1, pp. 115–158.

[22] D. Saraswat, P. Bhattacharya, A. Verma, V.K. Prasad, S. Tanwar, G. Sharma, P.N. Bokoro, and R. Sharma. (2022). "Explainable AI for Healthcare 5.0: Opportunities and Challenges." *IEEE Access*, vol. 10, pp. 84486–84517. DOI: 10.1109/ACCESS. 2022.3197671.

[23] V.K. Prasad, P. Bhattacharya, M. Bhavsar, A. Verma, S. Tanwar, G. Sharma, Pitshou N. Bokoro, and R. Sharma. (2022). "ABV-CoViD: An Ensemble Forecasting Model to Predict Availability of Beds and Ventilators for COVID-19 Like Pandemics." *IEEE Access*, vol. 10, pp. 74131–74151.

[24] R. Gupta, A. Shukla, and S. Tanwar. (2020). "AaYusH: A Smart Contract-Based Telesurgery System for Healthcare 4.0." *2020 IEEE International Conference on Communications Workshops (ICC Workshops)*, pp. 1–6. DOI: 10.1109/ICCWork shops49005.2020.9145044.

[25] Venkata Yanambaka, Saraju Mohanty, Elias Kougianos, Deepak Puthal, and Laavanya Rachakonda. (2019). "PMsec: PUF-Based EnergyEfficient Authentication of Devices in the Internet of Medical Things (IoMT)." *2019 IEEE International Symposium on Smart Electronic Systems (iSES) (Formerly iNiS)*, pp. 320–321.

[26] P. Bhattacharya, S. Tanwar, U. Bodkhe, S. Tyagi, and N. Kumar. (2021). "Bindaas: Blockchain-Based Deep-Learning as-a-Service in Healthcare 4.0 Applications." *IEEE Transactions on Network Science and Engineering*, vol. 8, no. 2, pp. 1242–1255.

[27] K. Bonawitz, H. Eichner, W. Grieskamp, D. Huba, A. Ingerman, V. Ivanov, C. Kiddon, J. Konečný, S. Mazzocchi, H.B. McMahan, T.V. Overveldt, D. Petrou, D. Ramage, and J. Roselander. (2019). "Towards Federated Learning at Scale: System Design." *Proceedings of the 2 nd SysML Conference*, vol. 1, pp. 374–388. Google Inc., Mountain View, Palo Alto, USA.

[28] Stanislava Stanković. (2011). "Medical Applications of Wireless Sensor Networks: Who-Did-What." *Application & Multidisciplinary Aspects of Wireless Sensor Networks*, pp. 171–184.

[29] G. Acampora, D.J. Cook, P. Rashidi, and A.V. Vasilakos. (2013). "A Survey on Ambient Intelligence in Healthcare." *Proceedings of the IEEE*, vol. 101, no. 13, pp. 2470–2494.

[30] R. Wang, J. Lai, Z. Zhang, X. Li, P. Vijayakumar, and M. Karuppiah. (2022). "Privacy-Preserving Federated Learning for Internet of Medical Things Under Edge Computing." *IEEE Journal of Biomedical and Health Informatics*, pp. 2168–2208.

[31] V.A. Patel, Pronaya Bhattacharya, Sudeep Tanwar, Rajesh Gupta, Gulshan Sharma, Pitshou N. Bokoro, and Ravi Sharma. (2022). "Adoption of Federated Learning for Healthcare Informatics: Emerging Applications and Future Directions." *IEEE Access*, vol. 10, pp. 90792–90826. DOI: 10.1109/ACCESS.2022.3201876.

[32] J. Xu, B.S. Glicksberg, C. Su, P. Walker, J. Bian, and F. Wang. (2021). "Federated Learning for Healthcare Informatics." *Journal of Healthcare Informatics Research*, vol. 5, pp. 1–19.

[33] J. Li, X. Zhu, N. Tang, and J. Sui. (2010). "Study on ZigBee Network Architecture and Routing Algorithm." *2nd International Conference on Signal Processing Systems*, vol. 2, pp. 389–393. IEEE, Dalian, China.

# 4 IoMT Implementation
## Technological Overview for Healthcare Systems

Neha Sharma, Sadhana Tiwari, Md Ilyas,
Rajeev Raghuvanshi, and Ashwin Verma

## CONTENTS

DOI: 10.1201/9781003303374-4

## 4.1  INTRODUCTION

The healthcare system plays a crucial role in the Indian economy. Healthcare systems support individuals to manage the lifestyle, which is in turn important for society. Availability of doctors, hospitals, and specialists are various challenges faced by the healthcare domain. As per a 2020 Union Ministry of India (UMI) survey, the doctor-to-patient ratio in India is 0.62:1000 [1]. With each passing year, the demand for quality healthcare solutions for people is increasing across the globe. This issue is being addressed through the use of emerging technologies. The term "smart health-care" originated from "Smarter Planet" proposal by IBM in 2008 [46]. The smart healthcare unit consists of doctors, patients, medical research, medical devices, servers, and hospitals. With a smart healthcare system, monitoring and diagnosis of patients is easier for doctors, as it provides continuous monitoring of patients and confirms the state of patients. It facilitates retrieval of medical data in advance [2]. During the COVID-19 pandemic, the concept of the smart healthcare system is drastically increasing for remote and contactless patient appointments, better diagnosis of patients, and improvements to quality of life. According to the UMI, with smart healthcare, the mortality rate could be reduced by about 26%. According to market research, the market is expected to be worth USD 345.59 billion by 2028. Figure 4.1 shows different technologies that contribute to smart health systems.

IoT technology specific to the healthcare industry is known as Internet of Medical Things (IoMT) [3]. IoMT can be understood as a system consisting of several medical devices that are connected to an information technology (IT) server. With the help of IoT, real-time monitoring of patients, hospitals, and healthcare insurance policies can take place [3–5]. As the number of IoT-enabled devices increases, such technology which transmits huge data with low latency is increasingly needed. The developing fifth-generation (5G) technology standard for broadband cellular networks has also

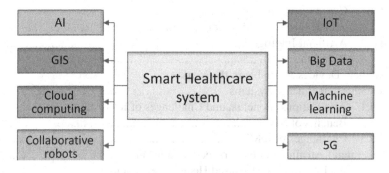

**FIGURE 4.1**  Overview of a smart healthcare system.

given the huge contribution in IoMT. 5G supports uninterrupted connectivity between the users, high speed data transmission between devices and servers in healthcare. Therefore, 5G-enabled IoT is the driver of the healthcare industry. Machine learning is used to predict hospitalization and improve customer services. The Geographical Information System (GIS) is used to track the spread of disease. From the patient point of view, different smart wearable devices are available in the market like 3D printed pills, smart pulse oximeters, and smartwatches [40]. Doctors manage medical information through different platforms like electronic health records (EHRs), laboratory information management systems, radio frequency identification (RFID), and picture archiving and communication systems. These medical platforms are used to improve patient experiences. With the use of technologies, smart healthcare systems are able to reduce costs and overcrowding in the hospital. It can also provide quick emergency services and improve collaboration between entities of smart healthcare systems [6].

Section 4.1 has been an introduction to the chapter topic, a technological overview of IoT implementation for healthcare systems. Section 4.2 presents an overview of literature on the topic, while Section 4.3 describes the contributions of IoMT in the various domains. Section 4.4 describes the architecture and technology involved in IoMT. Section 4.5 describes the application, benefits, and different challenges of IoMT. Federated learning (FL) as it relates to IoMT is addressed in Section 4.6. Different healthcare devices available in the market are described in Section 4.7. Section 4.8 concludes the chapter.

## 4.2 LITERATURE SURVEY

Much research is going on in the medical domain and researchers are trying to incorporate the emerging trends such as IoT and AI for healthcare application for the ease of medical professionals and patients both. Table 4.1 shows the review points of researchers who contributed their research in healthcare services.

## 4.3 IoMT OVERVIEW

The basic blocks for IoMT system architecture are its physical layer, network layer, and application layer [7, 13, 8, 10] which is depicted in Figure 4.2.

### 4.3.1 PHYSICAL LAYER OR PERCEPTION LAYER

This is the core layer of any IoMT system because all information is generated from the physical layer. Physical layer collects medical/health information of patients from different types of sensors and further transmits to a network layer. It includes various sensors, actuators, and micro-electronic-mechanical systems (MEMS) devices. Sensors are the devices that identify changes in the environment and include RFID, medical and infrared sensors, smart device sensors, global positioning systems (GPS), and cameras. Sensors identify information through location, object, and geographic and convert this information into digital signals. Physical layer consists of the following two sub-layers.

**TABLE 4.1**

**Existing Survey of IoT in Healthcare Services**

| References | Contribution |
|---|---|
| M. S. Islam et al. [1] | The authors discuss the application of IoT in different sectors like agriculture, smart homes, healthcare, etc. They also present the importance, applications, and benefits of IoT in healthcare. |
| M. Mamun-Ibn-Abdullah et al. [2] | The authors discuss the utility of cloud-based computing in the IoT-based smart healthcare system and also propose the cloud/IoT-based application in healthcare. |
| Ahad et al. [7] | The authors present architecture, taxonomy, and communication technology in context to smart health-care systems based on 5G. |
| J. Lloret [8] | The authors present the architecture of smart e-health monitoring of chronic patients using 5G technology, including wearable devices to measure the different parameters of the body and smartphones are used for the processing, and they propose machine learning in Big Data for the database. |
| Dalal et al. [9] | The authors discuss the importance of IoT in healthcare in the Indian economy. The authors also present the architecture, benefits, and applications of IoMT. |
| Tian et al. [10] | The authors discuss the existing problems in healthcare and propose solutions for smart healthcare. Finally, they discuss the different technologies involved in smart healthcare. |
| Javaid et al. [11] | The authors present the importance of Big Data and cloud computing technology involved in smart healthcare and how IoMT are applicable in the treatment of COVID-19 patients and smart hospitals. |
| Dwivedi et al. [12] | The authors present the role of IoMT applications case studies, advantages, and challenges for the healthcare system. |

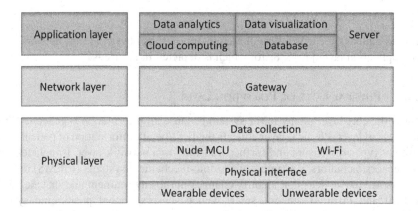

**FIGURE 4.2**   IoMT architecture.

#### 4.3.1.1 Physical Interface Layer

Physical layer collects medical information of patients and monitors environmental information from different types of sensors. Generally, sensors can be categorized into two types: wearable sensors and unwearable sensors. Each category of sensor is grouped into separate nodes or devices.

*4.3.1.1.1 Wearable Devices*

These are biosensors that monitor different parameters like blood pressure, oxygen level, glucose level, and temperature level of patients through wireless technology and send consistent information to doctors (see Figure 4.3). Doctors analyze patient health information and counsel the patients regularly with the help of wearable devices [14, 15].

*4.3.1.1.2 Unwearable Devices*

Unwearable node is used to detect environmental situations that surround patients to provide advanced healthcare services. It includes different sensors like temperature and humidity sensors, light sensors, and passive infrared sensors.

#### 4.3.1.2 Data Collection Layer

This layer collects the information/data from the physical interface and transfers that data to the network layer. Multipoint control unit and Wi-Fi are typically used in the data collection layer. Microcontrollers collect information from different types of sensors, perform data processing, and make the data ready for further transmission to a network layer.

### 4.3.2 NETWORK LAYER

This layer provides the interface between physical layer and application layer. Network layer includes wearable/unwearable devices, microcontrollers like Raspberry Pi (which acts as a gateway due to its higher capability) and mobile applications. Gateway collects information from different microcontroller units (MCUs)

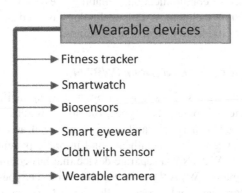

**FIGURE 4.3** Wearable devices.

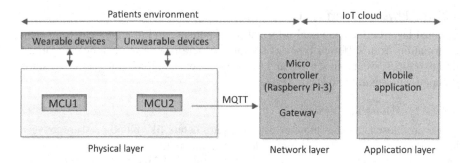

**FIGURE 4.4** IoMT network layer.

through message queue telemetry transport (MQTT) protocol. Figure 4.4 shows the components of IoMT network layer.

### 4.3.3 Application/User Interface Layer

This layer is the backend of any IoMT system. Application layer or user interface layer stores the data. Cloud computing processes, data analytics, and data processing can take place on this stored data.

## 4.4 TECHNOLOGICAL STACK INVOLVED IN IoMT

Various technologies are involved in IoMT development, such as RFID, sensor technology, fog computing, cloud computing, nanotechnology, and wireless communication and technology, as shown in Figure 4.5 [3, 10, 16, 11, 17, 18].

### 4.4.1 RFID Technology

This technology is based on radio frequency identification (RFID) tags, which communicate through radio waves or microwaves for automatic retrieval of information. RFID features wireless communication, reliability, less power consumption, and highly efficient antenna technology. This technology is used in supply chain management and logistics to identify objects in buildings.

### 4.4.2 Wireless Body Area Network (WBAN)

WBAN transfers data from sensors to a nearby processing facility. It is compatible with other wireless technologies like Zigbee, Bluetooth, wireless local area network (WLAN), wireless sensor network, and wireless personal area network (WPAN). WBAN can help reduce costs in healthcare and improve patient quality of life by using various sensors. WBAN is a separate device that has communication capability. Based on performance, WBAN can be classified in three types: personal devices, sensors, and actuators. Personal devices collect data from sensors, and communication can take place between two devices by activating the actuators. In WBAN

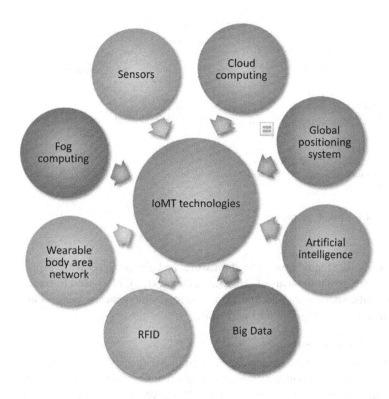

**FIGURE 4.5** Technology involved in IoMT.

application, nodes may be classified into different types such as implant node, surface node, external node, connector, storage node, and relay. End nodes are sensors, while a relay transfers data between different sensors.

### 4.4.3 FOG COMPUTING

Edge computing is the subset of fog computing. It is assumed that fog is the standard, while edge is the concept. It allows more effective data processing by eliminating propagation delay. Therefore, this technique can be used in emergency health services. Fog computing technique has significant advantages like data integrity, data security, and confidentiality. It plays a crucial role at the perception layer and the network layer of IoMT architecture. It enhances computer performance, and maintains and provides network services between end users and cloud data centers.

### 4.4.4 SENSOR TECHNOLOGY

Sensors are the backbone of IoMT systems. IoMT has various applications in terms of clinical and non-clinical contexts. IoMT is used to measure different parameters

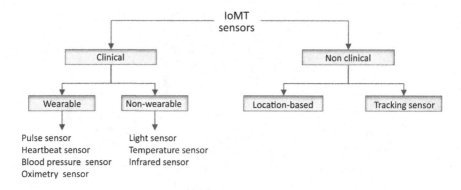

**FIGURE 4.6** IoMT sensors.

of a patient like temperature, blood pressure, and glucose level with respect to clinical contexts, while in terms of non-clinical context, IoMT is used to track locations of hospitals, specialists, and ambulances during emergencies. Sensors are broadly classified into two types (refer Figure 4.6).

### 4.4.4.1 Pulse Sensors

These measure the pulse, which can be used in emergency services like cardiac tests and remote patient monitoring systems. The wrist, fingertip, and earlobe are the contact points where pulse can be measured. Wrist-wearable devices are more popular as it is comfortable to wear any device on wrist as compared to earlobe or fingertip. Pulse can also be measured from other sensors such as pressure sensors, ultrasonic sensors, RFID sensors, and photoplethysmography (PPG) sensors.

### 4.4.4.2 Respiratory Rate Sensors

These measure the breath rate. It is used in critical situations like asthma attacks, lung cancer, tuberculosis, etc. Other sensors—like pressure sensors, fiber optic sensors, and stretch sensors—also measure respiratory rate, but according to researchers, stretch sensors provide more accuracy while other sensors suffer from noise interference.

### 4.4.4.3 Body Temperature Sensors

These measure the body temperature during fevers. According to researchers and doctors, thermistors-based sensors are preferred because they measure the body temperature while recognizing and accepting reading errors.

### 4.4.4.4 Blood Pressure Sensors

These measure blood pressure which arises due to hypertension, which can lead to a heart attack. Blood pressure can be measured by pulse transit time (PTT), the time taken for the pulse from heart to other parts of the body like the wrist, chest, finger, etc. PTT can be more accurate when it is measured between chest and wrist, while errors may be introduced in other cases.

#### 4.4.4.5 Pulse Oximeter Sensors

These measure oxygen level by retrieving PPG signals in the blood. This sensor can be used in diagnosis of COVID-19. PPG sensors contain two light-emitting diodes (LEDs) and are focused on the skin. Most of the light is absorbed by the hemoglobin, and that part which is not absorbed is calculated by photodiodes. These sensors are generally placed either on the fingertip or ear. Signal-to-noise ratio and PLL tracking methods are the two techniques that help in power reduction. It reduces power up to 6× with a minimal margin of error (approximately 2%).

#### 4.4.4.6 Passive Infrared Sensors

These are used to detect the position of a patient. They usually use radio waves and optical radiation to detect the presence of patients in its close proximity. The term passive sensor means that it does not participate in the process of identifying patients; apparently, it receives infrared radiation coming from the patient's body in its surroundings.

### 4.4.5 CLOUD COMPUTING

Cloud computing technique is used for the processing block in IoMT architecture. It provides a variety of services like software service, platform service, and infrastructure service. IoMT sensors generate large amounts of data. This data can be stored and processed with the help of a cloud network. The cloud provides an infinite amount of resources in the data center. By using these resources, the healthcare industry can benefit from the stored and analyzed data for future use. Physicians and doctors can monitor and diagnose patients remotely with the help of the cloud in IoMT. It has a significant advantage, but the drawback is latency. Analytically generated data from the cloud must be transmitted over the internet for access by medical devices. There are platforms whereby multiple cloud providers come together to provide better services to the user to store patients' sensitive information with competitive pricing [19]. This process takes a long time; therefore, cloud computing technique is not feasible in the emergency device. This drawback is eliminated by edge computing or fog computing.

### 4.4.6 GLOBAL POSITIONING SYSTEM

GPS is used by physicians and hospitals in the following ways.

1. **Track Fastest Route:** During emergency services, it is assumed that ambulance drivers must use the shortest path with minimal delay. GPS device is installed in the ambulance that helps drivers to choose an effective path to reach the destination.
2. **Calculate Time:** GPS devices have the feature to calculate arrival time. Using this feature, healthcare workers and physicians are able to collect valuable tools and medication in advance before the patients arrive.
3. **Temperature Monitoring:** Medicines are supposed to be kept at appropriate temperature; otherwise, temperature can destroy the valuable medicine.

GPS has the capability to detect the temperature. Therefore, this system ensures that the medicine should be kept at the correct temperature.

4. **Resource Allocation:** GPS enables allocation of resources to ensure the physicians and patients reach things on the time.
5. **Location Tracking:** In GPS, location is tracked through a navigation satellite. Therefore, the nearest ambulance is preferred to pick patients in order to save time and improve healthcare services.
6. **Equipment Tracking:** Hospital equipment is very costly and there is always the possibility of theft. Therefore, an indoor GPS system can solve the problem of theft and the stolen equipment can be recovered immediately.

### 4.4.7 ARTIFICIAL INTELLIGENCE

In healthcare, AI techniques are used to improve diagnosis (such as cancer therapy, computerized tomography [CT] scans, and X-rays), virtual healthcare assistants (VHAs), and healthcare bots. VHAs monitor patient information with the help of patient data, making it possible that doctors and patients are constantly in communication; informs pharmacies about prescription of patients; and reminds patients to take medication. Bots are mainly used for patient engagement. Healthcare bots incorporate the concept of image recognition, natural language programming, sentimental analysis, and data mining into the chat script.

### 4.4.8 BIG DATA

IoMT devices collect large amounts of patient information which needs to be analyzed properly to make a decision. An efficient solution to this problem is Big Data analysis and virtualization. Big Data collects large amounts of patient information on a variety of medical and climate sensors, temperature, locations, and geographical data. The data analytics process is performed by statistical analysis, cleaning, and extraction before referral to physician or patients [20].

## 4.5 MEDICAL DEVICES AVAILABLE IN THE MARKET FOR SMART HEALTHCARE SYSTEMS

Various examples of wearable devices used in healthcare include stationary medical devices, continuous glucose monitoring (CGM) systems, connected inhalers, OpenAPS closed-loop insulin delivery, activity trackers during cancer treatment, ingestible sensors, connected contact lenses, depression-fighting smartwatch apps, and coagulation testing, sometimes using platforms such as Apple's ResearchKit, Parkinson's Project Blue Sky, and LEAF Patient Monitoring System [14, 15].

1. **Wearable Devices:** These are biosensors that monitor different parameters like blood pressure, oxygen level, glucose level, and temperature level of patients constantly through wireless communication. By calculating these parameters, doctors can analyze and counsel patients remotely. Examples of wearable devices are Fitbits, smartwatches, and wearable monitors.

2. **OpenAPS Closed-Loop Insulin Delivery:** This system is designed to control insulin delivery by insulin pump. Using the OpenAPS system, glucose level can be adjusted for a certain range after a meal. It uses a CGM sensor to determine glucose level and issue commands to the insulin pump to maintain the temporary basal rate as per requirements.
3. **Smart Drill:** The smart drill is a brush that suggests the location and depth for drill operation during surgery. Drilling operation is based on resistance and bone density.
4. **Implant Devices:** Implant devices gather information and send it to cloud computing infrastructure. They send information from the patients to doctors regularly. These devices are placed either inside or the surface of the body. For example, brain implant devices are used to manipulate the brain and relieve pain or depression.
5. **Smart Inhalers:** IoT-based inhalers monitor the frequency of asthma attacks and also alert the patient when any alarming situation arises.
6. **Ingestible Sensors:** These can collect information such as stomach pH and gives insights into the digestive tract in a less invasive, non-surgical manner.
7. **Smart Contact Lenses:** These are mounted on the surface and can be controlled with eye blinking. With the help of these lenses, images can be captured and tasks can be carried by processing the acquired information.

### 4.5.1 APPLICATIONS, BENEFITS, AND CHALLENGES OF IoMT

Contribution of IoMT in various applications is listed in Table 4.2.

**TABLE 4.2**
**Applications of IoMT**

| S. No. | Author Name | Publishing Year | Application |
|---|---|---|---|
| 1. | Islam et al. [1] | 2020 | Monitoring of blood pressure, glucose level, oxygen saturation, body temperature and electrocardiogram. |
| 2. | Verma et al. [21] | 2020 | Maintain industrial mechanics, managing pharma supply chains and controlling drug manufacturing environments, sales and marketing, and patient access. |
| 3. | App Development Agency [22] | 2020 | Remote patient monitoring through wearable apps, sensor technology. |
| 4. | Applications of IoT In Healthcare System by Harshith [13] | 2020 | Emergency care, distribution of medical information, research application, insurance companies, detection of how many patients are remaining in quarantine during COVID-19. |
| 5. | Dwivedi et al. [12] | 2021 | Testing and tracing of disease spread, smart hospitals and smart operating rooms, tele-dentistry, 3-D scanning and printing, automatic robot-based healthcare automation, adverse drug reaction system. |

**TABLE 4.3**
**Benefits of IoMT**

| S. No. | Benefits | References |
|---|---|---|
| 1. | • Reduce cost | [14, 15] |
| | • Collection of accurate data and minimize error. | |
| | • Improved outcomes of treatment | |
| | • Improved diagnostic accuracy because they have real-time patient data | |
| | • Low patient interaction and adherence to medication | |
| | • Quality of life is improved | |
| | • Improvement of disease management and prevention | |
| | • End user experience and patient care is improved | |
| | • Discovery of new methods for disease prevention | |
| 2. | • Healthcare equipment is cheaper | [23] |
| | • More innovative | |
| | • Improve the economy of healthcare industry | |
| 3. | • Improve patient safety | [24–27] |
| | • Patient data are maintaining through EHRs | |
| | • Revenue-generating opportunity for different industry sectors like telecom, software, firmware, and many more | |

## 4.5.2 BENEFITS OF IoMT

IoT has various advantages such as agriculture, education, smart homes, business and consumers, society, environments, markets, and also individuals. IoMT has made large contributions in the medical field also. Using IoMT, remote monitoring and diagnosis of patients is possible. IoMT collects patient data accurately with minimal cost and minimizes error risk while maintaining privacy. The following benefits are listed in Table 4.3 based on the contributions of IoMT.

## 4.5.3 CHALLENGES OF IoMT

There are numerous challenges as listed in Table 4.4 based on the contribution of IoMT.

## 4.6 FEDERATED LEARNING AND ITS PERSPECTIVE IN IoMT

Artificial intelligence greatly assists physicians in diagnosing patients remotely by studying patterns in the data generated by these devices. Conventional machine learning/deep learning (ML/DL) models require sensor data generated at the test end, so all sensor data must be transmitted to the central server in order to train data using ML/DL models—but transferring patient data to central servers may create significant security and privacy issues [33].

FL is the latest variation of ML, in which the ML model is used on individual machines to train data rather than transferring data to central servers; the ML model itself is used on individual devices to train data. Parameters from models trained on

**TABLE 4.4**

**Challenges of IoT in the Healthcare System**

| S. No. | Challenges | References |
|---|---|---|
| 1. | • Security and privacy of data<br>• Amalgamation of various devices and protocols<br>• Scalability, upgradation, regulations and standardization<br>• Cost<br>• Energy limitation<br>• Massive amount of data generation<br>• Interoperability and manage device diversity<br>• Need for medical expertise | [1, 28, 29, 24] |
| 2. | • Computational limitation<br>• Memory limitation | [30] |
| 3. | • Needs high flexibility<br>• Data transmits from the sensor device to the cloud device and vice versa; as a result, quality degrades.<br>• Increasing the number of devices and sensors increases energy consumption/power consumption.<br>• Traditional approach in electrocardiograms (ECGs) increases the cost and possibilities of error | [31, 29] |
| 4. | • Intelligence in medical care<br>• Processing of data in real time<br>• System prediction | [32, 17, 24] |
| 5. | • Environment impact (Since in the IoMT system various biomedical sensors are designed through amalgamations of various semiconductor materials like earth metals and other toxic gas material, adverse effects in the environment result) | [12] |
| 6. | • Market impact:<br>• Physician and security policy compliance<br>• Overloading of data on healthcare facility | [25] |

individual devices may be exported to ML/DL intermediate models for global training. In this way, FL can help maintain the confidentiality of patient data by not disclosing sensitive information to potential attackers. Currently, COVID-19 has grown into a global health emergency and endangers millions. To combat the coronavirus, related researchers have used emerging ML technologies to train the model for diagnosis [34]. However, due to unreliable communication channels and potential attackers, a large amount of data collected may cause many security and privacy concerns during this time. With the aim to ensure the safety of the patient's record in the referral process and training, integrated confidentiality learning becomes the best option.

### 4.6.1 Architecture of FL-Based Healthcare Systems

Framework of FL consists of certain steps, as shown in Figure 4.7. Initially, the central server selects different related network parameters such as deciding whether the

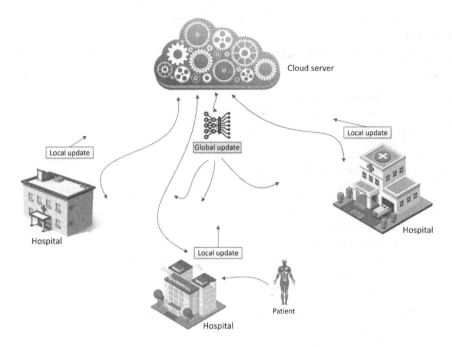

**FIGURE 4.7**   Architecture of a FL-based healthcare system.

identifying algorithm is based on prediction or classification, medical image processing, or some other human-related application. In addition, the ML is selected, based on different configurable parameters and learning rates. In addition, the central server determines clients participating in the FL process [35]. The central server determines the number of end nodes to participate in FL, then shares the first models between nodes. The end node trains the model based on different parameters such as local data and then the updated model is shared with the central model for aggregation. Sometimes, we could use a federated mid-range integrated model, whereby weights are assigned to local models based on data size availability. Finally, the new global model is used to share the data with end nodes. The learning process continues in a repetitive manner until the desired accuracy is reached.

## 4.6.2 Impact of FL in IoMT

New improved features for collaborative learning in FL allow its use in various fields, especially in IoMT. By adopting FL algorithms in IoMT, the local model parameters are connected or communicated, while the host data remains constant within local nodes [36]. This increases privacy and reduces information leakage. In addition, network training on a variety of data enhances the capability of FL. Communication costs are reduced by loading only gradients rather than large datasets. These actions taken by FL enable effective bandwidth utilization and avoid network congestion on large IoMT networks [37, 38].

### 4.6.3 APPLICATION OF FL IN IoMT SYSTEMS

| S. No. | Application | Reference |
|---|---|---|
| 1. | EHR management | [39–41, 24] |
| | Image processing | |
| | Security and privacy in IoMT | |
| 2. | Cyber physical systems in IoMT | [27, 42–45] |

## 4.7 MARKET IMPACT OF IoMT

IoMT is amalgamation of health system and services, software applications, and different healthcare devices. It enables patients to constantly consult their doctors through the internet, which helps patients to reduce hospital visits. IoT-enabled healthcare providers are also supporting different industries like the data management industry, the firmware industry, the telecom industry, and the software industry [46]. Some statistics are shown in Figure 4.8 which show that impact (in terms of percentage) of different industries in healthcare. This graph depicts why IoMT has become the digital health leader and will become and remain popular.

## 4.8 CONCLUSION

IoMT technology has potential to fulfill the demands of the healthcare industry. Sensors, RFID, AI, Big Data, and GPS are the main technological stacks of IoMT-based smart healthcare systems. All these entities are briefly described in this chapter. Whole systems are virtually composed of a physical layer, a virtualization layer and a network layer. Each layer has a significant role in the system and is

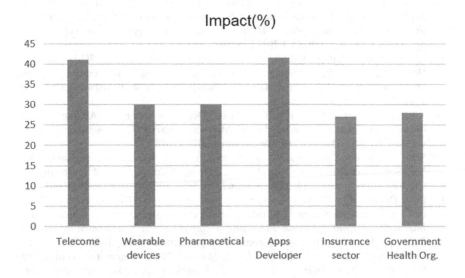

**FIGURE 4.8** Impact of different industries in IoMT.

also mentioned in this study. Several devices used for remote surgery, smart drills, implants, and emergency devices were presented in this chapter. Rehabilitation systems, drug manufacturing, and remote patient monitoring are the few applications of IoT in the healthcare domain. Cost reduction, improved disease monitoring, and safety are a few of the benefits. In spite of having many benefits and applications, there are some challenges. Data security, system scalability capabilities, environmental impacts, transmission, expertise availability and computational capabilities are major concerns. With all these facts, the market analysis of this technology in context to the healthcare domain is also performed. With above study, it is concluded that with the implementation of IoMT-based healthcare systems can result in better and timely measurement, real time monitoring, fast processing, and better medical data analysis.

## REFERENCES

[1] M.S. Islam, F. Humaira, and F.N. Nur. (February 2020). "Healthcare Applications in IoT." *Global Journal of Medical Research*, vol. 20, no. 2. https://medicalresearchjournal.org/index.php/GJMR/article/view/1960.

[2] M. Mamun-Ibn-Abdullah, M. Shahinuzzaman, S.M. Abdur Rahim, and M. Humayun Kabir. (August 2020). "Convergence Platform of Cloud Computing and Internet of Things (IoT) for Smart Healthcare Application." *Journal of Computer and Communications*, vol. 8, no. 8. DOI: 10.4236/jcc.2020.88001.

[3] White Paper. "How IoT Is Transforming the Future of Healthcare." https://www.keysight.com/in/en/assets/3120-1073/white-papers/How-IoT-is-Transforming-the-Future-of-Healthcare.pdf.

[4] IoT WORM. https://iotworm.com/internet-of-things-healthcare-devices/. Accessed 27 December 2021.

[5] Smart City. https://www.smartcity.press/smart-healthcare-for-smart-cities/. Accessed 23 December 2021.

[6] Rafael Molina-Masegosa, and Javier Gozalvez. (December 2017). "LTE-V for Sidelink 5G V2X Vehicular Communications: A New 5G Technology for Short-Range Vehicle-to-Everything Communications." *IEEE Vehicular Technology Magazine*, vol. 12, no. 4, pp. 30–39. DOI: 10.1109/MVT.2017.2752798.

[7] Abdul Ahad, Mohammad Tahir, and Akok-Lim Alvin Yau. (2016). "5G-Based Smart Healthcare Network: Architecture, Taxonomy, Challenges and Future Research Directions." *IEEE Access*, vol. 4, pp. 100747–100762. DOI: 10.1109/ACCESS.2019.2930628.

[8] J. Lloret, L. Parra, M. Taha, and J. Tomas. (December 2017). "An Architecture and Protocol for Smart Continuous eHealth Monitoring Using 5G." *Computer Networks*, vol. 129, pp. 340–351. DOI: 10.1016/j.comnet.2017.05.018.

[9] Shuo Tian, Wenbo Yang, Jehane Michael, Le Grange, Peng Wang, Wei Huang, and Zhewei Ye. (September 2019). "Smarthealthcare: Making Medical Care More Intelligent." *Global Health Journal*, vol. 3, no. 3, pp. 62–65. DOI: 10.1016/j.glohj.2019.07.001.

[10] Priya Dalal, Gaurav Aggarwal, and Sanjay Tejasvee. (April 2020). "Internet of Things (IoT) in Healthcare System: IA3 (Idea, Architecture, Advantages and Applications)." *International Conference on Innovative Computing and Communication (ICICC 2020)*, pp. 1–6. https://papers.ssrn.com/sol3/papers.cfm?abstract_id=3566282.

[11] Mohd Javaid, and Ibrahim Haleem Khan. (January 2021). "Internet of Things (IoT) Enabled Healthcare Helps to Take the Challenges of COVID-19 Pandemic." *Oral Biology and Craniofacial Research*, vol. 11, no. 2. DOI: 10.1016/j.jobcr.2021.01.015.

[12] Ruby Dwivedi, Divya Mehrotra, and Shaleen Chandra. (November 2021). "Potential of Internet of Medical Things (IoMT) Applications in Building A Smart Healthcare System: A Systematic Review." *Journal of Oral Biology and Craniofacial Research.* DOI: 10.1016/j.jobcr.2021.11.010.

[13] J.M.C. Brito. (July 2016). "Trends in Wireless Communications Towards 5G Networks-The Influence of e-Health and IoT Applications." *2016 International Multidisciplinary Conference Computer. Energy Science (SpliTech).* DOI: 10.1109/SpliTech.2016.7555949.

[14] CONTUS. (2020). https://blog.contus.com/iot-healthcare-applications-benefits/. Accessed 20 November 2021.

[15] https://cprimestudios.com/blog/benefits-internet-things-hospitals-and-healthcare. Accessed 21 November 2021.

[16] https://www2.deloitte.com/us/en/insights/industry/health-care/smart-technology-in-health-care-medicaid- programs.html. Accessed 20 November 2021.

[17] D. Saraswat, P. Bhattacharya, A. Verma, V.K. Prasad, S. Tanwar, G. Sharma, P.N. Bokoro, and R. Sharma. (2022). "Explainable AI for Healthcare 5.0: Opportunities and Challenges." *IEEE Access*, vol. 10, pp. 84486–84517. DOI: 10.1109/ACCESS.2022. 3197671.

[18] https://iotbusinessnews.com/2020/03/25/05014-how-to-apply-iot-in-healthcare-best-approaches-and-use-cases/. Accessed 15 January 2021.

[19] A. Verma, P. Bhattacharya, U. Bodkhe, D. Saraswat, S. Tanwar, and K. Dev. (2022). "FedRec: Trusted Rank-Based Recommender Scheme for Service Provisioning in Federated Cloud Environment." *Digital Communications and Networks*, pp. 2352–8648. DOI: 10.1016/j.dcan.2022.06.003.

[20] Sushruta Mishra, Brojo Kishore Mishra, Hrudaya Kumar Tripathy, and Arijit Dutta. (2020). "Analysis of the Role and Scope of Big Data Analytics with IoT in Health Care Domain." *Handbook of Data Science Approaches for Biomedical Engineering*, pp. 1–23. DOI: 10.1016/B978-0-12-818318-2.00001-5.

[21] Arushi Verma: IOT, Advancing Healthcare Sector Like Never Before, Scrutiny Tip. (August 2020). https://orcid.org/0000-0002-0303-8368.

[22] www.appdevelopmentagency.com/possibilities-of-iot-in-healthcare/. Accessed 24 April 2021.

[23] https://kalypso.com/files/docs/Axendia_WhitePaper_IOMT_Kalypso.pdf. Accessed 15 November 2021.

[24] Chao-Hsi Huang, and Kung-Wei Cheng. (January 2014). "RFID Technology Combined with IoT Application in Medical Nursing System, Bulletin of Networking." *Computing, Systems, and Software*, vol. 3, no. 1, pp. 20–24. ISSN: 2186-5140. www.bncss.org/index. php/bncss/article/view/31/32.

[25] www.aranca.com/assets/uploads/resources/special-reports/Internet-of-Medical-Things-IoMT_Aranca-Special-Report.pdf. Accessed 24 December 2021.

[26] P. Bhattacharya, P. Mehta, S. Tanwar, M.S. Obaidat, and K.F. Hsiao. (November 2020). "HeaL: A Blockchain-Envisioned Signcryption Scheme for Healthcare IoT Ecosystems." *2020 International Conference on Communications, Computing, Cybersecurity, and Informatics (CCCI)*, pp. 1–6.

[27] M. Zuhair, F. Patel, D. Navapara, P. Bhattacharya, and D. Saraswat. (April 2021). "BloCoV6: A Blockchain-Based 6G-Assisted UAV Contact Tracing Scheme for COVID-19 Pandemic." *2021 2nd International Conference on Intelligent Engineering and Management (ICIEM)*, pp. 271–276.

[28] https://iot4beginners.com/applications-of-internet-of-things-in-healthcare. Accessed 24 April 2021.

[29] Sureshkumar Selvaraj, and Suresh Sundaravaradhan. (2019). "Challenges and Opportunities in IoT Healthcare Systems: A Systematic Review." *SN Applied Sciences.* https://link.springer.com/article/10.1007/s42452-019-1925-y.

[30] Gonçalo J.F. Carnaz, and Vitor Nogueira. (2019). "An Overview of IoT and Healthcare." *International Conference of the IEEE Engineering in Medicine and Biology Society*, pp. 1455–1458.

[31] A. Verma, P. Bhattacharya, U. Bodkhe, A. Ladha, and S. Tanwar. (March 2020). "Dams: Dynamic Association for View Materialization Based on Rule Mining Scheme." In *The International Conference on Recent Innovations in Computing* (pp. 529–544). Springer, Singapore.

[32] A. Verma, P. Bhattacharya, Y. Patel, K. Shah, S. Tanwar, and B. Khan. (2022). "Data Localization and Privacy-Preserving Healthcare for Big Data Applications: Architecture and Future Directions." In *Emerging Technologies for Computing, Communication and Smart Cities* (pp. 233–244). Springer, Singapore.

[33] D. Saraswat, A. Verma, P. Bhattacharya, S. Tanwar, G. Sharma, P.N. Bokoro, and R. Sharma. (2022). "Blockchain-Based Federated Learning in UAVs Beyond 5G Networks: A Solution Taxonomy and Future Directions." *IEEE Access*, vol. 10, pp. 33154–33182.

[34] V.K. Prasad, P. Bhattacharya, M. Bhavsar, A. Verma, S. Tanwar, G. Sharma, Pitshou N. Bokoro, and R. Sharma. (2022). "ABV-CoViD: An Ensemble Forecasting Model to Predict Availability of Beds and Ventilators for COVID-19 Like Pandemics." *IEEE Access*, vol. 10, pp. 74131–74151.

[35] V.A. Patel, P. Bhattacharya, S. Tanwar, N.K. Jadav, and R. Gupta. (2022). "BFLEdge: Blockchain Based Federated Edge Learning Scheme in V2X Underlying 6G Communications." *2022 12th International Conference on Cloud Computing, Data Science & Engineering (Confluence)*, pp. 146–152. DOI: 10.1109/Confluence52989. 2022.9734213.

[36] V.A. Patel, Pronaya Bhattacharya, Sudeep Tanwar, Rajesh Gupta, Gulshan Sharma, Pitshou N. Bokoro, and Ravi Sharma. (2022). "Adoption of Federated Learning for Healthcare Informatics: Emerging Applications and Future Directions." *IEEE Access*, vol. 10, pp. 90792–90826. DOI: 10.1109/ACCESS.2022.3201876.

[37] A. Verma, P. Bhattacharya, M. Zuhair, S. Tanwar, and N. Kumar. (2021). "Vacochain: Blockchain-Based 5G-Assisted UAV Vaccine Distribution Scheme for Future Pandemics." *IEEE Journal of Biomedical and Health Informatics*, vol. 26, no. 5, pp. 1997–2007.

[38] U. Bodkhe, S. Tanwar, P. Bhattacharya, and A. Verma. (2021). "Blockchain Adoption for Trusted Medical Records in Healthcare 4.0 Applications: A Survey." In *Proceedings of Second International Conference on Computing, Communications, and Cyber-Security* (pp. 759–774). Springer, Singapore.

[39] A. Verma, P. Bhattacharya, D. Saraswat, S. Tanwar, N. Kumar, and R. Sharma. (2023). "SanJeeVni: Secure UAV-Envisioned Massive Vaccine Distribution for COVID-19 Underlying 6G Network." *IEEE Sensors Journal*, vol. 23, no. 2, pp. 955–968. DOI: 10.1109/JSEN.2022.3188929.

[40] https://aicorespot.io/iot-within-healthcare-applications-advantages-and-challenges/. Accessed 15 January 2021.

[41] www.peerbits.com/blog/internet-of-things-healthcare-applications-benefits-and-chal lenges.html. Accessed 15 November 2021.

[42] Impact of IoT in the Healthcare Industry in India. https://healthcare.siliconindia.com/ viewpoint/cxoinsights/impact-of-iot-inthe-healthcare-industry-in-india-nwid-18364. html. Accessed 24 April 2021.

[43] www.transparencymarketresearch.com/internet-of-medical-things-iomt-market.html Accessed 24 December 2021.

[44] Mansoor Ali, Faisal Naeem, Muhammad Tariq, and Geroges Kaddoum. "Federated Learning for Privacy Preservation in Smart Healthcare Systems: A Comprehensive Survey." https://arxiv.org/abs/2203.09702.

[45] V.A. Patel, Pronaya Bhattacharya, Sudeep Tanwar, Rajesh Gupta, Gulshan Sharma, Pitshou N. Bokoro, and Ravi Sharma. (2022). "Adoption of Federated Learning for Healthcare Informatics: Emerging Applications and Future Directions." *IEEE Access*, vol. 10, pp. 90792–90826. DOI: 10.1109/ACCESS.2022.3201876.

[46] S.J. Palmisano. (2008). "A Smarter Planet: The Next Leadership Agenda." IBM: https://www.ibm.com/ibm/history/ibm100/us/en/icons/smarterplanet/

# 5 A New Method of 5G-Based Mobile Computing for IoMT Applications

*Javaid A. Sheikh, Sakeena Akhtar, and Rehana Amin*

## CONTENTS

## 5.1 INTRODUCTION

Our modern societies have greatly been affected by mobile communications over the past few decades. The developing technology standards for broadband cellular mobile communications (1G–4G) have drastically changed the ways of sharing, accessing, and exchange of information among humans. The increase in mobile communications generates huge data traffic, and there is always a need for new and updated standards of communication that fulfil the ever-increasing rate of data from one device to another. This has ultimately led towards the higher generations of mobile communication world with higher data traffic and bulk connected devices.

5G communications are rapidly developing to undertake the challenges due to an increased growth in wireless data traffic. Among such tasks, the most difficult one for the future generation networks is to deal with how various devices like cameras,

DOI: 10.1201/9781003303374-5

connected sensors, smart-home grid appliances, etc., will connect to networks. The two leading market drivers for 5G networks are mobile internet and IoT.

Thus, in general, mobile internet and IoT applications can be classified into three use-cases, i.e., mMTC (massive machine-type communications), eMBB (enhanced mobile broadband) and URLLC (ultrareliable and low-latency communications). The main aspects of 5G currently being visualized are as follows.

- Fog computing
- Device-to-device communication
- Machine-to-machine communication
- e-health and m-health services

### 5.1.1 Fog Computing

The term "fog computing" was first introduced by Cisco in 2012 [1]. It spreads the cloud-based internet with a midway layer among mobile devices and the cloud. The low latency and smooth service delivery between cloud and mobile is only possible because of fog computing. The geo-distributed fog servers that are the intermediate fog layer are installed at the edge of networks like bus terminals, parks, etc. A fog server resembles a cloud server which is light in weight with highly virtualized computing system having capacity to store high volumes of data and facilitate efficient wireless communication. The gap between mobile users and the cloud is overcome by the use of fog servers. It directly communicates with users using Wi-Fi and Bluetooth. The important applications and functions of the cloud can be easily accessed with the help of fog servers. Thus, edge computing can broadly be used through fog computing with main focus on the local application that provide services and computational request.

The example and techniques in [2, 3] can be included in a fog computing framework.

#### 5.1.1.1 Device-to-Device Communication

The incomparable number of connected devices in 5G communication networks is likely to reach 50 billion by 2020 and to assist such an enormous number of connected devices, we require data rates to grow by a factor of 1,000. Some of the main requirements of 5G wireless networks includes e-health, e-banking, e-learning, and device-to-device (D2D) communication [4, 5]. The long two-hop route across the base station is replaced by a short one-hop route with less latency, reduced consumption of power and greater spectral efficiency using D2D links. The transmission schemes for D2D cellular systems is constructed using geometric tools [6–8] and game theory [9, 10], and it can also be used for cellular offloading [11, 12]. Thus, in general, all these above techniques reveal that D2D communication links increase the overall network throughput provided.

#### 5.1.1.2 Machine-to-Machine Communication

With the introduction of IoT, especially machine-to-machine (M2M) communications also known as 3GPP (3rd Generation Partnership Project), machine-type communications (MTC) has a special requirement. Like the previous mobile generations, MTC calls for more capacity for human-type traffic (HTC). MTC simply refers to swapping of information among machines and the ecosystem. The exchange of information can be in between (one end M2M—other end M2M). Fundamentally, M2M communication is necessarily having one end as a machine, constituting it to be a fundamental part of the IoT services [13, 14].

### 5.1.1.3   e-Health and m-Health Services

In recent times, wearable technology has been introduced. The most recent trend for the growth of IoT services is interaction with humans with the help of sensors and actuators. The actuators which need to be installed at the patient's home and its associated centralized servers that are installed at hospitals enables automated communication between in-body or on-body sensors. With the help of this process, a patient can be remotely diagnosed for any kind of illness and based upon the diagnosis, drug dosage can be suggested to the patient, which is considered a big sub-domain of wearable technology. Similarly, another sub-domain of e-health service is m-health. Mobile health (m-health) states the use of medicine and public health by the mobile devices for health services, information, and data collection. The mobile device is used to collect all the relevant and related clinical health data of the community, including mobile telemedicine [15]. Thus, m-health operates within a range of objectives that include improved access to healthcare and health-associated information (especially for those areas which are hard to reach), enhanced skills to identify and track diseases and prolonged access to current medical education, and better guidance for health workers.

Although there are countless applications of 5G and IoT networks, such as delivering vaccine with UAV on 5G or 6G communication channels [16–18], and few of which were introduced in Section 5.1, the focus in this chapter has been laid on m-health services only. The chapter proposes an efficient, reliable watermarked data hiding and data transmission technique in 5G Networks for m-health services. The chapter has been structured as: Section 5.2 briefly introduces the filter bank multicarrier (FBMC) modulation technique used as a signal processing technique in 5G Networks. Section 5.3 describes the watermarking model used in this chapter. Section 5.4 gives the details of the medical data (information about each medical image that has been used for test purposes in this chapter). A block diagram and description of the proposed technique is given in Section 5.5. Section 5.6 displays the simulation results, and finally, the chapter is concluded in Section 5.7.

### 5.1.1.4   Federated Computing and IoMT

Recent advancements in communication technologies and IoMT have transformed healthcare by exploiting artificial Intelligence (AI)-driven machines and systems. Centralized data collection and processing traditionally is core in the case of AI-based systems, but this is not feasible in the current scenario large volumes of patient records and privacy concerns related to sensitive information in the connected network of hospitals [19]. In this context, federated learning (FL) can prove an emerging paradigm that enhance healthcare services by providing security for the sensitive data. This is possible by training the hospitals with local data and creating a model at the local level to take decision for furthering these local models now sent to the global aggregator to generate a global updated model and further share the global model to all the local hospitals so all local models are updated and trained via all the data of different hospitals. FL can be used in data management, health monitoring, and COVID-19 management [20, 21]. In this chapter, we analyze several FL-based projects and the key findings.

## 5.2  FILTER BANK MULTICARRIER MODULATION

Filter bank multicarrier (FBMC) transmission has an added advantage over the OFDM (orthogonal frequency-division multiplexing) modulation technique. It overcomes the main drawbacks (synchronization requirements and reduced spectral efficiency) of OFDM modulation. Due to the benefits, FBMC is considered as the most capable techniques of modulations for 5G networks. In OFDM, orthogonality is maintained for all the subcarriers, whereas in FBMC orthogonality is maintained in neighbouring sub-channels only. In FBMC, besides the IFFT/FFT operations, additional filtering is done at both the transmitting and receiving sides with the help of a filter bank called a prototype filter. The filter bank in FBMC overcomes the limitations of OFDM systems. There is no need to insert a cyclic prefix between the sub-channels in FBMC [22]. Moreover, for the generation of several carrier frequencies, the zero frequency is exploited in the FBMC. This type of FBMC filter is categorized based upon the overlapping factor k. Such a filter has the order which is given by $2 \times (k-1)$, where k = 2, 3, 4. Further, k is basically a integer in time domain and number of frequency coefficients in the frequency domain as FFT filter coefficients. Figure 5.1 shows the prototype filter with frequency response for K = 4. The frequency spreading technique is employed in the existing FBMC modulation technique. Therefore, with FBMC, it is easy to analyze as compared with other modulation techniques [23].

### 5.2.1  FILTER BANK IMPLEMENTATION

The block diagram of the filter bank is depicted in Figure 5.2. The filter bank (shown in Figure 5.1) with overlapping factor K, 2(K − 1) carriers needs to be

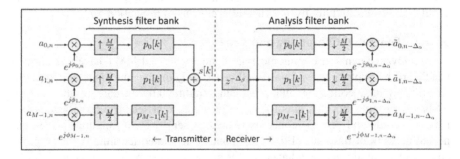

**FIGURE 5.1**   Prototype filter frequency coefficients and frequency response for K = 4.

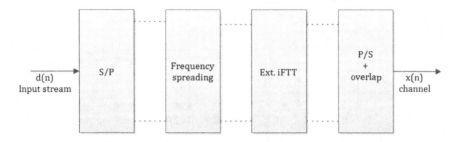

**FIGURE 5.2**  Filter bank implementation in transmitter.

modulated by the data element, but in Figure 5.2, the filter bank needs to be modelled as the following.

- IFFT size of KM, used to generate the carriers.
- The filter frequency coefficients are multiplied by data element [$di(mM)$] where M is multicarrier symbol and m is symbol index.
- $2(K - 1)$ inputs of the IFFT are fed by the data elements.
- IFFT gives a block of KM samples for each set of data. Since symbol rate is 1/M, K consecutive IFFT outputs overlap in time domain.
- The overlap and sum operations are basically the output of the filter bank as shown in Figure 5.2:

Figure 5.3 shows the detailed process of implementation. The indices i and I + 2 of the sub-channels do not overlap with indies I + 1. Thus, real and imaginary parts need to be processed separately in order to maintain orthogonality, and hence, offset quadrature amplitude modulation (OQAM) is the efficient technique to be used here. The complex data symbol consisting of real and imaginary data parts are transmitted separately with imaginary parts delayed by N/2. Therefore, real part of IFFT of the filter bank is used for i and I + 2, and imaginary part for I + 1, or vice versa [24].

At the receiver, the extended FFT of size KM is basically the implementation method of filter bank. Therefore, at the output of FFT, the data elements are convalesced by weighted de-spreading operation as shown in Figure 5.4.

## 5.3   WATERMARKING MODEL

During transmission of any kind of message in a wireless environment, the transmitted message needs to be protected from any intentional or unintentional manipulation. This is done by a robust way of hiding and securing information called digital speech watermarking in a host speech signal [25]. With advancement from 2G–5G networks, preservation of intellectual property rights is the need of the hour [26, 27]. Intellectual property protection is currently the main driving force for copyright protection, authentication, and other digital rights management (DRM) purposes. A watermarking model consists of two main important blocks: a watermark embedder and watermark detector. The watermarked message is embedded into the host/

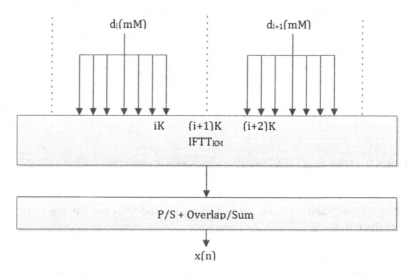

**FIGURE 5.3**  Frequency spreading with extended IFFT.

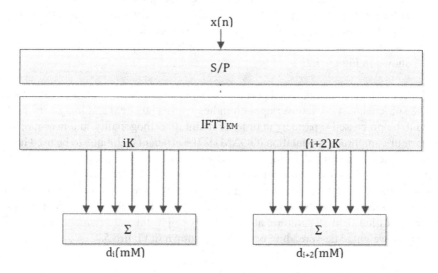

**FIGURE 5.4**  Frequency dispreading with extended FFT at receiver.

cover signal, which is then called as watermarked signal. This watermarked signal is then given to the watermark embedded as an input signal. In this chapter, the proposed watermarking model takes a 64 × 64-bit medical image (consisting of vital information related to a patient's health) as a watermark message, and the cover signal consists of 4,096 samples of a speech signal. The schematic of the implemented technique is shown in Figure 5.5. In this scheme, the 64 × 64-bit watermarked signal is embedded in to the least significant bits of the speech signal. In the cover signal

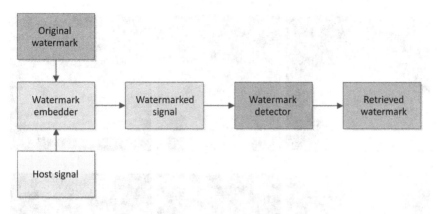

**FIGURE 5.5**   Watermark model.

(speech signal), the LSB is modified due to the fact that it has least impact to the appearance of the carrier signal [28].

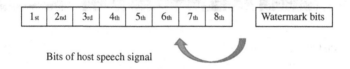

The mathematical description of the watermarking process is basically adding watermark signal *wm(k)* with host signal *hs(k):*

Where *wm(k)* is a 64 × 64-bit medical image
*hs(k)* is a test cover signal with 4,096 samples size.

$$Z(k) = hs(k) + wm(k; m, hs[k])$$

Where *m* is the message and *hs(k)* denotes the set (frame) of samples adjacent to the *k*th sample *hs(k)* [15].

## 5.4   MEDICAL IMAGES USED

Figure 5.6 depicts the medical images used for test purposed in this chapter. In total six standard medical images have been used for embedding purposes. The description of each of the image used is as follows.

## Figure 5.6: Image 1

**Diagnosis:** Spondylolysis and Spondylolisthesis (Smith ABS—MedPix (2006]).

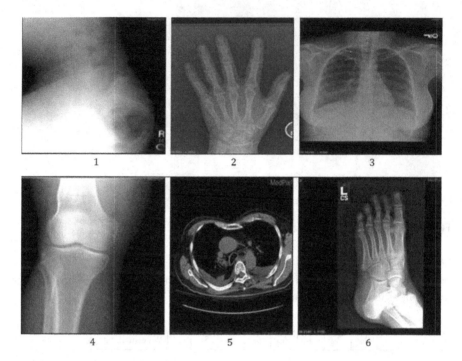

**FIGURE 5.6**   Medical images used.

**History:** A male in his 40s with the history of chronic back pain.
**Findings:** A grade II spondylolisthesis demonstrated with lateral radiograph

## Figure 5.6: Image 2

**Diagnosis:** Chondrocalcinosis (Long JRL—MedPix [2008]).
**History:** 60-year-old male with left thumb pain.
**Findings:** Frontal, lateral, and oblique radiographs of the left hand demonstrate chondrocalcinosis within the triangular fibrocartilage complex, as well as degenerative changes at the scaphotrapezial joint evidenced by joint space narrowing and subchondral sclerosis. The remainder of the osseous and soft tissue structures is unremarkable.

## Figure 5.6: Image 3

**Diagnosis:** Azygous lobe (azygous fissure) (Long JRL—MedPix [2007]).
**History:** 26-year-old woman with a positive PPD (purified protein derivative, used to test for tuberclerosis), otherwise asymptomatic.
**Findings:** PA chest radiograph demonstrating a thin line extending from the right lung apex to an ovoid opacity in the right paratracheal region (denoted with two arrows) in a curvilinear fashion consistent with an azygous fissure, a normal variant.

## Figure 5.6: Image 4

**Diagnosis:** Intraosseous lipoma of the distal femur confirmed by MRI (Carlson CLC—MedPix).

**History:** 50-year-old female with bilateral knee pain.

**Findings:** A geographic, lobulated, well marginated, radiolucent, expansile, medullary lesion with a thin rim of sclerosis and central calcific densities is seen on plain radiograph in the posterior aspect of the metadiaphysis of the distal right femur without cortical destruction. T1 and T2 weighted magnetic resonance images show the lesion to have signal isointense to fat and a sclerotic rim.

## Figure 5.6: Image 5

**Diagnosis:** Persistent Left SVC (Barfield LB—MedPix).

**History:** A 63-year-old male with placement of a left subclavian line.

## Figure 5.6: Image 6

**Diagnosis:** Freiberg infraction (Kang PK—MedPix [2007]).

**History:** Foot pain.

**Findings:** Flattening of the articular surface, subchondral lucency, and subchondral sclerosis are seen at the head of the second metatarsal bone.

## 5.5 PROPOSED TECHNIQUE

The schematic of the proposed new method of 5G-based mobile computing for e-health applications is shown in Figure 5.7. A test recorded medical image is first processed and transformed into digital form, after which the watermark is embedded into the test recorded digital speech signal. As per the system requirements, the parameters are defined. A speech signal consisting of 4,096 samples acts as host signal in which a $64 \times 64$-bit medical image having 4,096 samples is embedded. This $64 \times 64$-bit medical image contains the vital information about the patient's health. The most common and widely used method for watermarking is the least significant bit algorithm (LSB), and this has been used in the proposed technique. In the host signal, the bits which are watermarked are embedded in the last position. The frame synchronization is not needed since it is not the frame-based technique. Moreover, the signal size determines the capacity of the watermark bits to be embedded. The algorithm first checks capacity and compatibility of the watermark based on the parameters set in the system. The FBMC modulation—both at the transmitting end and the receiving end—modulated the speech signal, i.e., combined (watermark and host signal) and subsequently to demodulate it using the receiver. The schematic of both the FBMC receiver and transmitter is depicted in Figure 5.8. The watermarked speech signal is given to symbol mapper which uses OQAM scheme to map symbols. The data bits are divided into two parts—one is real and another imaginary—and both parts are forwarded to extended IFFT filter. The sums of overlapped carriers are sent through the additive white Gaussian noise (AWGN) channels. At the

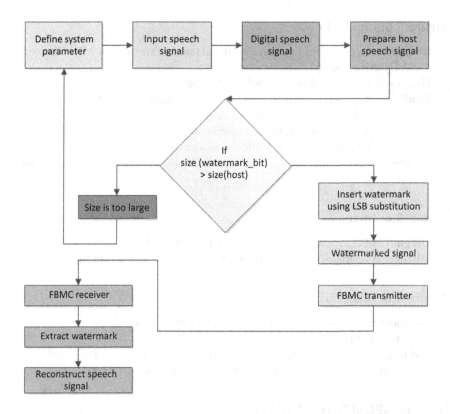

**FIGURE 5.7** Block diagram of the proposed technique.

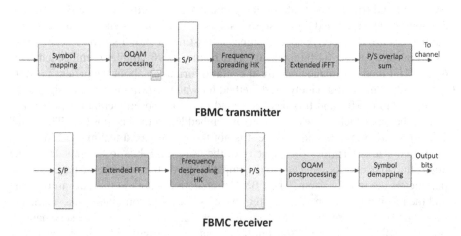

**FIGURE 5.8** Implementation of transmitter and receiver [1].

FBMC receiver, the signal is extended using fast Fourier transformation (FFT) and frequency de-spreaded through the prototype filter. The post processing of the filtered symbols are being carried and watermark bits are taken out from de-mapped and speech signals. The retrieved and original watermarks are compared, and the signal processing modification is calculated.

## 5.6   SIMULATION AND RESULT ANALYSIS

Figure 5.9 depicts the original and watermarked speech signals. The graph clearly shows that there is no change in the pictorial representation of the original and retrieved speech signals. Figure 5.10 and Figure 5.11 give the comparison between spectral densities of FBMC and OFDM. The low out-of-band leakage is highlighted by plotting the power spectral density of the transmitted signal. FBMC has lower side lobes. This allows the usage of allocated spectrum, which helps in increasing the spectral efficiency in comparison with OFDM.

Tables 5.1–5.6 give the BER analysis of the retrieved watermarked medical images. In this technique, multicarrier modulation is used to process the signal, which consists of bank of prototype filters. The resultant FBMC signal is passed through the AWGN channel with different SNRs (signal-to-noise ratios). By analyzing the results, it has been observed that despite severe attacks, the performance was found to be satisfactory. Figure 5.12 gives graphical representation of bit error rate (BER) analysis of retrieved watermarks.

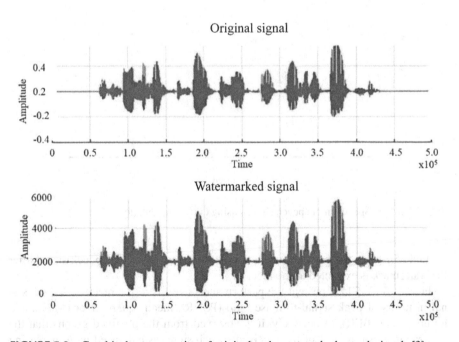

**FIGURE 5.9**   Graphical representation of original and watermarked speech signals [3].

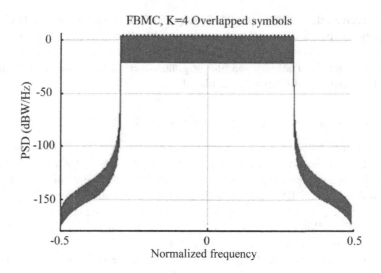

**FIGURE 5.10** Spectrum of speech signals using FBMC modulation.

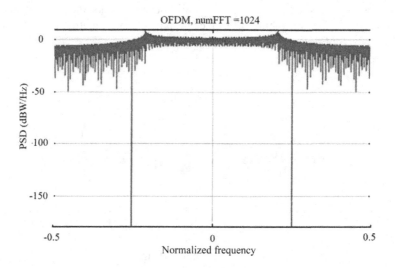

**FIGURE 5.11** Spectrum of speech signals using OFDM modulation.

Table 5.7 gives the performance analysis of the reconstructed speech signal after the watermark is extracted at the receiver.

Figures 5.13–5.15 represent the performance analysis of the received speech signal in terms of peak signal-to-noise ratio (PSNR), mean square error (MSE), and bit error rate (BER), respectively. It is observed from the obtained graphs that the performance parameters of the received speech signal is enhanced with increasing SNR value.

**TABLE 5.1**

**BER of the Extracted Watermark for Image 1**

| Attack (AWGN) | BER | BER% |
|---|---|---|
| SNR of 1 | 0.0710 | 7.1 |
| SNR of 2 | 0.04856 | 4.856 |
| SNR of 3 | 0.03181 | 3.181 |
| SNR of 4 | 0.01863 | 1.863 |
| SNR of 5 | 0.00991 | 0.991 |
| SNR of 6 | 0.00471 | 0.471 |
| SNR of 7 | 0.00172 | 0.172 |
| SNR of 8 | 0.00041 | 0.041 |
| SNR of 9 | 0.00021 | 0.021 |
| SNR of 10 | 0.000 | 0.00 |

**TABLE 5.2**

**BER of the Extracted Watermark for Image 2**

| Attack (AWGN) | BER | BER% |
|---|---|---|
| SNR of 1 (dB) | 0.08100 | 8.1 |
| SNR of 2 (dB) | 0.0576 | 5.76 |
| SNR of 3 (dB) | 0.0429 | 4.29 |
| SNR of 4 (dB) | 0.0294 | 2.94 |
| SNR of 5 (dB) | 0.0150 | 1.5 |
| SNR of 6 (dB) | 0.0095 | 0.95 |
| SNR of 7 (dB) | 0.0029 | 0.29 |
| SNR of 8 (dB) | 0.0010 | 0.1 |
| SNR of 9 (dB) | 0.0007 | 0.07 |
| SNR of 10 (dB) | 0.0001 | 0.01 |

**TABLE 5.3**

**BER of the Extracted Watermark for Image 3**

| Attack (AWGN) | BER | BER% |
|---|---|---|
| SNR of 1 (dB) | 0.0621 | 6.21 |
| SNR of 2 (dB) | 0.0534 | 5.34 |
| SNR of 3 (dB) | 0.0492 | 4.92 |
| SNR of 4 (dB) | 0.0249 | 2.49 |
| SNR of 5 (dB) | 0.0120 | 1.2 |
| SNR of 6 (dB) | 0.0085 | 0.85 |
| SNR of 7 (dB) | 0.0049 | 0.49 |
| SNR of 8 (dB) | 0.0026 | 0.26 |
| SNR of 9 (dB) | 0.0013 | 0.13 |
| SNR of 10 (dB) | 0.0008 | 0.08 |

## TABLE 5.4
### BER of the Extracted Watermark for Image 4

| Attack (AWGN) | BER | BER% |
|---|---|---|
| SNR of 1 (dB) | 0.0928 | 9.28 |
| SNR of 2 (dB) | 0.0865 | 8.65 |
| SNR of 3 (dB) | 0.0741 | 7.41 |
| SNR of 4 (dB) | 0.0690 | 6.90 |
| SNR of 5 (dB) | 0.0417 | 4.17 |
| SNR of 6 (dB) | 0.0376 | 3.76 |
| SNR of 7 (dB) | 0.0129 | 1.29 |
| SNR of 8 (dB) | 0.0098 | 0.98 |
| SNR of 9 (dB) | 0.0023 | 0.23 |
| SNR of 10 (dB) | 0.0009 | 0.09 |

## TABLE 5.5
### BER of the Extracted Watermark for Image 5

| Attack (AWGN) | BER | BER% |
|---|---|---|
| SNR of 1 (dB) | 0.0865 | 8.65 |
| SNR of 2 (dB) | 0.0789 | 7.89 |
| SNR of 3 (dB) | 0.0620 | 6.20 |
| SNR of 4 (dB) | 0.0543 | 5.43 |
| SNR of 5 (dB) | 0.0399 | 3.99 |
| SNR of 6 (dB) | 0.0156 | 1.56 |
| SNR of 7 (dB) | 0.0094 | 0.94 |
| SNR of 8 (dB) | 0.0045 | 0.45 |
| SNR of 9 (dB) | 0.0007 | 0.07 |
| SNR of 10 (dB) | 0.0001 | 0.01 |

## TABLE 5.6
### BER of the Extracted Watermark for Image 6

| Attack (AWGN) | BER | BER% |
|---|---|---|
| SNR of 1 (dB) | 0.1045 | 10.45 |
| SNR of 2 (dB) | 0.0908 | 9.08 |
| SNR of 3 (dB) | 0.0861 | 8.61 |
| SNR of 4 (dB) | 0.0776 | 7.76 |
| SNR of 5 (dB) | 0.0610 | 6.10 |
| SNR of 6 (dB) | 0.0545 | 5.45 |
| SNR of 7 (dB) | 0.0373 | 3.73 |
| SNR of 8 (dB) | 0.0189 | 1.89 |
| SNR of 9 (dB) | 0.0088 | 0.88 |
| SNR of 10 (dB) | 0.0024 | 0.24 |

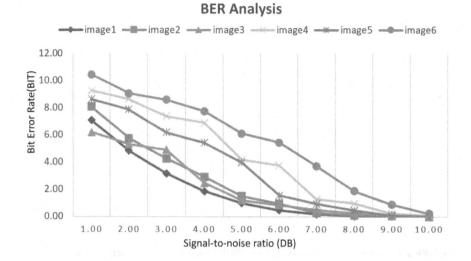

**FIGURE 5.12** BER analysis of the extracted watermarks.

**TABLE 5.7**
**Performance Analysis of the Reconstructed Speech Signal at the Receiver**

| SNR (dB) | PSNR | MSE % | BER% |
|---|---|---|---|
| 1 | 58.45 | 11.45 | 14.7 |
| 2 | 60.44 | 7.4 | 10.4 |
| 3 | 63.23 | 3.61 | 6.03 |
| 4 | 67.72 | 1.54 | 4.63 |
| 5 | 71.90 | 0.65 | 2.11 |
| 6 | 75.68 | 0.25 | 1.4 |
| 7 | 80.38 | 0.07 | 0.40 |
| 8 | 84.23 | 0.05 | 0.19 |
| 9 | 87.56 | 0.03 | 0.14 |
| 10 | 89.76 | 0.01 | 0.09 |

## 5.7 CONCLUSION

Technology has intensely changed the scenarios of today's world. The greater freedom and mobility offered by the wireless technologies compel organizations that depend on computers and wired technology to opt for wireless technology. One of leading regions of research within academia and industry growing at a faster rate is 5G wireless technology. In this chapter, we present a novel approach that significantly improve features of digital speech watermarking system in 5G networks for m-health services. In this chapter, a new technique of speech watermarking is proposed using

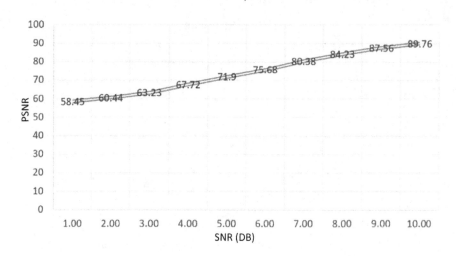

**FIGURE 5.13**    Peak signal-to-noise ratio (PSNR) of the received speech signal.

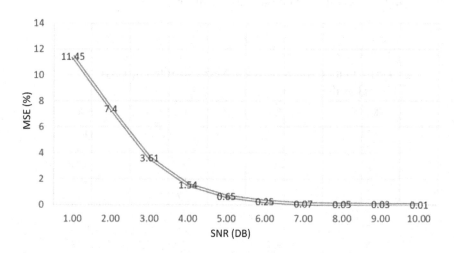

**FIGURE 5.14**    Mean square error (MSE) of the received speech signal.

5G network. The techniques is simulated in the MATLAB environment against different variations of signal processing and channel attacks. With the obtained results, we conclude that proposed techniques which use least significant bit substitution and multicarrier modulation allows efficient receiving of watermarks, maintaining quality with less error rate.

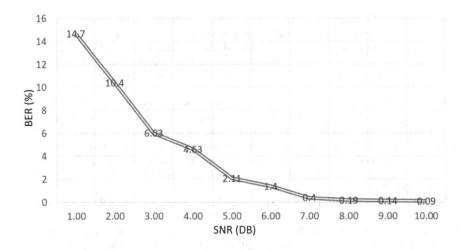

**FIGURE 5.15**   Bit error rate (BER) of the received speech signal.

## REFERENCES

[1] F. Bonomi, R. Milito, J. Zhu, and S. Addepalli. (2012). "Fog Computing and Its Role in the Internet of Things." *Proceedings of ACM MCC*, pp. 13–16; U. Bodkhe, and S. Tanwar. (2020). "Secure Data Dissemination Techniques for IOT Applications: Research Challenges and Opportunities." *Software Practice and Experience*, pp. 1–23.

[2] M. Satyanarayanan, Z. Chen, K. Ha, W. Hu, W. Richter, and P. Pillai. (2014). "Cloudlets: At the Leading Edge of Mobilecloud Convergence." *Proceedings of MobiCASE*. DOI: 10.4108/icst.mobicase.2014.257757

[3] Y. Zhang, and Y. Zhou. (2006). "Transparent Computing: A New Paradigm for Pervasive Computing, in Ubiquitous Intelligence and Computing." In *Third International Conference* (pp. 1–11). Springer, Berlin, Heidelberg.

[4] S. Andreev, A. Pyattaev, K. Johnsson, O. Galinina, and Y. Koucheryavy. (2014). "Cellular Traffic Offloading onto Network-Assisted Device-to-Device Connections." *IEEE Communications Magazine*, vol. 52, no. 4, pp. 20–31. DOI: 10.1109/MCOM.2014.6807943.

[5] M. Tehrani, M. Uysal, and H. Yanikomeroglu. (2014). "Device-to-Device Communication in 5G Cellular Networks: Challenges, Solutions, and Future Directions." *IEEE Communications Magazine*, vol. 52, no. 5, pp. 86–92. DOI: 10.1109/MCOM.2014.6815897.

[6] Javaid A. Sheikh, Sakeena Akhtar, Shabir A. Parah, and G.M. Bhat. (2018). "Blind Digital Speech Watermarking Using Filter Bank Multicarrier Modulation for 5G and IoT Driven Networks." *International Journal of Speech Technology*, vol. 21, no. 3, pp. 715–722.

[7] Javaid A. Sheikh, Sakeena Akhtar, Shabir A. Parah, and G.M. Bhat. (2018). "A New Method of Speech Transmission Over Space Time Block Coded Co-Operative MIMO–OFDM Networks Using Time and Space Diversity." *International Journal of Speech Technology*, vol. 21, no. 1, pp. 65–77.

[8] G. George, R.K. Mungara, and A. Lozano. (2014). "An Analytical Framework for Device-to-Device Communication in Cellular Networks." http://arxiv.org/abs/1407.2201.

[9] N. Lee, X. Lin, J.G. Andrews, and R.W. Heath, Jr. (2015). "Power Control for D2D Underlaid Cellular Networks: Modeling, Algorithms and Analysis." *IEEE Journal on Selected Areas in Communications*, vol. 33, no. 1, pp. 1–13. DOI: 10.1109/JSAC.2014.2369612.

[10] X. Lin, J.G. Andrews, and A. Ghosh. (2014). "Spectrum Sharing for Device-To-Device Communication in Cellular Networks." *IEEE Transactions on Wireless Communications*, vol. 13, no. 12, pp. 6727–6740. DOI: 10.1109/TWC.2014.2360202.

[11] Y. Li, D. Jin, J. Yuan, and Z. Han. (2014). "Coalitional Games for Resource Allocation in the Device-To-Device Uplink Underlaying Cellular Networks." *IEEE Transactions on Wireless Communications*, vol. 13, no. 7, pp. 3965–3977. DOI: 10.1109/TWC.2014.2325552.

[12] D. Wu, J. Wang, R. Hu, Y. Cai, and L. Zhou. (2014). "Energy-Efficient Resource Sharing for Mobile Device-to-Device Multimedia Communications." *IEEE Transactions on Vehicular Technology*, vol. 63, no. 5, pp. 2093–2103. DOI: 10.1109/TVT.2014.2311580.

[13] L. Al-Kanj, H.V. Poor, and Z. Dawy. (2014). "Optimal Cellular Offloading via Device-To-Device Communication Networks with Fairness Constraints." *IEEE Transactions on Wireless Communications*, vol. 13, no. 8, pp. 4628–4643. DOI: 10.1109/TWC.2014.2320492.

[14] A. Asadi, Q. Wang, and V. Mancuso. (2014). "A Survey on Device-To-Device Communication in Cellular Networks." *IEEE Communications Surveys & Tutorials*, vol. 16, no. 4, pp. 1801–1819. DOI: 10.1109/COMST.2014.2319555.

[15] Saeed Sarreshtedari, Mohammad Ali Akhaee, and Aliazam Abbasfar. (November 2015). "A Watermarking Method for Digital Speech Self-Recovery." *IEEE/ACM Transactions on Audio, Speech, and Language Processing*, vol. 23, no. 11.

[16] A. Verma, P. Bhattacharya, D. Saraswat, S. Tanwar, N. Kumar, and R. Sharma. (2023). "SanJeeVni: Secure UAV-Envisioned Massive Vaccine Distribution for COVID-19 Underlying 6G Network." *IEEE Sensors Journal*, vol. 23, no. 2, pp. 955–968. DOI: 10.1109/JSEN.2022.3188929.

[17] R. Gupta, Arpit Shukla, Parimal Mehta, Pronaya Bhattacharya, Sudeep Tanwar, Sudhanshu Tyagi, and Neeraj Kumar. (2020). "VAHAK: A Blockchain-Based Outdoor Delivery Scheme Using UAV for Healthcare 4.0 Services." *IEEE INFOCOM 2020 — IEEE Conference on Computer Communications Workshops (INFOCOM WKSHPS)*, pp. 255–260. DOI: 10.1109/INFOCOMWKSHPS50562.2020.9162738.

[18] R. Gupta, A. Shukla, and S. Tanwar. (1 October–December. 2021). "BATS: A Blockchain and AI-Empowered Drone-Assisted Telesurgery System Towards 6G." *IEEE Transactions on Network Science and Engineering*, vol. 8, no. 4, pp. 2958–2967. DOI: 10.1109/TNSE.2020.3043262.

[19] D. Saraswat, P. Bhattacharya, A. Verma, V.K. Prasad, S. Tanwar, G. Sharma, P.N. Bokoro, and R. Sharma. (2022). "Explainable AI for Healthcare 5.0: Opportunities and Challenges." *IEEE Access*, vol. 10, pp. 84486–84517. DOI: 10.1109/ACCESS.2022.3197671.

[20] V.K. Prasad, P. Bhattacharya, M. Bhavsar, A. Verma, S. Tanwar, G. Sharma, Pitshou N. Bokoro, and R. Sharma. (2022). "ABV-CoViD: An Ensemble Forecasting Model to Predict Availability of Beds and Ventilators for COVID-19 Like Pandemics." *IEEE Access*, vol. 10, pp. 74131–74151.

[21] M. Zuhair, F. Patel, D. Navapara, P. Bhattacharya, and D. Saraswat. (April 2021). "BloCoV6: A Blockchain-Based 6G-Assisted UAV Contact Tracing Scheme for COVID-19 Pandemic." *2021 2nd International Conference on Intelligent Engineering and Management (ICIEM)*, pp. 271–276. IEEE, London, UK.

[22] K. Zheng, S. Ou, J. Alonso-Zarate, M. Dohler, F. Liu, and H. Zhu. (2014). "Challenges of Massive Access in Highly Dense LTE-Advanced Networks with Machine-to-Machine Communications." *IEEE Wireless Communications*, vol. 21, no. 3, pp. 12–18.

[23] A.N. Ibrahim, and M.F.L. Abdullah. (2017). "The Potential of FBMC Over OFDM for the Future 5G Mobile Communication Technology." In *AIP Conference Proceedings 1883*. American Institute of Physics, College Park, MD.

[24] Juan Fang, Zihao You, I-Tai Lu, Jialing Li, and Rui Yang. (2013). "Comparisons of Filter Bank Multicarrier Systems." *Systems, Applications and Technology Conference (LISAT), 2013 IEEE Xplore.* http://ieeexplore.ieee.org/abstract/document/6578232/.

[25] Kai Shao, Juuso Alhava, Juha Yli-Kaakinen, and Markku Renfors. (2015). "Fast-Convolution Implementation of Filter Bank Multicarrier Waveform Processing." *Circuits and Systems (ISCAS), 2015 IEEE International Symposium on IEEE Xplore.* https://ieeexplore.ieee.org/document/7168799.

[26] Mohammad Ali Nematollahi, and S.A. Al-Haddad. (December 2013). "An Overview of Digital Speech Watermarking." *International Journal of Speech Technology*, vol. 16, no. 4, pp. 471–488.

[27] Harald Gruber, and Pantelis Koutroumpis. (2010). "Mobile Communications: Diffusion Facts and Prospects." *Communications & Strategies*, vol. 77, first quarter.

[28] Shraddha S. Katariya. (February 2012). "Digital Watermarking: Review." *International Journal of Engineering and Innovative Technoloy (IJEIT)*, vol. 1, no. 2.

# 6 Trusted Federated Learning Solutions for Internet of Medical Things

*Sagar Lakhanotra, Jaimik Chauhan,*
*Vivek Kumar Prasad, and Pronaya Bhattacharya*

## CONTENTS

DOI: 10.1201/9781003303374-6

## 6.1 INTRODUCTION

In simple terms, cloud computing is the sharing of computing resources across the internet, resources that are adaptable, and economies of scale. Cloud computing refers to the circulation of computing services such as servers, storage, databases, networks, software, statistics, intelligence, and more with the cloud [1]. The mobility that cloud technology gives—both to the heavy user and to the commercial and business user—is another of the most significant outer uses of cloud computing. In cloud computing, the phrase "cloud" refers to a cluster of networks, analogous to a data centre, like the way real clouds are formed of water molecules. Cloud computing refers to any technology that provides hosted services through the internet. A cloud can be private or public. Virtualization and automated technologies are heavily used in cloud computing. In cloud services, users often pick a mediator provider for internet access rather than building up personal infrastructure. Users are required to pay a subscription fee to utilize the cloud, and computing burden can be shifted to the cloud in order to reduce load. Figure 6.1 shows the network on a cloud framework.

Government and private industry both can benefit from the scalability and flexibility of cloud computing services [2]. Concerns have also been raised about whether cloud users can trust cloud services to maintain cloud tenant data, and whether could computing services can prevent malicious disclosure of sensitive or private data [3, 4].

**FIGURE 6.1** Network on cloud [5].

### 6.1.1 COMPONENTS OF CLOUD COMPUTING

Cloud computing consists of the following three basic components [6, 7, 8].

- **Client End Devices:** End users can interact with the cloud via client PCs.
- **Servers Locations in a Distributed Manner:** The servers are scattered around the world, yet they appear to be talking with one another.
- **Data Centres:** A collection of servers is called data centre.

### 6.1.2 CLOUD COMPUTING ECOSYSTEM AND ITS ASSOCIATED SERVICES

- **Software as a Service (SaaS):** The process of providing end applications as a service through the public internet is referred to as software as a service. Rather than introduce the software on their computer, the user can just connect to it through the internet. It relieves the user of the burden of maintaining complex software and hardware. SaaS users are not required to purchase, maintain, or update software or hardware. The only thing the user needs is an internet connection, and then accessing the software is pretty straightforward. Examples include Google Drive, Amazon Cloud, etc. [9].
- **Platform as a Service (PaaS):** Through PaaS, the customer can construct their personal applications and codes using a platform as a service. Customer can build their own apps to run on the cloud computing environment. PaaS gives a specific mix of application servers and operating systems to obtain application management capacity. Examples include LAMP (Linux, Apache, MySQL, and PHP), J2EE, Ruby, etc. [1].
- **Infrastructure as a Service (IaaS):** IaaS delivers on-demand computer resources such as a storehouse for storing data, networking, operating systems, hardware, and storage devices. Customers who use IaaS can access services via a broad area network, such as the internet. By logging into web-based management systems, the users can access the IaaS platform; a cloud customer, for example, can create virtual computers or machines [10, 11].

### 6.1.3 KINDS OF CLOUD COMPUTING DEPLOYMENT MODELS AND THEIR CHARACTERISTICS

**Public Cloud:** A public cloud is a computer service supplied by third-party provider enterprises through the public internet. All users who want to utilize these services are able to access them.

**Private Cloud:** Private cloud encompasses computing services distributed through the public internet or a private network, with services accessed by group of users rather than the general public. Private clouds provide greater security and privacy by utilizing a network security and internal hosting [12].

**Hybrid Cloud:** The phrase "hybrid cloud" relates to the combination of private and public cloud services. Each cloud in the hybrid cloud can be independently controlled, yet information and applications can be shared between them [13].

## 6.1.4 Cloud Computing Architecture

Cloud computing uses web-based tools and applications to retrieve resources from the internet. This allows the users to work remotely because the cloud can be used as "internet". Therefore, it is not processed as traditional outsourcing, and this is also knows as massive computing. The application allocation should be dynamic in this case. There is no requirement to install or purchase any of the hardware or software. The goal of cloud computing is to enable users to access data from all technologies and applications without requiring extensive knowledge of them. This is reflected in the previous points—that to run a web-based application in the cloud ecosystem, the requirement of a high computational computer is not necessary [14]. In the architecture of the cloud ecosystem, the task, information, and its various forms of services, such as XaaS (everything as a service) and others, are migrated into the cloud systems via the internet [15]. These services are then made available to the end users via the specific integrated software and are used in an on-demand manner. The architecture of the cloud ecosystem can be denoted as a stack of the layered model. This layered architecture is shown in Figure 6.2 and consists of the application functionality layer, platform functionality layer, infrastructure functionality layer, and bare metal hardware functionality layer.

The description of each layer is defined as follows.

**Hardware Layer:** It manages the cloud's physical and hardware resources. The hardware layer is in charge of trying to control physical servers, switches, adapters, and the power system. The hardware layer implementation is provided in the data centre. This data centre contains several servers that are linked together by routers and switches. Fault tolerance, hardware configuration, traffic management, and resource management are some of the issues that arise in the hardware layer.

**Infrastructure Layer:** in cloud computing, the infrastructure layer is also referred to as the "virtualization layer". It is a critical object of cloud computing. The infrastructure layer is based on key features such as virtualization technology's assignment of dynamic resources.

**Platform Layer:** The platform layer is composed of a operating system and the application framework. It stands at the top the infrastructure layer. The platform layer's main purpose is to reduce the operating costs of directly installing apps into virtual machine containers if possible.

**Application Layer:** This layer is on the highest level of cloud architecture. It is formed of actual cloud applications. Cloud applications must have some of the characteristics such as lower operating costs, accessibility, and scalability in order to achieve better performance.

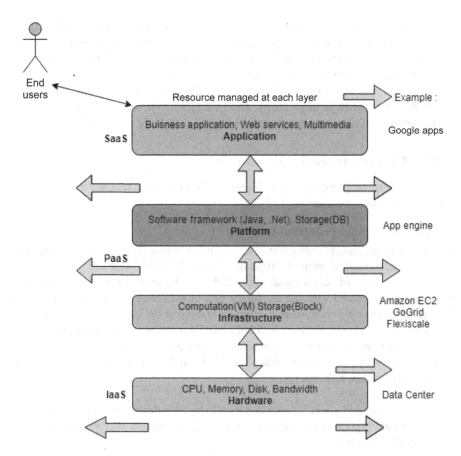

**FIGURE 6.2**   Cloud computing architecture [16].

## 6.2   FEDERATED LEARNING

Federated learning (FL) is a newly introduced technology that has piqued the interest of researchers eager to investigate its potential and applicability. Federated learning simply tries to answer the question: "Can we prepare the model without trying to transfer data to a central location?". Furthermore, federated learning allows for training without the need for data dissemination, which was not previously available with typical machine learning (ML) techniques. Google, Amazon, and Microsoft dominate the artificial intelligence (AI) market by providing cloud-based API and AI solutions [17]. Traditional AI approaches provide confidential user data to servers whereby models are trained. Federated learning emerges from the confluence of on-device AI and ML, blockchain technology, and cloud technologies and Internet of Things (IoT) [18].

Suppose that our centralized ML implementation will mean that all devices will have a local copy, which users will be able to use as needed [19]. The model will now begin to learn and train itself based on the data available by the users, gradually growing wiser. The systems are then allowed to transfer training effectiveness from the local copy of the ML app to the central server. The same issue happens on many devices that have a local copy of the app. The findings will be collected on the centralized server, but this time without any user data [20].

Nowadays, the number of modern devices is rapidly increasing, resulting in data being generated in large amounts by data generation. These devices are now used with numerous sensors to generate data, which is critical for client-users.

## 6.2.1 FEDERATED LEARNING ARCHITECTURE

In this section, we present federated learning architecture examples and introduce each architecture type independently.

### 6.2.1.1 Horizontal Federated Learning

A horizontal federated learning network standard structure is illustrated in Figure 6.3. Using this architecture, multiple firms have multiple clients who see themselves as much as K number of peoples who responded with the same sort of data and jointly train on an ML model with the assistance of a cloud server or parameter. Because in horizontal learning framework machine is trained at the local site with their local data and only gradients are sent to global server that aggregate the different updates from the different location, in this way no personal information is shared. This ensure the privacy of the patients data. The following four stages are often part of the preparation for such an event [21].

- The training gradient is computed locally by edge devices picking gradients using encryption and secret sharing, and masked results are then sent to the cloud platform.

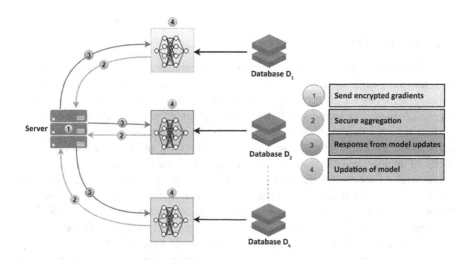

**FIGURE 6.3**   Horizontal FL.

- The encrypted aggregation that occurs on the server with no understanding of the edge devices.
- When the aggregated results are received by the server, they are sent back to the edge devices.
- The unencrypted gradients are then used to tailor the edge device's learning.

### 6.2.1.2 Vertical Federated Learning

Assume that two companies, Company X and Company Y, would like to train a ML model together, and each company is responsible for its own data within its own business systems. This is a critical component of cloud computing. Infrastructure layer is based on key features such as virtualization technology's dynamic resource assignment. However, Company Y has marked information that the algorithm must model. Both companies X and Y are unable to share data directly due to data protection and confidentiality concerns. To ensure security of the results, a third-party person C is introduced into the training process of companies X and Y. We believe that individual C is trustworthy and does not work for Company X or Y, and that teams X and Y are both reputable but have a mutual interest in each other. Person C could be operated with the system like authorities or replaced with secured computer nodes like Intel Software Guard Extensions, so that Team X, a trustworthy third-party C, is a fair inference (SGXs). This FL system is divided into two parts, which are depicted in Figure 6.4.

### 6.2.1.3 Federated Transfer Learning

Transfer learning (TL) is a method to reuse a previously learned model for a new task, and it has lately been employed in surveillance, biometrics, medical, and

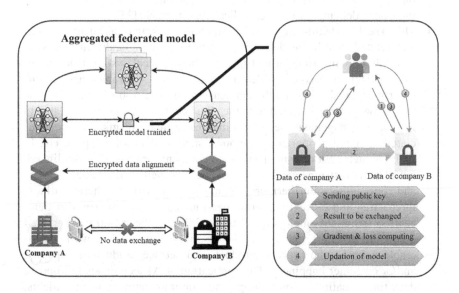

**FIGURE 6.4** Vertical FL [22].

agricultural applications, to name a few. As shown in the vertical federated learning example presented above, Company Y has overlapping examples or samples, but these are extremely rare, and then this is attempting to learn the labels for all data about Company X. TL uses the same illustration of a feature between firms X and Y and assists in reducing label prediction error for the target company with the help of a source company, such as Company Y in the present case.

## 6.3  HEALTHCARE

**Healthcare 1.0:** The basic patient–clinician relationship is often referred to as Healthcare 1.0. The patient attends visits a hospital and consults a doctor and other healthcare stakeholders of the care team during such an encounter. Based on the consultation, test report, and diagnosis, the medical officer writes a prescription for pharmaceuticals and develops a treatment plan for an illness, as well as follow-up plans [23].

**Healthcare 2.0:** Along with substantial advances in the fields of health, life science, and biotechnology, a slew of innovative medical devices and equipment have been designed, manufactured, and tested, and these are becoming more popular, being employed in delivery of healthcare. Image testing equipment, and also surgical and life-associated equipment, is increasingly being used to aid in diagnosis, treatment, and monitoring at hospitals and other patient care settings. This is known as Healthcare 2.0 [24].

**Healthcare 3.0:** Many electronic health record (EHR) actions are time-stamped and stored, and many manual tasks have been computerized and digitalized. Furthermore, telemedicine and remote care are now possible via the use of existing computer networks, and electronic visits are starting to replace certain face-to-face meetings. The COVID-19 pandemic is increasing demand for remote medical appointments [23].

**Healthcare 4.0:** Healthcare 4.0 is coming into focus. In order to attain smart and related healthcare delivery, the current set of healthcare delivery methods is being transformed into a cyber-physical system made up of IoT, RFID (radio frequency identification devices), wearables, and various other medical devices, intelligent sensors, medical robots, etc. All these technologies are associated with the cloud ecosystems, analysis related to Big Data management, deep learning–based mechanisms, and the associated artificial supported techniques, such as decision support, etc. In such a system, not only are healthcare companies and institutions linked, but also all instruments and technologies, as well as the patient's home and communities. Furthermore, we may foresee proactive therapy, illness forecasting and prevention, customized medicine, and improved patient-centred treatment employing AI tools [23]. Healthcare 4.0 has heralded a new era of smart, cybernate, and sustainable production, with considerable gains in the process, product, and service productivity, quality, and/or customer happiness. The application of AI techniques to improve detecting, treating, coordinating, and communicating among patients, physicians, and other related and associated end users and stakeholders in order to achieve personalized and patient-based and patient-centred smart healthcare administration, which encompasses the following views on classification and stratification.

1. **Prediction Analysis:** To aid in diagnosis and prognosis, accurate forecasts of illness progress and consequences created on stratification and categorization can be generated for each patient. Such models should not only estimate risk levels, but also rank and interpret the elements that influence this prediction.
2. **Preventive and Proactive Care:** The results of forecast analysis can be used to create preventive and proactive treatment programmes. Aside from preventing or reducing disease progression, we can increase prescription error prevention and patient safety [16].
3. **Monitoring, Involvement, and Finest Treatment:** Continuous monitoring of dangerous signs and other healthcare-related patient-specific serious factors, continuous analysis and prediction of patient condition, and dynamic updating of care complications and diagnosis plans, are necessary to improve patient outcomes and to support healthcare professionals in making the best decisions for each patient.

**Healthcare 5.0:** The fifth generation of healthcare acknowledges the critical role of customers and shifts industry operational models forward into adapting to customer processes. It is a shift in mindset, from relationship management to customer-managed relationships. Instead of the other way around, health service providers in Healthcare 5.0 are trying to ask where they can fit into the lives of their customers [25–27]. The emphasis is on customer models, fully understanding the healthcare industry's customers [24]. Digital wellness will emerge as a result of Healthcare 5.0. Participants in the industry will shift their focus from simply treating patients to establishing long-term relationships with individuals, making treatment an exception rather than the norm [24].

The new emphasis on digital wellness will create new ways of improving care quality [24].

**Responsiveness:** The proactive approach will accelerate the progression of preventive healthcare, for example, by encouraging us to change our ways and thus avoid adverse health scenarios through smart devices. In the event of an accident, self-driving cars may communicate with emergency services and share actual information about the condition of their passengers, possibly even sparking the production of customized body parts.

**Fairness Financing:** The digital economy's players continue to astound us with new business models. If we can predict anything about the future of the health industry, it is that many health services will become available for free, while the financial models of others will change dramatically. Many more business models will emerge than those which rely on outright payments such as Medicare systems or insurance schemes. Digital wellness will largely eliminate geographical boundaries, allowing for the greater contest between many service providers and, ideally, better patient outcomes.

### 6.3.1 HEALTHCARE AND FEDERATED LEARNING

There is a greater emphasis on data security these days as a result of an unmatched increase in the number of exposed records, which will reach 8.4 million in the first quarter of 2020. IBM claims that in 2019–2020 reports, the average global price of a data breach reached 3.86 million, with the health industry leaderboard first at 7.13 million. FL is an interesting technique that protects privacy and thereby lowers data leaks. Also, it corresponds to the distributed nature of healthcare data. Deep federated learning leverages deep learning technologies, as well as a number of supplementary and high-performance models, to handle complicated and intensive FL tasks. This really is especially important in healthcare, a sector in which the amount of data is large and continually changing [28].

Deep learning would thus eliminate the necessity for featuring engineering approaches by employing the neural network stacking methodology in FL. As a result of the method being totally automated and requiring no human interaction, local training on edge devices will be improved [28–30].

### 6.3.2 FEDERATED LEARNING INFORMATION FOR HEALTHCARE DATA STUDY AND ITS ANALYSIS: A FRAMEWORK TOWARDS THE HEALTHCARE DOMAIN

This subsection provides a decentralized FL framework for analyzing use of IoT for healthcare data, prompted by the need to ensure data privacy for patient populations that utilize IoT devices using AI technologies to monitor their overall health status and conditions while enabling a decentralized structure. IoT devices will be involved in the data capture, acquisition, and analytical techniques in this framework [31]. The previous global interconnected model version is then used to analyze healthcare data in order to detect any issues. Following this, a local model training process must be completed and healthcare data collected and analyzed to identify any errors or problems. Following that, using data from the same IoT device, a local model learning process must be carried out autonomously of the modelling framework. After the local training process is completed, the model's modification will be summed up as updates or sent to a cloud server without uncovering any kind of information that may related to personal or public data. Because the data is stored on the user's device and the user is the only one who has access to it, the customer's privacy will be protected. As only model updates are available on the centralized cloud server, the attack on it will not disclose any personal information of the patient. During the global model training phase, these notifications will be averaged. The model output global training programme will continually enhance performance and include new user scenarios. Following the learning of the global model, an enhanced version will be provided to the IoT devices that are participating [32]. The entire FL process will be repeated to keep the model up to date. Following training of the global model, the another updated tasks will be delivered to the participating IoT nodes [33]. The whole federated learning procedure would be continued to keep the model up to date.

### 6.3.3 IMPLEMENTATION

This subsection recommends carrying out an experiment involving the use of DFL for skin disease diagnosis utilizing data received from IoT devices. The research is broken into two sections: constructing a global deep learning model that identifies skin illnesses via TL, and then utilizing FL to safeguard data privacy and enable decentralization. A dermatology dataset of roughly 10,000 photos was used to construct a model for trying to detect skin disorders. This model will act as a modelling framework throughout the first phase of the process and will be shared with the participants. This will be considered as the first round of iteration where local participant entity uses the global model.

> **Algorithms:** To put in place a fully automated DFL procedure, the community education data acquisition process must be addressed. This part is crucial for the IoT device local training phase. Algorithms 1–3 combine to build an improved FL algorithm that governs the input collection and learning stages of locally and globally deep learning models. During the first task cycle, the deep learning model that has been pre-trained will be shared with the IoT side, allowing users to diagnose skin conditions utilizing the approach (Algorithm 1). The data acquisition round (Algorithm 2) begins once the prediction procedure is complete. The user is requested to score the outcome on a 5-point scale in order to get training examples for local training since the model performs training using a picture with a label. If the rate is too high, the sample will be utilized as a training sample. Otherwise, the sample data will be rejected, and no local training will take place. Furthermore, until at least one training sample is provided, this user will be unable to participate in the federated average round, which is Algorithm 3. As a result, if just one member has completed the data-collecting procedure, the federated average round will begin. This step also ensures that the training data is of good quality and involves the client in the model output validation process [34]. The model performs well in the federated average round (Algorithm 3); output weight values would be broadcast to the participants for use in instantiating the local model, and the local training will then begin.

### 6.3.3.1 Experimental Setup and Results

#### 6.3.3.1.1 Dataset

The Interactive Dermatology Atlas dataset [35] was used to train the skin disease identification model. The collection contains around 10,000 photos divided into 361 categories. The images have been scaled to fit the dimensions $224 \times 224 \times 3$. The algorithm for the same has been discussed herein.

## Algorithm 1: Starting Assignment Round

**Input:** Tpre-traine
**Output:** Tg
Tg: global model weights.
Tpre-trained: pre-trained model of weights
    1: function Initial Round(Tpre-trained)
    2:   Tg ¡- Tpre-trained
    3:   send global weights(Tg) to all users
    4: End
    5: Return Tg

## Algorithm 2: Initial Assignment Round

**Input:** users
**Output:** USERS
**Training Sample**: the image captured by the user(x) and the high rated.
USERS: a subset of users performed the data acquisition round.
  1:    fun Data acqu(F(x))
  2:      for U users perform
  3:        Prediction Process Yi-F(X)
  4:          if(user rating for Yi=3) then
  5:            Training sample ¡-(x,y)
  6:            USERS Users
  7:          End
  8:        End
  9:      Return USERS
 10:    End

### 6.3.3.2  Experimenting with Federated Learning

First, the global model output weights will be disseminated to participants. Second, on the participant's data, a local training process using the broadcast weights will be performed to update each participant model's weights. Next, the global model weights will be changed as an average of the participant model modifications.

### 6.3.3.3  Results and Evaluation Strategy

This segment describes the evolution of the deep learning prototype from the initial model to four federated current average rounds based on accuracy, classification report parameters, receiver-operating characteristic curve and the area beneath the curve, timeframes, and ultimately adaptation period. It also contrasts the level of secrecy and operating cost vs. process complexity services supplied by DFL models and centralized models.

### 6.3.3.4   Performance Calculations

Get the confusion matrix first, then compute the ML assessment metrics. A test method that completely describes a model's performance is the confusion matrix. In comparison to the actual class instances, it indicates the expected class instances. True positive, true negative, false positive, and false negative findings are produced by the confusion matrix [36].

**Accuracy:** This is the percentage of correct prediction samples from across all sample data that represent true positives and true negatives is referred to as accuracy. It counts the number of times this same model correctly classifies a data sample.

**Classification Report:** This is a report that summarizes the three major evaluations of ML to ensure comprehensive accuracy: precision, recall, and F1 score.

**Precision:** This is the model's reliability in making positive future predictions.

**Recall:** This is the percentage of identified positive data samples among all positive samples.

**Macro Average:** This measures the typical categorization measurement for every without taking into consideration the total number of items in the dataset for each category.

---

### Algorithm 3: Federated Average Round

W: weights of user's local model. R: Rate of learning
L: Loss function
V: if found weight value (option).
**Input:** USERS, Wx,Wy, training sample varibale R,L,V
**Output:** USERS, Wx

```
 1: function Federated learning round1(Wx)
 2:     if(USERS!= empty) then
 3:         send global weights (Wx) to all USERS end
 4:         for U in USERS do
 5:             Wy ¡- Wx
 6:             B ¡- (small-batches of training samples)
 7:             for e in epochs do
 8:                 for k in k do
 9:                     Wy ¡ – Wy * –R * L(Wu,k)
10:                 end
11:         end
12:         return Wy
13:     end
14:     public function Federated learning average(Wu,Wu)
15:         Wx ¡- ∀USERS(Wy * V y)/USERS    Wy
16: Return Wx =0
```

---

## 6.4  FL SYSTEMS: CASE STUDY

In this case study, we will describe steganography and steganalysis, implementation of steganography on healthcare data, and finally, we will move towards naïve approaches to advanced approaches for steganography.

### 6.4.1  WHAT IS STEGANOGRAPHY?

Steganography is the process of hiding messages or information within non-secret text or data.

### 6.4.2  DIFFERENCE BETWEEN STEGANALYSIS AND STEGANOGRAPHY

Steganography is the encoding of information on a viable object source, and steganalysis is the decoding of information from the encoded object.

Stegano is a Python steganography module that we can use to encode and decode messages in an image, as shown in Figure 6.5.

We just hide a message in our image with two lines of code. Let's try looking at the images to observe if there is any difference (see Figure 6.6). Figure 6.7 shows the original image vs stago image. Figures 6.8 and 6.9 show the RGB graph and extracted data from the main image respectively.

Surprised? Can't tell the difference, can we?

Stegano also provides a function for decoding the message hidden in our image. Next, let's try that.

#### 6.4.2.1  We Can See the Text We Hide, But What Is Going On under the Hood?

The module makes use of a technology that produces a concealed channel in sections of the cover image where changes are expected to be low when compared to the human visual system (HVS). It conceals the information in the picture data's least significant bit (LSB). This embedding method is basically based on the fact that the least significant bits in an image can be thought of as random noise, and they consequently become not responsive to any changes on the image; this is one of the first and classical ways of doing steganography on images. In terms of how they conceal information, the well-known steganographic tools based on LSB embedding differ. Some of them alter the LSB of pixels at random, others modify pixels in specific

```
from stegano import lsb
image = cv2.imread("/content/drive/MyDrive/Stegnalysis_Data/term.png")
message = "hello"

secret=lsb.hide("/content/drive/MyDrive/Stegnalysis_Data/IM-0001-
0001.jpeg",message)

secret.save("/content/drive/MyDrive/Stegnalysis_Data/output.png")
```

FIGURE 6.5   Hiding data.

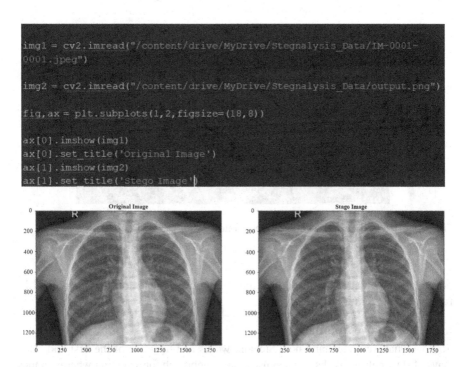

```
img1 = cv2.imread("/content/drive/MyDrive/Stegnalysis_Data/IM-0001-
0001.jpeg")

img2 = cv2.imread("/content/drive/MyDrive/Stegnalysis_Data/output.png")

fig,ax = plt.subplots(1,2,figsize=(18,8))

ax[0].imshow(img1)
ax[0].set_title('Original Image')
ax[1].imshow(img2)
ax[1].set_title('Stego Image')
```

**FIGURE 6.6 AND FIGURE 6.7**  Original image and stago image, comparing RGB values of both images.

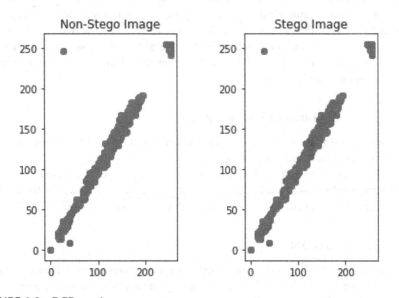

**FIGURE 6.8**  RGB graph.

```
msg = lsb.reveal("/content/drive/MyDrive/Stegnalysis_Data/output.png")

print(msg)
```

**FIGURE 6.9**   Extracted data from image.

```
vec1 = np.reshape(img1,5749245)
vec2 = np.reshape(img2,5749245)
```

**FIGURE 6.10**   Converting Vec-1 and Vec-2 into a NumPy array.

portions of the image, and still others increase or decrease the pixel value of the LSB rather than changing the value.

### 6.4.2.2   K-Naïve Approach

So now what we understand how Stegano works and how one of the first and oldest ways of steganalysis works, we can use a naïve approach for detecting whether a message has been encoded in a image file or not. The following presents a naïve approach.

- An RGB (red, green, and blue) image is stored in a form of 3-D NumPy array whereby each dimensions contains pixels of RGB colours. The values in this vary between 0 and 255. We can flatten the NumPy array into a vector of rdim × gdim × bdim. This will get us a feature vector for an image.
- Now we can find the cosine similarity between the two vectors of our normal image and encoded image, if they are alike then cosine dissimilarity (1-similarity) must be 1; else, it will be less than 1 and we can get an idea that something is wrong.

### 6.4.3   Let's Do This and See the Results

- We can see that we can find whether an information is hidden or not using a naïve approach without much effort.
- This naïve approach is not wrong, but not exactly correct because the information is hidden in the DCT coefficients of the image rather than the RGB pixels. Figures 6.10–6.13 show the result of the performed operation.

## 6.5   CONCLUSION

We propose in this chapter a security feature in Internet of Medical Things (IoMT) using FL. In IoMT, FL can help with healthcare analytics using user-generated data. It depicts a DFL proof-of-concept experiment for X-ray images.

```
print(1 - spatial.distance.cosine(vec1,vec1))

1.0
```

**FIGURE 6.11** Verifying cosine similarity between same vectors.

```
print(1 - spatial.distance.cosine(vec1,vec2))

0.9999999524490734
```

**FIGURE 6.12** Verifying cosine similarity between same vectors.

```
print(spatial.distance.cosine(vec2, vec1))

4.755092664066041e-08
```

**FIGURE 6.13** Verifying cosine similarity between same vectors.

The evaluation showed promising results for providing security. We implement code on X-ray images, and it showed promising results which will help in securing patient X-ray images and data. To that end, the proposed model may make possible the efficient and feasible integration of user-generated wellness and behavioral data.

## REFERENCES

[1] C. Chen, E.W. Loh, K.N. Kuo, and K.W. Tam. (2020). "The Times They Are a-Changin'–Healthcare 4.0 Is Coming!." *Journal of Medical Systems*, vol. 44, no. 2, pp. 1–4.
[2] V.K. Prasad, P. Bhattacharya, M. Bhavsar, A. Verma, S. Tanwar, G. Sharma, Pitshou N. Bokoro, and R. Sharma. (2022). "ABV-CoViD: An Ensemble Forecasting Model to Predict Availability of Beds and Ventilators for COVID-19 Like Pandemics." *IEEE Access*, vol. 10, pp. 74131–74151.
[3] J. Xu, B.S. Glicksberg, C. Su, P. Walker, J. Bian, and F. Wang. (2021). "Federated Learning for Healthcare Informatics." *Journal of Healthcare Informatics Research*, vol. 5, pp. 1–19. DOI: 10.1007/s41666-020-00082-4.
[4] Unlocking the Potential of the Internet of Things. (2015). www.mckinsey.com/business-functions/mckinsey-digital/our-insights/the-internet-of-things-the-value-of-digitizing-the-physical-world.

[5] A. Verma, P. Bhattacharya, D. Saraswat, S. Tanwar, N. Kumar, and R. Sharma. (2023). "SanJeeVni: Secure UAV-Envisioned Massive Vaccine Distribution for COVID-19 Underlying 6G Network." *IEEE Sensors Journal*, vol. 23, no. 2, pp. 955–968. DOI: 10.1109/JSEN.2022.3188929.

[6] W. Voorsluys, J. Broberg, and R. Buyya. (2011). "Introduction to Cloud Computing." *Cloud Computing: Principles and Paradigms*, pp. 1–44.

[7] K. Stanoevska-Slabeva, and T. Wozniak. (2010). "Cloud Basics–an Introduction to Cloud Computing." In *Grid and Cloud Computing* (pp. 47–61). Springer, Berlin, Heidelberg.

[8] F. Rahman, M. Slepian, and A. Mitra. (5–8 December 2016). "A Novel Big-Data Processing Framwork for Healthcare Applications: Big-Data-Healthcare-in-a-Box." *Proceedings of the 2016 IEEE International Conference on Big Data (Big Data)*, pp. 3548–3555.

[9] Saqib Hakak, Wazir Zada Khan, and Erik Scheme. (2020). "A Framework for Edge-Assisted Healthcare Data Analytics using Federated Learning." *2020 IEEE International Conference on Big Data (Big Data)*. https://ieeexplore.ieee.org/document/9377873.

[10] Gaurav Dhiman, Sapna Juneja, Hamidreza Mohafez, Ibrahim El-Bayoumy, Lokesh Kumar Sharma, Maryam Hadizadeh, Mohammad Aminul Islam, Wattana Viriyasitavat, and Mayeen Uddin Khandaker. "Federated Learning Approach to Protect Healthcare Data Over Big Data Scenario." https://ideas.repec.org/a/gam/jsusta/v14y2022i5p2500-d755691.html.

[11] D. Remédios, A. Teofilo, H. Paulino, and J. Lourenço. (August 2015). "Mobile Device-to-Device Distributed Computing Using Data Sets." *Proceedings of the 12th EAI International Conference on Mobile and Ubiquitous Systems: Computing, Networking and Services on 12th EAI International Conference on Mobile and Ubiquitous System.* DOI: 10.4108/eai.22-7-2015.2260273.

[12] C.N. Höfer, and G. Karagiannis. (2011). "Cloud Computing Services: Taxonomy and Comparison." *Journal of Internet Services and Applications*, vol. 2, no. 2, pp. 81–94.

[13] W. Kim. (2013). "Cloud Computing Architecture." *International Journal of Web and Grid Services*, vol. 9, no. 3, pp. 287–303.

[14] M. Jouini, and L.B.A. Rabai. (December 2017). "A Security Risk Management Model for Cloud Computing Systems: Infrastructure as a Service." In *International Conference on Security, Privacy and Anonymity in Computation, Communication and Storage* (pp. 594–608). Springer, Cham.

[15] T. Taleb, K. Samdanis, B. Mada, H. Flinck, S. Dutta, and D. Sabella. (2017). "On Multi-Access Edge Computing: A Survey of the Emerging 5G Network Edge Cloud Architecture and Orchestration." *IEEE Communications Surveys & Tutorials*, vol. 19, no. 3, pp. 1657–1681.

[16] M. Mian, A. Teredesai, D. Hazel, S. Pokuri, and K. Uppala. (27 June–2 July 2014). "Work inProgress–In-Memory Analysis for Healthcare Big Data." *Proceedings of the 2014 IEEE International Congress on Big Data, Anchorage, AK*, pp. 778–779. IEEE, Anchorage, AK.

[17] S.K. Garg, S. Versteeg, and R. Buyya. (2013). "A Framework for Ranking of Cloud Computing Services." *Future Generation Computer Systems*, vol. 29, no. 4, pp. 1012–1023.

[18] Haya Elayan, and Moayad Aloqaily. "Member, IEEE, and Mohsen Guizani, Fellow, IEEE. Sustainability of Healthcare Data Analysis IoT-Based Systems Using Deep Federated Learning." https://ieeexplore.ieee.org/iel7/6488907/9770336/09509396.pdf.

[19] Dinh C. Nguyen, Quoc-Viet Pham, Pubudu N. Pathirana, Aruna Senevi-Ratne, Zihuai Lin, Octavia Dobre, and Won-Joo Hwang. "Federated Learning for Smart Healthcare: A Survey." https://arxiv.org/abs/2111.08834.

[20] "A Fairness-Aware Incentive Scheme for Federated Learning—Proceedings of the AAAI/ACM Conference on AI, Ethics, and Society." https://dl.acm.org/doi/abs/10.1145/3375627.3375840. Accessed 12 November 2020.

[21] M. Zuhair, F. Patel, D. Navapara, P. Bhattacharya, and D. Saraswat. (April 2021). "BloCoV6: A Blockchain-Based 6G-Assisted UAV Contact Tracing Scheme for COVID-19 Pandemic." *2021 2nd International Conference on Intelligent Engineering and Management (ICIEM)*, pp. 271–276.

[22] S. Lin, G. Yang, and J. Zhang. (May 2020). "Real-Time Edge Intelligence in the Making–A Collaborative Learning Framework via Federated Meta-Learning." arXiv200103229 Cs Stat. http://arxiv.org/abs/2001.03229. Accessed 12 November 2020.

[23] S.M. Riazul Islam, Daehan Kwak, M.D. Humaun Kabir, Mahmud Hossain, and Kyung-Sup Kwak. (2015). "The Internet of Things for Health Care: A Comprehensive Survey." *IEEE Access*, vol. 3, pp. 678–708.

[24] Q. Yang, Y. Liu, T. Chen, and Y. Tong. (February 2019). "Federated Machine Learning–Concept and Applications." arXiv190204885 Cs. http://arxiv.org/abs/1902.04885. Accessed 3 November 2020.

[25] J. Chanchaichujit, A. Tan, F. Meng, and S. Eaimkhong. (2019). "An Introduction to Healthcare 4.0." In *Healthcare 4.0* (pp. 1–15). Palgrave Pivot, Singapore.

[26] A. Verma, P. Bhattacharya, M. Zuhair, S. Tanwar, and N. Kumar. (2021). "Vacochain: Blockchain-Based 5G-Assisted UAV Vaccine Distribution Scheme for Future Pandemics." *IEEE Journal of Biomedical and Health Informatics*, vol. 26, no. 5, pp. 1997–2007.

[27] J.J. Hathaliya, R. Gupta, S. Tanwar, and P. Sharma. (2021). "A Smart Contract-Based Secure Data Sharing Scheme in Healthcare 5.0." *2021 IEEE Globecom Workshops (GC Wkshps)*, pp. 1–6. DOI: 10.1109/GCWkshps52748.2021.9681956.

[28] P. Sareen. (2013). "Cloud Computing: Types, Architecture, Applications, Concerns, Virtualization and Role of IT Governance in Cloud." *International Journal of Advanced Research in Computer Science and Software Engineering*, vol. 3, no. 3.

[29] V.A. Patel, Pronaya Bhattacharya, Sudeep Tanwar, Rajesh Gupta, Gulshan Sharma, Pitshou N. Bokoro, and Ravi Sharma. (2022). "Adoption of Federated Learning for Healthcare Informatics: Emerging Applications and Future Directions." *IEEE Access*, vol. 10, pp. 90792–90826. DOI: 10.1109/ACCESS.2022.3201876.

[30] P. Bhattacharya, S. Tanwar, U. Bodkhe, S. Tyagi, and N. Kumar. (1 April–June 2021). "BinDaaS: Blockchain-Based Deep-Learning as-a-Service in Healthcare 4.0 Applications." *IEEE Transactions on Network Science and Engineering*, vol. 8, no. 2, pp. 1242–1255. DOI: 10.1109/TNSE.2019.2961932.

[31] Rodolfo Stoffel Antunes, Cristiano André da Costa, Arne Küderle, Imrana Abdullahi Yari, and Björn Eskofier. (November 2021). "Federated Learning for Healthcare: Systematic Review and Architecture Proposal." *ACM Transactions on Intelligent Systems and Technology, Just Accepted.* DOI: 10.1145/3501813.

[32] D. Saraswat, P. Bhattacharya, A. Verma, V.K. Prasad, S. Tanwar, G. Sharma, P.N. Bokoro, and R. Sharma. (2022). "Explainable AI for Healthcare 5.0: Opportunities and Challenges." *IEEE Access*, vol. 10, pp. 84486–84517. DOI: 10.1109/ACCESS.2022.3197671.

[33] V.A. Patel, P. Bhattacharya, S. Tanwar, N.K. Jadav, and R. Gupta. (2022). "BFLEdge: Blockchain Based Federated Edge Learning Scheme in V2X Underlying 6G Communications." *2022 12th International Conference on Cloud Computing, Data Science & Engineering (Confluence)*, pp. 146–152. DOI: 10.1109/Confluence52989.2022.9734213.

[34] A. Verma, P. Bhattacharya, Y. Patel, K. Shah, S. Tanwar, and B. Khan. (2022). "Data Localization and Privacy-Preserving Healthcare for Big Data Applications: Architecture

and Future Directions." In Singh, P.K., Kolekar, M.H., Tanwar, S., Wierzchoń, S.T., and Bhatnagar, R.K. (Eds.), *Emerging Technologies for Computing, Communication and Smart Cities: Lecture Notes in Electrical Engineering* (vol. 875). Springer, Singapore. DOI: 10.1007/978-981-19-0284-0_18.

[35] Richard P. Usatine, B. D. (2019). "Interactive Dermatology Atlas." Dermatlas: https://www.dermatlas.net/

[36] Fahad Ahmed KhoKhar, Jamal Hussain Shah, Muhammad Attique Khan, Muhammad Sharif, Usman Tariq, and Seifedine Kadry. "A Review on Federated Learning Towards Image Processing." https://www.sciencedirect.com/science/article/abs/pii/S0045790622001161.

# 7 Early Prediction of Prevalent Diseases Using IoMT

*Jigna Patel, Jitali Patel, Rupal Kapdi, and Shital Patel*

## CONTENTS

## 7.1 INTRODUCTION

A person's health is critical for living a pleasant and productive life. Healthcare is the way of improving one's health through disease identification, treatment, and prevention. The World Health Organization (WHO) defines health as "a condition of complete mentally and physically well-being free of sickness and disability" [1]. The majority of existing healthcare employs administrative management and monitors patient case history, demographic data, drug stock maintenance diagnostics, billing, and prescriptions, which may end in manual errors that show a negative impact on patients. By integrating all decision support systems and critical data surveillance equipment through a network, smart healthcare based on Internet of Things (IoT) minimizes human errors and supports clinicians in detecting diseases more quickly and precisely. Internet of Medical Things (IoMT) refers to medical devices that may communicate data over a network without involving human efforts or computer interaction [2]. According to Gartner [3], a research and consultancy firm, 27 billion devices will be connected to the internet by 2025. In addition, the global IoT market will grow at a 16.9% annual rate. This substantial sum of money also involves the development of IoMT systems. IoMT has the potential to deliver cost-effective and novel services to the healthcare industry, notably by enabling further effective monitoring of patients hospitalized or those with

DOI: 10.1201/9781003303374-7

chronic conditions. The platform also offers a smart system that primarily consists of sensors and electronic control systems to procure biomedical signals through a patient, a peripheral device to handle the sensor information, a permanent or temporary storage unit, a piece of network equipment to transfer the biomedical information over a network, and a visualization platform of artificial intelligence programmers to make decisions based on professional medical ease [4] and predict the future based on the past medical history [5, 6]. This study reviews IoMT-based remote health monitoring, smart hospitals, FDA-approved sensor tracking and improved chronic illness therapy. IoMT makes use of mobile technology and linked healthcare equipment that is now available in the end-user market at reasonable rates.

However, because of a shortage of compatibility among smart devices, the necessity to integrate numerous systems, and data security, the adoption of IoMT solutions faces significant hurdles. To fully realize the promise of IoMT, designers of these applications need to be given tools that protect them from the intricacies that come with these issues [7, 8]. IoMT is also alternately known as the Medical Internet of Things (MIoT). It is a health-specific version of IoT whereby a physician can remotely and instantly measure various metrics of a patient's health like body temperature, heart rate, and oxygen level, using a sensor system deposited on the body of a patient [9]. Figure 7.1 depicts several IoMT entities.

One of the most common diseases is diabetes. It causes adverse effects on many human organs, resulting in macrovascular alterations. Diabetes is a disease that occurs when blood sugar levels are abnormally high. Our bodies get their energy from glucose. Our carbohydrates are broken down into a minor form of glucose

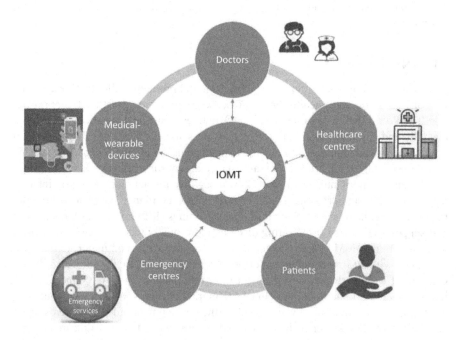

**FIGURE 7.1**　IoMT system.

through metabolism. The concentration of glucose in the blood in diabetes can cause catastrophic damage to different body areas, including the eyes, kidneys, and heart. Diabetic retinopathy (DR), cataracts, glaucoma, and other vision problems can develop over time due to diabetes. According to statistics [10], about 382 million individuals have been diagnosed with diabetes, with the number potentially rising to 592 million, as shown in Figure 7.2. Diabetes affects people's lives around the world, with women accounting for more than 50% of those affected. According to researchers [10], a group of Indian states been identified as having the highest prevalence of diabetes among women. Diabetes affects 1 in 10 women in the 35–49 age group in at least half of the 640 regions surveyed. The districts with more prevalence rate are in the states of Kerala, Tamil Nadu, Odisha, and Andhra Pradesh. In total, 254 electoral districts have a very severe diabetes burden, whereas 130 have a moderately high burden (range: 8.7%–10.6%). The weight is heaviest towards the south and east and lightest in the centre. The figure comes from a survey conducted in 2015–2016 (National Family Health Survey) which includes district-level indicators. The demographic information of 2,35,056 people from 36 states and union territories was examined in order to determine disease prevalence and investigate relationships between disease and socioeconomic status, number of children, obesity, hypertension, and location, among other factors. Samples are collected to capture blood glucose levels in both men and women, aiding in diabetes diagnosis.

Diabetes affected 10.5% of the population in 2020, according to diabetes statistics, and 45% of diabetic patients are completely unaware of their condition, as depicted in Figure 7.3 [9]. In 2045, diabetes patients are expected to increase by 12.2%, compared to 11.35% in 2030 as shown in Figure 7.4 [11]. In terms of spending, 966 billion US dollars were expended in 2021, as shown in Figure 7.5 [12].

Thyroid disease is a broad term for a chronic condition in which a person's thyroid does not produce adequate hormones. Normally, the thyroid produces hormones essential to keep the human body running smoothly. The human body requires

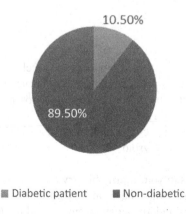

## Diabetes worldwide

10.50%

89.50%

■ Diabetic patient        ■ Non-diabetic

**FIGURE 7.2**  Diabetes worldwide.

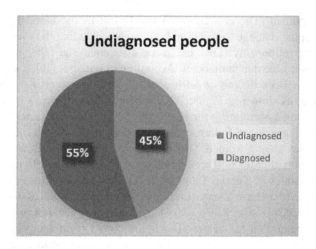

**FIGURE 7.3**   Undiagnosed people.

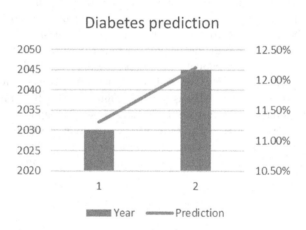

**FIGURE 7.4**   Diabetes future.

energy extremely faster if your thyroid produces too much thyroid hormone. Thyroid hyperthyroidism is the term for this condition. Newborns, teenagers, men, women, and the elderly all be affected by thyroid disease. It is possible that it is present from birth. It can also worsen as you become older. A woman is 5–8 times significantly more likely than a man to be detected with thyroid disease. Following are the significant heredity symptoms of the thyroid.

- Thyroid disease runs in your family history.
- Type 1 diabetes, pernicious anaemia, lupus, rheumatoid arthritis, primary adrenal insufficiency, and Turner syndrome are all medical conditions.
- Taking an iodine-rich dietary supplement (amiodarone).

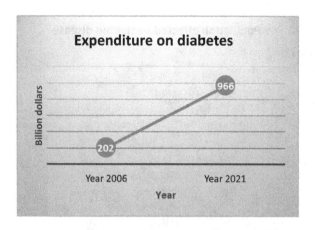

**FIGURE 7.5** Expenditure on diabetes.

- Age greater than 60.
- Radiation or thyroidectomy type treatment for cancer or a past thyroid condition.

Thyroid diseases are frequently induced by autoimmune reactions, which occur when the body's immune system begins to target its own cells [13]. Diabetes puts a person at a larger chance of acquiring thyroid disease than persons who do not have it. Type 1 diabetes is an autoimmune condition. We are more prone to acquire another autoimmune condition if we have one already. The risk is reduced for persons having Type 2 diabetes, but it still exists. You are more likely to develop thyroid disease later in your life if you have Type 2 diabetes. Thyroid disease affects around 1 in 8 women at some stage in life. The risk is nearly 10 times higher in women than in men. Figure 7.6 shows the thyroid patient statistics in India [14].

## 7.2 CASE STUDIES

### 7.2.1 INTELLIGENT GLUCOSE METER (IGLU) WITH IOMT

Continuous glucose measurement (CGM) is required to treat diabetes with insulin secretion or medicines. A solution for measuring glucose levels in patients with diabetes is needed. Controlling diabetes through insulin secretion or dosing requires CGM device. At present, there are no smart healthcare solutions available to measure glucose. Diabetes patients need a solution for glucose monitoring. People will become more aware of dietary control through CGM. A diabetic patient may need to measure his glucose level from time to time. Blood glucose is typically measured using the traditional method, which is by pricking a blood drop. Currently available CGM devices do not always give accurate results, and also they are not cost-effective. To address these difficulties, This chapter employs a non-invasive device, iGLU, that works with IoMT architecture to deliver a cutting-edge smart healthcare solution [15]. The iGLU is a new non-invasive testing gadget that uses an optical detecting

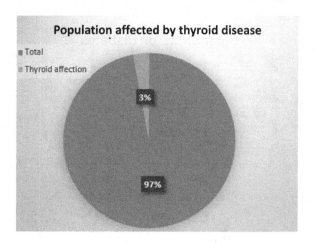

**FIGURE 7.6**    Population affected by thyroid disease.

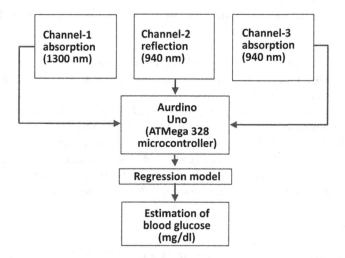

**FIGURE 7.7**    Model iGLU with IoMT.

approach to estimate continuous blood glucose levels. A non-invasive iGLU device that works with IoMT architecture to deliver a cutting-edge smart healthcare solution is proposed in this chapter, as shown in Figure 7.7. The iGLU is a new non-invasive testing gadget integrated with the IoMT framework enabling diabetic patients in remote areas to help them with diet and medication.

The proposed iGLU device employs a near-infrared (NIR) spectroscopy technique with various short wavelengths. The gadget has three channels, each equipped with an emitter and detector for a specific wavelength. The reflectance and absorption spectroscopy are taken into account in order to detect the glucose molecules. This device fits best as it is cost-effective and gives high accuracy. Three channels of the output voltage can be used to estimate blood glucose values with the optimization of the regression model. In order to predict the blood glucose level, the output voltages are used as input vectors. Testing the device on healthy, prediabetic, and diabetic patients by following the protocol confirms the accuracy of the trained regression model. The proposed device best suits measurement as it is also tested on age groups of 17–75, and the non-invasive blood glucose level measurement is accurate in the range of 80–420 mg/dl. Additionally, prototypes of iGLU were developed having a system on chip (SoC) that included light-emitting diodes (LEDs), an analogue-to-digital (ADC) converter with noise filtering capabilities, and detectors and frame acquisition controllability. A 16-bit ADC was used to process the collected data at a sampling rate of 128 samples per second. These data have been stabilized by coherence averaging, and the blood glucose levels are predicted using a deep neural network (DNN). Levenberg–Marquardt back propagation is used to train the sigmoid activation for DNN. Based on a comparison with a standard SD Check glucometer, the mean absolute relative difference (mARD) is 4.66%, the mean error (AvgE) is 4.61%, and the regression coefficient is 0.81.

In summary, iGLU is a new non-invasive glucose meter for smart healthcare. The device prototype uses specific wavelengths of NIR light to detect glucose molecules. For monitoring of patients, glucose values are stored in the cloud for later access by caregivers who use the IoMT framework.

### 7.2.2 IoMT-Enabled Blood Glucose Prediction with Deep Learning and Edge Computing

Predicting blood glucose (BG) levels is important for successful glycemic control in managing Type 1 diabetes (T1D). CGM and deep learning techniques have been shown as depicted in Figure 7.8 to be capable of improving BG prediction with the advent of IoMT. The chronic disease diabetes is characterized by hyperglycemia, affecting nearly 500 million people worldwide. People who have Type 1 diabetes (T1D) can receive lifelong treatment to keep their BG levels within safe limits because of the autoimmune destruction, which leads to absolute insulin deficiency. In order to accomplish this, the patient must consistently adhere to a set of self-care behaviors,

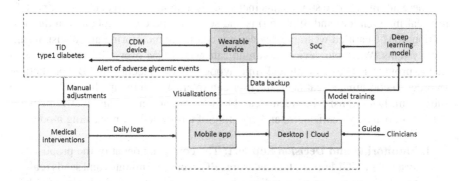

**FIGURE 7.8** Blood glucose prediction with deep learning.

such as keeping track of BG levels, administering extrinsic insulin, and careful planning of diet and exercise [16]. Failure to do so increases the risk of hyperglycemia and hypoglycemia, resulting in a variety of temporary or deep-rooted complications. With the advancement in IoT, many CGM devices have been developed. The wide use of CGM has generated data in huge amounts and promising the development of artificial intelligence (AI) technology, mostly in the prediction of BG in machine learning algorithms [17]. Recent advances in deep learning–based models have brought them to the cutting edge in terms of accuracy. However, due to the increasing demand for computational resources, these algorithms are difficult to implement for sustainable decision support in real-world clinical settings. Smartphone-based implementations, on the other hand, are limited due to their short span of battery life, and the fact that users need to carry their devices. Therefore, this chapter introduces a new deep learning model that uses attention-based stochastic recurrent neural networks to design IoMT-enabled wearable devices and implement embedded models. It includes a low-cost, low-power SoC that uses Bluetooth connectivity and edge computing to perform real-time BG prediction and hypoglycemia detection. In addition, a smartphone app is developed for visualizing BG trajectories and forecasts and a cloud and desktop platform for backing up and fine-tuning models.

Existing methodologies to implement deep learning models for BG prediction are primarily based on customized smartphone apps. However, these methods have some limitations, such as lack of portability, battery limitations, and mobile operating system reliance. In this task, you will develop a new IoMT-enabled wearable device to implement how to use SoC for Bluetooth low energy (BLE) connectivity and edge computing. An attention mechanism is introduced for obtaining accurate BG predictions by a computationally efficient recurrent neural network (RNN). Evidential regression is used to improve the diagnosis of hypoglycemia and compute model uncertainty. The trained model was then implemented into the SoC of the reflected wearable device using improved circuitry to reduce the consumption of energy. After obtaining CGM measurements, the non-invasive wearable device uses real-time model inference to produce BG forecasts and hypoglycemia warnings to support a decision, which can later be integrated into APsystems. Finally, the predictive correctness of embedded models, performance analysis and edge computing execution, and testing of the effectiveness of wearable devices in ten simulations are evaluated.

There are in all three subsystems included: 1) monitoring and decision support, 2) medical intervention, and 3) platforms and servers. These are explained in the next section. IoMT-entitled wearable devices are central to monitoring and decision support systems. Wearable devices communicate with CGM over a Bluetooth connection to provide T1D users with real-time hypoglycemia detection and BG prediction. In order to coordinate treatment, the user can interact with the medical intervention subsystem. Data transfer between wearable devices and servers and platforms is for data backup, data visualization, and updating of embedded deep learning models.

1. **Monitoring and Decision Support:** The core component of the proposed system is a CGM sensor that measures BG every five minutes and sends real-time measurements to a dedicated wearable bracelet via BLE (Bluetooth low energy).

2. **Medical Interventions:** In this task, the use of insulin pumps is not common among people with T1D, so manual control of various clinical scenarios is considered. After receiving predictions and alerts from the wearable device, T1D patients can search for the necessary interventions in advance and manually adjust existing treatments.

3. **Platforms and Servers:** A smartphone app can connect to the bracelet via Bluetooth to visualize existing CGM measurements, forecasts, and past BG history while recording day-to-day activities such as meals, exercise, and health status. Train deep learning models and protect the data collected using a desktop application with a specially designed graphical user interface (GUI). You can communicate with the bracelet via the universal serial bus (USB) port and transfer data to the Amazon cloud storage, i.e., AWSS3 bucket.

In summary, this case study focuses on E3NN, a RNN model based on GRU with proof regression and attention mechanism, and develops a new IoMT-compatible wearable device that uses deep learning algorithms for predicting BG dynamically and hypoglycemic alert implementation edge computing on the SoC. As tested on three clinical datasets, the suggested model gained the best prediction accuracy for future BG levels as well as for impending hypoglycemia events with the fewest amount of floating point operations per second (FLOPs) and model parameters when compared to the deep learning–based approaches analyzed. The results of the in silico study showed that integrating a wearable device with a T1D management system significantly improved the results of glycemic-controlled glycemic levels. In the future, wearable devices will be evaluated with the proposed algorithms in real-world clinical trials, further investigation of hardware and software performance in real-world environments, and the modification of features and GUIs will be done according to user feedback.

### 7.2.3 REFLECTIVE BELIEF DESIGN–BASED BIG DATA ANALYTICS IN IoMT FOR DIABETES

As the global population grows, the main challenge for society is to have a better healthcare system. IoMT aspires to deliver a more comprehensive and pervasive health monitoring system. The most difficult issue has been the time required for web services in recent days. By keeping up with the current technological advances, three-dimensional (3D) videos can be downloaded at random intervals. The acquired voluminous data is obtained with minimum time for reliable data measurement. It will improve the ability of devices to allocate resources and provide faster speeds for diverse networks. The vital features of an intelligent healthcare system are high throughput, low delay, and reliability, all of which are critical for accurate and successful consultation and diagnosis [18]. Currently, Big Data is widely used for analyzing large amounts of data for business people, predictors, and academics to make more accurate forecasts than traditional analysis [19–21]. Big data in healthcare aids in predicting epidemics, the treatment of diseases, the improvement of survival rates, and the avoidance of avoidable deaths [22]. As the world's population grows and people live longer lives, fast advances in medical treatment occur, and many decisions are made due to these changes. Patients can make the best decisions at the appropriate moments because of Big Data. Metaheuristic algorithms face a new challenge from Big Data. As a result, this chapter proposes a metaheuristic optimization algorithm for Big Data processing in IoMT (DBN [deep belief network], CNN [convolutional neural network]) by integrating a gravity search optimization algorithm (GSOA) and a belief network that reflects a CNN. The architecture of the reflective belief design–based IoMT model is shown in Figure 7.9. According to the performance analysis, the GSOA-DBN CNN is effective at predicting diseases. Therefore, the purpose of this study is to provide a metaheuristic method for the optimization and predictive analytics of diabetes data to predict the risk of a heart attack. The IoMT module is used in collecting the data, which is subsequently optimized using a gravitational algorithm, followed by data categorization using a DBN-based CNN. Finally, SVM (support vector machine) will be used to do predictive analysis based on the predictive image analysis.

For the proposed model, the dataset is collected from public healthcare, which comprises over 100,000 records with 55 different attributes: gender, age, race, number of drugs, number of procedures, readmissions, and number of diagnoses are only a few of them. The data was initially acquired using the IoMT module, and it was then clustered to improve the processing of the data. A metaheuristic algorithm is used for data optimization, including the gravitational search optimization technique. The diabetes data were then categorized using these optimized data to determine the abnormal range. Then, a DBN was created in which CNN was used to perform categorization. The normal and pathological ranges of diabetes have been classified using this classification. It updated the hospital database to include the

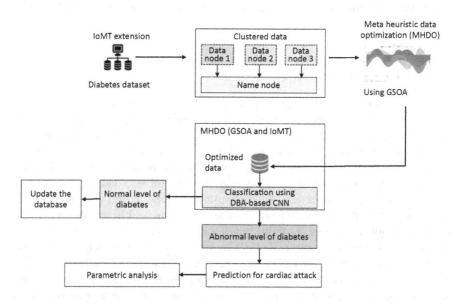

**FIGURE 7.9**   Reflective belief design–based IoMT model.

normal diabetes range. It used a predictive image algorithm based on SVMs to analyze the abnormal diabetes range for the cardiac nerves and blood vessels. A dataset
for diabetes is collected in the IoMT module. The data from the dataset is grouped
in the data clustering phase, followed by data optimization using metaheuristic data
optimization utilizing GSOA. The DBN-based CNN classification technique is used
to classify the optimized data. The regular variety of diabetes is given to the sanato-
rium database, while an atypical variety of diabetes is despatched to the evaluation of
predicting cardiac assault risk, with a purpose to be performed the use of numerous
factors, primarily based completely on the categorization results.

The proposed method is implemented using the MATLAB program for performance evaluation. A few parameters of measures—including precision, accuracy,
recall, and F1 score—are used to assess the efficiency of the suggested strategy. The
quantization error was calculated using the U-matrix error rate of the topological
error. The diabetes dataset was chosen as the basis for estimation. Data was randomly selected from the dataset to test the model's performance. They compared
the approach with ACO, WOA, GA, and HA. In comparison with existing artificial
neural network (ANN), KNN (k-nearest number), and NN, the suggested technique
achieves 98% accuracy, 96% precision, 94% recall, and 92% F1 score. The comparable results were that the suggested GSOA-DBN CNN outperformed ANN, NN, and
KNN by more than 2%, 3%, and 4%, respectively. More than 2% of ANN precision,
3% of NN precision, and 6% of KNN precision were attained. The F1 score reached
is 2% of ANN, 3% of NN, and 4% of KNN, and the recall acquired is higher than 2%
of ANN, 3% of NN, and 4% of KNN. The suggested GSOA-DBN CNN technique
outperforms the existing AWO, WOA, and GA strategies by 0.2 peak signal-to-noise
ratio (PSNR). Hybrid deep learning methods may be used in the future to improve
the model's efficiency.

## 7.3  LITERATURE SURVEY

This section explores strategies implemented using IoMT on diabetes and thyroid
disease. According to research, a new health platform featuring humanoid robots has
been created to assist an arising highly complex treatment approach to take care of
diabetes. This same platform's framework transforms the IoT technologies into an
internet concept by leveraging current internet protocols to access and operate core
network items. It contains microvascular channels, all of which contain a collection
of clinical sensors attached remotely to a robotic system connected (through the web)
to an internet illness management centre. A highly optimized model is developed,
and its edge features and acceptance are effectively assessed in a health professional
research study, demonstrating that patients and families are open to the suggested
system's implementation [23].

Under this research, a physics method is proposed based on electrodynamics,
which describes all abnormal albumin fluxing mechanisms in the early stages of
diabetic kidney disease (DKD) and is evaluated using the Monte Carlo approach.
As per the computer models, the output could be acknowledged throughout cases in
which a nanosensor would be expected to be capable of significantly defeating noise
or background noise. Researchers have assigned a simulation error of the order of

15% to these experiments [24]. The study examines Zion China's technological solution E-Follow Up, primarily based on conventional business analytics and information collected from locations, gadgets, and the online cloud. They wished for a more intelligent, faster, and cheaper way to constantly and consistently serve data from the cloud and other forms of different information in this process. Its results show how they efficiently handled enormous data quantities and improved data analysis [25].

Researchers presented Saleem as an architecture for a diabetic management system in this chapter. Its goal is to collect data on diabetic patients' behaviour and health. The data is then evaluated and mined so that doctors and patients may see it. As a result, real-time data is used to assist judgments. Saleem only has the visualization layer at this point. As a result, this version lacks the prediction layer. In the future, researchers will integrate a prediction layer that analyzes diabetes patients' vital signs and compares them to other patients with similar symptoms using machine learning to forecast complications. The system should also give doctors recommendations to their patients based on their behaviour and lifestyle to avert future difficulties [26].

This study describes the architecture of DAMON, a tracking system that takes recorded and captured client information as input and operates it by using an standard template library (STL) framework that includes two monitoring strategies and reasons for its fundamental validity to get more appropriate decision guidance. The consumer can also be required to offer side-channel verification if it is proven that a selective admission is suspicious because it violates defined physiological standards or conflicts with other information sources. The system captures an entry of the authenticity of the data in a questionnaire based on the person's extra response. Rather than raw data, authenticated data will now be used to make judgments [27].

This study aims to present a semantic-driven complex event processing technique for diabetic individuals who are at risk of cardiovascular disease (CVD). They have concentrated on the semantic modelling of medical events, in particular, proposing various processing criteria. There are four phases to the planned architecture. The first was concerned with collecting clinical information from diverse and dispersed MCOs. The data was transformed from an ambiguous and unclear layout to a fully integrated and specific format within the second step. The third stage was also offered as an analysis of the patient's condition, prediction of severe health complications, recommendation of appropriate treatment, and finally, notification of choice to the patient. The final phase is devoted to developing diagnostic and therapeutic choice assistance for clients, clinicians, and managers [28].

Researchers presented an IoT and machine learning–based healthcare platform to minimize the chances of diabetes by constant monitoring and forecasting. The no-contact IoT-based glucose detector and its interaction with the mobile application allow for handy and reduced continuous tracking and measuring of blood sugar levels. They looked at a variety of machine learning models. They discovered that SVM significantly improved for diabetes estimation, with an accuracy of 80.5%, using a source data called practice fusion that contains more than 10,000 occurrences. Besides that, approaches such as grid search and K-fold cross-validation were used to optimize SVM-based machine learning model parameters, which enhanced effectiveness by up to 82%. This same machine learning model's prediction aids the user in keeping track of their health and making lifestyle modifications to minimize their chances of diabetes. The designed methodology is among the most successful strategies for constantly monitoring and measuring a person's critical data to reduce diabetes risk [29]. Generated by IoMT, the whole study establishes the concept of remote health monitoring and ambient assisted living. This study presents the FreeStyle Free sensor, which uses IoT technology that would allow CGM. It is a low-cost device that will enable doctors and caregivers to access information from afar. Libre monitoring processes the data obtained from various sensors and stores it in the cloud for future study. During the same time period, the glucose levels can be measured and analyzed using FreeStyle Libre software. Researchers suggest an IoMT-based framework for clinicians to monitor and evaluate glucose levels of people with diabetes from far-away locations, which is precise and minimal in terms of cost [30].

A screening approach for a better successful thyroid illness assessment is given throughout the research work. A fundamental goal was also to increase the understanding of thyroid illness treatment. They used AI to get a diagnosis of thyroid illness. Using the machine learning approach, the method achieved 94.82% prediction performance. The findings showed that this suggested technique could efficiently understand the thyroid by computationally identifying and categorizing it using the suggested method. Furthermore, this finding confirmed that this method would be suitable to detect thyroid activity results of scientific testing and would therefore pave the road for different diagnoses to be supported by utilizing fresh diagnostic experiment records, which they are currently doing [31] In Simulink®, an upturned technique is utilized to construct a model of the sensing element that would be applied during thyroid surveillance. The suggested design was shown to be resource-intensive, with a temperature precision of +0.1°C in the 25°C–40°C bands. Additional study will focus on the execution of this framework, as well as the integration of several more similar modules for IoT [32]. This chapter has suggested a technique for identifying thyroid cancer predicated using AI in the suggested system. This strategy for thyroid cancer identification was already performed in Apache Spark utilizing MLlib, which is mainly developed with deep learning. Finally, medical imaging analytics grades were listed. Both the test results are a good fit for this position, with 72.9% accuracy and a 78.7% sensitivity. Moreover, such results are also based on a relatively small number of entries [33]. As a result, this study aims to test the efficiency of computer-aided diagnosis and AI algorithms for thyroid nodule detection from bump pics. On the single side, researchers devised a radiomics approach for obtaining 302-sized summary statistics from already screened visuals with wide bandwidth. This overall result has been obtained after feature minimization using respondent agreed and LDA, accordingly. AI-based technique, from a different side, was created and verified by preprocessing and shaping a convolutional architecture. Radiology and computer learning–based algorithms recorded the maximum precision on the validation dataset, with 66.81% and 74.69%. The comparative result revealed that the AI-based approach outperforms the physical in terms of quality [34].

These discussed approaches lack comprehensive solutions and suggestions. These approaches do not address the recommendation module. Hence to overcome this lacuna, we proposed a model that provides personalized recommendations to deal with prevalent diseases.

## 7.4 PROPOSED MODEL

We proposed an architecture to provide the chances of occurrence of prevalent diseases like diabetes and thyroid disease, along with personalized recommendations and preventive measures helpful for each person in India, as shown in Figure 7.10. IoMT delivers a cost-effective system for real-time data maintenance, as depicted in Figure 7.11. The cloud computing framework is the most suitable technology to reach each system stakeholder. The data repository module, early prediction module, recommendation, preventive measures module, and visualization module are important cornerstones of the proposed project [35]. The functional need for the prediction module is the early body symptoms of patients. Support for the same will be availed from a team of doctors and public and private health organizations. Supervised and unsupervised deep learning methodology will be applied to attain better prediction at an early stage for women. Verification and analysis of the developed model will be used to enhance the performance. Various visualization elements such as graphs, reports, rules, and charts are deliverable to stakeholders.

The government has launched various schemes to improve women's health. In this work, we are planning to aid Pradhmantri Jan Arogya Yojana (PJAY) [36, 37]. The cloud computing framework is proposed to share computing resources and provide our model's reachability to individuals, public and private health organizations, general practitioners, super specialists, and pathology and image providers as stakeholders. As depicted in Figure 7.12, the proposed system architecture offers online services to stakeholders and PJAY. Online services consist of four modules: data repository, prediction, prevention, and visualization modules. Structured, unstructured and semi-structured data are pre-processed and aggregated into a data repository. The prediction module will use advanced machine learning methods to detect the primary level of prediction and deep learning techniques to predict the secondary level. The primary level of early prediction requires basic attributes from pathology tests. Less than 50% of the occurrence with the disease is notified as low-risk patient. Patients diagnosed with above 50% chances of disease are asked for further necessary tests. Deep learning models will train specialized test results to give better accuracy. Preventive modules suggest preventive measures and personalized recommendations on a day-to-day life diet and exercise. The visualization module represents knowledge in a remarkable graphical format. An intended project can collaborate with PJAY to identify low-risk patients and high-risk patients for insurance purposes, and hence, it will reduce the nation's economic burden.

The study of research papers approves that disease prediction is achieved through well-known machine learning methods, as shown in Figure 7.12. SVM, random forest with k-fold cross verification, and Naïve Bayes classifier on Pap smear test are well-known methods for detection of cervical cancer [38]. Disproportional distribution of data will lead to low accuracy in existing methods for the detection of cervical cancer. Data preprocessing and the CNN model of deep learning are the most suitable futuristic techniques to achieve worthy accuracy. Association rule mining, k-means clustering, random forest, and ANN assure good results in diabetes and thyroid disease research. ANN is the most suitable method for the prediction model, and it has achieved 75.5% accuracy. An RNN of deep learning model is applicable

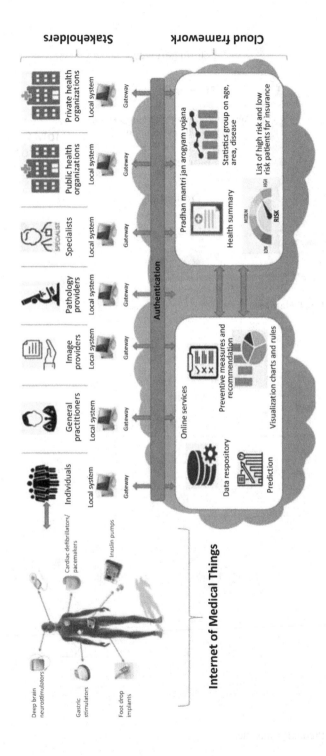

**FIGURE 7.10** Proposed architecture.

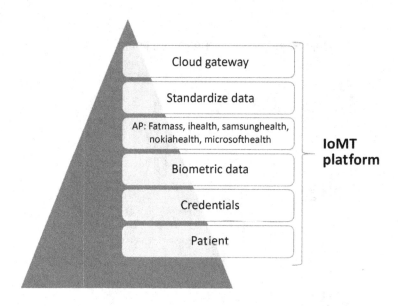

**FIGURE 7.11**   IoMT platform.

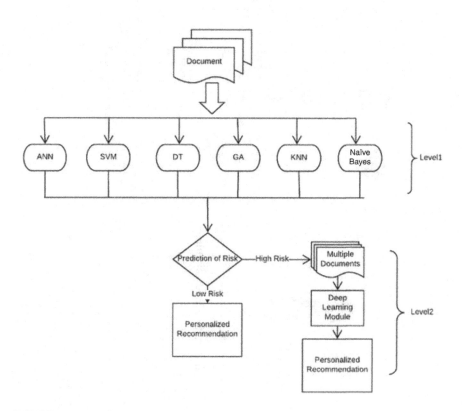

**FIGURE 7.12**   Prediction module.

here to deal with a larger dataset and automatic feature extraction. Two of the biggest challenges with traditional machine learning techniques are feature extraction and high-dimensional databases. In this project, we proposed to predict prevalent diseases in any person at an early age using deep learning models [39, 40].

Cloud framework interfaced with each stakeholder and proposed model consist of web portal for collecting online data and to provide user-friendly environment to the end-user. The online functionality process consists of the development of a data repository module, prediction module, prevention module, and visualization module. Adapted machine learning methods will be applicable for primary-level prediction of said diseases, and new approaches to be invented or hybrid techniques to be applied for secondary level of prediction [41]. Python, Java, and PHP programming languages will be used to achieve the same. SQL and NoSQL databases will be used to manage the data repository module. The developed technology can be clubbed as a module in PJAY for early detection of disease for corrective action on time and to reduce the economic burden on the nation. The intended work will provide health statistics and a list of low-risk and high-risk patients for insurance. Increased collaboration, resource availability, and simple ways to access data repositories, prediction modules, prevention modules, and visualization modules for stakeholders and PJAY is more effective by using cloud framework. Data mining and machine learning techniques are proven methodologies to detect and predict the primary level of diagnosis for prevalent diseases in women. Convolution deep neural networks and other deep learning methods are more suitable for a large volume of image data. By selecting Big Data platforms like Apache Spark and Apache, Hadoop provides distributed implementation environment for parallel processing.

## 7.5  CONCLUSION AND FUTURE WORK

This chapter examines and summarizes IoMT-based systems for early prediction of prevalent diseases like diabetes and thyroid disease. It also tracks ingestible sensors, smart hospitals, mobile health, and a cloud-based enhanced framework for chronic illness treatment approaches and treatment and patient tracking systems connected with PJAY. Each user will be restricted in the future by security and privacy concerns. The proposed project will provide a single platform to all stakeholders, which will be both time-effective and cost-effective. Public and private health organizations can identify low-risk patients and high-risk patients for prevention and hospitalization purposes, along with prevention measures from all super specialists and experts for each patient. Early prediction of disease will warn each future patient about a healthy diet and lifestyle. Healthy people lead to a healthy nation, and the early prediction will reduce the cost of insurance for PJAY.

## REFERENCES

[1] S. Joshi, and S. Joshi. (September 2019). "A Sensor Based Secured Health Monitoring and Alert Technique Using IOMT." *2019 2nd International Conference on Intelligent Communication and Computational Techniques (ICCT)*, pp. 152–156.

[2] A.A. Jolfaei, S.F. Aghili, and D. Singelee. (2021). "A Survey on Blockchain-Based IoMT Systems: Towards Scalability." *IEEE Access*, vol. 9, pp. 148948–148975.

[3] Leading the IoT - Gartner. (2017). gartner.com: https://www.gartner.com/imagesrv/books/iot/iotEbook_digital.pdf

[4] N. Boutros-Saikali, K. Saikali, and R. Abou Naoum. (April 2018). "An IoMT Platform to Simplify the Development of Healthcare Monitoring Applications." *2018 Third International Conference on Electrical and Biomedical Engineering, Clean Energy and Green Computing (EBECEGC)*, pp. 6–11.

[5] D. Saraswat, P. Bhattacharya, A. Verma, V.K. Prasad, S. Tanwar, G. Sharma, P.N. Bokoro, and R. Sharma. (2022). "Explainable AI for Healthcare 5.0: Opportunities and Challenges." *IEEE Access*, vol. 10, pp. 84486–84517. DOI: 10.1109/ACCESS.2022.3197671.

[6] V.K. Prasad, P. Bhattacharya, M. Bhavsar, A. Verma, S. Tanwar, G. Sharma, Pitshou N. Bokoro, and R. Sharma. (2022). "ABV-CoViD: An Ensemble Forecasting Model to Predict Availability of Beds and Ventilators for COVID-19 Like Pandemics." *IEEE Access*, vol. 10, pp. 74131–74151.

[7] S. Vishnu, S.J. Ramson, and R. Jegan. (March 2020). "Internet of Medical Things (IoMT)-An Overview." *2020 5th International Conference on Devices, Circuits and Systems (ICDCS)*, pp. 101–104.

[8] A. Ghubaish, T. Salman, M. Zolanvari, D. Unal, A. Al-Ali, and R. Jain. (2020). "Recent Advances in the Internet-of-Medical-Things (IoMT) Systems Security." *IEEE Internet of Things Journal*, vol. 8, no. 11, pp. 8707–8718.

[9] www.who.int/health-topics/diabetes#tab=tab_1. Accessed 12 April 2022.

[10] J. Elflein. (2022). "Diabetes Statistics & Facts." Statista: https://www.statista.com/topics/1723/diabetes/

[11] https://idf.org/aboutdiabetes/what-is-diabetes/facts-figures.html. Accessed 12 April 2022.

[12] www.cdc.gov/diabetes/data/statistics-report/index.html. Accessed 12 April 2022.

[13] www.ncbi.nlm.nih.gov/pmc/articles/PMC3743364/. Accessed 12 April 2022.

[14] A. Begum, and A. Parkavi. (March 2019). "Prediction of Thyroid Disease Using Data Mining Techniques." *2019 5th International Conference on Advanced Computing & Communication Systems (ICACCS)*, pp. 342–345.

[15] A.M. Joshi, P. Jain, and S.P. Mohanty. (July 2020). "iGLU: Non-invasive Device for Continuous Glucose Measurement with IoMT Framework." In *2020 IEEE Computer Society Annual Symposium on VLSI (ISVLSI)* (pp. 598–599). IEEE. https://te.booksc.org/book/83495786/8ce94c.

[16] T. Zhu, L. Kuang, J. Daniels, P. Herrero, K. Li, and P. Georgiou. (2022). "IoMT-Enabled Real-time Blood Glucose Prediction with Deep Learning and Edge Computing." *IEEE Internet of Things Journal*. DOI: 10.1109/JIOT.2022.3143375.

[17] A. Farhad, S. Woolley, and P. Andras. (August 2021). "Federated Learning for AI to Improve Patient Care Using Wearable and IoMT Sensors." *2021 IEEE 9th International Conference on Healthcare Informatics (ICHI)*, pp. 434–434.

[18] A. Sampathkumar, M. Tesfayohani, S.K. Shandilya, S.B. Goyal, S. Shaukat Jamal, P.K. Shukla, P. Bedi, and M. Albeedan. (2022). "Internet of Medical Things (IoMT) and Reflective Belief Design-Based Big Data Analytics with Convolution Neural Network-Metaheuristic Optimization Procedure (CNN-MOP)." *Computational Intelligence and Neuroscience*.

[19] J.A. Patel, and P. Sharma. (2020). "Online Analytical Processing for Business Intelligence in Big Data." *Big Data*, vol. 8, no. 6, pp. 501–518.

[20] A. Mehta, V. Vandriwala, J. Patel, and J. Patel. (2021). "Indexing on Healthcare Big Data." In *Soft Computing for Problem Solving* (pp. 271–283). Springer, Singapore.

[21] A. Verma, P. Bhattacharya, Y. Patel, K. Shah, S. Tanwar, and B. Khan. (2022). "Data Localization and Privacy-Preserving Healthcare for Big Data Applications: Architecture and Future Directions." In *Emerging Technologies for Computing, Communication and Smart Cities* (pp. 233–244). Springer, Singapore.

[22] J.A. Patel, and P. Sharma. (August 2014). "Big Data for Better Health Planning." *2014 International Conference on Advances in Engineering & Technology Research (ICAETR-2014)*, pp. 1–5.

[23] M.A. Al-Taee, W. Al-Nuaimy, Z.J. Muhsin, and A. Al-Ataby. (2016). "Robot Assistant in Management of Diabetes in Children Based on the Internet of Things." *IEEE Internet of Things Journal*, vol. 4, no. 2, pp. 437–445.

[24] H. Nieto-Chaupis. (October 2017). "Monte Carlo Simulation for the Very Anticipated Detection of Charged Giants Proteins in Type-2 Diabetes Patients Based on the Internet of Bio-Nano Things." *2017 CHILEAN Conference on Electrical, Electronics Engineering, Information and Communication Technologies (CHILECON)*, pp. 1–4.

[25] A. Ara, and A. Ara. (August 2017). "Case Study: Integrating IoT, Streaming Analytics and Machine Learning to Improve Intelligent Diabetes Management System." *2017 International Conference on Energy, Communication, Data Analytics and Soft Computing (ICECDS)*, pp. 3179–3182.

[26] S. Alelyani, and A. Ibrahim. (February 2018). "Internet-of-Things in Telemedicine for Diabetes Management." *2018 15th Learning and Technology Conference (L&T)*, pp. 20–23.

[27] W. Young, J. Corbett, M.S. Gerber, S. Patek, and L. Feng. (April 2018). "Damon: A Data Authenticity Monitoring System for Diabetes Management." *2018 IEEE/ACM Third International Conference on Internet-of-Things Design and Implementation (IoTDI)*, pp. 25–36.

[28] A. Rhayem, M.B.A. Mhiri, and F. Gargouri. (December 2019). "Complex-Event Processing for Diabetic Patients in the Internet of Medical Things: Semantic-Based Approach." *2019 7th International Conference on ICT & Accessibility (ICTA)*, pp. 1–6.

[29] A. Hebbale, G.H.R. Vinay, B.V. Krishna, and J. Shah. (October 2021). "IoT and Machine Learning Based Self Care System for Diabetes Monitoring and Prediction." *2021 2nd Global Conference for Advancement in Technology (GCAT)*, pp. 1–7.

[30] A. Joy, T.H. Hafsiya, and G. King. (March 2021). "A Review on Glucose Monitoring Using Enabling Technologies of Internet of Things." *2021 7th International Conference on Advanced Computing and Communication Systems (ICACCS)*, vol. 1, pp. 270–273.

[31] H. Kodaz, İ. Babaoğlu, and H. İşcan. (November 2009). "Thyroid Disease Diagnosis Using Artificial Immune Recognition System (AIRS)." *Proceedings of the 2nd International Conference on Interaction Sciences: Information Technology, Culture and Human*, pp. 756–761.

[32] P. Sundaravadivel, S.P. Mohanty, E. Kougianos, and U. Albalawi. (April 2016). "An Energy Efficient Sensor for Thyroid Monitoring Through the IOT." *2016 17th International Conference on Thermal, Mechanical and Multi-Physics Simulation and Experiments in Microelectronics and Microsystems (EuroSimE)*, pp. 1–4.

[33] D. Ivanova. (September 2018). "Artificial Intelligence in Internet of Medical Imaging Things: The Power of Thyroid Cancer Detection." *2018 International Conference on Information Technologies (InfoTech)*, pp. 1–4.

[34] Y. Wang, W. Yue, X. Li, S. Liu, L. Guo, H. Xu, H. Zhang, and G. Yang. (2020). "Comparison Study of Radiomics and Deep Learning-Based Methods for Thyroid Nodules Classification Using Ultrasound Images." *IEEE Access*, vol. 8, pp. 52010–52017.

[35] J. Mulani, S. Heda, K. Tumdi, J. Patel, H. Chhinkaniwala, and J. Patel. (2020). "Deep Reinforcement Learning Based Personalized Health Recommendations." In *Deep Learning Techniques for Biomedical and Health Informatics* (pp. 231–255). Springer, Cham.

[36] www.optum.in/thought-leadership/library/internet-healthcare-things.html. Accessed 12 April 2022.

[37] https://transformingindia.mygov.in/scheme/pradhan-mantri-jan-arogya-yojana/. Accessed 12 April 2022.

[38] J.A. Patel. (2015). "Classification Algorithms and Comparison in Data Mining." *International Journal of Innovations & Advancement in Computer Science*, vol. 4.

[39] H. Brawijaya, and S. Widodo. (August 2018). "Improving the Accuracy of Neural Network Technique with Genetic Algorithm for Cervical Cancer Prediction." *2018 6th International Conference on Cyber and IT Service Management (CITSM)*, pp. 1–7.

[40] K. Manikandan. (2019). "Diagnosis of Diabetes Diseases Using Optimized Fuzzy Rule Set by Grey Wolf Optimization." *Pattern Recognition Letters*, vol. 125, pp. 432–438.

[41] https://community.nasscom.in/communities/digital-transformation/healthtech-and-life-sciences/the-internet-of-medical-things-and-positive-disruption-in-the-healthcare-sector.html. Accessed 12 April 2022.

# 8 Trusted Federated Learning for Internet of Medical Things
## Solutions and Challenges

*Sajid Nazir, Yan Zhang, and Hua Tianfield*

## CONTENTS

DOI: 10.1201/9781003303374-8

## 8.1  INTRODUCTION

Internet of Things (IoT) devices can collect data in real time and communicate it wirelessly to a gateway device for onward transmission to a central server with the required computing, storage, and data analytics capability. The vital signs monitoring through IoT for hospitalized patients offers many advantages compared to manual data collection [1]. Electronic health records (EHRs) can comprise clinical readings, symptoms, monitored data, etc., for a patient [2]. The data stored in spreadsheets or other systems does not form part of patient EHR and can often be discarded [1]. A recent trend is to collect healthcare data through always-on low power devices termed as Internet of Medical Things (IoMT) [3]. IoMT allows wireless and remote devices to securely communicate over the network and thus data can be collected automatically and analyzed using machine learning (ML) techniques for predictions and determining future issues [1]. There are five segments in IoMT: on-body IoMT, in-home IoMT, community IoMT, in-clinic IoMT, and in-hospital IoMT [4]. On-body IoMT uses wearable devices such as smartwatches, smart glasses, and wristbands for health monitoring. In-home IoMT includes private emergency response systems, virtual telehealth services, and distance patient monitoring systems mainly used to manage chronic diseases. Community IoMT includes devices spread across a town or broader geographic area, for example, mobility services and emergency response intelligence systems. In-clinic IoMT devices are used for functional and therapeutic purposes. In-hospital IoMT utilizes devices presenting in the hospital for clinical and administrative use including product management, personnel emergency management, resource management, environmental and energy monitoring, etc. [4].

    The data collected by IoMT devices could be kept private to a patient, a department, or a hospital and yet be part of a collaborative effort to train a global model. However, it would be more common for the data sharing to be at the hospital level [5]. The collected data can help with both the diagnosis of a disease and for long-term health indicators monitoring both at homes and hospitals. The personal healthcare data is sensitive considering privacy, and restricted due to regulations, limiting the sharing of data [3]. In addition, there are risks posed due to connected medical devices of privacy leakage, cyber-attacks, and theft of personal data. The existing privacy preservation techniques are not sufficient for ensuring privacy due to statistical and linkage-based attacks that can compromise the privacy of patients' healthcare data [6]. Privacy issues, risks, and regulations limit the utilization of IoMT data [7].

    Advances in artificial intelligence (AI) and deep learning have revolutionized medical healthcare in radiology, genomics, pathology, and other fields [8, 9]. One of the challenges facing AI is that for most domains, data exists in local storage [10]. Thus, despite having AI algorithms with performance rivalling those of human domain experts, a model can be only as good as the data it is trained on and a lot of training data is required before model learning can take place [11]. The importance of hyper-parameters, which define a model's parameters, cannot be overlooked as these determine the model performance [12]. Healthcare systems and processes are complicated by their very nature. Due to data security and privacy protection rules, it is difficult for a medical institution to access and/or analyze medical data from other institutions. A robust ML model, on the other hand, can only be trained with enough data, which in most cases involves a significant quantity of data, especially for deep learning [13].

Following this introductory Section 8.1, the rest of this chapter is organized as follows. Section 8.2 explains the motivation to integrate federated learning and IoMT. Section 8.3 describes related work, which includes an in-depth literature review on federated learning. Section 8.4 discusses trusted federated learning. New architectures are discussed in Section 8.5 for a trusted federated learning for IoMT. Finally, Section 8.6 provides the conclusion.

## 8.2 MOTIVATION

### 8.2.1 IoMT Data Sharing for Smart Healthcare

IoMT can be used for health monitoring in hospitals and homes. IoMT could include wearable devices, environmental sensors, and medical monitors [5]. In order to guard against the challenges facing data sharing through IoMT, each healthcare establishment can avoid sharing its data with other research organizations and instead focus on developing its own custom models on its own data. This approach has several limitations. The medical data due to lack of trust and privacy remains fragmented in the different silos, missing the benefits of sharing the data to improve the model training and prediction process. The trained models thus would have biases due to data collection procedures, at time be unbalanced, and in any case, not taking advantage of medical data elsewhere. The need therefore is not only to build trust in data sharing but also to provide for mechanisms for model improvement by incorporating diverse data [13].

Medical data is collected and held in various formats and—regardless of its particular format—can render improvement in disease diagnosis through sharing. Machine learning has proved its importance for disease diagnosis through use of high quality and abundant data. The medical data could be time series data such as electrocardiogram (ECG) data; electronic health records (EHRs); medical IoT data comprising blood pressure, heart rate, etc.; and image data. The intelligent deployment of IoT devices can provide around-the-clock and real-time data acquisition from remote and inaccessible places. In general, there are two types of things in IoMT. One is the sensors and devices that are attached to the patients, and the other is the specialized medical equipment and devices that are interconnected to the network.

Within the same institution, it is efficient to integrate and manage the data from IoMT via a cloud platform, which will improve the productivity of healthcare

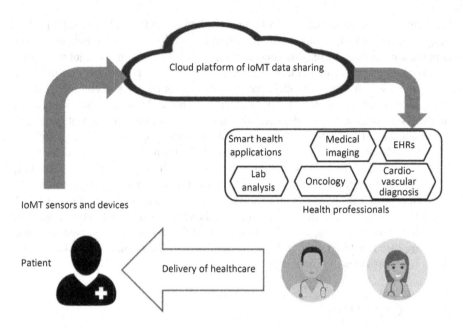

**FIGURE 8.1**   Cloud platform of IoMT data sharing for smart health applications.

delivery processes supported by the smart health applications. This can be illustrated as shown in Figure 8.1. However, when it is in a cross-organizational environment, due to policy control, regulations compliance and data protection, data sharing would become unrealistic and unfeasible, even if technologically it may be possible, e.g., with cloud computing.

### 8.2.2   Model Cooperation with Federated Learning

The data from different organizations cannot be transmitted and stored at a central location due to privacy and computation issues [14, 15]. Instead, the data can stay local and yet contribute to building better trained models with better classification accuracy and generalization using federated learning. In federated learning, a server orchestrates the sharing of the model parameters between the participating devices [14]. Federated learning models may require training of models on low-power devices or machines which could be incapable of processing large datasets compared to a high-end server [14].

The basic steps in training a model through federated learning are as follows.

- **Model Selection:** The model is selected and can then be shared with the individual participating devices for the federated learning algorithm. The server also selects the contributing devices or clients.
- **Local Model Training:** The model will be trained at each participating device with its local data. The server sends the model to the participating nodes for model training.

- **Model Aggregation:** The model parameters are then sent to the central server and are used to train a global model.
- **Mode Improvement:** The trained model can then be shared again with the participating devices for improving the model's accuracy.

Figure 8.2 shows the model training locally at the participating hospitals with local data and sharing updates with a central server for updates to a global model. The model cooperation through trusted federated learning also helps to reduce the model biases due to different data acquisition equipment, data collection protocols, age and gender parameters, etc., and can result in better trained models useful by all. Thus, the trusted federated learning approaches facilitate sharing the trained AI models across different participating healthcare organizations by breaking down barriers, increasing trust, and preserving privacy for better disease predictions that can increase deployment of AI models in clinical practice. However, there are still issues for federated learning adoption relating to technical and security aspects [14]. Federated learning has gained prominence for privacy preservation in IoMT data sharing [5].

Federated learning as a solution is a decentralization approach for privacy preserving, and sharing of data to train a model [16]. Thus, federated learning seeks to address data governance without the exchange of private data [8]. The distributed nature of federated learning is a good fit for the IoT data at the edge, as the collected

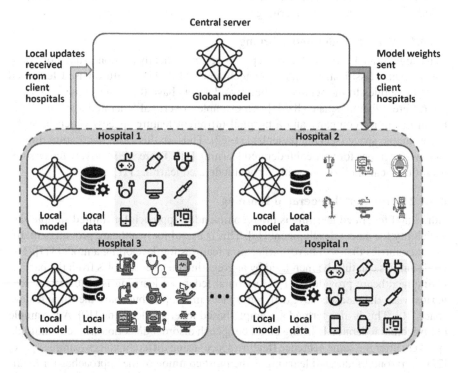

**FIGURE 8.2**    Model cooperation with federated learning.

data remains private local to the IoT device [3]. Compliance with the healthcare regulations is thus ensured by avoiding a centralized model. Thus, the federated learning system architecture follows a client–server model with one central server facilitating cooperation in the model development with clients training the model on their local datasets, distributing the model, and ultimately sharing the model with an acceptable accuracy [17].

## 8.3   RELATED WORK, FRAMEWORKS, AND CHALLENGES

The term federated learning [18] describes a distributed ML approach by taking advantage of parallelism [17, 19]. With federated learning, the training can take place by the contributing users on the user data in a privacy-preserving way without sharing the private data with others. Instead, the model parameters are shared which can be aggregated to create a joint or global trained model [5, 17, 19]. An advantage of the federated learning approach is the decoupling of direct access to the training data and the model training [18].

### 8.3.1   Categories of Federated Learning

A survey of federated learning in data mining is provided in [20]. A categorization of federated learning systems using privacy mechanisms, communication architecture, scale of federation, data distribution, ML model, and motivation of federation is provided in [21]. The federated learning can be categorized as follows.

#### 8.3.1.1   Vertical Federated Learning

Vertical federated learning has been proposed for vertically portioned data for gradient descent, classification, and other techniques [10]. This feature-based federated learning applies to the scenario when two datasets have the same sample ID space but different feature space [10, 11]. An example of vertical federated learning could be an insurance company and a hospital (different feature spaces) which have the same sample space (serving patients) [11, 22]. Thus, in this case, the feature dimension will increase for vertical federated learning [11]. There are relatively fewer studies for medical applications with vertical federated learning [11].

#### 8.3.1.2   Horizontal Federated Learning

Horizontal federated learning is the recommended approach for limited sample size variability for model development [11]. This is useful for healthcare providers in different countries that will have similar user features for developing a model [11]. The total samples can thus be increased by aggregating the user samples from the participating healthcare providers [11]. Horizontal federated learning is required for scenarios when the datasets have different spaces in samples but share the same feature space [10]. This is also termed as sample-based federated learning [10]. An example of horizontal federated learning could be speech disorder detection whereby multiple speakers utter the same sentence (feature space) using different voices (sample space) [22]. Horizontal federated learning is the most common of the approaches for medical applications [11].

### 8.3.1.3   Federated Transfer Learning

This is applicable to scenarios when the two datasets differ in terms of the samples and the feature space [10]. Federated transfer learning can use the shared AI models for better diagnosis accuracy [22]. For smart healthcare, an example could be disease diagnosis involving multiple participating countries' hospitals with different patients (sample space) and different therapeutic programmes (feature space) [22]. It was found that the federated transfer learning as a technique was applied more often compared to vertical and horizontal federated learning [23]. A model for human activity recognition was extended to Parkinson's disease classification using transfer learning in the Fedhealth [24].

### 8.3.2   OPEN FRAMEWORKS FOR FEDERATED LEARNING

Federated learning provides the possibility to decouple the ability to do ML from the need to access centralized significant amounts of data. However, federated learning is not easy to implement realistically, both in terms of scale and system heterogeneity [25]. A number of research frameworks are available to support the study of scalable federated learning on healthcare data. Google proposed an open-source framework TFF (TensorFlow Federated) for ML and other computations on decentralized data [26]. The latest version (0.20.0) of TFF was released in February 2022. Developers can either use the federated learning algorithms included in TFF or experiment with new algorithms using TFF. TFF's interfaces are composed of two layers: federated learning (FL) API and federated core (FC) API. TFF is distributed under the Apache 2.0 licence.

FATE (Federated AI Technology Enabler) is an open-source project initiated by Webank's AI Department to provide a secure computing framework to support the federated AI ecosystem [27]. FATE can be deployed on a single host or on multiple nodes. It has six major modules: FederatedML, FATE Serving, FATE Flow, FATE Board, Federated Network, and KubeFATE. Many common federated ML algorithms, encryption tools, and secure protocols are implemented in the FederatedML module. FATE supports analysis of horizontal (homogeneous) and vertical (heterogeneous) data partitions. FATE provides algorithm level interfaces. Practitioners have to modify the source code of FATE to implement their own federated algorithms, which is not easy for non-expert users [21]. FATE is also distributed under the Apache 2.0 licence. Flower is a comprehensive federated learning framework that offers facilities to execute large-scale federated learning experiments, and considers richly heterogeneous federated learning device scenarios [25]. Flower core framework architecture includes both Edge Client Engine and Virtual Client Engine. Edge clients live on real edge devices and communicate with the server over remote procedure call (RPC). Virtual clients consume close to zero resources when inactive and only load models and data into memory when the client is being selected for training or evaluation [25]. With Flower, researchers are able to build experimental blocks both on the global and the local levels to quantify the system costs associated with running federated learning on real heterogeneous edge devices and to identify bottlenecks in real-world federated training. Again, Flower is open-sourced under Apache 2.0 licence.

IBM Federated Learning is a Python framework with the main drivers as confidentiality and privacy, provisions to move the data to the central server, and compliance with regulatory requirements [13]. IBM Federated Learning can be extended by easily incorporating advanced features. It supports different ML technologies and is independent of ML frameworks, such as support for models (TensorFlow, Keras), deep reinforcement learning algorithms, decision trees, and linear classifiers [13]. IBM Federated Learning provides a foundation for development in enterprise and in academic and industry research, and can be used for private, public, and hybrid clouds [13].

PaddleFL is an open-source framework that makes it easy to deploy federated learning models in distributed clusters, and comparison and replication of federated learning algorithms [28]. PySyft is a Python library which can work with PyTorch and Tensorflow [29]. Federated learning and differential privacy (FL & DP) framework is an open-source framework for federated learning and differential-privacy experimentation [30]. Some other federated learning frameworks proposed by researchers are a low-code federated learning platform (EasyFL) [31], a tier-based federated learning system (TiFL) [32], a self-adaptive federated learning framework for heterogeneous systems (FedSAE) [33], and a fair and accurate federated learning under heterogeneous targets with ordered dropout (FjORD) [34].

### 8.3.3 FEDERATED LEARNING HEALTHCARE SOLUTIONS AND APPLICATIONS

Federated learning provides privacy-preserving data sharing. Federated learning has been proposed as a promising method to bridge the gap between the separation of medical data to protect patient privacy and training a strong deep learning model with a vast quantity of data. A summary of federated learning architectures for healthcare data is provided in Table 8.1. A framework termed deep federated learning was proposed for IoT healthcare data collection and analysis for a skin disease detection, showing an improvement in the model performance [35]. An architecture for smart healthcare is proposed with an edge node and user layer [36]. The use of federated learning in healthcare applications are described in the following sections.

#### 8.3.3.1 Federated Learning with EHR Data

Healthcare monitoring could be used through medical devices in the hospitals and wearable devices for in-house patients. A key application for the emerging communications standards is in healthcare for patients' medical records [37]. Federated learning has been applied to address the various types of healthcare data. A review of federated learning for EHR is provided in [38], highlighting the extensive research on privacy and confidentially of data. It was reported that deep learning was the most common technique, with almost 79% of case studies using it. The authors also proposed an architecture for federated learning of EHR data [38].

An algorithm termed FT-IoMT Health was proposed for data aggregation from the participating clients, ensuring security and privacy by employing transfer learning [37]. The proposed model was validated using human activity detection and showed improved results compared to traditional ML models [37]. In a study by NVIDIA in collaboration with King's College London, the successful development of a global

**TABLE 8.1**

**Summary of Federated Learning Architectures for IoMT Data**

| Type of Data | Issues | Evaluation and Results | Reference |
|---|---|---|---|
| **IoMT device data** | Adaptive differential-privacy algorithm/edge nodes to avoid a single point of failure. | Diabetic dataset, better accuracy, resistance to poisoning attacks, and acceptable running time. | [36] |
| | Ethereum smart contracts for data provenance and encryption for security and privacy. | COVID-19 detection on public datasets, attained above 90% accuracy in training and above 85% in testing. | [39] |
| | Deep federated learning framework. | Skin disease detection on Dermatology Atlas dataset, with an area under the ROC curve (AUC) of the model as 97%. | [35] |
| **Wearable device data** | Fedhealth framework for data aggregation and transfer learning. | Parkinson's disease diagnosis achieved personalized healthcare ensuring privacy. 5.3% improvement over a no-federation model. | [24] |
| | Heart activity data collected from smart bands. | Three datasets; better accuracy (87.55%) compared to the other selected models. | [7] |
| **EHR** | Enables healthcare institutions for distributed data analysis, preserving patient confidentiality. | Leverages federated learning methodologies and practices. | [38] |
| **Image data** | Brain tumour segmentation (BraTS) simulation of 32 institutions with six subjects per institution. | BraTS challenge dataset, federated learning segmentation of multi-modal data (Dice = 0.852) similar to models with shared data. | [40] |
| | Fusion-based federated learning for COVID-19 detection. | Better performance compared to default setting for accuracy, and communications efficiency. | [15] |
| | Ethereum blockchain–based secure framework for 5G networks using differential privacy. | Image classification on MNIST and CIFAR-10 can deter membership inference and poisoning attack. | [41] |
| **Multi-modal data, chest X-rays, lab data, vital signs** | COVID-19 oxygen requirement prediction. | AUC improvement of 16% across participating sites and an increase in generalizability of 38% compared to models trained at a single site. | [42, 43] |
| **General data** | Privacy protection with addition of differential-privacy noise. | MNIST dataset prevented a single point of failure and provided better protection against malicious interference. | [44] |

model was demonstrated by sharing the small client datasets for a segmentation task using BraTS 2018 dataset [45]. The federated learning model achieved similar performance to that achieved without sharing the data [45]. The study also prevented restoration and reverse engineering of the dataset by using complex mathematical algorithms [45]. The patient data was encoded before sharing it with other clients using differential-privacy technique [45]. It was shown that it is possible to achieve similar performance as that of a large dataset by using the federated learning model without sharing the small datasets at the institutional level [45]. Many medical institutions can thus overcome the problem of data paucity by following the combined sharing and use of the small datasets in encoded form [45].

### 8.3.3.2 Medical Imaging via Federated Learning

Federated learning can be a solution for healthcare organizations with small image datasets which they are willing to use in conjunction with other healthcare organizations in order to develop better medical imaging AI models [45]. There are challenges for medical image classification using federated learning, as it is hard to quantify the contribution of different participating devices which could be based on image quantity, quality, or diversity [45]. A research study at the University of Pennsylvania in collaboration with 29 other collaborating institutions around the world is developing a federated learning framework focusing on tumour segmentation in collaboration with Intel [46]. This was presented as the first use of federated learning techniques to real-world imaging data [46]. The performance of federated learning on a brain tumour segmentation (BraTS) dataset was compared with two other collaborative learning methods, institutional incremental learning (IIL) and cyclic institutional incremental learning (CIIL) and was found to perform better [40].

The recent outbreak of COVID-19 highlighted the importance for disease diagnosis with chest computerized tomography (CT) imaging [47]. However, the data sharing across the clinical storage has its challenges for ML-based models [47]. The challenges of data heterogeneity can be overcome as shown for a real-world project for COVID-19 region segmentation in chest CT images from China, Italy, and Japan [47]. The proposed framework with semi-supervised leaning was shown to have better results compared to the conventional data sharing [47]. A dynamic fusion-based federated learning model is proposed for COVID-19 diagnostics on medical images [15]. The fusion method was used to select the participating clients based on local model performance in order to schedule the model fusion determined by the participating clients' training time [15]. The proposed model was evaluated on a COVID-19 detection dataset comprising X-ray and CT imaging [15].

### 8.3.3.3 Federated Learning with Medical IoT Data

A framework termed Fedhealth was proposed for wearable healthcare data using transfer learning for creating personalized models [24]. The personalized models are useful for solving personalized healthcare situations as a federated learning global model lacks personalization [24]. For the evaluation of Fedhealth, a public human activity recognition dataset comprising six activities collected from 30 users was used [24]. The results for Fedhealth were compared against the traditional ML models and it was shown that Fedhealth had the best classification accuracy [24]. The wearable devices data can help to diagnose Parkinson's disease [24]. The Parkinson's disease dataset was used for diagnosis, and it was shown that the proposed federated transfer learning approach achieved effective symptom classification [24]. The authors concluded that the model updating with incremental learning—that is, a model updating with the arrival of new data—can further improve the proposed Fedhealth model [24].

A federated learning deep learning algorithm was proposed for heart activity IoT data [7]. The algorithms were tested on two different scenarios for a case study on stress recognition on photoplethysmography (PPG)-based heart activity signals [7]. The scenarios related to a centralized processing of data as in non-federated approach and the other was through federated learning for local training of model [7]. The results showed that the performance was improved without sacrificing privacy [7].

### 8.3.3.4 Health Text Mining via Federated Learning

Google has introduced natural language processing (NLP) through Pixel phones, Android messages and Gboard mobile keyboards [41]. A survey of the federated learning algorithm for NLP covered language modelling, speech recognition, text classification, recommendation system, sequence tagging, and health text mining [41]. Due to the privacy concerns, federated learning is a favoured approach for health text mining and some of the tasks reported were patient representation learning and phenotyping, similarity learning, and predictive modelling [41]. The health data can exhibit bias towards communities, hospitals, and diseases and can be challenging for federated learning [41]. A benchmarking framework, FedNLP, was proposed for evaluating the federated learning techniques on different tasks, that is, seq2seq, text classification, question answering, and sequence tagging [48]. The framework provided an interface for other models under different non-IID (non–independent and identically distributed) strategies for partitioning [48]. FedNLP can be used for evaluating and analyzing NLP tasks with federated learning [48]. NLP can also be useful for generating image labels consistently across different participating clients for ML, which can improve standardization [45].

### 8.3.3.5 Federated Learning with Multi-Modal Data

A federated learning model termed EXAM (electronic medical record [EMR] chest X-ray AI model) was proposed that collected data across 20 institutes for oxygen requirement prediction for COVID-19 patients by using inputs from chest X-rays, laboratory data and vital signs [42]. The use of federated learning enhanced the data science collaboration amongst the institutes for model development from heterogeneous datasets [42]. The federated learning global model was found to perform better as compared to the local models, improving area under the RUC curve (AUC) from 0.75 to 0.920, and model generalization from 0.667 to 0.920, providing an AUC improvement of 16% across participating sites and an increase in generalizability of 38% compared to trained model for a single site with its own data [42]. A biosensing application was developed for Parkinson's disease diagnosis by combining the acceleration and gyroscope signals [37]. Each of the symptoms of walking, postural normal tremor, resting tremor, arm swing, and balance were divided into five levels ranging from normal to severe [37]. Data from three hospitals was used for evaluation, and the proposed model showed optimum results [37].

## 8.3.4 CURRENT CHALLENGES FOR FEDERATED LEARNING

### 8.3.4.1 DATA QUALITY

Data quality could vary widely across the different participating users and devices. Some participants may only have few samples, whereas others could have large datasets of high quality to contribute [19]. The quality of data can suffer from clutter and there is a possibility to get poor quality data which can drastically reduce the effectiveness of the trained model [22, 46]. It is important to safeguard the model parameters and the model while these are being shared over the network. A balance between the privacy and data sharing has to be maintained [19].

### 8.3.4.2 DATA DISTRIBUTION AND HETEROGENEITY

Different calibrations, diverse medical equipment manufacturers, and different data acquisition techniques in various hospitals results in different data distributions [11, 19]. The data of the participating devices is not uniformly distributed and is non-IID [46]. This was exemplified into different categories: (i) feature distribution skew, (ii) label distribution skew, (iii) same label but different features, (iv) same features but different labels, and (v) quantity skew [49]. These factors can violate the data consistency [50]. It was reported that in the initial stages of COVID-19 patients were provided high flow oxygen regardless of the need which could skew the model predictions [42].

With different participating devices having different data modalities, such as text, images, time series, etc., it is important that the central server should be able to intelligently handle the data heterogeneity through, for example, ensemble learning [22]. The data heterogeneity challenge can be mitigated by considering the heterogeneity aspects before the start of model training [3]. Data heterogeneity across the participating clients can result in difficulties in the model parameter selection, and algorithms are therefore needed to address this [11, 14].

### 8.3.4.3 LEARNING ALGORITHMS

A model trained on a centralized dataset can be improved in accuracy by improving the data quality and by improving the model performance through hyperparameter tuning [12]. Federated learning—due to its very nature of decentralized data—does not provide insights into the data, and hyperparameter tuning would require tuning many models to select optimal hyperparameter values which would not work for the low-power participating devices [19]. Flexibility in configuration can help the participating devices [22].

### 8.3.4.4 MODEL PRECISION

The performance of a trained model can deteriorate over time, and the model would need to be trained again [19]. Therefore, alternative techniques such as continual learning, progressive learning, and meta learning will be important [19]. For healthcare, the requirements are quite stringent for model predictions, and there is therefore a need to improve the prediction accuracy of the federated learning models to compete against the trained models from the large medical datasets [50]. Semi-supervised learning was shown to produce better results and improved model generalizability by leveraging the supervision from labelled data and the available information of unlabelled data [47]. There is a trade-off between the model performance and privacy, and it can affect the final model's accuracy [8].

### 8.3.4.5 MODEL AGGREGATION AND CONSISTENCY

The model's parameters are aggregated by the central server to create a global model. For this, the individual contributing devices have to write the parameters to the global server. The variation in data—that is, data heterogeneity—can result in the failure of the global model to converge to a single global model [46]. This could be due to low-performing nodes taking inordinately long time intervals before they can write to the central server [19]. The limited power and storage constraints of the IoT devices should be considered for the processing time and the model's nature for these devices [3]. This challenge can be helped by use of lightweight ML models for the IoT devices [3].

### 8.3.4.6 COMMUNICATIONS

The participating devices may be located at varying distances from each other, and in the case of large distances, the communication latency can be significant [5]. Edge devices are low powered and have limited communications facilities onboard. There is a requirement for an iterative exchange of the model's parameters and the trained model [22]. This can easily be facilitated using optical communications networks; however, there is a need for optimization techniques for wireless communications [14]. In some cases, the low bandwidth and connection quality can result in significant latency [19]. The transfer of the model updates introduces a heavy communication cost [15]. It is thus important to develop efficient algorithms for communicating the data, which can become problematic otherwise due to large number of model parameters and participating nodes [19, 22]. Due to the differences in the networking and communications, the running of federated learning algorithms on different participating clients can vary which results in training time and weights updating [45]. This can make the debugging and optimization difficult [45]. The reduced bandwidth for the wireless devices makes the communications difficult between the central server and the participating clients, and in an extreme case, the model updates might fail during an update iteration [3].

The communications cost can be reduced through P2P (peer-to-peer) learning, model compression, and by the reduction of updates [50]. The data sharing and model exchange in a federated learning system can result in a computation and communication burden for the power-constrained IoMT devices [5]. Collection of personal data using IoMT and then processing it at a central server has privacy and communications challenges, especially for large datasets [19].

### 8.3.4.7  DEVICE HETEROGENEITY

The participating devices can differ based on network connectivity, computing power, and hardware settings [46]. Due to heterogeneity of the participating devices, there is a need to reconcile the differences in storage, processing, and communication capability of the devices in federated learning [22]. There is a need to devise the model quantization, and one way to address is to admit devices based on their storage and processing capabilities, as otherwise it can increase the time for model convergence [14]. Much of the research has focused on mobile devices which have sufficient computing, storage, and power for training deep learning models, but novel algorithms are needed that can reduce the amount of processing and communications needs [19]. Device heterogeneity lowers the model performance due to the increased communications overhead for the transfer of model updates [15]. A dynamic fusion-based ML approach was proposed to improve model performance and communication efficiency [15].

### 8.3.4.8  CLIENT MANAGEMENT

In a decentralized model such as federated learning, the admittance and management of participating devices becomes a challenge to be managed [46]. The clients with smaller datasets have the incentive to get a global model trained on a collaborative larger dataset [42].

IoMT devices such as smartwatches and medical wearable devices can collect a lot of medical data such as blood pressure and heart rate [11]. This data can be used for device federated learning, but there is lack of communications and computing resources in wearable devices required for participating in federated learning training [11]. These devices have to be provided with incentive mechanism with rewards for good quality healthcare data and with penalties for harmful data contribution [11]. Before the federated learning becomes mainstream, some form of incentive mechanism has to be developed [10]. The model's performance can be recorded and can encourage other organizations to participate by sharing the data and computation resources for the model training [10]. There are also incentives required for the organizations possessing high quality data to contribute [50]. Also, the participating clients—especially the mobile devices—require commitment of significant computation and communication resources and can be incentivized to participate [22, 50]. Data owners should also be incentivized to contribute the data [51]. Client management by the central server has a single point of failure, as the central server could fail. Therefore, decentralized federated learning models have also been explored for IoMT [51]. It was shown that the centralized server could be replaced by blockchain that can prevent a single point of failure [44].

## 8.4  TRUSTED FEDERATED LEARNING

A lossless privacy-preserving tree-boosting system termed SecureBoost has been proposed for federated learning [52]. The proposed method constructs boosting trees across multiple participating parties using a privacy-preserving protocol [52]. The authors proposed ways for reducing the information leakage and concluded their proposed framework to be as accurate as a non-federated version on two credit scoring public datasets [52]. A lightweight scheme based on software-defined networking (SDN) is proposed to handle the federated learning communications for clients and central server based on data sharing using k-nearest neighbour (KNN) algorithm [53]. The proposed scheme was shown to provide better resource adjustment and Quality of Service (QoS) compared to conventional schemes [53].

### 8.4.1 ATTACKS ON DATA AND MODEL

The collection of data from IoMT and its communication to a central server provides a very large attack surface that can be exploited by malicious agents [19]. Data is susceptible to adversarial attacks, as the data received cannot be validated against the source data, and the training phase attacks can be more serious than the inference phase attacks [46]. A taxonomy of privacy preservation techniques, such as homomorphic encryption, for healthcare data and description of the chosen techniques are provided by [6]. The security against the data updates can be ensured through the use of blockchain to select updates only from the trusted devices [52].

#### 8.4.1.1 Model Inversion

The cooperation of trained models makes these susceptible to interception and de-identification by the malicious nodes that are taking part in the training or model aggregation [39]. The risk of data interception during the client–server communication in a federated learning system should be safeguarded to enhance the security and privacy of healthcare data to mitigate the risk of model inversion [42]. Model inversion attack is aimed at recreating data and can leak the patient's data in the model training process [11]. The model inversion is aimed at exploiting a sensitive feature from the information about the other features and the predicted probability [11].

#### 8.4.1.2 Model and Data Poisoning

An adversarial attack could affect the model by providing updates that alter the global model, thus poisoning the model to affect the model predictions [19, 22]. This could be achieved by manipulating the model gradients or training rules [46]. The integrity of the training data can be compromised through data poisoning attacks [46]. Poisoning attacks can result in the failure of the global model construction through submission of an error update by an unreliable device [54]. One of the types of data poisoning attack is label flipping during training, which can offset the model's prediction by ascribing a wrong label to data [46].

#### 8.4.1.3 Model Inference Attack

Inference attacks are aimed at accessing private data by inferring the private training data through system leakage by manipulation [46]. Prevention of these attacks can be achieved through homomorphic encryption, differential privacy, and multi-party computation [46]. The membership inference attacks can be carried out by the malicious participants and can result in the federated learning model privacy leakage [54].

This can happen through reverse engineering of the intermediate gradients to access sensitive information [54]. In spite of the local user data not leaving the device to the central server, it could still be possible to use the weights and gradients to reconstruct the original data [41]. Blockchain technology was used to implement a decentralized federated learning system to safeguard against the inference attack [44].

### 8.4.1.3.1 Differential Privacy

Differential privacy provides a privacy-preserving safeguard, and the mechanism will return statistically indistinguishable results for similar datasets [19]. This could be achieved by introducing some noise in the model [10, 19, 44]. The noise added before sending the updates obscures the samples presence in the dataset, and the model thus has a differential privacy [40]. Two random noises used for medical applications are Gaussian and Laplace [11]. The noise addition to the updates can generally slow down the training [40]. There is a trade-off between model performance and data leakage protection [50]. It was shown that partial weight-sharing scheme could reduce the risk of model inversion [42].

### 8.4.1.3.2 Homomorphic Encryption

Homomorphic encryption can ensure data privacy by parameter encryption during the exchange in the aggregation process [11]. Homomorphic encryption can offer protection against the model attacks but can result in an increase in the training time and the message size [42]. The federated learning model for IoMT was shared with the participants using homomorphic encryption to prevent the chances of information leakage [37].

## 8.5  A CASE STUDY ON BLOCKCHAIN-BASED TRUSTED FEDERATED LEARNING

### 8.5.1  Trusted Federated Learning with Blockchain

Federated learning faces the fairness challenges due to multi-party involvement; one of the challenges is to achieve trustworthiness [55]. The central server has to be trusted by all the participating devices [56]. However, the assumption that the central server in a plain federated learning can be trustworthy is flawed [39]. Blockchain has a decentralized mechanism and can ensure secure transactions through strong cryptography [39]. A blockchain-based trustworthy federated learning architecture was proposed for enhancing the fairness with each client, and the central server had a blockchain node installed to hold a replica of the transaction data [55]. In federated learning collaboration, the trust level can vary between the parties [8]. The participating parties in a federated learning consortium can be considered trustworthy, and therefore, the malicious activities such as extracting sensitive information can be disregarded [8]. This can reduce the need for countermeasures [8]. However, for large-scale federated learning systems, it is difficult to enforce a collaborative agreement, and some clients can attempt to degrade performance, necessitating the need for encryption and authentication of the clients [8]. The trust and validation of the shared model and model parameters has to be ensured because a set of tampered model parameters can affect the quality of the trained aggregated model [14]. It is important to have a trust in the generated global model by incorporating the explainability of the model [46]. Blockchain technology can play a useful role in enabling trusted federated learning using decentralized architecture for secure sharing and validation of data [14]. The use of blockchain is important for IoMT data, as it can enhance trust in the system [57]. Blockchain technology is a natural fit for federated learning due to its decentralization and traceability [5]. Blockchain technologies are increasingly being used for problems relating to image retrieval, industrial equipment, and patient health records [23].

The model cooperation in federated learning can be viewed as a process of transactions of the locally trained models completed by the federated learning nodes. As such, we can replace the central server with a blockchain platform. After the local nodes complete their local model trainings, they submit their locally trained models as transactions to the blockchain platform and the new global model will be determined according to the consensus protocol on the blockchain platform. The model cooperation process is shown in Figure 8.3.

Although the above process ensures that the data remains private but sharing of model parameters in this process can be subject to interception and change [14]. Blockchain can help with the decentralization of the data and model cooperation for federated learning. The blockchain technology makes the protected records as tamper-proof and can therefore preserve the data integrity. Many different types of blockchains exist, and notable ones are private, public and consortium. A consortium based blockchain would be a preferable approach for blockchain-based federated learning as that prevents the uninvited devices from joining the collaborating devices. Blockchain can be used to prevent network anomalies and intrusion aspects for the training and aggregation of the models [23].

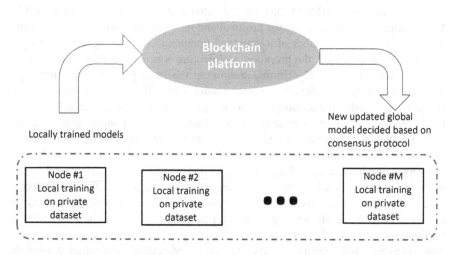

**FIGURE 8.3** Model cooperation in federated learning as transactions of locally trained models via blockchain platform.

Zero-knowledge proof (ZKP) is an encryption method to prove a given statement with zero knowledge about the content of the statement and the identity of the prover [58]. ZKP can be used for implementation of blockchain [59]. Messaging is the prime application in the blockchain. The use of ZKP creates an end-to-end trust for parties of the messaging without leaking additional information. However, scalability can be a disadvantage due to the extensive overheads incurred in the interaction of ZKP.

### 8.5.2 BLOCKCHAIN-BASED FRAMEWORKS

We next describe some pertinent blockchain-based federated learning architectures that have been proposed to overcome the trust challenges. A blockchain-based federated learning model is proposed aimed at preventing the malicious users being involved in the federated learning model using smart contracts [54, 60]. An architecture for smart healthcare is proposed with an IoT blockchain cloud platform with a case study for medical data [16]. A framework for privacy preserving federated learning used blockchain for electronic health data for tracking the incentive mechanisms for quality data contribution [51] and vaccine distribution to prevent fraud [61, 62]. The federated learning model was proposed for intelligent AI processing of IoMT with blockchain [51].

For the processing of medical images with patients related information stored on the images such as X-rays, it was proposed to store the patient's related information in the form of blockchain transactions [51]. The proposed model was tested on medical image data and it was concluded that it improved the performance of the convolutional neural network (CNN) model compared to a non-federated approach [52]. A blockchain-based federated learning model (MPBC) was proposed that avoided the use of a centralized server, by storing the trained local model on the Interplanetary File System (IPFS) [44, 63]. The global model was stored in the blockchain [44]. The privacy protection was ensured through differential-privacy noise [44]. A cross cluster blockchain federated learning system was proposed for IoMT using cross-chain consensus protocol and the multiple clusters were connected together to limit the number of aggregated updates [5, 64]. Using image recognition as the learning task, the proposed architecture was evaluated by implementing the proposed consensus algorithms, simulating the latency by adding a delay [5]. The blockchain-based federated learning models can suffer due to problems of data sparsity [5]. A federated learning approach with blockchain for decentralized learning is proposed for training models with local and distributed patient data for IoMT [52]. A lightweight federated learning framework is proposed with blockchain smart contracts for trust management, authentication of participating federated nodes, and reputation of edge nodes, and distribution of the models [39]. The proposed framework also included differential privacy for anonymization of COVID-19 patients' data [39]. A blockchain-based Deep Learning–as-a-Service framework, BinDaaS in Healthcare 4.0 applications was proposed for sharing EHR records between multiple participating clients. The proposed architecture provided for disease prediction in addition to ensuring security for EHR. The proposed system was evaluated using the medical EHR dataset SemVal 2013 task 9.2 and showed improved results compared to traditional models [2].

### 8.5.3 Proposed Framework

We propose a trusted federated learning framework by combining the use of block-chain, explainable AI (XAI) technologies and federated learning for IoMT data. The proposed architecture is shown in Figure 8.4. The medical data is collected by IoMT devices and communicated to the edge devices such as Raspberry Pi that have sufficient processing, storage and communications resources to run deep learning models. These edge devices can also provide security by running advanced cryptographic algorithms. We propose the use of a permissioned blockchain for privacy protection, trustworthy data sharing, and data security for the collaborating hospitals. A consortium blockchain suits the sharing of healthcare data, as clients can only participate if permitted, precluding any malicious or untrusted sources. The local updates are then sent to the central server using the blockchain and the global model updates are thereafter propagated to all the participating clients. We also propose use of an explainable artificial intelligence (XAI) [63] module at the central server that can help to enable a trusted framework. The collaborating clients can thus have a better understanding of why a global model is making certain predictions which can increase the trust and adoption of the global model. With IoMT, it is important that the latency of the federated learning training is reduced. Fog computing can also be used to reduce the communications overhead and latency between the participating devices and the central server [19].

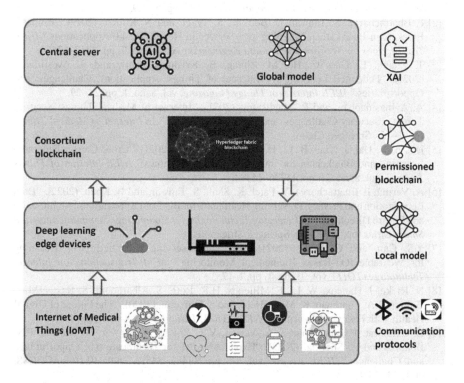

**FIGURE 8.4** Trusted FL model for IoMT.

## 8.6   CONCLUSION

In this chapter, we have covered the state-of-the-art applications and challenges of federated learning for healthcare applications. Federated learning provides many benefits for privacy preservation of healthcare data. There is no need to share the local private data, yet the model can be trained by sharing and aggregating the parameters for the participating devices. However, the machine learning model's parameters can be altered and updated maliciously to negatively affect the model. We have proposed an architecture showing that further privacy and trust safeguards can be accomplished through the use of blockchain and explainable artificial intelligence to validate the data sharing during communications.

There are issues surrounding the low power devices to reliably share the computing resources for the model training. Certain challenges would have to be circumvented for federated learning to become a mainstream technique. Trust in the global model's predictions can be improved through explainability of the model's predictions; however, explainability is an open issue and a harder problem as the global model is an aggregate of local models.

## REFERENCES

[1] C.A. Da Costa, C.F. Pasluosta, B. Eskofier, D.B. Da Silva, and R. da Rosa Righi. (2018). "Internet of Health Things: Toward Intelligent Vital Signs Monitoring in Hospital Wards." *Artificial Intelligence in Medicine*, vol. 89, pp. 61–69.

[2] P. Bhattacharya, S. Tanwar, U. Bodkhe, S. Tyagi, and N. Kumar. (2019). "Bindaas: Blockchain-Based Deep-Learning as-a-Service in Healthcare 4.0 Applications." *IEEE Transactions on Network Science and Engineering*, vol. 8, no. 2, pp. 1242–1255.

[3] T. Zhang, L. Gao, C. He, M. Zhang, B. Krishnamachari, and S. Avestimehr. (2021). "Federated Learning for Internet of Things: Applications, Challenges, and Opportunities." *IEEE Internet of Things Magazine*, vol. 5, no. 1, pp. 24–29.

[4] A. Avinashiappan, and B. Mayilsamy. (2021). "Internet of Medical Things: Security Threats, Security Challenges, and Potential Solutions." In *Internet of Medical Things* (pp. 1–16). Springer, Cham.

[5] H. Jin, X. Dai, J. Xiao, B. Li, H. Li, and Y. Zhang. (2021). "Cross-Cluster Federated Learning and Blockchain for Internet of Medical Things." *IEEE Internet of Things Journal*, vol. 8, no. 21, pp. 15776–15784.

[6] A. Verma, P. Bhattacharya, Y. Patel, K. Shah, S. Tanwar, and B. Khan. (2022). "Data Localization and Privacy-Preserving Healthcare for Big Data Applications: Architecture and Future Directions." In *Emerging Technologies for Computing, Communication and Smart Cities* (pp. 233–244). Springer, Singapore.

[7] Y.S. Can, and C. Ersoy. (2021). "Privacy-Preserving Federated Deep Learning for Wearable IOT-Based Biomedical Monitoring." *ACM Transactions on Internet Technology (TOIT)*, vol. 21, no. 1, pp. 1–17.

[8] N. Rieke, J. Hancox, W. Li, F. Milletari, H.R. Roth, S. Albarqouni, S. Bakas, M.N. Galtier, B.A. Landman, K. Maier-Hein, and S. Ourselin. (2020). "The Future of Digital Health with Federated Learning." *NPJ Digital Medicine*, vol. 3, no. 1, pp. 1–7.

[9] D. Saraswat, P. Bhattacharya, A. Verma, V.K. Prasad, S. Tanwar, G. Sharma, P.N. Bokoro, and R. Sharma. (2022). "Explainable AI for Healthcare 5.0: Opportunities and Challenges." *IEEE Access*, vol. 10, pp. 84486–84517. DOI: 10.1109/ACCESS.2022.3197671.

[10] Q. Yang, Y. Liu, T. Chen, and Y. Tong. (2019). "Federated Machine Learning: Concept and Applications." *ACM Transactions on Intelligent Systems and Technology (TIST)*, vol. 10, no. 2, pp. 1–19.

[11] Prayitno, C.R. Shyu, K.T. Putra, H.C. Chen, Y.Y. Tsai, K.S.M. Hossain, W. Jiang, and Z.Y. Shae. (2021). "A Systematic Review of Federated Learning in the Healthcare Area: From the Perspective of Data Properties and Applications." *Applied Sciences*, vol. 11, no. 23, p. 11191.

[12] S. Nazir, S. Patel, and D. Patel. (2018). "Hyper Parameters Selection for Image Classification in Convolutional Neural Networks." *IEEE 17th International Conference on Cognitive Informatics & Cognitive Computing (ICCI\* CC)*, pp. 401–407.

[13] IBM Federated Learning. https://ibmfl.mybluemix.net/. Accessed 12 August 2022.

[14] M. Ali, H. Karimipour, and M. Tariq. (2021). "Integration of Blockchain and Federated Learning for Internet of Things: Recent Advances and Future Challenges." *Computers & Security*, vol. 108, p. 102355.

[15] W. Zhang, T. Zhou, Q. Lu, X. Wang, C. Zhu, H. Sun, Z. Wang, S.K. Lo, and F.Y. Wang. (2021). "Dynamic-Fusion-Based Federated Learning for COVID-19 Detection." *IEEE Internet of Things Journal*, vol. 8, no. 21, pp. 15884–15891.

[16] S. Singh, S. Rathore, O. Alfarraj, A. Tolba, and B. Yoon. (2022). "A Framework for Privacy-Preservation of IoT Healthcare Data Using Federated Learning and Blockchain Technology." *Future Generation Computer Systems*, vol. 129, pp. 380–388.

[17] B. Pfitzner, N. Steckhan, and B. Arnrich. (2021). "Federated Learning in a Medical Context: A Systematic Literature Review." *ACM Transactions on Internet Technology (TOIT)*, vol. 21, no. 2, pp. 1–31.

[18] H.B. McMahan, E. Moore, D. Ramage, and B.A. Arcas. (2016). "Federated Learning of Deep Networks Using Model Averaging." arXiv:1602.05629. https://uk.arxiv.org/abs/1602.05629v1.

[19] C. Briggs, Z. Fan, and P. Andras. (2021). "A Review of Privacy-Preserving Federated Learning for the Internet-of-Things." *Federated Learning Systems*, pp. 21–50.

[20] B. Yu, W. Mao, Y. Lv, C. Zhang, and Y. Xie. (2022). "A Survey on Federated Learning in Data Mining." *Wiley Interdisciplinary Reviews: Data Mining and Knowledge Discovery*, vol. 12, no. 1.

[21] Q. Li, Z. Wen, Z. Wu, S. Hu, N. Wang, Y. Li, X. Liu, and B. He. (2021). "A Survey on Federated Learning Systems: Vision, Hype and Reality for Data Privacy and Protection." *IEEE Transactions on Knowledge and Data Engineering*.

[22] D.C. Nguyen, Q.V. Pham, P.N. Pathirana, M. Ding, A. Seneviratne, Z. Lin, O. Dobre, and W.J. Hwang. (2022). "Federated Learning for Smart Healthcare: A Survey." *ACM Computing Surveys (CSUR)*, vol. 55, no. 3, pp. 1–37.

[23] D. Li, Z. Luo, and B. Cao. (2021). "Blockchain-Based Federated Learning Methodologies in Smart Environments." *Cluster Computing*, pp. 1–15.

[24] Y. Chen, X. Qin, J. Wang, C. Yu, and W. Gao. (2020). "Fedhealth: A Federated Transfer Learning Framework for Wearable Healthcare." *IEEE Intelligent Systems*, vol. 35, no. 4, pp. 83–93.

[25] D.J. Beutel, T. Topal, A. Mathur, X. Qiu, T. Parcollet, P.P. de Gusmão, and N.D. Lane. (2020). "Flower: A Friendly Federated Learning Research Framework." arXiv:2007.14390. https://arxiv.org/abs/2007.14390.

[26] Tensorflow Federated: Machine Learning on Decentralized Data. (2020). www.tensorflow.org/federated. Accessed 12 August 2022.

[27] FedAI. "An Industrial Grade Federated Learning Framework." https://fate.fedai.org/. Accessed 12 August 2022.

[28] PaddleFL. https://paddlefl.readthedocs.io/en/latest/introduction.html. Accessed 12 August 2022.

[29] Openmined. https://docs.openmined.org/pysyft/. Accessed 12 August 2022.

[30] Federated Learning and Differential Privacy (FL & DP) Framework. https://developers. sherpa.ai/privacy-technology/overview. Accessed 12 August 2022.

[31] W. Zhuang, X. Gan, Y. Wen, and S. Zhang. (2022). "Easyfl: A Low-Code Federated Learning Platform for Dummies." *IEEE Internet of Things Journal*, vol. 9, no. 15, pp. 13740–13754. DOI: 10.1109/JIOT.2022.3143842.

[32] Z. Chai, A. Ali, S. Zawad, S. Truex, A. Anwar, N. Baracaldo, Y. Zhou, H. Ludwig, F. Yan, and Y. Cheng. (2020). "Tifl: A Tier-Based Federated Learning System." *Proceedings of the 29th International Symposium on High-Performance Parallel and Distributed Computing*, pp. 125–136.

[33] L. Li, M. Duan, D. Liu, Y. Zhang, A. Ren, X. Chen, Y. Tan, and C. Wang. (2021). "FedSAE: A Novel Self-Adaptive Federated Learning Framework in Heterogeneous Systems." *2021 International Joint Conference on Neural Networks (IJCNN)*, pp. 1–10.

[34] S. Horvath, S. Laskaridis, M. Almeida, I. Leontiadis, S. Venieris, and N. Lane. (2021). "Fjord: Fair and Accurate Federated Learning Under Heterogeneous Targets with Ordered Dropout." *Advances in Neural Information Processing Systems*, vol. 34.

[35] H. Elayan, M. Aloqaily, and M. Guizani. (2021). "Sustainability of Healthcare Data Analysis IoT-Based Systems Using Deep Federated Learning." *IEEE Internet of Things Journal*, vol. 9, no. 10, pp. 7338–7346.

[36] Y. Chang, C. Fang, and W. Sun. (2021). "A Blockchain-Based Federated Learning Method for Smart Healthcare." *Computational Intelligence and Neuroscience*.

[37] X. Zheng, S.B.H. Shah, X. Ren, F. Li, L. Nawaf, C. Chakraborty, and M. Fayaz. (2021). "Mobile Edge Computing Enabled Efficient Communication Based on Federated Learning in Internet of Medical Things." *Wireless Communications and Mobile Computing*. https://www.wjgnet.com/1007-9327/CitedArticlesInF6?id=10.1109%2Ft kde.2009.191.

[38] R.S. Antunes, C. André da Costa, A. Küderle, I.A. Yari, and B. Eskofier. (2022). "Federated Learning for Healthcare: Systematic Review and Architecture Proposal." *ACM Transactions on Intelligent Systems and Technology (TIST)*, vol. 13, no. 4, pp. 1–23.

[39] M.A. Rahman, M.S. Hossain, M.S. Islam, N.A. Alrajeh, and G. Muhammad. (2020). "Secure and Provenance Enhanced Internet of Health Things Framework: A Blockchain Managed Federated Learning Approach." *IEEE Access*, vol. 8, pp. 205071–205087.

[40] M.J. Sheller, G.A. Reina, B. Edwards, J. Martin, and S. Bakas. (2018). "Multi-Institutional Deep Learning Modeling Without Sharing Patient Data: A Feasibility Study on Brain Tumor Segmentation." In *International MICCAI Brainlesion Workshop* (pp. 92–104). Springer, Cham.

[41] M. Liu, S. Ho, M. Wang, L. Gao, Y. Jin, and H. Zhang. (2021). "Federated Learning Meets Natural Language Processing: A Survey." arXiv:2107.12603. https://www. researchgate.net/publication/353510646_Federated_Learning_Meets_Natural_ Language_Processing_A_Survey.

[42] I. Dayan, H.R. Roth, A. Zhong, A. Harouni, A. Gentili, A.Z. Abidin, A. Liu, A.B. Costa, B.J. Wood, C.S. Tsai, and C.H. Wang. (2021). "Federated Learning for Predicting Clinical Outcomes in Patients with COVID-19." *Nature Medicine*, vol. 27, no. 10, pp. 1735–1743.

[43] V.K. Prasad, P. Bhattacharya, M. Bhavsar, A. Verma, S. Tanwar, G. Sharma, Pitshou N. Bokoro, and R. Sharma. (2022). "ABV-CoViD: An Ensemble Forecasting Model to Predict Availability of Beds and Ventilators for COVID-19 Like Pandemics." *IEEE Access*, vol. 10, pp. 74131–74151.

[44] H. Zhang, G. Li, Y. Zhang, K. Gai, and M. Qiu. (2021). "Blockchain-Based Privacy-Preserving Medical Data Sharing Scheme Using Federated Learning." In *International*

*Conference on Knowledge Science, Engineering and Management* (pp. 634–646). Springer, Cham.

[45] D. Ng, X. Lan, M.M.S. Yao, W.P. Chan, and M. Feng. (2021). "Federated Learning: A Collaborative Effort to Achieve Better Medical Imaging Models for Individual Sites That Have Small Labelled Datasets." *Quantitative Imaging in Medicine and Surgery*, vol. 11, no. 2, p. 852.

[46] J.H. Yoo, H. Jeong, J. Lee, and T.M. Chung. (2021). "Federated Learning: Issues in Medical Application." In *International Conference on Future Data and Security Engineering* (pp. 3–22). Springer, Cham.

[47] Federated Learning in Medicine: Facilitating Multi-Institutional Collaboration Without Sharing Patient Data. www.med.upenn.edu/cbica/federated-learning-in-medicine-facil itating-multi-institutional-collaboration-without-sharing-patient-data.html. Accessed 12 August 2022.

[48] D. Yang, Z. Xu, W. Li, A. Myronenko, H.R. Roth, S. Harmon, S. Xu, B. Turkbey, E. Turkbey, X. Wang, and W. Zhu. (2021). "Federated Semi-Supervised Learning for COVID Region Segmentation in Chest CT Using Multi-National Data from China, Italy, Japan." *Medical Image Analysis*, vol. 70, p. 101992.

[49] B.Y. Lin, C. He, Z. Zeng, H. Wang, Y. Huang, M. Soltanolkotabi, X. Ren, and S. Avestimehr. (2021). "Fednlp: A Research Platform for Federated Learning in Natural Language Processing." arXiv:2104.08815. https://www.researchgate.net/publication/ 350991738_FedNLP_A_Research_Platform_for_Federated_Learning_in_Natural_ Language_Processing.

[50] J. Passerat-Palmbach, T. Farnan, M. McCoy, J.D. Harris, S.T. Manion, H.L. Flannery, and B. Gleim. (2020). "Blockchain-Orchestrated Machine Learning for Privacy Preserving Federated Learning in Electronic Health Data." *IEEE International Conference on Blockchain (Blockchain)*, pp. 550–555.

[51] J. Xu, B.S. Glicksberg, C. Su, P. Walker, J. Bian, and F. Wang. (2021). "Federated Learning for Healthcare Informatics." *Journal of Healthcare Informatics Research*, vol. 5, no. 1, pp. 1–19.

[52] D. Połap, G. Srivastava, A. Jolfaei, and R.M. Parizi. (2020). "Blockchain Technology and Neural Networks for the Internet of Medical Things." *IEEE INFOCOM 2020-IEEE Conference on Computer Communications Workshops (INFOCOM WKSHPS)*, pp. 508–513.

[53] K. Cheng, T. Fan, Y. Jin, Y. Liu, T. Chen, D. Papadopoulos, and Q. Yang. (2021). "Secureboost: A Lossless Federated Learning Framework." *IEEE Intelligent Systems*, vol. 36, no. 6, pp. 87–98.

[54] S. Math, P. Tam, and S. Kim. (2021). "Reliable Federated Learning Systems Based on Intelligent Resource Sharing Scheme for Big Data Internet of Things." *IEEE Access*, 9, pp. 108091–108100.

[55] Y. Liu, J. Peng, J. Kang, A.M. Iliyasu, D. Niyato, and A.A. Abd El-Latif. (2020). "A Secure Federated Learning Framework for 5G Networks." *IEEE Wireless Communications*, vol. 27, no. 4, pp. 24–31.

[56] S.K. Lo, Y. Liu, Q. Lu, C. Wang, X. Xu, H.Y. Paik, and L. Zhu. (2023). "Towards Trustworthy AI: Blockchain-Based Architecture Design for Accountability and Fairness of Federated Learning Systems." *IEEE Internet of Things Journal*, vol. 10, no. 4, pp. 3276–3284. DOI: 10.1109/JIOT.2022.3144450.

[57] D. Li, D. Han, T.H. Weng, Z. Zheng, H. Li, H. Liu, A. Castiglione, and K.C. Li. (2022). "Blockchain for Federated Learning Toward Secure Distributed Machine Learning Systems: A Systemic Survey." *Soft Computing*, vol. 26, no. 9, pp. 4423–4440.

[58] S. Nazir, M. Kaleem, M. Hamdoun, J. Alzubi, and H. Tianfield. (2022). "Blockchain of Things for Healthcare Asset Management." In *Healthcare Monitoring and Data*

*Analysis Using IoT: Technologies and Applications* (pp. 199–209). Institution of Engineering and Technology (IET). https://digital-library.theiet.org/content/books/he/pbhe038e.

[59] S. Goldwasser, S. Micali, and C. Rackoff. (1989). "The Knowledge Complexity of Interactive Proof Systems." *SIAM Journal on Computing*, vol. 18, no. 1, pp. 186–208.

[60] X. Sun, F.R. Yu, P. Zhang, Z. Sun, W. Xie, and X. Peng. (2021). "A Survey on Zero-Knowledge Proof in Blockchain." *IEEE Network*, vol. 35, no. 4, pp. 198–205.

[61] R. Gupta, A. Shukla, and S. Tanwar. (1 October–December 2021). "BATS: A Blockchain and AI-Empowered Drone-Assisted Telesurgery System Towards 6G." *IEEE Transactions on Network Science and Engineering*, vol. 8, no. 4, pp. 2958–2967. DOI: 10.1109/TNSE.2020.3043262.

[62] A. Verma, P. Bhattacharya, M. Zuhair, S. Tanwar, and N. Kumar. (2021). "Vacochain: Blockchain-Based 5G-Assisted UAV Vaccine Distribution Scheme for Future Pandemics." *IEEE Journal of Biomedical and Health Informatics*, vol. 26, no. 5, pp. 1997–2007.

[63] A. Verma, P. Bhattacharya, D. Saraswat, S. Tanwar, N. Kumar, and R. Sharma. (2023). "SanJeeVni: Secure UAV-Envisioned Massive Vaccine Distribution for COVID-19 Underlying 6G Network." *IEEE Sensors Journal*, vol. 23, no. 2, pp. 955–968. DOI: 10.1109/JSEN.2022.3188929.

[64] H. Mankodiya, M.S. Obaidat, R. Gupta, and S. Tanwar. (2021). "XAI-AV: Explainable Artificial Intelligence for Trust Management in Autonomous Vehicles." *2021 International Conference on Communications, Computing, Cybersecurity, and Informatics (CCCI)*, pp. 1–5. DOI: 10.1109/CCCI52664.2021.9583190.

[65] R. Gupta, Arpit Shukla, Parimal Mehta, Pronaya Bhattacharya, Sudeep Tanwar, Sudhanshu Tyagi, and Neeraj Kumar. (2020). "VAHAK: A Blockchain-Based Outdoor Delivery Scheme Using UAV for Healthcare 4.0 Services." *IEEE INFOCOM 2020 — IEEE Conference on Computer Communications Workshops (INFOCOM WKSHPS)*, pp. 255–260. DOI: 10.1109/INFOCOMWKSHPS50562.2020.9162738.

# 9 Security and Privacy Solutions for Healthcare Informatics

*Pranshav Gajjar, Shivani Desai,*
*Akash Vegada, Pooja Shah, and Tarjni Vyas*

## CONTENTS

## 9.1 INTRODUCTION

The world as we know it in this day and age is being increasingly affected by imminent technologies. Many technologies have become so paramount that they maintain unparalleled influence over people's lives. With the evolution of information technology (IT), its in-depth understanding has advanced as well, increasing the threat to data security and becoming the foremost concern for any institution. Domains such as healthcare informatics and defence become particularly vulnerable to data breaches. With the number of data infringements on the rise, the need is felt to reinforce the network to make data communication more secure and reliable. Data security encompasses varying levels of protection such as encryption, authentication, intrusion detection, virtual private networks (VPNs), and many more, with the primary pursuit of ensuring the integrity and privacy of the data. The healthcare information domain is an industry that relies immensely on data security, and its development has witnessed the enhancement of the healthcare system in almost every aspect [1]. Healthcare information systems are one of the most significant factors in improving the quality

DOI: 10.1201/9781003303374-9

of healthcare systems. Electronic health records (EHRs) are one such application of healthcare informatics aimed to mitigate the conventional difficulties by creating a decentralized system of patient records to provide universal data access, prompt medical assistance, and remote surveillance, to name a few benefits. These systems can not only organize patient records but may also improve the quality of service for the patient, reduce costs, and boost the overall performance of healthcare systems.

However, the privacy and security of health records are difficult to manage in the healthcare system. Patients must protect the privacy of their health records while consulting with healthcare stakeholders, while healthcare personnel must confirm the credibility of health reports received from labs. Similarly, the medical reports filed for insurance claims must be confirmed by insurance companies, and any unauthorized access to the sensitive health records of patients should be denied. Moreover, confidentiality, integrity, and privacy of healthcare data needs utmost attention while transmission over the internet and/or retaining data on a third-party server [2]. The last decade has witnessed a myriad of incorporations of IoT (Internet of Things) in the medical domain. Internet of Medical Things (IoMT) apparatuses like pacemakers, glucose monitors, thermometers, and more are facilitating patients self-monitoring their health, simplifying subsequent doctor visits. IoMT devices allow remote surveillance of less critical and infectious patients in the comfort of their own homes and let patients schedule their appointments. Healthcare informatics permits doctors to access and maintain patient records through apps from any part of the world. The COVID-19 pandemic illuminated many critical problems in the traditional healthcare system and emphasized the advantages of IoMT in the medical industry. The number of IoMT devices is anticipated to surpass seven million by 2026, according to Juniper Research [3]. The international market potential for IoMT is envisioned to surge to an astounding $158 billion evaluation by 2022 [4]. With such an expanse of IoMT, data security and protection become exceptionally crucial with the requirement to devise robust methods to protect the sensitive data of patients.

EHRs [5] prove to be extremely beneficial in the medical industry but are subject to various problems such as ownership as well as security and integrity of patient health records. The adoption of blockchain technology can aid in addressing these challenges by providing a secure and impenetrable medium for storing sensitive medical data. Blockchain [5–7] is a remarkable field of study finding applications in various domains, with finance being the most notable. The medical industry can likewise gain enormously from blockchain technology because of its aspects like security, confidentiality, privacy, and decentralization. Blockchain technology can be used to store EHRs by providing a secure platform and controlling user access to make patient data records decentralized and globally accessible. Moreover, we store vaccination records on blockchain to prevent vaccine forgery [8]. Explainable artificial intelligence is used nowadays to improve the predictions [9, 10]. Research describes blockchain technology as a distributed ledger that is mutual, immutable, and capable of being verified publicly, used for documenting the record of trades or transactions [2]. The sample utility of such an enhanced system can be seen below in Figure 9.1.

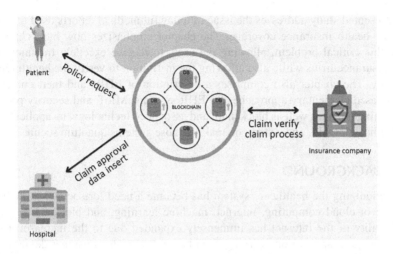

**FIGURE 9.1** Sample blockchain-induced healthcare technology [2].

In terms of protection, privacy, efficiency, clarity, and fault tolerance, blockchain has gained significant prominence in the financial domain, having the potential to change domains like e-governance, healthcare, and supply chains. Some key characteristics that make blockchain technology extremely beneficial are the following.

1. **Transparency**: All participants interested in the arrangement can use agreement, confirmation, and acceptance contracts to initiate and complete transactions on the blockchain, making the system transparent in its activities.
2. **Immutability**: Immutable transactions can aid process parties to maintain transparency while also bypassing unauthorized alterations.
3. **Authenticity**: The digital signatures of the initiator and responder are usually required in a blockchain transaction. In some applications, smart contracts are also utilized to ensure transaction legitimacy.
4. **Verifiability**: Insiders and outsiders can both confirm the completed transactions using blockchain technology with the sharing and consensus processes.
5. **Ownership**: In blockchain-based systems, the immutability of transactions in blocks, as well as the linkability of blocks, may give ownership control and accountability.

### 9.1.1 Chapter Layout

The chapter provides a novel study on blockchain-based protocols and associated technologies like federated learning for safeguarding the healthcare system, with a focus on patient data insurance, diagnosis statements, and the responsibility and clarity of assistance provided by various entities concerned in the medical domain.

The presented study addresses the issue of unlawful medical reports used to acquire or deny health insurance coverage. The chapter emphasizes how blockchain may solve this critical problem, allowing the users to receive excellent treatment from their insurance firms while also allowing the institution to verify the health report's integrity. The chapter also comprises a description of EHRs and their challenges, cloud-based elementary approaches for EHR systems, MIoT, and security problems concerning them, as well as blockchain and associated technology, its applications in the medical domain, and a study on making those systems quantum secure.

## 9.2   BACKGROUND

Revolutionizing the healthcare system has become a need for societal growth with the rise of cloud computing, internet, machine learning, and blockchain, and the reachability of the internet has immensely expanded due to the increased mobile phone usage in applications varying from home devices to consumer devices [2]. It has improved the connectivity between service providers and consumers and formed a virtual link around the globe via networks and other means. Employing the tremendous capabilities of blockchain, cloud computing, and edge technology, one might create a backend support application that would assist with responsibility, right, and elasticity attributes. Governing data permits, safeguarding privacy, and building connections are also important characteristics in influencing patients and service providers to encourage and use services in the healthcare domain [11]. Blockchain technology can be used to create a data-focused and disjointed architecture for handling the safety of healthcare applications with separate servicing units controlling their actions recorded in distributed verifiable ledgers [2]. In a blockchain-driven healthcare system, various service units can be channelled through several edges that can manage resources intelligently using the cloud, which is powered by decentralized immutable and public ledgers, making medical services visible, accountable, and auditable. In this chapter, we look at how blockchain technology can be used to protect health records and the domain of healthcare informatics in general in terms of tamper-proofing, responsibility, data rights, and privacy in the sector.

## 9.3   ELECTRONIC HEALTH RECORDS

Health or medical records can be defined as the overview of a patient's medical records, allergies, and prescriptions. This section provides a synopsis on EHRs as described in [12]. Health records were once documented on paper and kept in folders according to conventional approaches. However, the evolution of computers in the 1960s laid the foundation for EHRs. They have altered the format of health documents and revolutionized healthcare systems. They have made patients' medical data easier to read and attain from virtually anywhere. EHRs are a primary focus of contemporary health informatics research, although the necessity for research from many viewpoints has also been noted. Recent EHR research has focused on the capabilities of existing approaches and underlying frameworks, as well as the use of medical records as a basis for proof-based medicine.

The employment of EHRs quickly resulted in large magnitudes of healthcare data being discovered to be useful for epidemiologic research. On the other hand, secondary use of EHR data quickly indicated difficulties with the information's rate for analysis and assessment. Numerous distortions have resulted due to the dissatisfactory nature of the data. Moreover, there have been various circumstances when the data has been used for purposes other than that for which it was obtained. Medical data from health records could be used for clinical decision support (CDS), resulting in a unique significant field of healthcare informatics. When data storage and sharing over computer networks were envisioned, ownership and privacy became widespread concerns. Despite these impediments, there were numerous healthcare community networks that were in early steps of construction or functional to differing extents. Different healthcare providers—as well as administrative employees such as doctors, nurses, apothecaries, laboratory technicians, and radiologists—utilize various features of the EHRs. Large healthcare institutions and government bodies are acknowledging the significance of EHRs in deciding best suitable treatments. However, issues such as medical coverage, data privacy, and protection of EHRs remain major impediments to their utility. With the rising urge in reducing patient's approval before using their medical information, patients might feel reluctant if confidentiality is not guaranteed. Mental health data is particularly susceptible and conceivably detrimental if privacy is broken. Due to differences in the state, country, and international rules, gaining permit to behavioural health records turns out to be even more challenging. The growing amount and reachability of EHRs also extends up further aspects for identifying novel disease information. The last decade has witnessed an advancement in Big Data and text mining concentrated on the identification of illness associations. Large-scale EHR information analysis of outcomes, patterns, temporal trends, and correlations are possible with Big Data. Numerous individuals consider that EHRs will be utilized in the expansion of Big Data analytics, bringing us from illness definition and documenting to prognosis, anticipative modelling, and conclusion optimization. Several nations, including Australia, Canada, England, Finland, and the United States, are working on developing a framework for national health data [13]. The same research also states that these projects intend to achieve the following goals.

1. To make patients a part of decision-making in the usage of their medical data.
2. The necessity to describe the fundamental data of these documents.
3. The selection and execution of norms, terminologies, regulations, and naming conventions.
4 The requirement to devise essential data protection framework and guidelines.
5. The goal of creating unrestricted, consistent, and interoperable EHR techniques for information interaction and data administration.

## 9.4   CLOUD-BASED EHR SYSTEMS

The cloud computing paradigm presents a possibility for electronic health systems to improve their quality and functionality. The risks of establishing EHRs on a third-party CSP (cloud service provider) are emphasized in this section as examined in research [14], which also remarks on some recommendations for healthcare personnel to assure the privacy of medical data and make the process more manageable. Security concerns that CSPs need to decipher in their platforms are taken into account, as well. Cloud computing offers an excellent platform that is both effective and simple to deliver electronic health assistance in various situations. The elasticity of a cloud infrastructure gives numerous advantages, along with certain limitations that must be overcome. The authors of this research also stated that the capacity to intercommunicate medical data with other healthcare organizations and the incorporation of all the EHRs of a cluster of healthcare organizations to aid personnel to execute their tasks are the key benefits of employing a cloud-driven EHR administration approach. The use of this layered service can be leveraged efficiently and the graphical description and use of the analogous services and related technologies are illustrated in Figure 9.2.

So, how can healthcare practitioners and clinical centres ensure that their patient data is secure, private, and confidential? The key challenge that a cloud-based electronic healthcare approach needs to address is the protection and privacy of information hosted on the cloud [14]. This goal must be accomplished by both medical professionals and cloud providers, as positioning EHRs on the cloud requires a transition in perspective. The research also states that privacy and data security is of utmost importance when a medical service provider wants to use an electronic healthcare administration system based on the cloud, and that by assuring the data protection aspects of the healthcare forum, the security of patients' sensitive data can be guaranteed [14]. To safeguard data from external attacks, transmission and network security procedures must be implemented. When patient data is hosted on the cloud, the medical records are stored on the CSP's servers. What exactly does this imply? These businesses must ensure that their databases are secure so that unauthorized people cannot access or modify the information. The research [14] also explains that due to the sensitivity of nature of patient data, it is critical to be conscious of the fact that security and privacy agreements are required when health records are

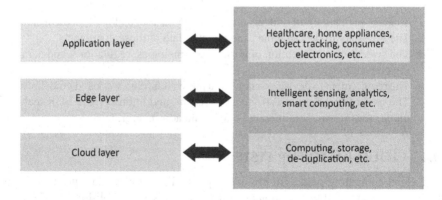

**FIGURE 9.2** The available layered services and their related domain specific utilities [2].

moved to the cloud. CSPs must provide verification criteria that safeguard the security of patient data to prevent unauthorized access. Governments must impose strict privacy rules on CSPs to safeguard patient data. The implementation of a legislative framework will aid in the creation of a safe environment. In some nations, privacy regulations have been enacted to govern and protect the privacy of patient records. The Health Insurance Portability and Accountability Act (HIPAA), for example, governs the safety of patient information in the United States, but each country's policies are unique. Furthermore, to ensure data security and privacy, EHRs are governed by standards that contain data protection provisions such as the international standard HL7 (Health Level 7). A safe "health cloud" scenario will be accomplished by integrating these measures with cloud practices and protection measures enforced by CSPs.

This section provides a condensed view of the research article [14], whose authors describe the implementation of EHR administration techniques as a significant breakthrough in the healthcare system of the contemporary era. The number of people using these technologies is steadily increasing. This type of practice is widely used in the majority of developed nations. They defined an EHR as documentation that contains details concerning the medical development in the treatment process of a patient, according to Spanish statute 41/2002. The uses of EHRs are outlined in this ordinance, which demands medical workers protect patients' privacy. This type of data is ranked as "specially safeguarded" under Spanish legislation. The 15/1999 law established this type of nomenclature to safeguard the privacy of sensitive patient information such that, excluding the circumstance of a crisis when the life of the patient is at stake, the patient's authorization is mandated to collect and utilize this information. The research also describes that HIPAA handles and documents pertaining to patient data protection conditions in the United States. The Privacy Rule and the Security Rule are two provinces of this law that address the improper use of personal information. The HIPAA Privacy Rule states that protected health information (PHI) needs to be made unrestricted to deliver medical treatment to the patient, either with a court order or with the consent of the patient. The research also states that this rule requires informing patients about the utilization of their PHI by concerned entities. Also, it is required by the Privacy Rule that entities having access to PHI be granted access to the smallest amount of patient information required to satisfy their tasks. As previously said, the healthcare personnel need to ensure and maintain the safety of EHRs, as well as install the necessary security methods to maintain patient data securely in the cloud.

### 9.4.1 Challenges in Cloud-Based EHRs

The adoption of cloud-based EHRs represents a significant advancement in the evolution of healthcare. As per the same research [14], cloud-based solutions make it possible to devise elastic platforms that are tailored to the requirements of users. This overall transformation is aided by the cost conservation provided by a cloud computing system (pay-per-use approach). Another significant benefit of storing EHRs in the cloud is that medical personnel or patients can access the data via the internet from virtually anywhere and at any time. With the current international financial concerns, a compelling motivation for a corporation to migrate its health-care framework to the cloud could be cost savings. As a result, when selling the benefits of cloud-based systems to prospective clients, CSPs must capitalize on this point. The research [14] states that to ensure the safety of their platforms, CSPs must implement various protection measures to ensure the safeguard of their clients' data. The following sections present different measures incorporated by a CSP to ensure data protection in the context of EHR security. The exact level of data privacy must be maintained in a cloud-based her, as data is kept on the healthcare provider's servers. Patients and medical staffers should be aware that their data will be maintained by a third-party service provider. Although the process of shifting sensitive health records to the cloud does not involve patients, healthcare professionals should educate them about this data migration. Patients should be made aware of all of the benefits that a cloud-based approach provides for the administration of their healthcare data, not just the notifications. Patients should be aware that data management is the duty of the CSP, as well as—to a lesser extent—the medical practitioner or healthcare organization. Privacy concerns should be addressed by both, patients and healthcare providers. Following is a condensation of major issues with cloud computing security [15].

- In cloud computing, CSPs provide all the services to the consumers, giving them complete authority over users' data, known as a centralized system of management.
- The lack of standards among CSPs may compromise the migration of user data, causing reduced portability and data lock-ins, making users greatly dependent on the CSP.
- There is always a risk of data breach from internal management.
- Whenever clients ask for data to be wiped, it raises the issue of whether the desired portion of their data segment can be deleted accurately, resulting in "insecure or incomplete data deletion" [15].
- All the data in cloud computing is divided and transmitted, unlike in conventional computing systems where it is stored locally. This data is prone to reply assaults and "sniffing" from malicious attackers during transmission, posing immense risks to data privacy.

These challenges make quite challenging the application of cloud computing in the healthcare domain, where security of sensitive patient data is of greatest importance.

## 9.5 INTERNET OF MEDICAL THINGS (IoMT)

As a worldwide network infrastructure in which everything linked to the internet has an identification and may intercommunicate with other gadgets connected to the internet, IoT will lead a substantial part in the internet's future. Computers, cell phones, tablets, washing machines, and other electronic equipment are just a few examples. IoT is a vast network of interconnected gadgets having microchips that connects them all. These microchips monitor their environment and report back to the network and humans. One of the most beneficial qualities of IoT is that it allows any physical entity to interact via the internet. The low-cost internet provides an excellent platform for an abundance of IoT devices. However, integrity, confidentiality, availability, and authenticity of data remain some of the main issues in IoT [16]. IoMT is an IoT application in the medical area that aims to improve the healthcare system's accuracy, reliability, and productivity.

It has developed into a distinct field of research and has resulted in significant changes to healthcare systems. It has aided in remote patient–physician interaction, as well as the development of rehabilitation devices for people with diseases or disabilities. Medical equipment can send a patient's vital parameters to a platform, such as a secure cloud, where they can be stored and evaluated. The elderly and people with chronic diseases can receive special attention. electrocardiogram (ECG) monitors, temperature monitors, glucose level monitors, medication management devices, and other MIoT devices are some of a few examples.

### 9.5.1 SECURITY CHALLENGES OF IoMT

IoMT devices and applications handle sensitive personal data, such as private health information, and they can be linked to a global information network to make them available at any time and from any location. MIoT devices encounter several issues, including the privacy of patient data records and virus assaults on devices that cause them to malfunction. If not addressed appropriately, these issues could obstruct the complete integration of IoT in the healthcare arena. As a result, to deliver more robust platforms, it is necessary to thoroughly identify and analyze various IoT safety challenges. Following are some of the security concerns with MIoT [16, 17]:

**Data Modification:** If patient medical data is intercepted by a malicious actor, either from the source node of an IoT-based device or during data exchange between nodes, that person could modify the data, thereby presenting the wrong data to caregivers who respond based on the wrong data, and this could spell disaster for the patient whose health is monitored using this device.

**Impersonation:** Every node on the network has an identity, and IoT-based network devices are no exception, as they all have their unique identities which possibly may contain some of the patient's information. If an intruder is able to steal this identity, that person could use it to spy on the patient's health records.

**Replay Attack:** an attacker can retransmit the data exchanged between nodes on the network, and this may likely lead to treatment malfunction.

**Eavesdropping:** IoT devices make use of wireless channels to communicate, which makes it easier for an intruder to be able to listen to the communications between nodes—thus compromising the confidentiality of the patients' data, which can then be used for more dangerous attacks than stealing the patient's private information.

Other attacks may be based on host and network properties, which include the following.

**Hardware Attacks:** An attacker can physically take and tamper with the device, removing the device's program codes, security codes, and data, as well as reprogram the device's program code with malicious codes, causing it to malfunction.

**Software Attacks:** A malicious virus may attack the software (operating system, application software), causing IoT-based healthcare devices to malfunction.

**Standard Protocol Attacks:** An attacker could breach the confidentiality, authenticity, availability, and integrity of sensitive data by exploiting conventional applications and network protocols.

## 9.6   DECENTRALIZED SECURITY

This section summarizes blockchain technology and its components as stated in research [2], which posits that transactions in a blockchain are aggregated into clusters known as blocks. A point or a node in the chain typically broadcasts a fresh transaction to all points. A point that discovers an answer to the system's agreement rules transmits it to all the other points, and the chain accepts the block only if it obeys all regulations. Eventually, the timestamp, hash of the accepted block, and agreement methods that connect to prior blocks are used to create a chain of blocks. The previous block's hash value is used to connect the blocks in the chain. This acts as a timestamp, proving that the referenced block was present at the time the block that refers to it was created. The chronological sequence and validity of prior blocks are reinforced with each recent block added to the blockchain. The research defines blockchain as a data structure that may be used to create an immutable ledger which is publicly verifiable—that is, shared among the system's distributed nodes. A typical blockchain system is made up of numerous nodes that do not trust each other completely. The transactions are agreed upon by all nodes in the system established on certain agreement rules and their order, which cannot be changed after they are complete. A typical blockchain data structure is shown in Figure 9.3 [2].

There are two types of blockchain systems: public and private. Any node in a public blockchain system may connect or disconnect from the blockchain, making the chain distributed and decentralized. The blockchain governs membership and who can join private blockchains, so implied authentication of nodes is familiar to the rest of the nodes. Following are descriptions of the underlying technologies [1].

**Hash Function:** A cryptographic hash function is used in a blockchain system to ensure that all transactions recorded in the blockchain are immutable. RIPEMD-160 and SHA-256 are widely employed hash algorithms in many blockchains out of several accessible hash algorithms in the literature. A cryptographic hash function is a pseudo-random process that meets one-way and collision-resistant features.

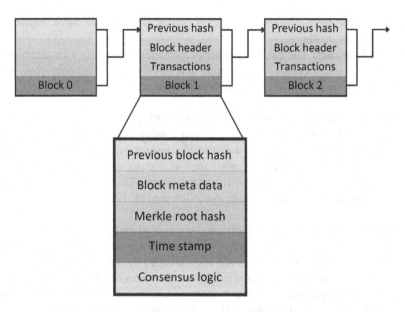

**FIGURE 9.3** Visual representation of standard blockchain architecture [2].

**Hash Tree:** The Merkle tree accommodates a configurable number of transactions in a block. A safe hash technique is employed in hashing transactions of the Merkle tree. A hash tree is a tree network in which the leaf nodes hold information, and the inside nodes are hashes of concatenation of their child nodes. Such a layout is extremely beneficial in determining whether information exists or if any modifications have transpired in particular nodes. To safeguard the credibility of the ledgers, a blockchain utilizes a hash (Merkle) tree. Bucket hash trees are utilized in a hyperledger wherein states are clustered into a pre-set quantity of buckets [1]; Patricia Merkle Tree is used by Ethereum, which looks like a tree and includes key-value states as leaves. The hash tree's main approach is to connect the blocks with a chain of cryptographic hash pointers, the contents of a block include the hash of its previous block. Any change to the previous block nullifies all following blocks immediately. Blockchain systems deliver secure and effective data architecture that can track all previous modifications to block states in a blockchain system by integrating hash pointers and Merkle trees.

**Digital Signature:** The authors of [2] also describe a digital signature as "a cryptographic method" for verifying the validity and source of data, as well as its integrity and nonrepudiation. The digital signature scheme is usually a 3-tuple algorithm. The signature verification pipeline takes the inscribed message and the associated public key and determines if it is true or false.

**Consensus Protocol:** As per the research [2], the contents of the ledger reflect past and present states, maintained using an agreement process decided upon by all parts of the blockchain. PoS (proof of space), PBFT (practical

Byzantine fault tolerance), and PoW (proof of work) are three important agreement methods.

**Smart Contract:** The calculation performed when executing a transaction is called a smart contract. Each node agrees on the intakes, outcomes, and states influenced by the smart contract implementation.

Given the possibility of blockchain in transforming the landscape of many applications currently controlled by a centralized database, healthcare is one of those sectors that demand transparent, accountable, testable services which can benefit consumers, patients, medical personnel such as doctors and nurses, and healthcare organizations like hospitals and insurance companies. The fundamental characteristics of blockchain technology include the following [18, 19].

1. **Decentralization:** Unlike traditional systems whereby data is reserved centrally, blockchain uses nodes to distribute data across the grid. It causes the authority of data to be dispersed and managed by agreement arrived upon by intercommunicated information from the nodes linked on the network.
2. **Data Transparency:** Since any information on the blockchain is not centrally stored, and the rights to the data are shared by the entire blockchain of nodes, it cannot be altered by a single party, making it secure from unauthorized access.
3. **Data Security and Privacy:** Cryptographic operations and secure hashing algorithms (SHAs) are employed to safeguard the data stored on the blockchain. A barrier for digital data can be created using one-way functions known as cryptographic hashes, making blockchain technology extremely robust and providing high security to sensitive data.

The predicaments encountered in blockchain technology include those mentioned in what follows [18].

1. **Absence of Universally Described Standards:** There is an absence of defined sets of protocols and standards, making it difficult to incorporate this technology in different domains.
2. **Scarcity of Social Aptitudes:** The faint awareness of blockchain could be a potential issue due to the technology still being in its early phases, and not fully understood by many.
3. **Storage and Scalability:** Since all the nodes can observe the data on the blockchain, sensitive information about patients such as medications, medical history, and health conditions become susceptible. Moreover, this data could be extremely substantial, impeding the repository of blockchain.

## 9.7 FEDERATED LEARNING APPLICATIONS

This section offers a deeper insight into the domain and paradigm of federated learning (FL) [20] and its application to healthcare, its various underlying digitized counterparts, and the concept of blockchain-based federated learning. The inclusion of blockchain in this learning paradigm facilitates an enhanced security experience as mentioned before in the relevant sections. As described in the article [21], federated learning is an approach to model training whereby machines learn from a shared model collectively. Using proxy or representative data, the shared model is initially trained on the server. This model is then downloaded on each device, where it improves based on the federated data of the said device. The model is trained using locally accessible data by the device. The model changes are recapitulated in a version upgrade, which is then delivered to the cloud. Individual updates and training data are saved on the device. The model is compressed using quantization and randomized rotations to facilitate downloads of these changes in a rapid fashion.

A unified model is produced by averaging the models communicated by all the devices to the server. This process is repeated numerous times to obtain a high-quality model [21]. The standard method for training for any machine learning model can be explained as uploading data to a server and then utilizing the obtained data to train models. This kind of training suffices when data security is not concerned, but when extremely sensitive data is at stake, this training method turns out to be problematic. To minimize data breaches, training models on a centralized server require huge storage capacity and exceptional protection [21].

Federated learning (FL) demonstrates a perspective transformation away from localized and centralized data lakes. Clinicians, patients, hospitals, and healthcare professionals in general are examples of stakeholders. Patients are often treated on a local level. FL implementation on a worldwide scale might assure optimum medical decisions independent of the treatment site. Patients in rural places, for example, might profit from the exact outstanding machine learning–aided diagnostics accessible in clinics with plenty of cases [21]. The same is valid for unique or geographically unusual illnesses, which are more likely to have lesser repercussions if quicker and more precise examinations are possible. Federated learning might even lessen the barrier to being a data contributor by assuring patients that their information will remain with their organization and that data authorization may be cancelled. The standard topology and compute plans or the traditional version are graphically presented in Figure 9.4 [21].

Concerning the scope of this chapter, an interesting parallel and utility can be obtained for blockchain systems to enhance the federated learning methodologies in their totality. The conventional mechanisms associated with federated learning have a substantial degree of related predicaments. These can be remedied by using an underlying blockchain methodology and can be further explained by the following [22].

1. By using blockchain in place of a central aggregator, single-point failure may be prevented. In a blockchain FL system, the model aggregation will be performed by several clients.
2. The verification technique can filter out untrustworthy data. Unreliable data will be recognized prior to the aggregation of local model updates, and only valid information gets included in the global model.
3. Through incentive systems, more individuals and computational resources may be drawn. Economic incentives (for example, Bitcoin) might motivate

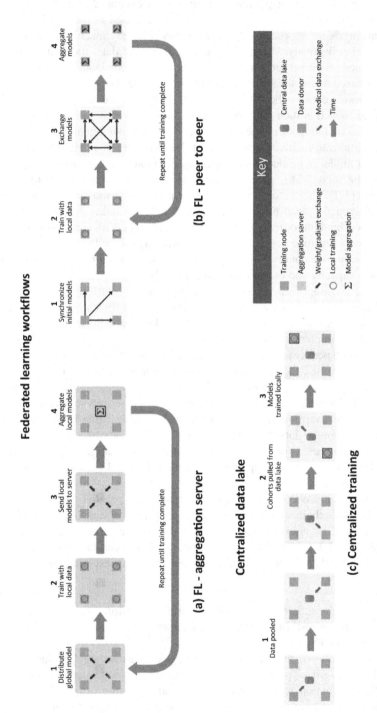

**FIGURE 9.4** Sample FL topologies and compute plans [21].

not just additional machines to partake in model training, and customers to behave by obeying the regulations.

4. On the distributed ledger, learning data may be saved and shared. Once the data is stored on the distributed ledger, it is difficult to tamper with it. Meanwhile, authorized clients may get public data from the distributed ledger, increasing training efficiency.

To implement these techniques and successfully use a blockchain-induced FL model, the completely connected federated learning model (FuC-BCFL) based on the blockchain [22] framework is developed. FL clients operate as blockchain nodes in this situation, which means they not just prepare local models but furthermore validate updates and develop new blocks. The federated learning model is decentralized as specified by the FuC-BCFL specification as each node of the chain has the option to partake in local training and a global model collection, and so the blockchain may serve as the central aggregator [22]. In such a system, there are two techniques for averaging the global model: one in which certain designated vertices gather the verified local model amendments and then run the collection algorithm, and the other in which all vertices partake in the global model accumulation [22]. The training data, consisting of validated global model updates, local model updates, and other information generated during the learning procedure, is stored in the distributed ledger. Typically, the FuC-BCFL procedure may be characterized as clients gathering data and training models locally. Selected clients proceed by verifying the local model changes. Selected clients acquire confirmed local changes, which are subsequently used to update the global model. A new block that holds confirmed model changes is included in the dispersed log (distributed ledger) and eventually acts in accordance with the incentive system in which incentives are dispersed to participants [22].

When such a system is implemented in a real-time scenario, certain merits and demerits are observed. When every node contains a copy of the distributed ledger as the system is decentralized, the single-point failure can be avoided. The transfer of data to any central server is not needed, bypassing data privacy leakage and lowering transmission expenditures. However, more computational resources are required because both FL and blockchain run on one network. Local training, as well as integration of the global model, is carried out to clients. The latency of transmission might be an issue to FuC-BCFL, as the bandwidth of blockchain is narrow. The literature also offers other implementations for a blockchain-induced FL system; other technologies, like Loosely Coupled BCFL and Flexibly Coupled BCFL, also propose certain merits and should be assessed carefully to make an informed decision for a specific utility [22].

## 9.8   QUANTUM-SAFE TECHNOLOGIES

The preceding sections offered a balanced viewpoint on security- and privacy-based necessities specific to smart healthcare and EHRs. When considering the MIoT paradigm and the use of decentralized security, the sparsely correlated technologies of federated learning offer an interesting novel area of research. When the security of such systems is considered, there is an evident need to make them secure enough and develop them according to cutting-edge quantum technologies. This section offers a novel and thorough understanding of quantum-safe methodologies for a blockchain system or blockchain-enhanced technology [23]. Many encryption methods now in use are vulnerable to quantum computing. It is estimated that the critical encryption method RSA2048 could possibly be broken by a quantum computer. Cryptographic protocols underpin many of the key subroutines in blockchain systems. Many of these protocols are vulnerable to quantum invasions. In this section, we look at various cryptocurrencies based on blockchains—such as Ethereum, Bitcoin, ZCash, and Litecoin—and see how vulnerable they are to quantum attacks. We conclude by comparing the investigated cryptocurrencies and their underlying blockchain platform, and their levels of susceptibility to quantum attacks [24].

As presented in the earlier sections, blockchain technology is based on two one-way computational technologies, namely cryptographic hash functions and digital signatures. To produce a digital signature, most blockchain platforms use ECDSA (elliptic curve public-key cryptography) or RSA (the big integer factorization problem) [23]. The security of these methods is predicated on the idea that certain mathematical problems are computationally difficult [25]. A universal quantum computer might be able to solve these issues efficiently, rendering equivalent digital or virtual signature methods—including those employed in blockchain systems—less secure [23]. The quantum algorithm as mentioned in the original research article [26], in particular, solves the problem of discrete logarithms or the factorization of big integers in polynomial time. Another safety concern is connected with Grover's search method [27], allowing for a quadratic speedup in generating the inverse hash function. This will allow a 51-percent assault, in which a coalition of malevolent actors regulating a majority of the network's computer capacity monopolizes the mining of new blocks.

Transactions of other nodes could be damaged by such attacks, rendering the recordings of their spending transaction on the blockchain incomplete. More quantum attacks on the blockchain and the potential functions of quantum algorithms in the mining operation are discussed in recent articles [28, 29]. Signing transactions can employ post-quantum digital signature techniques [30, 31] to improve the security of the blockchain system due to their resistance to quantum computer assaults [23]. This resilience, however, is based on untested hypotheses. Also, post-quantum digital signatures are expensive computationally, making them ineffective against quantum assaults to control the mining hash rate of the network. Other techniques for distributed ledger maintenance, such as Byzantine fault tolerance (BFT) replication [32] and practical BFT replication [23], exist in addition to blockchains based on mining principles. To the best of our understanding, all of the presented systems involve the use of digital signatures, making them susceptible to quantum attacks or pairwise authenticated channels. We should remark that the pairwise genuine channel assures tamper-proof transit of each message, but does not address the transferability [23]. To provide verification in the quantum age, quantum key distribution (QKD) should be employed, which provides unconditional (information-theoretic) protection established on quantum physics laws [33, 34]. QKD can produce a private key among two parties linked by a quantum channel (for communicating quantum states) and a public classical channel (for post-processing). The machinery that enables QKD networks has been shown in several trials [35, 36] and is now widely accessible from a variety of commercial sources.

Research [23] describes a blockchain medium that fuses the initial BFT state-machine reproduction without the need for digital signatures QKD for providing authentication.

The newer blockchain system can be understood by the following example (Figure 9.5).

The technique is considered resistant to not just the quantum computer's currently known capabilities, but those that may be developed in the future, as well, making post-quantum cryptography schemes powerless. The value held by QKD for blockchain systems may look contradictory, as QKD networks depend on node confidence, yet many blockchains lack such trust. It can also be contended that QKD cannot be employed for authentication, as it demands an established classical channel to operate. Every QKD transmission session, on the other hand, creates a huge quantity of shared secret material, a portion of which may be utilized for authentication in the

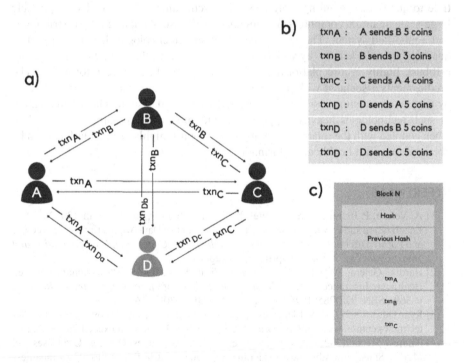

**FIGURE 9.5** Creating a quantum-safe blockchain implementation [23, 38]: a) Each node that wishes to implement a transaction sends identical copies of that transaction to all other nodes; txnA, txnB, and txnC denote the transactions of nodes A, B, and C, respectively, that follow the protocol. Node D is an attacker trying to transmit corrupted renditions txnDa, txnDb, and txnDc to the nodes. b) Transaction contents. c) The parties enforce the broadcast rule to negotiate the unverified transactions and construct the block. They realize that the transactions commenced by node D are illegal and deny it [37].

following sessions. As a result, a modest quantity of "seed" secret keys shared by the partakers prior to their first QKD session assures safe authentication for all forthcoming transmissions [39]. QKD can therefore be operated in place of traditional digital signatures.

## 9.9 CONCLUSION

The chapter aimed to explore a robust and feasible solution for healthcare security, and privacy-driven methodologies that offer an enhanced security experience for the broad domain of smart healthcare. After assessing the recent literature and the available data on security solutions, this chapter offers a novel study on decentralized techniques that are extremely relevant to the current digitized era and healthcare associations. Initiating with IoMT, the need for a decentralized storage methodology can be understood, which heavily implicated federated methods for enhancing the stakeholder experience. The induction of a blockchain-based method also presents sufficient utility and is explored thoroughly. Due to the underlying methods of these systems being dependent on a blockchain storage technique, they are highly susceptible to quantum computing platforms. The predicaments associated with possible large-scale quantum computers are remedied by the use of quantum key distributions and a modified system. The amalgamation of such technologies heavily supports a quantum-safe blockchain, by which—when coupled with the related technologies— a robust, highly secure platform can be obtained for healthcare informatics. The predicaments associated with possible large-scale quantum computers are remedied by the use of quantum key distributions and a modified system. The amalgamation of such technologies heavily supports a quantum-safe blockchain, from which— when coupled with the related technologies—a robust, highly secure platform can be obtained for smart healthcare informatics.

## REFERENCES

[1] A. Verma, P. Bhattacharya, Y. Patel, K. Shah, S. Tanwar, and B. Khan. (2022). "Data Localization and Privacy-Preserving Healthcare for Big Data Applications: Architecture and Future Directions." In *Emerging Technologies for Computing, Communication and Smart Cities* (pp. 233–244). Springer, Singapore.

[2] Hardik Gajera, Manik Lal Das, and Viral Shah. (2019). "Blockchain-Powered Healthcare Insurance System." *Security and Privacy of Electronic Healthcare Records*, p. 369. ISBN: 9781785618987. DOI: 10.1049/PBHE020Ech16.

[3] Ryan Daws. (2022). "IoMT Devices in Smart Hospitals to Exceed 7M by 2026." https://iot technews.com/news/2022/jan/04/iomt-devices-smart-hospitals-toexceed-7m-by-2026/.

[4] Andrew Meola. (2020). "IoT Healthcare in 2020: Companies, Devices, Use Cases and Market Stats." www.businessinsider.in/science/news/iot-healthcarein-2020companies-devices-use-cases-and-market-stats/articleshow/74126142.cms.

[5] Sudeep Tanwar, Karan Parekh, and Richard Evans. (February 2020). "Blockchain-Based Electronic Healthcare Record System for Healthcare 4.0 Applications." *Journal of Information Security and Applications*, vol. 50, p. 102407. ISSN: 2214-2126. DOI: 10.1016/j.jisa.2019.102407.

[6] Deepti Saraswat, Ashwin Verma, Pronaya Bhattacharya, Sudeep Tanwar, Gulshan Sharma, Pitshou N. Bokoro, and Ravi Sharma. (2022). "Blockchain-Based Federated

Learning in UAVs Beyond 5G Networks: A Solution Taxonomy and Future Directions." *IEEE Access*, vol. 10, pp. 33154–33182. ISSN: 2169-3536. DOI: 10.1109/ access.2022.3161132.

[7] Umesh Bodkhe, Sudeep Tanwar, Karan Parekh, Pimal Khanpara, Sudhanshu Tyagi, Neeraj Kumar, and Mamoun Alazab. (2020). "Blockchain for Industry 4.0: A Comprehensive Review." *IEEE Access*, vol. 8, pp. 79764–79800. ISSN: 2169-3536. DOI: 10.1109/access.2020.2988579.

[8] A. Verma, P. Bhattacharya, D. Saraswat, S. Tanwar, N. Kumar, and R. Sharma. (2023). "SanJeeVni: Secure UAV-Envisioned Massive Vaccine Distribution for COVID-19 Underlying 6G Network." *IEEE Sensors Journal*, vol. 23, no. 2, pp. 955–968. DOI: 10.1109/JSEN.2022.3188929.

[9] D. Saraswat, P. Bhattacharya, A. Verma, V.K. Prasad, S. Tanwar, G. Sharma, P.N. Bokoro, and R. Sharma. (2022). "Explainable AI for Healthcare 5.0: Opportunities and Challenges." *IEEE Access*, vol. 10, pp. 84486–84517. DOI: 10.1109/ACCESS. 2022.3197671.

[10] V.K. Prasad, P. Bhattacharya, M. Bhavsar, A. Verma, S. Tanwar, G. Sharma, Pitshou N. Bokoro, and R. Sharma. (2022). "ABV-CoViD: An Ensemble Forecasting Model to Predict Availability of Beds and Ventilators for COVID-19 Like Pandemics." *IEEE Access*, vol. 10, pp. 74131–74151.

[11] Pronaya Bhattacharya, Sudeep Tanwar, Umesh Bodkhe, Sudhanshu Tyagi, and Neeraj Kumar. (April 2021). "BinDaaS: Blockchain-Based Deep-Learning as-a-Service in Healthcare 4.0 Applications." *IEEE Transactions on Network Science and Engineering*, vol. 8, no. 2, pp. 1242–1255. ISSN: 2327-4697. DOI: 10.1109/tnse.2019.2961932.

[12] R.S. Evans. (May 2016). "Electronic Health Records: Then, Now, and in the Future." *Yearbook of Medical Informatics*, Suppl 1, pp. S48–S61. ISSN: 0943-4747. DOI: 10.15265/IYS-2016-s006.

[13] K. Häyrinen, K. Saranto, and P. Nykänen. (5 May 2008). "Definition, Structure, Content, Use and Impacts of Electronic Health Records: A Review of the Research Literature." *International Journal of Medical Informatics*, vol. 77, pp. 291–304. ISSN: 1386-5056. DOI: 10.1016/j.ijmedinf.2007.09.001.

[14] J.J. Rodrigues, Isabel de la Torre, Gonzalo Fernández, and Miguel López-Coronado. (8 August 2013). "Analysis of the Security and Privacy Requirements of Cloud-Based Electronic Health Records Systems." *Journal of Medical Internet Research*, vol. 15, p. e186. ISSN: 1439-4456. DOI: 10.2196/jmir.2494.

[15] Ahmed Albugmi, Madini O. Alassafi, Robert Walters, and Gary Wills. (2016). "Data Security in Cloud Computing." *2016 Fifth International Conference on Future Generation Communication Technologies (FGCT)*. Page: 57, DOI: 10.1109/ FGCT.2016.7605062. https://ieeexplore.ieee.org/stamp/stamp.jsp?tp=&arnumber=790 5270&isnumber=7905252.

[16] Md Husamuddin, and Mohammed Qayyum. (2017). "Internet of Things: A Study on Security and Privacy Threats." DOI: 10.1109/Anti-Cybercrime.2017.7905270. https:// ieeexplore.ieee.org/stamp/stamp.jsp?tp=&arnumber=7905270&isnumber=7905252.

[17] S. Banerjee, Vanga Odelu, Ashok Kumar Das, Samiran Chattopadhyay, Neeraj Kumar, Youngho Park, and Sudeep Tanwar. (2018). "Design of an Anonymity-Preserving Group Formation Based Authentication Protocol in Global Mobility Networks." *IEEE Access*, vol. 6, pp. 20673–20693. DOI: 10.1109/ACCESS.2018.2827027.

[18] Ayesha Shahnaz, Usman Qamar, and Ayesha Khalid. (2019). "Using Blockchain for Electronic Health Records." *IEEE Access*. DOI: 10.1109/ACCESS.2019.2946373. https://ieeexplore.ieee.org/document/8863359.

[19] R. Gupta, A. Kumari, and S. Tanwar. (2021). "A Taxonomy of Blockchain Envisioned Edge-as-a-Connected Autonomous Vehicles." *Transactions on Emerging Telecommunications Technologies*, vol. 32, p. e4009. DOI: 10.1002/ett.4009.

[20] Guodong Long, Tao Shen, Yue Tan, Leah Gerrard, Allison Clarke, and Jing Jiang. (December 2021). "Federated Learning for Privacy-Preserving Open Innovation Future on Digital Health." In *Humanity Driven AI* (pp. 113–133). Springer, Cham. ISBN: 9783030721879. DOI: 10.1007/978-3-030-72188-6_6.

[21] N. Rieke, J. Hancox, W. Li, F. Milletari, H.R. Roth, S. Albarqouni, S. Bakas, M.N. Galtier, B.A. Landman, K. Maier-Hein, and S. Ourselin. (2020). "The Future of Digital Health with Federated Learning." *NPJ Digital Medicine*, vol. 3, p. 119. DOI: 10.1038/s41746-020-00323-1.

[22] Zhilin Wang, and Qin Hu. (October 2021). "Blockchain-Based Federated Learning: A Comprehensive Survey." arXiv: 2110.02182v1 [cs.CR]. http://arxiv.org/abs/2110.02182v1.

[23] E.O. Kiktenko, N.O. Pozhar, M.N. Anufriev, A.S. Trushechkin, R.R. Yunusov, Yu V. Kurochkin, A.I. Lvovsky, and A.K. Fedorov. (May 2018). "Quantum-Secured Blockchain." *Quantum Science and Technology*, vol. 3, no. 3, p. 035004. ISSN: 2058-9565. DOI: 10.1088/2058-9565/aabc6b.

[24] Joseph J. Kearney, and Carlos A. Perez-Delgado. (July 2021). "Vulnerability of Blockchain Technologies to Quantum Attacks." *Array 10*, p. 100065. ISSN: 2590-0056. DOI: 10.1016/j.array.2021.100065.

[25] Raju Singh. (November 2020). "Applied Cryptography." DOI: 10.31219/osf.io/r4u8n. https://www.researchgate.net/publication/346888930_Applied_Cryptography.

[26] Peter W. Shor. (October 1997). "Polynomial-Time Algorithms for Prime Factorization and Discrete Logarithms on a Quantum Computer." *SIAM Journal on Computing*, vol. 26, no. 5, pp. 1484–1509. ISSN: 0097-5397. DOI: 10.1137/s0097539795293172.

[27] Lov K. Grover. (1996). "A Fast Quantum Mechanical Algorithm for Database Search." In *Proceedings of the Twenty-Eighth Annual ACM Symposium on Theory of Computing—STOC'96*. ACM Press, New York. DOI: 10.1145/237814.237866.

[28] Divesh Aggarwal, G.K. Brennen, T. Lee, M. Santha, and M. Tomamichel. (October 2018). "Quantum Attacks on Bitcoin, and How to Protect Against Them." *Ledger*, vol. 3. ISSN: 2379-5980. DOI: 10.5195/ledger.2018.127.

[29] F.M. Ablayev, D.A. Bulychkov, D.A. Sapaev, A.V. Vasiliev, and M.T. Ziatdinov. (September 2018). "Quantum-Assisted Blockchain." *Lobachevskii Journal of Mathematics*, vol. 39, no. 7, pp. 957–960. ISSN: 1995-0802. DOI: 10.1134/s1995080218070028.

[30] Daniel J. Bernstein. (n.d.). "Introduction to Post-Quantum Cryptography." In *Post-Quantum Cryptography* (pp. 1–14). Springer, Berlin, Heidelberg. ISBN: 9783540887010. DOI: 10.1007/978-3-540-88702-7_1.

[31] Chris Christensen. (2009). "Reviews of Two Post-Quantum Cryptography Books." In Bernstein, Daniel J., Buchmann, Johannes, and Dahmen, Erik (Eds.), *Post-Quantum Cryptography* (p. 245). Springer-Verlag, Berlin, Heidleberg. hardcover; Buchmann, Johannes, and Ding, J. (July 2009). "Quantum Cryptography: Second International Workshop, 2008 Proceedings, Lecture, Paperback." In *Cryptologiapp* (pp. 271–273). Verlag, Berlin, Heidleberg. ISSN: 0161-1194. DOI: 10.1080/01611190902742749.

[32] Leslie Lamport, Robert Shostak, and Marshall Pease. (July 1982). "The Byzantine Generals Problem." *ACM Transactions on Programming Languages and Systems*, vol. 4, no. 3, pp. 382–401. ISSN: 0164-0925. DOI: 10.1145/357172.357176.

[33] Nicolas Gisin, Grégoire Ribordy, Wolfgang Tittel, and Hugo Zbinden. (March 2002). "Quantum Cryptography." *Reviews of Modern Physics*, vol. 74, no. 1, pp. 145–195. ISSN: 0034-8861. DOI: 10.1103/revmodphys.74.145.

[34] Valerio Scarani, Helle Bechmann-Pasquinucci, Nicolas J. Cerf, Miloslav Dušek, Norbert Lütkenhaus, and Momtchil Peev. (September 2009). "The Security of Practical Quantum Key Distribution." *Reviews of Modern Physics*, vol. 81, no. 3, pp. 1301–1350. ISSN: 0034-8861. DOI: 10.1103/revmodphys.81.1301.

[35] D. Stucki, M. Legre, F. Buntschu, B. Clausen, N. Felber, N. Gisin, L. Henzen, P. Junod, G. Litzistorf, P. Monbaron, and L. Monat. (December 2011). "Long-Term Performance of the SwissQuantum Quantum Key Distribution Network in a Field Environment." *New Journal of Physics*, vol. 13, no. 12, p. 123001. ISSN: 1367-2630. DOI: 10.1088/1367-2630/13/12/123001.

[36] Teng-Yun Chen, Hao Liang, Yang Liu, Wen-Qi Cai, Lei Ju, Wei-Yue Liu, Jian Wang, H. Yin, K. Chen, Z.B. Chen, and C.Z. Peng. (April 2009). "Field Test of a Practical Secure Communication Network with Decoy-State Quantum Cryptography." *Optics Express*, vol. 17, no. 8, p. 6540. ISSN: 1094-4087. DOI: 10.1364/oe.17.006540.

[37] E.O. Kiktenko, N.O. Pozhar, A.V.E. Duplinskiy, A.A. Kanapin, A.S. Sokolov, S.S. Vorobey, A.V.E. Miller, V.E.E. Ustimchik, M.N. Anufriev, A.T. Trushechkin, and R.R. Yunusov. (September 2017). "Demonstration of a Quantum Key Distribution Network in Urban Fibre-Optic Communication Lines." *Quantum Electronics*, vol. 47, no. 9, pp. 798–802. ISSN: 1063-7818. DOI: 10.1070/qel16469.

[38] V.K. Ralegankar, Jagruti Bagul, Bhaumikkumar Thakkar, Rajesh Gupta, Sudeep Tanwar, Gulshan Sharma, and Innocent E. Davidson. (2022). "Quantum Cryptography-as-a-Service for Secure UAV Communication: Applications, Challenges, and Case Study." *IEEE Access*, vol. 10, pp. 1475–1492. DOI: 10.1109/ACCESS.2021.3138753.

[39] Piotr K. Tysowski, Xinhua Ling, Norbert Lütkenhaus, and Michele Mosca. (November 2017). "The Engineering of a Scalable Multi-Site Communications System Utilizing Quantum Key Distribution (QKD)." *Quantum Science and Technology*. ISSN: 2058-9565. DOI: 10.1088/2058-9565/aa9a5d.

# 10 IoT-Based Life-Saving Devices Equipped with Ambu Bags for SARS-CoV-2 Patients

*Ankit Jain and Anita Shukla*

## CONTENTS

## 10.1 INTRODUCTION

The COVID-19 epidemic has caused an unimaginable amount of fatalities since its outbreak. Due to the rising number of patients suffering from COVID-19, the need for ventilators has grown daily. Available resources and facilities are unable to cover the insurmountable gap between demand and supply, particularly in India. As a result,

DOI: 10.1201/9781003303374-10

individuals perished during the second wave because they were unable to even reach hospitals. This severe acute respiratory syndrome (SARS) originated in Wuhan city in China's Hubei Province, from where it spread to the rest of the world [1]. This illness can spread from asymptomatic people before symptoms even appear [2]. Large droplets released by sick patients during coughing and sneezing are used to transmit it. There is no difference in viral load between symptomatic and asymptomatic people, and viral loads are greater in the nasal cavity than in the throat, per research [3]. Patients with COVID-19 may also feel fever, breathlessness, a decrease in oxygen saturation, dry cough, nausea, vomiting, sore throat, headache, loss of taste, and physical pain [4]. If a patient has a high fever, low oxygen saturation, and an irregular pulse rate, they are regarded as critical patients. Shortness of breath and low oxygen saturation levels are symptoms of hypoxemia and hypoxia, respectively. The likelihood of the patient surviving is decreased when hypoxemia and low pulse rate are combined. Patients occasionally fail to notice hypoxemia and an accelerating pulse, and as a result, they pass away without receiving the appropriate care. Therefore, it is crucial that COVID-19 patients' health conditions—particularly their body temperature, heart rate, and oxygen saturation ($SpO_2$) level—are regularly assessed. In such circumstances, IoT-based solutions may be advantageous to people for routine health examinations and ongoing patient health parameter monitoring [5, 6]. IoT technology has emerged as a crucial invention with multiple uses. It specifically indicates to any arrangement of physical objects which acquire and swap data across wireless networks without the involvement of a person [7, 8]. Nearly every country during the second wave was unable to handle the situation. For COVID-19 patients, regular body temperature and pulse rate monitoring is required. The number of pulses or beats per minute (bpm) is known as the pulse rate or beat rate. The average pulse rate for healthy people is determined to be between 60–100 beats per minute, while it is 70–75 bpm for adult males and females, respectively. Typically, the pulse rates of women older than 12 are higher than those of men [9, 10]. The pulse rate is observed to be abnormal in COVID-19 individuals, necessitating the assistance of an emergency medical assistant. In a healthy adult, the body temperature ranges from 97.8°F (36.5°C) to 99°F (37.2°C) [10–12]. In addition to these causes, diseases like influenza, low-temperature hypothermia, and others can also affect body temperature. Hence, it becomes crucial to regularly check the body temperature of a patient with COVID-19. Now, in addition to heart rate and body temperature, oxygen saturation is a vital factor for treatment of COVID-19 patients. The usual range of the human body's oxygen saturation ($SpO_2$) is 95–100%. A COVID-19 patient needs emergency medical attention if their $SpO_2$ level is less than 95%. Silent hypoxia is caused by SARS-CoV-2 and is defined as $SpO_2$ of 90% without shortness of breath. Using a pulse oximeter to measure $SpO_2$, silent hypoxia can be identified [11, 12]. A patient with COVID-19 who has low oxygen saturation is at higher risk of death. Monitoring of early symptoms including fever, cough, heart rate, and $SpO_2$ levels becomes crucial for managing this contagious and fatal illness. To measure these values, a variety of tools and gadgets are on the market. For instance, most nations have easy access to fingertip pulse oximeters, which monitor $SpO_2$ and pulse rate [13]. The deluxe handheld pulse oximeter, which costs around USD 299 [14] and determines $SpO_2$ and heart rate, is also an option. A wrist-worn pulse oximeter that measures $SpO_2$ and heart rate is available over the counter. Like above listed devices, this one lacks features for measuring body temperature. The wrist-worn pulse oximeter is somewhat pricey, coming in at USD 179. Analogue and digital thermometers are also sold on the market for measuring body temperature [15], although the majority of them are pricey [13]. The disadvantage of the currently available traditional equipment is that it is not Internet of Things (IoT)-based. Therefore, when patients are arriving in droves, it becomes challenging for a doctor to gather updates from every patient at once. Patients with significant symptoms of COVID-19 are in need of immediate monitoring. Patients can obtain COVID-19 treatment utilizing their mobile phones at home thanks to technology [16]. The pulse rate of an individual is influenced by their age, physical stature, cardiovascular health, and emotional stability [17]. Since oxygen saturation and pulse rate are inversely correlated, when oxygen level of a patient drops, their pulse rate rises. All of these problems are resolved by using IoT technology. The IoT-based smart healthcare system functions as a real-time patient monitoring system, which can considerably benefit the current healthcare sector [18]. This is the rationale behind the rise in research interest in IoT-based smart healthcare equipment. In a study, the examined literature outlines the creation of smart healthcare monitoring systems in an IoT setting [19]. In this investigation, a temperature, $SpO_2$, and heart rate sensor-equipped pulse monitoring system with an Android operating system was used. The measured data from a different investigation, in which the $SpO_2$ measurement sensor was not employed, was posted online [20]. An IoT-based lung function monitoring system that did not take temperature, $SpO_2$, or pulse rate into account could be helpful for asthma patients [21]. Systems for monitoring heart rate using an Arduino, Android, or microcontrollers have been suggested in [22, 23]. The system [24] is based on cloud computing and the Arduino Uno, for which only a hardware prototype was created. There are not any statistics from actual testing, though. A mobile app-based heart rate monitoring system was established in [25]. The device detected the patient's pulse rate using a pulse rate sensor, and Arduino was used to interpret the results. The experiment only employed a small number of sensors [25]. Additionally, research is at its height, and using their creative working theories, several authors have suggested various IoT-based wireless health-monitoring systems. IoT-based smart solutions for estimating various health parameters for COVID-19 patients—like temperature, heart rate, and $SpO_2$—have apparently not yet been introduced. In a study, a brand-new IoT-based smart health monitoring system is developed and used for COVID-19 patients to evaluate various vital signs like body temperature, pulse, and $SpO_2$. Through a mobile application, the device may monitor and show measured values for human body temperature, oxygen saturation level, and pulse rate, enabling the patient to seek medical assistance even if a doctor is not physically present. Doctors must inquire about the patient's medical issues when caring for COVID-19 patients (including oxygen saturation level and pulse rate). Patients with COVID-19 and other illnesses, including asthma and chronic obstructive pulmonary disease (COPD), can both benefit from this gadget. COPD contributed to 5% of all fatalities globally in 2005, and is expected to continue to be a global health issue in the future [26]. Because COVID-19–related mortality and morbidity have increased throughout the pandemic, there is a greater demand for ventilators. The hospitals have been burdened as a result of the hospitals being unable to provide ventilator assistance to the acute respiratory distress syndrome (ARDS) patients who need it. A straightforward, manually operated bag valve mask (BVM) can also be used to ventilate patients in place of modern ventilators, which are computerized devices. A BVM must deliver from 500–800 millilitres of air to an average male adult patient's lungs in order for it to be successful, while 400 ml might still be sufficient if additional oxygen is given [27]. An acceptable breathing rate is determined by squeezing the bag; for adults, this is 10–12 breaths per minute, whereas for children or infants, this is 20–25 [28]. In this pandemic, we have also been unable to locate any full protective-assisted ventilating equipment that may be employed prior to intubation, while patients are waiting for invasive mechanical ventilation, or after intubation [29]. The Indian Institute of Technology (IIT), Hyderabad, has recommended using an Ambu bag or BVM as an alternative to traditional ventilators for COVID-19 patients in life-threatening situations [30].

## 10.2   DIFFERENCE IN MANUAL VENTILATION

### 10.2.1   SELF-INFLATING VENTILATION BAG VS. FREE FLOW INFLATING BAG

In case of manually operated ventilators having a BVM device, good mask seal against the face is required so that the required pressure to inflate the lungs can be generated. At the same time, knowledge of using ventilation devices effectively in order to deliver a breath is also required. Understanding of these differences is prerequisite and important.

### 10.2.2   SPONTANEOUS VS. MANUAL VENTILATION

With the help of a manual switch, the breathing mechanics can be changed from spontaneous ventilation to manual ventilation.

#### 10.2.2.1   Spontaneous Ventilation

The diaphragm and the muscles between the ribs (intercostal muscles) contract during inhaling during spontaneous breathing (Figure 10.1). The chest cavity is made larger by the movement of the ribs in an upward and outward direction caused by the contraction of the intercostal muscles, and it is also made larger by the movement of the diaphragm in a downward direction. Since pressure and volume are inversely related, the inner pressure of a container decreases as volume rises. The use of a syringe as an example makes the entire procedure easier to comprehend. When a syringe's plunger is pulled back, the interior chamber expands, the interior pressure decreases as a result of the lower volume, and fluid is drawn into the chamber. In contrast to this contraction process, chest expansion causes the intrathoracic pressure to fall below atmospheric pressure, which allows air to enter the lungs if the airway is open, until the two pressures are equal. The rib cage is compressed during exhale by the natural elastic rebound of our chest wall. As the volume lowers and the pressure rises, the diaphragm relaxes and the chest cavity shrinks. Let us use the instance of inserting the syringe plunger inward to better comprehend the same. The remaining air is forced out through an unobstructed airway as intrathoracic pressure climbs above atmospheric pressure (minus some oxygen and carbon dioxide content).

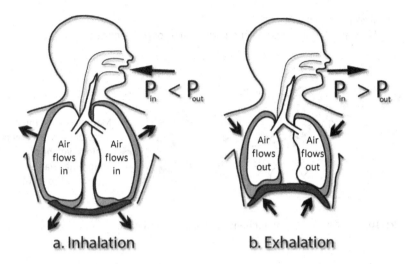

$P_{in} < P_{out}$

$P_{in} > P_{out}$

a. Inhalation          b. Exhalation

**FIGURE 10.1**   Change of air pressure inside the thoracic cavity in spontaneous breathing during (a) inhalation and (b) exhalation.

### 10.2.2.2   Manual Ventilation

Because a patient is mechanically ventilated, gas no longer passively flows into the lungs under the effect of negative intrathoracic pressure, and therefore, positive pressure is necessary to inflate the lungs. As an alternative, you must use positive pressure to expand the lungs. Your manual breath must lift the chest wall, force the contents of your abdomen and diaphragm downward, and overcome the first alveolar surface tension in order to expand your lungs. In individuals with bronchospasm or pneumonia, it is more difficult to overcome lower lung compliance to produce an adequate tidal volume because their lungs are stiffer. Additionally, a supine patient's higher diaphragm works against them when the bag is squeezed; as a result, more pressure is needed to move the diaphragms—and the abdominal contents beneath them—down and out of the way in a supine patient than in an upright one. Ventilation is also hampered by the patient's obesity, which adds to the weight of the belly wall and its contents. Manual ventilation must account for the fact that the diaphragm rests higher in the chest, the weight of the abdominal contents and chest wall, and the compliance of the lungs (Figure 10.2).

#### 10.2.2.2.1 Bag-Valve-Mask Devices

If the seal is improper, ventilation will not occur. When ventilating a patient, it is crucial to make sure the patient is getting a good ventilation. Understanding the variations between the two types of BVM devices in use is the first step in doing this. Figure 10.3 depicts a BVM device, which contains flexible bag connected to either an endotracheal tube or ventilation mask by a pressure control valve.

Air is pumped into the lungs through a mask or artificial airway by compressing the bag, which opens valves. On the other hand, by opening the bag, the pressure

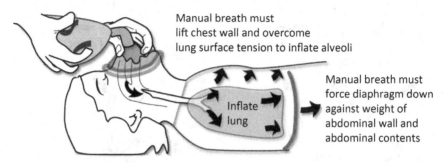

**FIGURE 10.2**   Effect of lung compliance in manual ventilation.

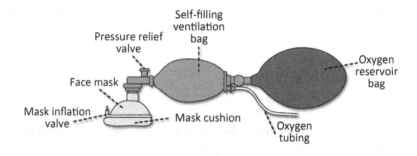

**FIGURE 10.3**   Common parts for bag-valve-mask devices.

inside the device is reduced. The patient in this situation exhales passively through a one-way valve. The clinician can usually compensate for the patient's lungs' compliance (ease of inflation) by adjusting the pop-off valve to release at either higher or lower pressures. Additionally, it aids in preventing potential barotrauma by not overpressurizing the lungs.

There are two different kinds of ventilation bags: self-inflating and free-flowing bag types.

### 10.2.2.2.2 Self-Inflating Ventilation Bags

When we stop squeezing the self-inflating bag, it refills itself. The Ambu bag is the proprietary name for these self-inflating resuscitation bags. One can expand their lungs by squeezing the bag. If an oxygen source is attached, releasing pressure allows the bag to refill with both air and oxygen. Without additional oxygen, a self-inflating bag can give an oxygen concentration of 21%, but most sick or injured individuals need more oxygen than that. The bag has the ability to give $O_2$ levels of 40%–60% when oxygen is supplied at a rate of 10–12 litres per minute. By adding a reservoir bag and running $O_2$ at 12–15 litres per minute, the concentration can be increased by up to 100%, providing the reservoir is given time to fill. A flow-inflation bag, on the other hand, is continuously filled with 100% oxygen.

Using a self-inflating bag requires that the bag be squeezed in a way that maximizes oxygen concentration. When the bag is empty and abruptly allowed to reload, it usually does so with ambient air rather than oxygen, whose inflow duration is constrained. It is best to release pressure on your hand gradually over the course of 3–4 seconds to allow the bag to fill. Breakage of the mask seal should be prevented during the refilling procedure to prevent the bag from filling with ambient air instead of oxygen. Self-inflating bags cannot be used for successful "blow by" unless they are squeezed to push oxygen toward the patient.

### 10.2.2.2.3 Free-Flow–Inflating Ventilation Bags

An empty free flow inflation ventilation bag resembles a deflated balloon, while a self-inflating bag when not in use looks like a softly inflated football. The flow-inflating bag must have an uninterrupted fresh oxygen flow. The flow-inflation bags will not automatically refill after the oxygen source is gone or disconnected. In order to prevent bag deflation and allow the patient to breathe, it is important to maintain a good seal between the ventilation mask and the face. Even flow-inflation or inflow dependent bags are often employed on anaesthetic machines and in other intensive care unit (ICU)-like settings because they enable finer control of tidal volume, better ventilation monitoring, and higher fraction of inspired oxygen ($FiO_2$), the concentration of oxygen in the mix. However, they can be more challenging to utilize. The flow-inflating bag's softness makes it easy to perceive changes in resistance and lung compliance.

While ventilating a neonate with a 500 ml bag, extremely fine tidal volume control is achievable, even if it is less than 50 ml. With each breath, the bag partially deflates—which is easily felt and seen—before it re-inflates by flow of gas during spontaneous ventilation. The degree of deflation can be used to estimate tidal volume. If the seal is broken, it is instantly apparent since the bag collapses. Contrary to self-filling bags, which may give you a fake sense of security as they are usually full even when filling of lungs is not proper, this type is filled all the time.

In contrast to self-filling bags, a flow-inflation bag cannot deliver positive pressure without a tight seal of the mask against the face. The flow-inflation bag deflates like a huge balloon when there is a poor seal. Emergency ventilation in flow-inflation bags is typically delivered by self-inflating bags because flow-inflation bags depend on an oxygen source and require more training. It does not matter what kind of ventilation gear is being utilized; what matters is making sure that the ventilation being done is sufficient. Chest rise, mask fogging, breath sounds, and end-tidal $CO_2$ should always be periodically checked.

## 10.3   HISTORY OF AMBU BAGS

Following their early work on a suction pump, the Danish anaesthesiologist Henning Ruben and the German engineer Dr. Holder Hesse created the idea of the BVM in 1953. Their resuscitator, later known as an Ambu bag, was put into production starting in 1956 by their own business, also known as Ambu. As a result, all bag valve masks are now referred to together under the trademarked name Ambu.

### 10.3.1  HOW TO USE AMBU BAGS

The Air-Shields Manual Breathing Unit Bag is referred to as the Ambu. A person having difficulty breathing is helped with a particular kind of BVM. A procedure known as "bagging" is employed to use this, which is held and handled with the hand, to continuously give oxygen to a person's lungs. The components of a BVM are a face mask and a non-rebreathing valve. A source of oxygen is connected to the bag's other end (or air). Manual holding is used to keep the mask in place. Before intubation can be performed, the bag is squeezed to give the patient breathing through their mouth and nose (Figure 10.4).

### 10.3.2  COMPONENTS OF AN AMBU BAG

The BVM features a pliable air chamber. The chamber, which has a diameter comparable to an American football, is attached to the face mask by a shutter valve. Air is forced into the patient's lungs by the machine when the face mask is securely fastened and the air chamber, or "bag," is squeezed. The bag self-inflates when it is released, drawing in ambient air or low-pressure oxygen flow from a controlled cylinder, and the patient's lungs expand to the air through the one-way valve. The size requirements for various Ambu bag components for patients in various age groups are listed in Table 10.1.

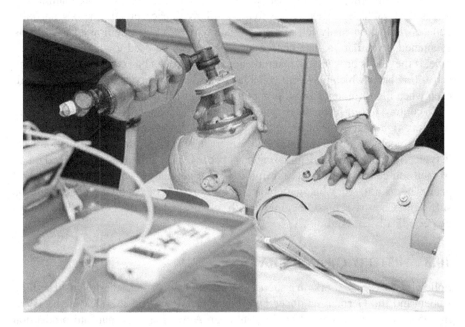

**FIGURE 10.4**   How an Ambu bag is used.

**TABLE 10.1**

**Required Sizes of Ambu Bag Parts for Different Age Groups**

|  | Adult | Child | Infant |
|---|---|---|---|
| **Sizes** | 1600 ml | 500 ml | 500ml |
| Mask | Size 4 | Size 2 | Size 1 |
| Reservoir | 1600 ml. bag | 500 ml. bag | 500 ml. Bag |
| Tubing | Having suitable connectors at both ends for easy and safe connections | | |

## Indications

- A severe asthma attack, respiratory failure, or drug overdose.
- Brain injury or imminent drowning.
- If a patient starts breathing on their own but the breathing is laboured or shallow, an Ambu bag may be used to make breathing more effective.

### 10.3.3 How to Use an Ambu Bag Manual Resuscitation Bag Valve Mask (BVM)

## Assemble Equipment

- If required, an oxygen supply with the proper tubing.
- As needed, adjust the mask's size.
- If necessary, attach an adaptor for a tracheostomy tube.
- Inform the patient of the operation if it is not an emergency.
- If an oxygen order is placed, secure the oxygen tubing to the resuscitation bag.
- Attach a tracheostomy tube to the resuscitation bag.
- If the patient is able to breathe on their own, match the patient's breaths to the manual breaths. Squeeze the resuscitation bag to provide air as the patient starts to breathe.
- Just enough bag pressure should cause the chest to elevate.
- The resuscitation bag should be squeezed at regular intervals to administer the recommended breaths per minute if the patient is unable to breathe on their own.
- Disconnect the tracheostomy tube from the resuscitation bag.
- Handwashing.

## Instructions

- If the patient is not breathing, one should first try to find a technique to get them to do so. If the patient continues to be non-responsive, use the Ambu bag.
- Before utilizing the device, one should make sure the patient's airways are clear of mucous.

- The patient must be lying flat on his back with their nose pointed upward. To assist in keeping this position, one can place a roll of a small towel beneath the patient's shoulders.
- Attachment of face mask to the bag adaptor, the oxygen tubing to the regulator on the tank, and the oxygen tubing to the bag must be verified. Hold the mask toward the patient's face while squeezing the bag firmly with your thumb to apply pressure.
- The mask should be worn tightly over the patient's mouth and nose. Make sure the chest of the patient rises when the Ambu bag is pressed, as it would if they were breathing normally.
- The Ambu bag should be squeezed once every 5–6 seconds for adult patients, compared to every 2–3 seconds for paediatric patient. If the patient is still having trouble breathing, keep bagging them up until either aid arrives or they start breathing properly.
- If the chest still does not rise, try moving the patient's head or the mask before adding a little more pressure to the Ambu bag. The patient should be revived if the condition continues and the chest still does not rise. If this is the case, there must be an obstruction blocking the patient's airway.

### Risks

- Hyperventilation can be brought on by squeezing the bag too quickly, and this can result in respiratory alkalosis. By compressing the bag at the proper rate, this situation can be mitigated or avoided.
- Danger can be reduced and the trapped air in the stomach can be evacuated by inserting a nasal gastric tube.

## 10.4 BACKGROUND OF THE PROPOSED SYSTEM

The world is still reeling from the rapidly growing pandemic. The SARS-CoV-2 virus causes COVID-19, an infectious sickness first identified in Wuhan, China, in December of that year. On March 11, 2020, the World Health Organization (WHO) declared it to be a pandemic. Symptoms of COVID-19 may appear 2–14 days after exposure. The incubation period is the period of time following exposure but before to the onset of symptoms. Even before one exhibits symptoms, COVID-19 can still spread (pre-symptomatic transmission). Respiratory issues, fever, coughing, and shortness of breath are a few common signs and symptoms. In severe situations, infection might result in pneumonia, SARS, and sometimes even death. As a result of their direct involvement in the diagnosis, treatment, and care of COVID-19 patients, healthcare workers become the subject of primary concern when treating such infectious diseases. As a result, they are constantly susceptible to infection and have a very high risk of contracting the SARS-CoV-2 virus. Many of the difficulties hospitals and their workers face can be solved without the use of technology.

The new strain of the virus in second wave was found to be more powerful and infectious, which left younger and healthy people in critical conditions as compared to first wave of COVID-19. People were gasping for breath. A shortage of doctors and healthcare workers gave rise to surge of cases; this was also having repercussions on the patients who were suffering with other critical illnesses as they face undue delays in getting treated.

The second COVID-19 wave in India exposed how ill-prepared the country's healthcare systems were to deal with the sudden rise in daily cases. The unexpected increase of cases collapsed the country's healthcare system. There was a shortage of hospital beds, oxygen, and medications. The shortage of oxygen supplies was also definitely a drawback. During first wave, there was shortage of personal protective equipment (PPE) kits, and in the second wave, more deaths were recorded due to the shortage of oxygen supplies and the hunt for medications by hospitals and relatives of patients. Cases were recorded en masse every day, and people in search of oxygen rushed to the hospitals and faced the problem of unavailability of ICU beds. People were struggling to gasp for breath. Because of limited resources/facilities to meet the emergency, a lot of people died. The major reason was that due to unavailability of hospital beds, people were bound to get treated at home—and when their situation worsened, they had to rush to the hospital, but in most of the cases, they could not make it because of scarcity of oxygen cylinders.

### 10.4.1 FEATURES OF THE PROPOSED SYSTEM

In the present work, we have developed an IoT-based wireless healthcare remote sensing device/system which could provide real-time online information about patients under observation either in home isolation or in hospital. Doctors at hospital and attendants at home can monitor their COVID-19 patients remotely. The system is smart enough to continuously sense a patient's oxygen level, body temperature, and pulse rate. All the readings taken can be displayed on liquid crystal displays (LCDs) and can be monitored remotely using IoT. The major advantage of the system is that the monitoring of all parameters can be done from anywhere in the world because of IoT technology. The system not only measures the oxygen level of the patient, but also provides the support to the patients in home isolation. The system is equipped with an Ambu bag, so that the patient struggling with lower oxygen level can buy time to reach a hospital safely. This Ambu bag is operated automatically by using a DC motor. The frequency of inhalation can also be adjusted in the system.

Numerous features built into the system increase its usefulness. Since COVID-19 is a highly infectious disease, the patient is being monitored remotely so that hospital staff and home caregivers have at least some interaction with the patient and have a lower risk of contracting the illness [31]. Through the use of a NodeMCU (node microcontroller unit, a low-cost open source IoT platform) Wi-Fi module, this system is connected to the internet and is capable of displaying real-time data that can be viewed and accessed via the internet via IoT technology from any location on the globe. The following is a list of the system's features.

- As the disease is highly infectious, the remote monitoring and management becomes necessary. The patient, if they are not critical, can also monitor the parameters like oxygen level, pulse value, and body temperature on their own.

- With the help of IoT technology, the healthcare workers at a hospital or attendants at home can also monitor the previously mentioned parameters remotely, as frequent monitoring of oxygen levels and body temperature is required for COVID-19 patients [32].
- If the patient is in home isolation and suffocates suddenly due to drop of oxygen level, there is provision of Ambu bag that can be used to save the patient's life while they are being rushed to the hospital. The Ambu bag is operated automatically—not manually—hence, it is user friendly.
- The frequency of inhalation in Ambu bag is also adjustable according to the requirement of patient's age group.

A block diagram of the proposed system is shown in Figure 10.5.
The main components which are used in this system are as follow.

- Ambu bag assembly
- NodeMCU
- Pulse oximeter Sensor MAX30100
- Temperature sensor DS18B20
- OLEDs (organic light-emitting diodes)
- DC motor 12V/1A
- Buzzer

Some major components are described in the following subsections.

### 10.4.1.1   NodeMCU ESP8266 Pin Out

ESP-based boards require the esp8266 package to be loaded into Arduino IDE, even though NodeMCU ESP8266 based boards initially arrived with LUA scripting

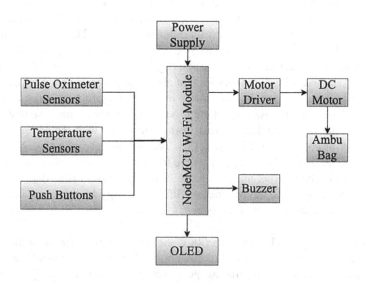

**FIGURE 10.5**   Block diagram of the proposed system.

language for programming. This is because Arduino IDE is the most common tool used by electronic hobbyists to program development boards. Since the NodeMCU ESP8266 boards were first constructed for a different architecture but later merged for Arduino IDE, we needed GPIO pin mapping for the NodeMCU pinout (Figure 10.6), which is marked on the board from D0-D8 but is utilized in code.

### 10.4.1.2 MAX30100 Pulse Oximeter Sensor

In Figure 10.7, the MAX30100 sensor module is seen. It is a straightforward module that interacts with the microcontroller via the I2C interface. It gives the linked

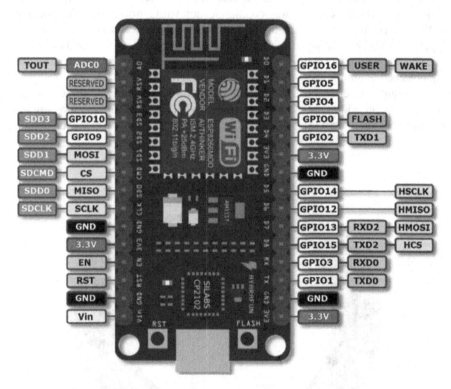

**FIGURE 10.6**   Pin mapping of NodeMCU.

**FIGURE 10.7**   MAX30100 pulse oximeter sensor.

microcontroller information about the SpO$_2$ and pulse rate. Simply said, this sensor is employed to measure oxygen saturation. As a result, this module can be used to non-invasively monitor the blood's oxygen saturation level and pulse rate. It makes use of optical components and photo detectors, with IR LEDs modulating the LED pulses. The LED current ranges from 0–50 mA. The power supply range for this pulse oximeter sensor is 1.8–5.5 volts.

### 10.4.1.3    Temperature Sensor DS18B20

Dallas Semiconductor Corp. makes a temperature sensor with a 1-Wire interface called the DS18B20. For two-way communication with a microcontroller, the novel 1-Wire interface just needs one digital pin. The sensor typically comes in two form types. A TO-92 packaging transistor has the same appearance as a standard transistor. The other is in the shape of a waterproof probe, which is more suited for measuring objects that are far away, submerged, or underground.

The temperature sensor in Figure 10.8 (the DS18B20) is fairly accurate and operates without any additional parts. It has a 0.5°C accuracy range and can measure temperatures between −55°C and +125°C. User configuration options for the temperature

**FIGURE 10.8**    MAX30100 pulse oximeter sensor.

sensor's resolution include 9, 10, 11, or 12 bits, but 12-bit resolution (i.e., 0.0625°C precision) is the default setting at startup.

### 10.4.1.4 OLED Display

The 0.96-inch SSD1306 mode with 12864 pixels OLED display that we utilized for this project is depicted in Figure 10.9.

Because the OLED display does not need a backlight, there is an excellent contrast in low light. Additionally, compared to other displays, it uses less electricity. There are four pins on the display we are utilizing. It utilizes the I2C protocol for communication. Figure 10.10 displays the proposed system's circuit diagram.

In Figure 10.10, the circuit diagram is shown the system is build with NodeMCU microcontroller board. NodeMCU is not able to provide that much current, which is required to operate DC motor; that is why an L298 motor driver module is used for operating the Ambu bag with the help of a 12V DC motor. This circuitry has three push buttons—one is used for any panic/emergency situation, the second for adult mode, and third for child mode. If any panic/emergency occurs, the patient will press the panic button; after pressing this button, the buzzer will blow and a notification/message will be sent to the concerned doctor or home healthcare provider using Blynk app. The second and third push buttons are used to set up the frequency of the Ambu bag in adult or child mode. By using pulse width modulation (PWM) signal, we can change the voltage level of the DC motor, and by changing the voltage level of the DC motor, we can operate the Ambu bag with different frequencies according

**FIGURE 10.9** OLED display.

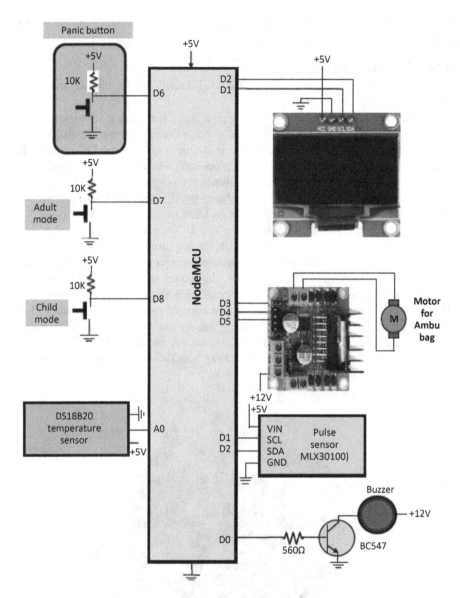

**FIGURE 10.10**   Circuit diagram of proposed system.

to the different age groups. We can monitor the heart rate and SpO$_2$ level with the help of MLX30100 pulse sensor module. the temperature of the patient can be measured by DS18B20 temperature sensor. All the measured values will be displayed on OLED. The MLX30100 pulse sensor module and OLED are connected with I2C protocol using SDA and SCL pin of NodeMCU D2 and D1 pin respectively. All the sensor data will be displayed over Blynk server using IoT and the range is all over the world.

## 10.4.2 SETTING UP BLYNK APPLICATION

Utilizing the Google Play Store or Apple's App Store, download the Blynk application for Android or iOS. Enter your email address and password to join up for the Blynk IoT cloud, and then click on the new project button to give the project a name. For instance, enter "IoT pulse oximeter" as the name, choose the NodeMCU board, and then pick Wi-Fi as the connection type. Finally, press the "Create" button as displayed in Figure 10.11(A).

**FIGURE 10.11(A)** Setting up the Blynk app.

The registered email address will receive the Blynk authentication token. This token will be necessary later when programming. To add two gauges and two value display widgets, tap the plus (+) icon on the main screen as illustrated in Figure 10.11(B).

**FIGURE 10.11(B)** Setting up gauge and display widget.

As indicated in Figure 10.11(C), one gauge will show the BPM values, while another gauge will show the oxygen saturation level (SpO$_2$). Choose virtual pin V1 for BPM and enter a value between 0 and 130.
Choose the virtual V2 pin for the oxygen level and enter values between 0 and 100.
Due to the fact that they both behave similarly, we will likewise add the identical values to the value display.

**FIGURE 10.11(C)** Setting up gauge and display widget.

After setting all the widgets, the final interface of "IoT pulse oximeter" using ESP8266 and Blynk server is shown in Figure 10.11(D).

**FIGURE 10.11(D)** Final user interface of the Blynk server.

### 10.4.3 PCB IMPLEMENTATION AND CIRCUIT

Figures 10.12(a)–(b) show lower and upper views of the printed circuit board (PCB) for the proposed system. DipTrace was used to prepare this PCB.

## 10.5 RESULTS AND DISCUSSION

The patient management issue with COVID-19 is addressed in this study in an electronic and environmentally responsible manner. The proposed system was put to the test in real time following its development, and the outcomes were good and appropriate. As is common knowledge, it is essential to often check the temperature and pulse rate of COVID-19 patients, and the system is able to do so precisely utilizing IoT and the Blynk server. The system has three push buttons: one for panic situations, a second for adult mode and a third for child mode. By using the panic button, the patient can inform about any panic/emergency situation to doctors or concerned persons using IoT. The adult and child mode push buttons are used to set the frequency by which Ambu bag should be pressed, according to patient age group. The Ambu bag is operated by a DC motor. By using pulse-width modulation (PWM) signal, we can adjust the frequency of pressing the Ambu bag for adult or child mode.

Figure 10.13(a) shows the original picture of the proposed system. The user would be able to see the heart rate, $SpO_2$, and temperature of patient in displayed results. This system transfers the data through IoT to the Blynk server, which is one of its crucial parts (Figure 10.13[b]). The system is found to work successfully and all sensors also worked satisfactorily. Five individuals, ranging in age from 23–56, used the gadget during the testing phase. For each feature included in the system, the exact values were discovered. Table 10.2 lists the $SpO_2$ level, pulse rate, and temperature measurements for five separate users. The majority of patients have $SpO_2$ levels of 97, which is

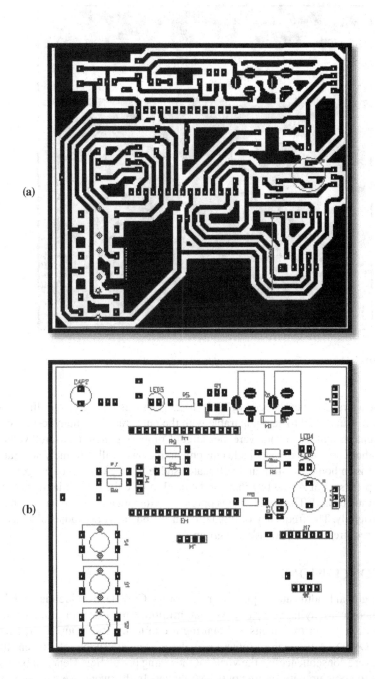

**FIGURE 10.12** PCB prepared using DipTrace: (a) lower view; (b) upper view.

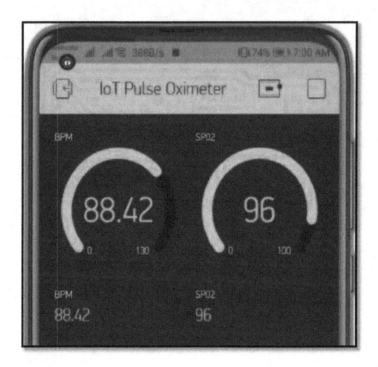

**FIGURE 10.13(A)**    Original photo of developed proposed system.

near to the average values, as seen in Table 10.2. The measured values for the various participants were found to be comparable with the pulse rate. For many test individuals, different physiological data were measured. Comparing these measured values to those of other commercially available equipment, they were all extremely accurate. If the patient is in home isolation and suffocates suddenly due to drop of oxygen level, there is a provision of Ambu bag that can be used to save the life while the patient is rushed to the hospital. The Ambu bag is operated automatically, not manually; hence, it is user friendly. The frequency of inhalation in Ambu bag is also adjustable according to the requirement of patient's age group.

## 10.6   CONCLUSIONS

There is a global health catastrophe as a result of the COVID-19 epidemic, and thousands of people are dying every day. We can minimize the losses or fatality rate by administrating proper treatments and making use of technology. During the second wave of COVID-19, the major problem was the inadequate supply of oxygen. India has had severe consequences as the virus hit the young population. Hence, it becomes necessary to come up with future control strategies. In this work, we have proposed a cost-effective and user friendly IoT-based life saving device equipped with Ambu bag for SARS-CoV-2 patients. The proposed system offers an excellent solution faced by COVID-19 patients when they gasp for breath for due to scarcity of oxygen

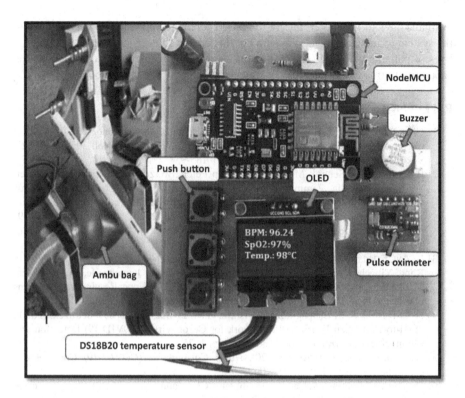

**FIGURE 10.13(B)** Original photo of displayed sensor data over the Blynk server.

**TABLE 10.2**

**Measured Values of SpO$_2$, Pulse Rate, and Temperature for Five Different Patients/Users**

| Patient/User | Age | SpO$_2$ (%) | Pulse (BPM) | Temperature (°C) |
|---|---|---|---|---|
| Patient 1 | 25 | 97 | 75 | 37 |
| Patient 2 | 32 | 97 | 73 | 36 |
| Patient 3 | 34 | 93 | 70 | 40 |
| Patient 4 | 56 | 97 | 74 | 37 |
| Patient 5 | 23 | 97 | 75 | 40 |

cylinders. The system is equipped with an Ambu bag, which works as a life-saving device when the patient suffers from a sudden drop of oxygen and making it to the hospital for an oxygen cylinder is not feasible. The system is capable of measuring/ monitoring of pulse rate, SpO$_2$ level, and temperature, which is very important for COVID-19 patients. The system was tested with five patients and measured values of all parameters were found to be in good agreement with the values measured using available devices in market. Future IoT-based sophisticated features can be added to the system to increase its use. To sum up, this approach is crucial for prolonging the lives of patients with COVID-19 over the world. Future upgrades could include the capability to track additional physiological functions of the human body.

## REFERENCES

[1] Chen Wang, Peter W. Horby, Frederick G. Hayden, and George F. Gao. (2020). "A Novel Coronavirus Outbreak of Global Health Concern." *The Lancet*, vol. 395, no. 10223, pp. 470–473. DOI: 10.1016/S0140-6736(20)30185-9.

[2] Rothe Camilla, Schunk Mirjam, Sothmann Peter, Bretzel Gisela, Froeschl Guenter, Wallrauch Claudia, Zimmer Thorbjörn, Thiel Verena, Janke Christian, Guggemos Wolfgang, Seilmaier Michael, Drosten Christian, Vollmar Patrick, Zwirglmaier Katrin, Zange Sabine, Wölfel Roman, and Hoelscher Michael. (2020). "Transmission of 2019-nCoV Infection from an Asymptomatic Contact in Germany." *New England Journal of Medicine*, vo. 382, no. 10, pp. 970–971. DOI: 10.1056/NEJMc2001468.

[3] L. Zou, F. Ruan, M. Huang, Lijun Liang, Huitao Huang, Zhongsi Hong, Jianxiang Yu, Min Kang, Yingchao Song, Jinyu Xia, Qianfang Guo, Tie Song, Jianfeng He, Hui-Ling Yen, Malik Peiris, and Jie Wu. (2020). "SARS-CoV-2 Viral Load in Upper Respiratory Specimens of Infected Patients." *New England Journal of Medicine*. DOI: 10.1056/NEJMc2001737.

[4] N. El-Rashid, S. El-Sappagh, S.M.R. Islam, H.M. El-Bakry, and S. Abdelrazek. (2020). "End-to-End Deep Learning Framework for Coronavirus (COVID-19) Detection and Monitoring." *Electronics*, vol. 9, no. 1439, pp. 1–25.

[5] D. Hongru, and T. Goyea. (2020). *Novel Coronavirus (COVID-19) Cases*. Johns Hopkins University, Baltimore, MD.

[6] Hypoxemia: Symptoms, Causes, Treatments. Cleveland Clinic. (2020). https://my.cleve landclinic.org/health/diseases/17727-hypoxemia.

[7] M. Pourhomayoun, N. Alshurafa, Foad Dabiri, Ehsan Ardestani, Ahsan Samiee, Hassan Ghasemzadeh, and Majid Sarrafzadeh. (2016). "Why Do We Need a Remote Human-Health Monitoring System? A Study on Predictive Analytics for Heart Failure Patients." *Proceedings of the 11th EAI International Conference on Body Area Networks*, pp. 171–172.

[8] D. Serpanos, and M. Wolf. (2019). "IoT System Architectures." In *Internet-of-Things (IoT) Systems Architectures, Algorithms, Methodologies*. Springer, Cham.

[9] Vital Signs (Body Temperature, Pulse Rate, Respiration Rate, Blood Pressure). https://www.hopkinsmedicine.org/health/conditions-and-diseases/vitalsigns-body-temperature-pulse-rate-respiration-rate-bloodpressure.

[10] Pulse Oximetry Training Manual. World Health Organization. (2011). www.who. int/patientsafety/safesurgery/pulse_oximetry/who_ps_pulse_oxymetry_training_manual_en.pdf?ua=1.

[11] Rizzo. "Silent Hypoxia and Its Role in COVID-19 Detection." www.news-medical.net/news/202006003/silenthypoxia- anditsrole-in-Covid-19-detection.aspx.

[12] M.A.A. Harun, M.M. Hossain, M.A. Bari, N.A.S. Rubel, M.E. Karim, N. Siddiquee, M.D. Hossain, F. Sultana, A. Taous, A.M. Islam, and S. Khatun. (2020). "Pulse Oximetry Is Essential in Home Management of Elderly COVID-19 Patients." *Bangladesh Journal of Otorhinolaryngology*, vol. 26, no. 1, pp. 55–67.

[13] PulseOximeter Price in Bangladesh: BMA Bazar. https://bmabazar.com/product-tag/pluse-oximeter-price-inbangladesh/?fbclid=IwAR0j6Qt5CLT46gIPo3p_upeRq WFASL80A8Z01uI0FwnIYVHik1q8NRxXo.

[14] Deluxe Handheld Pulse Oximeter: Concord Health Supply. www.concordhealthsupply. com/Deluxe-Handheld-Pulse-Oximeter-p/cci-300m.htm?fbclid=IwAR3JXUIjTJv6T9a WoeQwiBROTTU0ErD_Fqh429f0f_8FxXUr_AaZdQHsv0A.

[15] Wrist Worn Pulse Oximeter: Concord Health Supply. www.concordhealthsupply.com/Wrist-Oximeter-p/75006.html.

[16] M. Evans. (2020). "COVID-19: How to Treat Coronavirus at Home. Patient, UK." https://patient.info/news-and-features/covid-19-how-to-treat-coronavirus-at-home.

[17] T.S. Arulananth, and B. Shilpa. (2017). "Fingertip Based Heart Beat Monitoring System Using Embedded Systems." *Proceedings International Conference of Electronics, Communication and Aerospace Technology (ICECA)*, pp. 227–230.

[18] M.M. Khan. (2020). "IoT Based Smart Healthcare Services for Rural Unprivileged People in Bangladesh: Current Situation and Challenges." In *1st International Electronic Conference on Applied Science* (pp. 1–6). MDPI, Cham, Switzerland.

[19] M.M. Islam, A. Rahmanand, and M.R. Islam. (2020). "Development of Smart Healthcare Monitoring System in IoT Environment." *SN Computer Science*, vol. 1, no. 3.

[20] B. Srividya, and V. Satyanarayana. (2018). "Personal Lung Function Monitoring System for Asthma Patients Using Internet of Things (IOT)." *International Journal of Research in Electronics and Computer Engineering*, vol. 6.

[21] P. Srinivasan, A. Ayub Khan, T. Prabu, M. Manoj, M. Ranjan, and K. Karthik. (2020). "Heart Beat Sensor Using Fingertip Through Arduino." *Journal of Critical Reviews*, vol. 7, no. 7.

[22] P. Pierleoni, L. Pernini, A. Belli, and L. Palma. (2014). "An Android Based Heart Monitoring System for the Elderly and for Patients with Heart Disease." *International Journal of Telemedicine and Applications*, vol. 2014, Article ID 625156.

[23] J.S. Prasath. (2013). "Wireless Monitoring of Heart Rate Using Microcontroller." *International Journal of Advanced Research in Computer Science and Electronics Engineering (IJARCSEE)*, vol. 2.

[24] V. Tamilselvi, S. Sribalaji, P. Vigneshwaran, P. Vinu, and J. Geetha Ramani. (2020). "IoT Based Health Monitoring System." *2020 6th International Conference on Advanced Computing and Communication Systems (ICACCS)*. https://ieeexplore.ieee.org/document/9074192.

[25] T. Reza, S.B.A. Shoilee, S.M. Akhand, and M.M. Khan. (2017). "Development of Android Based Pulse Monitoring System." *2017 Second International Conference on Electrical, Computer and Communication Technologies (ICECCT)*. https://research.vu.nl/en/publications/development-of-android-based-pulse-monitoring-system.

[26] I. Sutradhar, G.R. Das, M. Hasan, A. Wazib, and M. Sarker. (2019). "Prevalence and Risk Factors of Chronic Obstructive Pulmonary Disease in Bangladesh: A Systematic Review." *Cureus*, vol. 11.

[27] Daniel Limmer, and Michael F. O'Keefe. (2005). *Emergency Care.* Edward T. Dickinson, Ed. (10th ed.). Pearson, Prentice Hall, Upper Saddle River, NJ.

[28] www.ahajournals.org/doi/full/10.1161/circ.102.suppl_1.1-22. Accessed 29 March 2022.

[29] Jumlongkul Arnon. (2021). "Automated AMBU Ventilator with Negative Pressure Headbox and Transporting Capsule for COVID-19 Patient Transfer." *Frontiers in Robotics and AI*, vol. 7. DOI:10.3389/frobt.2020.621580.

[30] https://mumbaimirror.indiatimes.com/coronavirus/news/bjp-mlc-prasad-lad-demands-the-opening-of-parels-gandhi-hospital/articleshow/74907481.cms. Accessed 29 March 2022.

[31] S. Tanwar, R. Gupta, M.M. Patel, A. Shukla, G. Sharma, and I.E. Davidson. (2021). "Blockchain and AI-Empowered Social Distancing Scheme to Combat COVID-19 Situations." *IEEE Access*, vol. 9, pp. 129830–129840. DOI: 10.1109/ACCESS.2021.3114098.

[32] Shah, Het, Saiyam Shah, Sudeep Tanwar, Rajesh Gupta, and Neeraj Kumar. (2022). "Fusion of AI Techniques to Tackle COVID-19 Pandemic: Models, Incidence Rates, and Future Trends." *Multimedia Systems*, vol. 28, pp. 1189–1222. DOI: 10.1007/s00530-021-00818.

# 11 Security and Privacy in Federated Learning– Based Internet of Medical Things

*Swathi J., G.R. Karpagam, and Raghvendra Singh*

## CONTENTS

## 11.1 INTRODUCTION

The development and advancements in the internet and Internet of Things (IoT) has led to increased communication among the various entities in a system to transfer

DOI: 10.1201/9781003303374-11

data for analytics purposes. Nowadays, the use of IoT devices for monitoring the health-related parameters has improved and it is commonly referred to as Medical IoT or IoMT (Internet of Medical Things). In recent years, the healthcare sector has development phenomenally and has been a major contributor to revenue, research and employment. The COVID-19 pandemic is unfortunately one of the top reasons for the boom in the healthcare sector. Improvements in embedded technologies, communication protocols and wireless sensors networks are enabling the development of smart hospitals with IoT [1]. Years back, a physical checkup in the hospital was necessary for the diagnosis of diseases and prediction of abnormality in the human body. The doctors had to monitor the patients throughout the course of treatment within the hospital premises. This resulted in increased financial stress for the patient. Nowadays, devices to monitor the oxygen level, glucose level, etc., are available at home and a visit to the hospital is made only if the condition of the patient is abnormal. The technological advancement has changed the healthcare industry into a patient-focused system [2, 3].

The most commonly used MIoT devices in the healthcare industry are smart-watches, fitness trackers, wearable medical devices, $SPO_2$ monitors, blood pressure monitors, blood glucose monitors, infusion pumps, ECG sensors, motion detection sensors, GPS enabled smart soles, embedded devices, radio frequency identification (RFID)-enabled monitoring devices, etc. Figure 11.1 shows few of the commonly used wearable devices that collect medical data from users. The data so collected

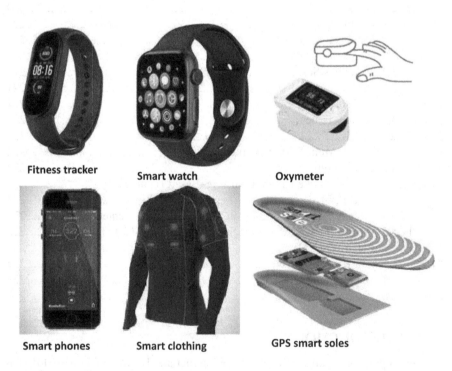

**Fitness tracker**     **Smart watch**        **Oxymeter**

**Smart phones**     **Smart clothing**     **GPS smart soles**

**FIGURE 11.1**   Wearable sensors.

may be analyzed to obtain meaningful inferences for assisting the doctors in providing better treatment plan.

A healthcare IoT solution not only monitors the health state of the patient but also helps to track details of all the people (nurses, technicians, specialists, intensive care units/intermediate care units [ICU/IMCU] in-charges, etc.) and assets associated with the hospital. GPS-enabled identification (ID) cards may be given to the users to monitor their movement. The assets may be enabled with RFID sensors which send data periodically to the cloud database. The medical IoT device has brought a significant transformation in the way healthcare systems work. Table 11.1 lists the areas of use of medical IoT devices and its benefits.

Hence, a smart healthcare framework may be developed by using IoT in two major aspects: i) IoT-based asset tracking and ii) IoMT-based disease prediction. First, highly expensive equipment can have embedded RFID chips to facilitate their tracking within and/or outside the hospital premises. Second, steps toward smart healthcare are smartphone-based appointment registration, mobile application–based test report inquiries and sending real-time signals to intelligent agents for diagnosis. Several research works are carried out for intelligent decision making by creating machine learning (ML) and deep learning models to make valuable predictions from the collected data [4, 5].

The above advantages of an IoMT-based healthcare system come at the cost of compromising the security and privacy of patient health-related data. Since it contains the personal data of patients, utmost importance should be given for the security and privacy of data. As per *HIPAA Journal* [6] of the U.S. Health Insurance Portability and Accountability Act, the largest data breach happened in 2021, where 715 times of 500 or more patients healthcare data is compromised. Hence, maintaining the sensitive personal information of patient is essential.

## TABLE 11.1
### Usage of IoMT and Its Advantages

| Use of IoMT | Advantage |
|---|---|
| **Automated asset tracking** | Periodic location monitoring of RFID-enabled assets |
| | Prevention of theft of assets |
| | Asset utilization management for optimized asset investments |
| **Patient and staff tracking** | Tracking location of patients and employees |
| | Assessment and prediction of patient flow |
| | Optimization of daily tasks of doctors, nurses and technicians |
| | Improvement in the safety of patients, doctors and other users of the system |
| **Patient health monitoring** | Monitoring and assessment of patients in their real-time environments |
| | Alerting healthcare professionals in case of abnormal health parameters |
| | Analysis of patient's data to improve treatment plan |
| **IoT-based components of a smart hospital** | Cloud-connected ward sensors for smart rooms lighting |
| | Efficient utilization of natural resources (use of sensors for water use, automatic power cutoff in empty rooms, etc.) |

### 11.1.1 Chapter Contributions

- A study on the various security and privacy issues associated with the federated learning framework is given.
- A privacy-preserving federated learning–based healthcare framework using Paillier cryptosystem is proposed.
- Agent-based realization of the privacy-preserving federated learning–based healthcare framework is discussed.
- Finally, a blockchain-based framework—along with future directions for further research in blockchain-enabled federated learning for healthcare systems—is discussed.

### 11.1.2 Chapter Layout

The chapter is organized as follows. Section 11.2 presents an overview of federated healthcare system. Section 11.3 provides the various security and privacy issues associated with the federated learning–based healthcare system. Section 11.4 deals with related work in the area. Section 11.5 discusses the proposed privacy-preserving federated learning–based healthcare framework. Section 11.6 explains the realization of privacy-preserving federated learning–based healthcare framework, and the agent-based system implementation is provided here. Section 11.7 deals with the blockchain-based federated learning environment. Section 11.8 deals with the conclusion and future scope of the suggested framework.

## 11.2 OVERVIEW OF FEDERATED LEARNING IN HEALTHCARE SYSTEMS

Advances in IoMT and communication technologies have generated huge volumes of medical data. Initially, AI techniques required centralized data collection and processing of data to make useful prediction. This may be difficult in realistic healthcare systems due to i) the voluminous data of modern healthcare networks and ii) data privacy concerns. Federated learning is a distributed platform that helps to maintain user privacy by creating and training a model at the end-devices rather than sending all patient information to centralized servers. Each data center and hospital stores patient details in the local server or private cloud and performs analysis of the data. After local training, the major inferences are shared among all the other entities which are part of the federated learning environment. Figure 11.2 shows an overview of the use of federated learning in healthcare systems. The patient-specific data collected in each hospital is maintained on the local server of each hospital. It contains the structured and unstructured data of the patients. It includes the X-ray, computerized tomography (CT) scan reports, magnetic resonance imaging (MRI) scan reports, prescriptions, lab reports, etc., of each patient. The local data pertaining to each patient is stored in a centralized server within each organization, which is used to make useful predictions.

The aggregation algorithm plays a major in federated learning. This algorithm runs on the global server. The global data center collects the local updates from all

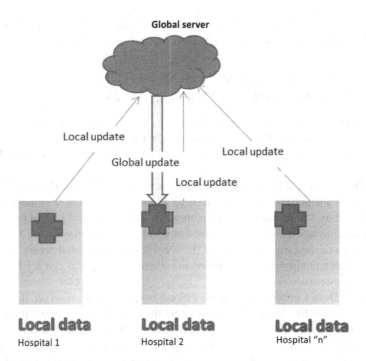

**FIGURE 11.2**    Overview of federated learning in healthcare systems.

the connected local entities periodically, runs the aggregation algorithm and comes up with the global update. The most commonly used techniques for aggregation are as follows.

1. **Federated Averaging Algorithm:** The device are trained with gradient decent algorithm and weights of the model are sent to the centralized server. The server returns the final weights by averaging the trained weights received from all the devices in the first cycle.
2. **Multi-Party Computation Averaging Algorithm:** This deals with two or more medical data centers that have varied privacy restrictions, and helps to hide the private data of each data center from the others. This algorithm deals with federated averaging algorithm, along with fully homomorphic encryption.
3. **FedProx:** This is used to handle heterogeneous data. It works by allowing varied amounts of work to be performed locally across devices dependent on their available systems resources, and then aggregating the partial solutions supplied from the stragglers (instead of omitting data obtained from them) [7, 8].
4. **FedMA:** This is designed to update the local parameter values of models that use CNN or LSTM in the local data center.

Federated averaging algorithm, SCM-Avg algorithm and FedProx could be used to handle structured data, while FedMA is used for unstructured data.

## 11.3 SECURITY AND PRIVACY ISSUES IN FEDERATED LEARNING–BASED HEALTHCARE SYSTEMS

While setting up a federated learning–based healthcare system, the confidentiality, integrity and availability of the data must be adhered since it deals with the private data of the patient. Security attacks can occur in any of the following three entities.

- **Within Hospital Premises:** A data breach may happen in the local data center if the patient data is not secured properly within the hospital premises. It may compromise the confidentiality and integrity of patient data.
- **Communication Network:** A wired or wireless system may be used as the medium of data transfer between the local server and global server in any distributed environment. It is prone to various security and privacy threats in the system.
- **Global Data Center:** This may be a cloud-based or physical server, depending upon the FL framework. It performs the role of aggregating data from all local servers and sending updated value to them. In certain cases, the global data center might be compromised and may tend to exchange the local data from a model with the other to generated revenue for itself. In such cases, data security of all data centers is compromised.

The *security threats* in federated learning environment that can cause high impact on the complete system developed are shown in Figure 11.3.

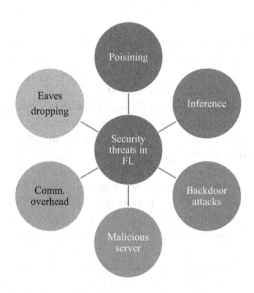

**FIGURE 11.3**  Security threats in FL framework.

### 11.3.1    POISONING ATTACKS

A hospital consists of multiple data centers. Several entities like lab technicians, nurses, physicians, specialists, doctors, etc., are associated with each medical center. All these entities have access to the training data, so there are high chances of data being modified. The local training dataset or the local model may be tampered with, leading to data poisoning and model poisoning, respectively; hence, it leads to propagation of incorrect parameters within the model.

### 11.3.2    INFERENCE ATTACKS

By probing an ML model with varied input data and weighing the result, inference attacks try to disclose secret information. Inference attacks can be in a variety of forms. Membership inference (MI) is a sort of attack in which the adversary attempts to reconstruct the records used to train the model. Attribute inference (AI) is another sort of inference attack in which an attacker has only a partial understanding of a training record and attempts to estimate the missing attributes by modifying them until the model reaches its peak performance.

### 11.3.3    BACKDOOR ATTACKS

A backdoor attack is a method of injecting a harmful task into an existing model while maintaining the task's correctness. Backdoor attacks are difficult and time-consuming to detect because they do not affect or modify the accuracy of the local model or the training data. It simply performs malicious tasks like collecting private data of patients and disclosing them to third parties. Trojan threats behave in a similar manner as backdoor attacks.

### 11.3.4    MALICIOUS SERVERS

The global central server contains the data parameters of all the local hospitals. Once these parameter values from centralized servers are captured and interpreted, it may lead to disruption of the entire FL system. The security of the entire system may be at risk. Several attackers may try to take control over the centralized server for easy access to complete data parameters. Such servers are referred to as malicious servers.

### 11.3.5    COMMUNICATION OVERHEAD

Any distributed system is a collection of multiple entities connected via wired or wireless medium. Transferring large amounts of raw data over the network may lead to bandwidth issues and may also lead to security issues in the system. Multiple nodes may try to send and receive data at the same time, leading to communication overhead. Several messages may be dropped due to communication network failure.

### 11.3.6    EAVESDROPPING

Theft of information from one device to another device while the user is sending or receiving data over a network is known as an eavesdropping attack. This type of attack is difficult to detect because the attacker silently steals the private data of the patients without affecting the regular transmission. This data can be used for organ theft, increased interest rates of medical insurance, etc. Although FL-based systems insist on sharing the local training model parameters instead of their actual data, the attackers try to extract meaning information of the original data with the available model parameter values that is being transmitted.

### 11.3.7 PRIVACY ISSUES

The major *privacy issues* in federated learning environment are as follows.

1. **Membership Inference Attacks:** The training data from the global server is hacked using sophisticated technologies and the same is used to predict the designed model. Once an inference about the global model is made, the same may be used to attack the local server—thereby leading to a crash of the entire system.
2. **Accidental Data Outflow and Rebuilding through Inference:** Patient data from the local center may be released accidentally. Using generative adversarial networks (GANs), the malicious client generates synthetic data that is similar to local training data. This helps to retrieve sensitive information from other clients [9].

## 11.4 RELATED WORK

Several research works have been carried out in the area of federated learning to preserve security and privacy of medical data [10]. The major ones are listed as follows.

### 11.4.1 SECURE MULTI-PARTY COMPUTATION

In secure multi-party computation (MPC) protocol, multiple data centers and hospitals train their model locally and exchange their model parameters without revealing their local data. In the first data center, an arbitrarily large number is added with the local parameter value and shared with the second data center. The second data center adds its local parameter value to the value obtained from first center and sends the result to the next. The same procedure is continued till the last data center. As a result, all nodes are aware of the average model parameters, but none of them can identify the local parameter of another node.

MPC protocol is secure because the data centers learn only the final global parameter value, and no other information about the patient's private data.

### 11.4.2 DIFFERENTIAL PRIVACY

Differential privacy is the concept that if the impact of making a random single substitution in the database is minimal enough, the query result cannot be used to infer much about a specific individual, and as a result, this helps to provide privacy of data.

Using the idea of differential privacy in federated learning helps to enhance privacy and security of the healthcare sector.

## 11.5  PRIVACY-PRESERVING FEDERATED LEARNING–BASED HEALTHCARE FRAMEWORK (PPFLHF)

The objective of the chapter is to propose a privacy-preserving federated learning–based healthcare framework (PPFLHF). Every hospital is associated with at least one medical data center. Medical data centers contain the structured and unstructured data of the patients. It includes the X-ray, CT and MRI scan reports, prescriptions, lab reports, etc., of each patient. The local data pertaining to each patient is stored in a centralized server within each organization, as shown in Figure 11.4.

First, useful predictions can be made with the available data in a medical data center by designing a model and training it locally. The same happens in every other medical data center. Second, the personal health data of individuals can be obtained from smartphones and other wearable devices. The data recorded by these devices is sent to a central location for storage and processing. Hence, the data from multiple vendors are collected, standardized and converted into a consistent format which could then be analyzed or used for ML training and inferencing. Finally, the data of a specific patient from the medical data center and the standardized third-party data center can be aggregated using a unique ID in the global data center.

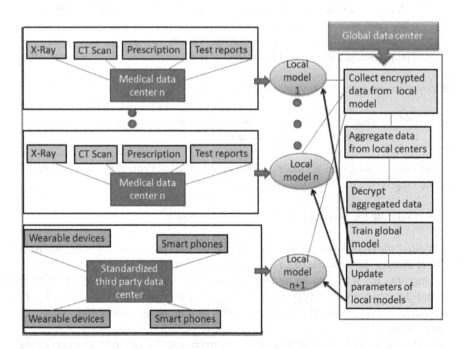

**FIGURE 11.4**  FL-based healthcare framework.

The global data model is then trained with the encrypted data from multiple data centers and the model parameters are passed back to local centers. The framework in Figure 11.4 would function efficiently if there is low computation overhead, and— more importantly—if the security and privacy preservation in the network, medical data center, standardized third-party data center and global data center is not compromised.

### 11.5.1 Privacy Preservation of Data in Medical Data Centers

To ensure the privacy of the patient's personal and health data in medical centers, a modified Paillier cryptosystem is used [11, 12]. Paillier cryptosystem is a combination of public key cryptography and additive homomorphism. The major operations on the cipher texts are i) two cipher texts can be added and ii) a cipher text can be multiplied by a plain text.

Key generation of an existing Paillier cryptosystem works as follows.

- Pick two large prime numbers p and q, randomly and independently. Confirm that gcd(pq, [p − 1][q − 1]) is 1. If not, start again.
- Compute n = p × q.
- Define function $L(x) = (x − 1)/n$.
- Compute λ as lcm (p − 1, q − 1).
- Pick a random integer g in the set $Z_{n^2}^*$ (integers between 1 and n2).
- Calculate the modular multiplicative inverse $\mu = (L\ (g^\lambda \bmod n^2))^{-1} \bmod n$. If μ does not exist, start again from step 1.
- The public key is (n, g). Use this for encryption.
- The private key is λ. Use this for decryption.

Encryption can work for any m in the range $0 \leq m < n$:

- Pick a random number r in the range $0 < r < n$.
- Compute cipher text $c = g^m .r^n \bmod n^2$.

Decryption presupposes a cipher text created by the encryption process, so that c is in the range 0 < c <n 2:

- Compute the plaintext $m = L(c^\lambda \bmod n^2).\mu \bmod n$.

A trusted party is involved to generate private and public keys for the local and global data centers. In the original Paillier cryptosystem, each medical data center encrypts the local model update parameters with the secret key $SK_p$ and the global data center can decrypt arbitrary ciphertexts with the public key $PK_p$. For this reason, it becomes infeasible to use this technique for secure multi-party data aggregation.

In the modified encryption algorithm, the parameter "n" in public key of the original Paillier $PK_p$ is split into "m parts" depending upon the number of medical centers that are part of the FL environment, then secret keys are generated with the split "n" for each data center.

$$n \rightarrow \{n_1, n_2; \ldots ; n_m\}$$

Generated secret keys : $SK_{MCi} = S_t^{\frac{i}{n}} \bmod n^2$

Here the $SK_P$ is replaced with a specific key $SK_{MCi}$ for each medical data center. Hence, the original Paillier secret key $SK_P$ cannot decrypt cipher texts encrypted with modified secret key $SK_{MCi}$. Specifically, each medical data center uses its secret key $SK_{MCi}$ to encrypt its local model attribute, which cannot be decrypted by central server. This helps to address the membership inference attacks and the unintentional data leakage at the global server.

Each local data center encrypts the local model parameters with the secret key generated. The data from each medical center $MC_1, MC_2 \ldots MC_M$ is encrypted with its own secret key $SK_{MCi}$ and is sent to the global data center. The global data center then aggregates the data obtained for all the medical centers, then use its key to decrypt the aggregated data. This prohibits the global data center from obtaining the parameter values from the local medical center. The global parameter values are then combined and delivered back to all medical data centers.

### 11.5.2 PRIVACY PRESERVATION IN THE STANDARDIZED THIRD-PARTY DATA CENTER

In the healthcare industry, there are numerous suppliers who produce a wide range of products. Most of these goods claim to follow traditional conventions and protocols during the design process. There is, however, a flaw in the logic. The third-party database collects health data from IoMT devices such smartwatches, fitness trackers, blood pressure monitors, blood glucose monitors, infusion pumps, ECG sensors, motion detection sensors, GPS equipped smart soles and so on. The information gathered by these devices is heterogeneous in nature. Thus, before the data can be used to train the prediction model, it must first be standardized [13].The data collected from the smart devices are connected to a server. Each organization has its own storage module, which varies from the others. In order to make useful predictions, the data from multiple industries are to be preprocessed and trained either by a centralized entity or by distributed entities.

To avoid an attack on IoMT devices, cryptographic algorithms may be used, along with identity authentication, authorization management and password encryption. Also, secure pairing protocols must all be evaluated and used by medical and sensor devices. Network protocols like Wi-Fi, Bluetooth, Zigbee, etc., must be integrated with secure routing algorithms and message integrity verification techniques [14].

## 11.6  REALIZATION OF PPFLHF

The privacy-preserving FL-based healthcare framework can be viewed as agent-based software system in which individual software agents interact with each other

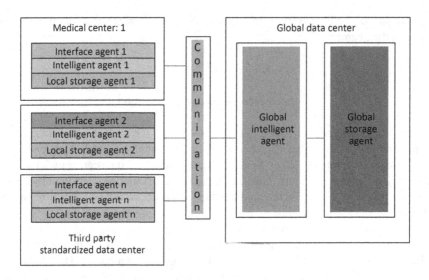

**FIGURE 11.5**    Agent-based PPFLHF system.

in a collaborative manner, autonomously following their individual objectives, gaining access to resources and services, and occasionally generating effects for the entities that instigated those software agents.

Figure 11.5 shows the various agents required for the implementation of the PPFLHF system. An *interface agent* is implemented in each medical data center to provide assistance to a user with computer-based tasks. It interacts with the users of the hospital system like the receptionist, lab technicians, specialists, doctors, nurses and patients. An *intelligent agent* is maintained in each medical data center. It does the collection of data and preprocessing of data, and it trains the local model in each data center. It encrypts the local parameter values of the model and sends it to the global intelligent agent via the communication agent.

The *communication agent* acts as an intermediator between the local and global intelligent agents. It should ensure secure communication of data and avoid communication overhead. The *global intelligent agent* aggregates the data from local agents and decrypts model parameter values. It validates the data sent by the local agents and then broadcasts the updated values to all the entities in the system. The local models are then trained with the updated values for better accuracy and prediction. A *local agent* and a *global storage agent* are required for storing the raw data collected from the users. A local server or cloud-based storage can be used within each medical center or hospital. Each agent communicates with another agent to accomplish the overall task.

Hence, the major roles of the various agents are as follows.

1. **Interface Agent**
   - **Role:** Collection of data.
   - **Input:** Obtained from IoMT devices, lab reports and prescriptions.
   - **Output:** Raw data passed to intelligent agent.

2. **Intelligent Agent**
   - **Role:** Preprocessing of data obtained from interface agent, training the local model with the data, calculating the model parameters, encrypting the local model parameters using Paillier encryption, and storing data and model predictions in local storage.
   - **Input:** Obtained from interface agent.
   - **Output:** Transferring encrypted data to communication agent.
3. **Communication Agent**
   - **Role:** Secure communication of local model parameters from local data center to global data center.
   - **Input:** Obtained from local intelligent agent.
   - **Output:** Transferring encrypted data to global intelligent agent.
4. **Global Intelligent Agent**
   - **Role:** Aggregation of encrypted messages from all medical centers, decrypting model parameter values using FedAvg algorithm, updating the global model with new values, transferring new parameter values to local agents and storing the values on an immutable global storage framework.
   - **Input:** Obtained from local intelligent agent via communication agent.
   - **Output:** Transferring updated parameters to individual data centers using communication agent.

## 11.7   BLOCKCHAIN-BASED PPFLHF

The blockchain framework is becoming popular these days due to its inherent features that make security and privacy an integral part of its framework. Since the medical data deals with the private information of patients, the privacy and security of data should not be compromised. The features of a blockchain-based system enable maintaining the security and privacy of data. The major features of blockchain that makes it adaptable with federated learning framework is that it is a distributed and decentralized framework that provides immutability and traceability of the stored records [15–19]. BinDaaS is a framework for integrating deep learning and blockchain for securing patient data which uses lattice key and signature verification to avoid quantum attacks [20].

The agent-based system discussed in the previous section may be deployed on a blockchain framework. The blockchain framework may be distributed across all the medical data centers and the centralized global server, as shown in Figure 11.6. Every medical data center may be considered as a node in the network. After a local training of the model, the parameter values are sent to the global server. The global server aggregates the value and comes up with the new value. Every updated model parameter value may be added as a new node in the blockchain network.

A block will consist of the header and the data fields. The major components are as follows.

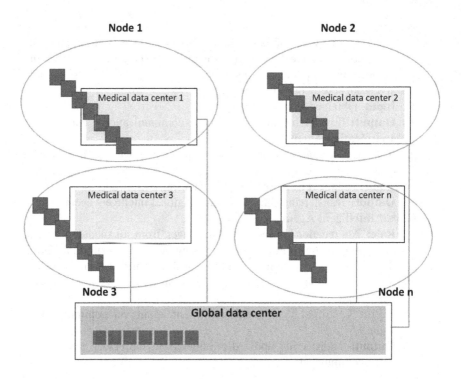

**FIGURE 11.6**   Blockchain-based PPFLHF system.

## Header

Time stamp, the time when the global server broadcasts the message to its local
   servers.
Hash of the previous block.

## Data

Model parameter values of the global medical center.
There are three major types of blockchain systems [21, 22]:
1.  Public blockchain.
2.  Private blockchain.
3.  Consortium blockchain.

Public blockchain is permissionless, i.e., anyone with an internet connection can
be a part of the system. The complete data may be available for all users who are
part of the system. A private blockchain works within an organization only and is
accessible for a group of people only. A consortium blockchain is a combination of
public and private blockchain. It provides more security when compared to public
blockchain and is less restrictive when compared to private blockchain. This framework is most suitable for a healthcare system. Since several entities are part of the

blockchain framework, the new blocks are to be validated using consensus mechanisms. Consensus mechanism is an agreement to be followed by all entities in the system to add a new block into the blockchain [23–28].

The following are the most often used platforms for building blockchain frameworks. One of the most popular open-source blockchain, Ethereum, serves as the foundation for the creation of other applications. The Linux Foundation's development of Hyperledger Fabric aims to boost the use of blockchain technology across several industries. IBM blockchain was designed only for personal use with the goal of building a platform for open business transactions. Permission networks are built using the multichain open-source blockchain framework. This is employed by several businesses, both internal and external. A joint project using Ethereum and brainbot technology is called Hydrachain. Since it is an extension of the Ethereum platform, private ledgers that are beneficial to businesses can be created using it. R3 Corda is a permissioned blockchain and it focuses on interoperability ease of integration with the legacy system. It is mainly used in healthcare, trade and finance, and supply chain management.

However, any of these platforms could be used to create the blockchain framework and integrate it with the existing healthcare systems.

## 11.8 CONCLUSION AND FUTURE SCOPE

This chapter gives a quick summary of how federated learning is used in healthcare systems. Attention is then shifted to the security and privacy concerns that may arise as a result of the development of a federated learning–based healthcare system. The use of a modified Paillier cryptosystem to create an efficient privacy-preserving federated learning–based healthcare system was discussed, then an agent-based realization of the system was examined and its implementation on a blockchain framework was introduced. As a future enhancement, the storage agent may be implemented using blockchain technology and its associated communication overhead may be analyzed. Appropriate consensus mechanisms may be proposed for federated learning healthcare frameworks to ensure security of private patient data.

## REFERENCES

[1] Z. Ali, M.S. Hossain, G. Muhammad, and A.K. Sangaiah. (2018). "An Intelligent Healthcare System for Detection and Classification to Discriminate Vocal Fold Disorders." *Future Generation Computer Systems*, vol. 85, pp. 19–28.

[2] G. Yang, L. Xie, M. Mantysalo, Xiaolin Zhou, Zhibo Pang, Li Da Xu, Sharon Kao-Walter, Qiang Chen, and Li-Rong Zheng. (2014). "A Health-IoT Platform Based on the Integration of Intelligent Packaging, Unobtrusive Bio-Sensor, and Intelligent Medicine Box." *IEEE Transactions on Industrial Informatics*, vol. 10, no. 4, pp. 2180–2191.

[3] Y. Yan. (2013). "A Home-Based Health Information Acquisition System." *Health Information Science and Systems*, vol. 1, p. 12.

[4] S. Syed, M.S. Jabeen, and A. Alsaeedi. (2019). "Smart Healthcare Framework for Ambient Assisted Living Using IoMT and Big Data Analytics Techniques." *Future Generation Computer Systems*, vol. 101, pp. 136–151.

[5] S.H. Almotiri, M.A. Khan, and M.A. Alghamdi. (2016). "Mobile Health (m-health) System in the Context of IoT." *IEEE 4th International Conference on Future Internet of Things and Cloud Workshops (Fi- CloudW)*, pp. 39–42.

[6] Hippa Journal. (2022). www.hippajournal.com: https://www.hipaajournal.com/2022-healthcare-data-breach-report/

[7] A. Nilsson, S. Smith, G. Ulm, E. Gustavsson, and M. Jirstrand. (2018). "A Performance Evaluation of Federated Learning Algorithms." In *Proceedings of the Second Workshop on Distributed Infrastructures for Deep Learning, DIDL 18*. ACM, New York.

[8] T. Li, A.K. Sahu, M. Zaheer, M. Sanjabi, A. Talwalkar, and V. Smith. (2018). "Federated Optimization in Heterogeneous Networks." arXiv:1812.06127. https://arxiv.org/pdf/1812.06127.

[9] Viraaji Mothukuri, Reza M. Parizi, Seyedamin Pouriyeh, Yan Huang, Ali Dehghantanha, and Gautam Srivastava. (2021). "A Survey on Security and Privacy of Federated Learning." *Future Generation Computer Systems*, vol. 115.

[10] J. Xu, B.S. Glicksberg, C. Su, P. Walker, J. Bian, and F. Wang. (2021). "Federated Learning for Healthcare Informatics." *Journal of Healthcare Informatics Research*, vol. 5, pp. 1–19. DOI: 10.1007/s41666-020-00082-4.

[11] A. Verma, P. Bhattacharya, Y. Patel, K. Shah, S. Tanwar, and B. Khan. (2022). "Data Localization and Privacy-Preserving Healthcare for Big Data Applications: Architecture and Future Directions." In Singh, P.K., Kolekar, M.H., Tanwar, S., Wierzchoń, S.T., and Bhatnagar, R.K. (Eds.), *Emerging Technologies for Computing, Communication and Smart Cities: Lecture Notes in Electrical Engineering* (vol. 875). Springer, Singapore. DOI: 10.1007/978-981-19-0284-0_18.

[12] Fengwei Wang, Rongxing Lu, Yandong Zheng, and Hui Li. (2021). "Achieve Efficient and Privacy-Preserving Disease Risk Assessment Over Multi-Outsourced Vertical Datasets." *IEEE Transactions on Dependable and Secure Computing*. https://www.researchgate.net/publication/345450417_Achieve_Efficient_and_Privacy-preserving_Disease_Risk_Assessment_over_Multi-outsourced_Vertical_Datasets.

[13] D.C. Nguyen, P. Cheng, M. Ding, D. Lopez-Perez, P.N. Pathirana, J. Li, A. Seneviratne, Y. Li, and H.V. Poor. (2021). "Enabling AI in Future Wireless Networks: A Data Life Cycle Perspective." *IEEE Communications Surveys & Tutorials*, vol. 23, pp. 553–595.

[14] Bikash Pradhan, Saugat Bhattacharyya, and Kunal Pal. (2021). "IoT-Based Applications in Healthcare Devices." *Journal of Healthcare Engineering*, vol. 2021, p. 6632599. DOI: 10.1155/2021/6632599

[15] J. Qiu, X. Liang, S. Shetty, and D. Bowden. (2018). "Towards Secure and Smart Healthcare in Smart Cities Using Blockchain." *IEEE International Smart Cities Conference*, pp. 1–4.

[16] Deloitte's 2019 Global Blockchain Survey: Blockchain Gets Down to Business. (2019). https://www2.deloitte.com/content/dam/Deloitte/se/Documents/risk/DI_2019-global-blockchainsurvey.pdf.

[17] E. Androulaki, A. Barger, V. Bortnikov, C. Cachin, K. Christidis, A. De Caro, D. Enyeart, C. Ferris, G. Laventman, Y. Manevich, and S. Muralidharan. (April 2018). "Hyperledger Fabric: A Distributed Operating System for Permissioned Blockchains." *Proceedings of the Thirteenth EuroSys Conference*, pp. 1–15.

[18] Zhilin Wang, and Qin Hu. "Blockchain-Based Federated Learning: A Comprehensive Survey." https://arxiv.org/abs/2110.02182.

[19] Umesh Bodkhe, Sudeep Tanwar, Karan Parekh, Pimal Khanpara, Sudhanshu Tyagi, Neeraj Kumar, and Mamoun Alazab. (2020). "Blockchain for Industry 4.0: A Comprehensive Review." *IEEE Access*, vol. 8, pp. 79764–79800.

[20] P. Bhattacharya, S. Tanwar, U. Bodkhe, S. Tyagi, and N. Kumar. (1 April–June 2021). "BinDaaS: Blockchain-Based Deep-Learning as-a-Service in Healthcare 4.0

Applications." *IEEE Transactions on Network Science and Engineering*, vol. 8, no. 2, pp. 1242–1255. DOI: 10.1109/TNSE.2019.2961932.

[21] R. Gupta, Arpit Shukla, Parimal Mehta, Pronaya Bhattacharya, Sudeep Tanwar, Sudhanshu Tyagi, and Neeraj Kumar. (2020). "VAHAK: A Blockchain-Based Outdoor Delivery Scheme Using UAV for Healthcare 4.0 Services." *IEEE INFOCOM 2020 — IEEE Conference on Computer Communications Workshops (INFOCOM WKSHPS)*, pp. 255–260. DOI: 10.1109/INFOCOMWKSHPS50562.2020.9162738.

[22] R. Singh, S. Tanwar, and T.P. Sharma. (2020). "Utilization of Blockchain for Mitigating the Distributed Denial of Service Attacks." *Security and Privacy*, vol. 3, p. e96. DOI: 10.1002/spy2.96.

[23] Kai Yang, Tao Jiang, Yuanming Shi, and Zhi Ding. (2020). "Federated Learning via Over-the-Air Computation." *IEEE Transactions on Wireless Communications*, vol. 19, no. 3, pp. 2022–2035.

[24] Qiang Yang, Yang Liu, Tianjian Chen, and Yongxin Tong. (2019). "Federated Machine Learning: Concept and Applications." *ACM Transactions on Intelligent Systems and Technology*, vol. 10, no. 2, pp. 1–19.

[25] Youyang Qu, Longxiang Gao, Tom H. Luan, Yong Xiang, Shui Yu, Bai Li, and Gavin Zheng. (2020). "Decentralized Privacy Using Blockchain-Enabled Federated Learning in Fog Computing." *IEEE Internet of Things Journal*, vol. 7, no. 6, pp. 5171–5183.

[26] V.A. Patel, P. Bhattacharya, S. Tanwar, N.K. Jadav, and R. Gupta. (2022). "BFLEdge: Blockchain Based Federated Edge Learning Scheme in V2X Underlying 6G Communications." *2022 12th International Conference on Cloud Computing, Data Science & Engineering (Confluence)*, pp. 146–152. DOI: 10.1109/Confluence52989.2022.9734213.

[27] Theodora S. Brisimi, Ruidi Chen, Theofanie Mela, Alex Olshevsky, Ioannis Ch Paschalidis, and Wei Shi. (2018). "Federated Learning of Predictive Models from Federated Electronic Health Records." *International Journal of Medical Informatics*, vol. 112, pp. 59–67.

[28] Qin Wang, Xinqi Zhu, Yiyang Ni, Li Gu, and Hongbo Zhu (2020). "Blockchain for the IoT and Industrial IoT: A Review." *Internet of Things*, vol. 10, p. 100081.

# 12 Use-Cases and Scenarios for Federated Learning Adoption in IoMT

*Jonathan Atrey and Ramani Selvanambi*

## CONTENTS

DOI: 10.1201/9781003303374-12

## 12.1 INTRODUCTION

The current medical scenario relies heavily on architecture that is either central server–based or utilizes the cloud for accessing data for purposes of analysis or processing. Due to the increase in the amount of data and the number of Internet of Medical Things (IoMT) devices to solve any given purpose corresponding to the current medical standards, this centralized method is neither appropriate nor efficient in terms of security and is also inefficient in terms of communication and networks with high scalability. When considered from a security perspective, significant concerns are raised, such as leakage of private or sensitive information. At times, centralized databases can even witness breaches which put the stored data at substantial risk. Thus, in order to eradicate these shortcomings, we use a decentralized artificial intelligence (AI) architecture called federated machine learning. By implementing federated machine learning, standing tasks can be implemented at a much more scalable level and can also be privacy-preserving. It is also very cost-effective and hence an up-and-coming solution for approaching the given traditional context while using AI techniques such as federated learning (FL).

Figure 12.1 represents a stated centralized machine learning (ML) architecture and a federated machine learning architecture.

The following are the primary steps involved when dealing with a federated learning network.

1. **Network Setup**
   - The first step in setting up a federated network is to choose a node for aggregation of all local outputs and updates.
   - Once chosen as an aggregation point, the remainder of the network requires local nodes for training its training data on locally run models. Thus, the aggregation server selects a number of underlying nodes

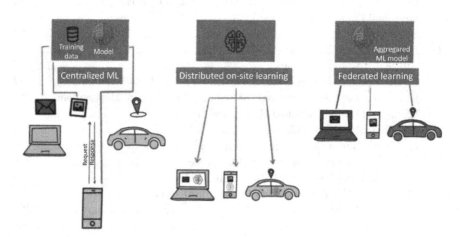

**FIGURE 12.1**    Centralized ML and FL overview.

to serve the stated purpose, which should be involved in the federated learning network.

2. **Training at Local Nodes**
   - After the set of local nodes and the convergence point is decided, the aggregation server distributes a model with all its corresponding required parameters to trigger the training of data locally within each local node of the network.
   - Each model that is trained locally keeps on producing updates; these may include values such as weights or other raw forms of data which are then offloaded onto the network to be passed on to the aggregation point.

3. **Aggregation of Updates**
   - All the updates received from the locally trained nodes then meet a point of convergence, i.e., the aggregation server.
   - Here, the aggregation server combines all the updates to form a resultant model.
   - The resultant model is achieved by averaging parameters received from local nodes of the federated network per element with renewed weights as per the data corresponding to the aggregation server.

4. **Repeat Until the Best Iteration Is Achieved**
   - Once the resultant model has been updated upon the first iteration of the network, it redistributes the combined parameters that were formed back to the local nodes for initializing the next iteration of training the data locally.
   - The network keeps on repeating this process till it has achieved its desired or optimal accuracy for its model.

Figure 12.2 represents a federated model that communicates with the aggregation server sending out a model for each local node to train on with global parameters, which are then altered based on the local training of data. It also depicts the transfer of each local node's updates being offloaded towards the aggregation server and the distribution of an updated global model post-aggregating the received parameters at the aggregation server.

To further emphasize the functioning of Figure 12.2, a key concept that brings about the working mechanism in federated learning is the FedAvg algorithm discussed further in Section 12.1.2. In Figure 12.3, federated network's steps are represented with examples of what can be considered a local training node. In the context of this chapter, a local data training node can be a hospital, home-based healthcare, or even personal gadgets like mobile phones, smartwatches, or other sensors.

## 12.1.1  RESEARCH CONTRIBUTIONS

In this chapter, the authors mainly aim to understand the various use-cases of federated learning with its integration in IoMT devices and deduce whether FL is a reliable concept based on multiple factors such as time, cost, scalability, and

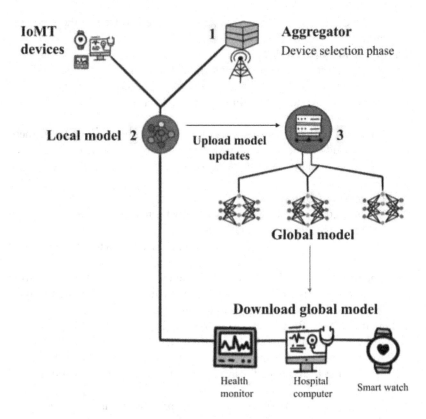

**FIGURE 12.2**   Communication between nodes in an FL network.

security. After an understanding of the significance of federated learning in the introduction section, the chapter initially presents information regarding the different types of federated learning, its requirements, and various limitations. Upon understanding the significance of federated learning and building a fundamental concept of understanding for readers, the authors present the essential scope of the chapter, i.e., use-cases of federated learning with IoMT. IoMT devices primarily help advance the field of healthcare. Thus, topics pertaining to healthcare such as managing electronic health records (EHRs), remote health monitoring, medical imaging, and other exceptional use-cases are discussed. The further sections discuss these use-cases in depth, followed by an additional section elaborating why federated learning can be a promising field from a healthcare perspective. A section based on real-world applications concludes the examination of the effectiveness and practicality of federated learning. Before concluding the chapter, based on the challenges required to be tended to, the future scope of federated learning is discussed in detail for an enhanced understanding of the topic. Finally, based on the different conclusions drawn from the various use-cases and empirical findings of recent use-cases, the authors state the conclusion drawn from the deductions proposed in the chapter.

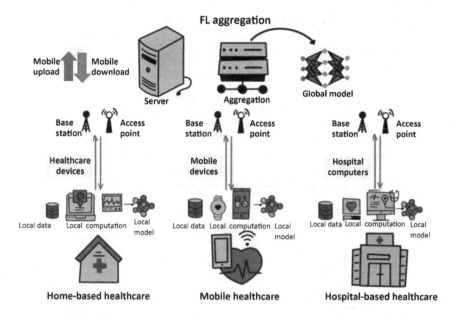

**FIGURE 12.3**   Medical-based FL architecture.

## 12.1.2   FEDAVG

Federated averaging (FedAvg) is an algorithm providing efficiency for communication for a vast sample space of clients holding distributed data for training models. In FedAvg, clients keep the data protected by training them locally and not sharing the actual data while creating a global model by passing their parameters onto an aggregation server. Stereotypically, most deep learning applications rely primarily on the alteration of their corresponding stochastic gradient descent (SGD). Thus, while developing FedAvg or federated averaging algorithm, authors in [1, 2] have applied SGD to an instance using federated optimization. In this case, a singular batch of gradient computation is applied every round of communication. This approach is efficient; however, it requires a large number of iterations for training a good model. Thus, [3] has utilized large-batch synchronous SGD similar to the experiments carried out in [4, 5]. In order to implement this approach, a fraction of clients is selected each round which computes the gradient of loss based on the data which these clients possess. This is referred to as FederatedSGD or FedSGD. Given such a set of FedSGD, the fraction of clients is considered a variable C equivalent to 1, and a set learning rate $\eta$ used by every client 'k' for computing the average gradient 'g' at the local models 'w'. The central server aggregates gradients and applies an update. Each locally trained client takes a single step of gradient descent on the current model using its local data and the server, then takes a weighted average of the resulting model as its parameters. After this, the local clients can be reiterated multiple times before taking the step, which involves calculating the weighted average. This approach is termed as FedAvg or federated averaging algorithm. Figure 12.1

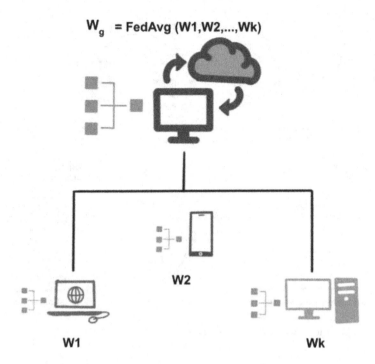

$$W_g = FedAvg\ (W1, W2, ..., Wk)$$

**FIGURE 12.4**    FedAvg.

and Figure 12.2 are the generalized illustrations of what goes behind the FedAvg algorithm. Figure 12.4 is another representation of the FedAvg.

In [4, 6], a number of challenges pertaining to federated learning algorithms have been reflected which include the following.

- **Statistical Challenges:** There is a significant difference between the distribution of the data. It is such that any available data value fails to be representative of the superset distribution.
- **The Efficiency of Communication:** The number of clients K is enormous, and it can exceed the average amount of training samples kept for inactive clients.
- **Security and Privacy:** For untrustworthy participants, further privacy safeguards are required. It's hard to guarantee that all clients are equally trustworthy.

### 12.1.3  TYPES OF FEDERATED LEARNING FOR IoMT

Following is a very commonly known categorization of forms of federated learning.

- Horizontal federated learning
- Vertical federated learning
- Federated transfer learning

These segregations mainly depend on the feature space and the sample space of the data being trained on the local node of the federated learning network.

A feature space is known as a set of all possible values from a selected feature or factors that make up a dataset. Furthermore, a sample space is the set of all possible outcomes for a test. Based on these terminologies and the differences between the types used by the local nodes in a federated learning network, we distinguish FL into different categories. For example, consider a classroom of people writing the same word on the chalkboard. In this case, the same word becomes our feature space which in this case is the same for all the students in the class, whereas the different handwriting of each student becomes our sample space.

Horizontal FL consists of IoMTs of the participant nodes training a global model shared with them by using data that consists of the same feature space but has a different sample space. It can be observed in Figure 12.5, which depicts the described scenario. This allows the local nodes on the federated network to implement the same learning model; for instance, a deep neural network model or a standard classification ML model for training data. From there, the trained models will then offload their parameters or learned outputs to be passed on to the primary server for aggregation and updating of the end model.

Vertical federated learning involves using data that have different feature spaces and the same sample space. An instance of VFL can be a smart healthcare environment in which multiple nodes of the system such as personal entities, government entities, hospitals, or insurance companies (different types of features) tend to the same crowd of patients (same sample space), wherein their combined training of data locally helps achieve creation of the final end model. Figure 12.5 and 12.6 is an illustration of what a Horizontal and vertical federated architecture looks like. Encryption methods are used for dealing with issues in the context of data overlapping and provide an additional layer of security for data exchange. Figure 12.7 represents the different FL categories and concepts of data overlapping.

The last of the most commonly used types of methods of federated learning is by using transfer learning. A transfer learning–based federated network consists of

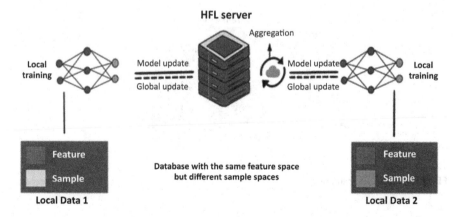

**FIGURE 12.5**   Horizontal FL.

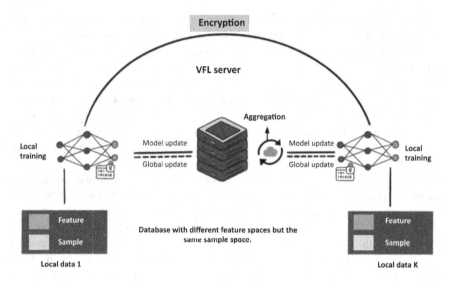

**FIGURE 12.6** Vertical FL.

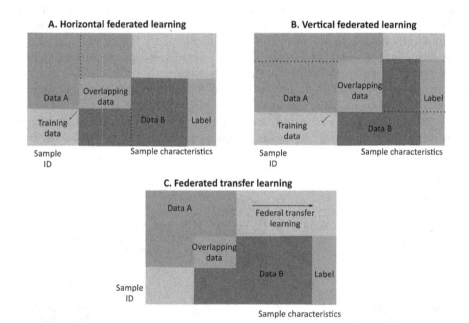

**FIGURE 12.7** FL categories.

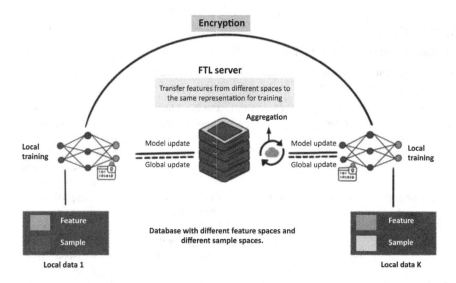

**FIGURE 12.8** Federated transfer learning.

different sample spaces and different feature spaces for each local training node. Thus, the transfer learning method helps reduce all the different values obtained and forge them into a common standard metric value for every local node on the federated network to train their model. Encryption is used to mask information of significant values in this type of federated network.

An example of federated transfer learning is having multiple medical centers which have different sets of patients (sample space) with different checkup facilities (feature space). Figure 12.8 is an illustration of transfer learning–based architecture.

## 12.2 LITERATURE REVIEW

Table 12.1 comprises a literature survey for federated learning for EHRs.
  Table 12.2 comprises a literature survey for FL for medical imaging.
  Table 12.3 comprises a literature survey for FL for remote monitoring using IoMT.
  Table 12.4 comprises a literature survey for FL for detection of COVID-19.

## 12.3 MOTIVATION

### 12.3.1 LIMITATIONS OF TRADITIONAL HEALTHCARE SCHEMATICS

- **Low-Security Aspects of Data:** A traditional artificial intelligence (AI) architecture makes use of central data warehouses or servers for the purpose of extracting resources for training data. This may contain data of significance to the patients which is at risk of being attacked. Since the server is centralized, in a situation where it is compromised, the compromised

**TABLE 12.1**

**Literature Survey: FL for EHRs**

| Ref. | Federated Learning Type | Local Training Nodes | Aggregation Servers | Observation | Drawbacks |
|------|------------------------|---------------------|---------------------|-------------|-----------|
| [1] | Horizontal | Healthcare center | Cloud-based | Combined learning approach used to train local nodes of the FL network | The conjunction of the stated algorithm for the local nodes must be ascertained effectively for the FL schematic |
| [3] | Horizontal | Mobile phones | Database server | Creating a model for predicting whether a patient should be admitted in the hospital using FL | Very simplistic approach and consists of a much less intricate analysis of the proposed scheme |
| [7] | Horizontal | Healthcare center | Database server | Differential confidentiality-based federated learning schematic is used for training the local nodes of the FL network | Requires several considerations for real-world implementation of the proposed model |
| [7] | Horizontal | Healthcare locations with radiology centers | Cloud-based | Utilizes split learning for training models of the local nodes in the federated learning network | Very simplistic and has no clear validity of the training difficulty |
| [8] | Horizontal | Healthcare center | Database server | Trained model, based on uncertain birth prediction using federated learning | Evaluation and analysis of the training difficulty are required at each local node |

server [26] under the influence of an untrustworthy party can lead to devastating effects. These effects include data leakage, which may be a threat to the privacy of sensitive and personal information. Even though these centralized servers have high efficiency in training huge amounts of data, the security aspects pertaining to them can be much better [27].

- **Lack of Training Datasets:** In order to build a machine learning model which can achieve good accuracy, it is crucial that it undergoes training on a good number of data samples so that it can know what to do with any test case. In some cases, the model may even adapt to figuring out outlier scenarios relatively well. However, in the case of medical-related aspects, datasets are very small and insufficient to produce properly fed models [28]. In

**TABLE 12.2**

**Literature Survey: FL for Medical Imaging**

| Ref. | Federated Learning Type | Local Training Nodes | Aggregation Servers | Observation | Drawbacks |
|------|------------------------|---------------------|--------------------|-------------|-----------|
| [9] | Vertical | Healthcare center | Cloud-based | A federated learning schematic for variations in types of the local nodes | The trained model learning must be ascertained |
| [10] | Horizontal | Magnetic resonance imaging (MRI) centers | Federated server | A schematic which offers better confidentiality for creating images of the brain | Improper evaluation of conjunction in the federated learning network |
| [11] | Horizontal | Websites with medical information | Database centers | Model trained for brain imaging using magnetic resonance imaging using federated learning | Various physical aspects of the proposed methodology need to be taken into consideration |
| [12] | Horizontal | Healthcare center | Database centers | Federated learning applied for identifying minor neuro-effects like headaches and loss of consciousness | A very simplistic approach that requires more dry runs and testing |
| [13] | Horizontal | Healthcare center | Database centers | Differential confidentiality-based federated learning schematic used for medical imaging | Improper comparison between traditional deep learning methods and federated learning techniques proposed |

desperate cases, the analyst must perform manual calculations, which may consume a fair amount of time and delay the data preprocessing period.

- **Low End-Model Performance:** As discussed previously, the issue of lack of sufficient training datasets may lead to a severe downfall in the required level of accuracy. Some medical test cases, such as cancer detection, can be based on very intricate details, and an incorrect prediction made for any patient may lead to extreme—even fatal—consequences for the patient. A very commonly known practice to increase the number of data samples is to apply data augmentation to the already existing dataset [29]; for instance, using general adversarial networks (GANs) for implementing data augmentation. However, data augmentation does not contribute much to very low-sampled datasets.

- **Network Latency:** There are several inconveniences caused during offloading of data within the network to different nodes. These inconveniences include the following.

**TABLE 12.3**

**Literature Survey: FL for Remote Monitoring**

| Ref. | Federated Learning Type | Local Training Nodes | Aggregation Servers | Observation | Drawbacks |
|------|-------------------------|----------------------|---------------------|-------------|-----------|
| [14] | Vertical | Mobile phones | Cloud-based | A federated learning approach for remotely monitoring and identifying activities of a person | Needs increased security standards |
| [15] | Federated transfer learning | Portable devices | Cloud-based | A federated learning approach for remotely monitoring and identifying activities of a person using transfer learning technique | No clarity regarding transmission costs and training for the proposed model |
| [16] | Horizontal | Healthcare center | Cloud-based | A federated learning approach that uses natural language processing (NLP) techniques for monitoring obesity | Needs increased security standards |
| [17] | Vertical | Mobile phones | Cloud-based | Using a mobile application for healthcare monitoring using a federated learning approach | Minimal comparison with independent and identically distributed (IID) learning techniques |
| [18] | Horizontal | Websites with medical information | Database center | Health insurance instance analysis for the entirety of the United States using federated learning | Terms and conditions for the acceptance of federal information use needs approval for real-world application |
| [19] | Horizontal | Mobile phones | Database centers | Sentiment analysis using mobile phones | Revision of policy for maintaining confidentiality in mobile-based federated learning and appropriate usage of data |

- Congestion of a network if the data is large in size; for instance, if it involves audio or video.
- Network latency is caused due to huge amounts of data.
- At times, the nodes in the network which train the data locally do not have sufficient transmission power to offload the data onto the network.

**TABLE 12.4**

**Literature Survey: FL for Detection of COVID-19**

| Ref. | Federated Learning Type | Local Training Nodes | Aggregation Servers | Observation | Drawbacks |
|------|------------------------|----------------------|---------------------|-------------|-----------|
| [20] | Horizontal | Healthcare center | Database centers | A combination learning-based federated network for detection of COVID-19 | The proposed model very simply lacks proper analysis |
| [21] | Horizontal | Healthcare center | Database centers | Presents multiple approaches in federated learning schematic for detection of COVID-19 | The conjunction of the algorithm used must be ascertained |
| [22] | Horizontal | Data clients | Data center | Identification of COVID-19 infections is done using a dynamic method of a combination-based federated learning schematic | Must be ascertained with respect to learning accuracy |
| [23] | Horizontal | Healthcare center | Database centers | A federated learning approach used for identifying COVID-19 using a model trained on X-ray imaging of the chest | The unclear mention of data leakage during transmission and required security standards |
| [24] | Vertical | Healthcare institution | Third-party aggregator | A federated learning approach used for identifying COVID-19 using a model trained on computerized tomography (CT) scans | Improper comments in context to latency during the training phase |
| [25] | Vertical | Healthcare institution | Cloud-based | A federated learning approach used for segmentation of COVID-19 area of the chest using an international standard dataset | Requires more comments in context of the conjunctions of updates and transmission of data in the federated network |

- **High Expense:** The offloading of a huge amount of data at a central server is very costly. All the above discussed issues caused during transmission can also require additional expenses to fix which makes it even costlier.

## 12.3.2 BENEFITS OF FL's INTEGRATION IN IoMT

- **Increased Data Security:** In a federated network, the local nodes only pass on the relevant parameters such as the gradient or weights for using it on the aggregated server, while the raw data remains at the local nodes. In comparison to a traditional AI centralized network, this is a much safer approach, since the compromising of any of the nodes might create far less damage to the overall network than the comparison of an entire central database. This significantly reduces the risk of major data leakage. Subsequently, if an attacker is to breach the network amidst data exchange, due to encryptions used and the different representations of the data, it becomes difficult for the attacker to make sense of the data obtained. This increases security drastically and keeps safer the sensitive and personal data relevant to each patient [30].

- **Minimal Loss of Performance:** In context with the change in the overall performance of the FL-based AI system and that of the traditional central AI system, there is very minimal performance change. The FL-based system allows us to perform tasks at a much higher scalability standard. The trade-off between the accuracy and utility of the system is very reasonable. However, the minimal change can be compensated by the security provided by the overall network, which is very significant.
- **Ease of Communication:** As far as the previously discussed transmission issues that are faced by traditional central server–based AI systems, an FL-based AI system significantly eradicates each issue. The parameters offloaded onto the network for transmission by each local node are generally much smaller in size [31] compared to raw data, and thus can be easily offloaded onto the network. Also, the power required to transmit these is significantly reduced while also improving the latency-related issues of the network due to the transmission data's smaller size. Furthermore, the network also saves a lot of bandwidth while reducing the risk of network congestion due to the scenario created.

### 12.3.3 REQUIREMENTS

- A trustworthy aggregation server.
- Secured transmission of data and parameters between the aggregation server and the local nodes of the federated network.
- Proper computational requirements for training the data at the local nodes must be met.
- Only the dataset with the proper number of instances for appropriate training must be considered for training the local nodes of the federated network.

### 12.3.4 KEY CHALLENGES

- Intercommunication between the local nodes.
- Balanced presetting of the local nodes such that each local node follows the same standard for training the datasets.
- Reduced quality of training of the local models due to lack of instances.
- Varying datasets are used by each local node for training and the data types such as audio/video or images.

- Issues of IID-less (not independent and identically distributed) data for the training of local nodes.
- Security concerns in a context, such as aggregation server attacks for sending off false updates by compromised local nodes.

## 12.4  FEDERATED LEARNING USE-CASES IN IoMT

In this section, we will shed light on the core federated learning applications corresponding to IoMT, such as the following.

- Federated EHR management
- Medical imaging using federated learning
- COVID-19 detection using FL
- Federated remote health monitoring

### 12.4.1  FEDERATED LEARNING FOR ELECTRONIC HEALTH RECORDS (EHR) MANAGEMENT

AI and deep learning have played crucial roles in identifying and gaining knowledge regarding various health-related issues and stages of disease development. These are made possible by using information that can be accessed from EHRs of various facilities such as hospitals and medical laboratories. These enable us to diagnose relevant diseases and carry out various research assessments for future use. The major issue pertaining to EHR is maintaining the privacy of the patients. The practice of removing the metadata of patients is not sufficient to maintain the required standard of privacy [32]. At times, other entities—apart from the hospitals—store the same sensitive or private information. These may include insurance companies, government databases, or private companies seeking personal information for health benefits, which results in making it difficult to conceal the relationship between the information and the patient.

Federated machine learning plays a vast role in fulfilling privacy-based shortcomings and helps carry out the solution searches just as effectively as traditional central-based AI systems using the data obtained from EHRs. Federated learning architectures also resolve the issue of handling privacy across multiple entities as mentioned before that use patients' sensitive and personal data. A very convincing approach to federated learning is proposed in [3], whereby multiple hospitals, along with a cloud-based server, implement a federated architecture that aims at preserving the privacy of the data as well as working on using data appropriately for creating a machine learning model. The methodology consists of using perturbation techniques used in machine learning on the training data. Each hospital trains its local neural network model using the prepared training data, and the output is pushed onto the federal learning architecture. In doing so, the creation of data that is very difficult to revert back to its original state—and also, the federated property of the system makes it difficult for the attackers to retrieve the information at the same time.

Another method introduced in [33] uses pre-recorded heart diagnosis–related data to predict whether or not a person fits the condition for being hospitalized. The training data obtained for serving the model comes from different sources, such as hospital diagnostic reports and patient gadgets like smartphones or smartwatches [34]. The models are trained locally on variables such as sex, age, and different physical characteristics of the patient. The configurations and the resultant outputs are then passed onto the federated scheme to a cloud server, where all these configurations and outputs of previously trained local models are combined to form a singular final model which uses a support vector machine classifier. The proposed method ensures that no private information is lost during an exchange of data from the local to the central cloud server—and thus, the original information remains undisclosed.

To add an extra layer of security, [35] proposed a methodology that integrates noise to conceal each update that takes place in the local models before it is transferred to the proceeding parts of the federated network. The network uses multiple prediction models to perform FL training in order to achieve variable accuracies and choose the best one of the lot. The method adopted in the chapter used is differential privacy-based federated learning, wherein privacy loss in each aspect is a measure that evaluates the performance of the network.

The methodology proposed in [7] uses a concept known as split neural networks (SplitNNs). As the name suggests, the local deep neural networks are split into different parts and are spread across different nodes of the federated network. The training data is trained at various radiology centers, and then the output generated is passed on to the network further. The training data is also split into different clients or can be retained at the corresponding client, as per the network's requirement. Each SplitNN prepares its corresponding weights, which are then passed around in the network. In this way, the nodes of the network prevent raw information from being passed around and hence withhold the security standards of the network.

A very reliable method of securing the data exchange between nodes of a federated learning network is by using blockchain [36]. The methodology proposed in [37] integrates a decentralized blockchain schematic to build federated learning networks. As we know, a common federated learning network may consist of local nodes which train the training set onto deep neural networks and the resulting data travels to a primary node for a final combination of the data obtained from various nodes to form an end model. However, when integrating blockchain, the concept of immutable ledger comes into play which is handled by the nodes of the federated learning network. This helps in secure communication and, if needed, data anonymity. Figure 12.8 consists of hospitals as its nodes that train medical or healthcare-related data onto deep learning neural nets or standard deep learning models from a blockchain-based federated learning network.

In a federated machine learning network, there are certain issues like the lack of a genuine method to validate transmissions, the lack of real-time monitoring of the communication in the network, and the lack of a particular algorithm enforced on the network for the selection of its local nodes for training. Thus, to deal with these issues, there have been several methodologies proposed [38] in which the authenticity of each node is evaluated in a given federated network. In a standard federated learning network, an aggregation server is selected which prepares the end model based on the updates it receives from all the local nodes training the datasets. However, as proposed in [39], a blockchain helps achieve further decentralization of the network and enables certain of its enhanced security aspects. Blockchain can also be used to store patients' personal information, along with their vaccination and medication details [40, 41]. The final model, which was originally prepared at the aggregation server, is now prepared at each local mode of the network using a block consensus mechanism in the federated learning network using a peer-to-peer method.

Research has proposed the increased security aspects offered by the integration of blockchain and how it works on eradicating any compromised nodes of the federated network and also prevents any potential attacks from taking place [42]. Here, the blockchain's key principles of competing to mine the next block are applied to the local nodes in the network, and every new block update is appended to the local ledgers. Figure 12.9 represents a single iteration of the blockchain-based federated learning network.

The following are the key steps involved in a blockchain-based FL (Figure 12.10).

1. Training data on local nodes using their local datasets.
2. After the preparation of each local model, the local nodes broadcast their trained models to all the other IoMTs (local nodes) of the network.

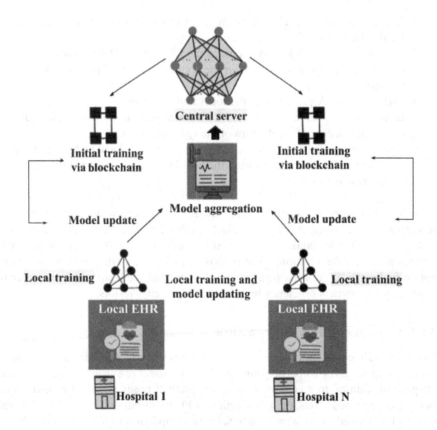

**FIGURE 12.9**   FL for EHR management using blockchain.

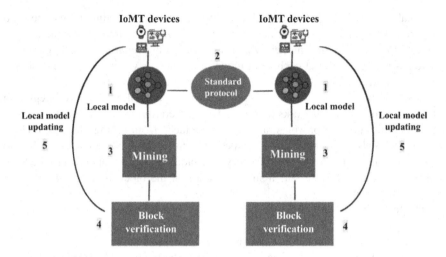

**FIGURE 12.10**   Single iteration of FL using blockchain.

3  In the exchange of each locally prepared model across the network, each
   local node verifies the model it receives.
4. After receiving each locally prepared model, each local node then focuses
   on mining the upcoming block for the chain based on all the models it has
   received.
5. If the new block prepared by the local nodes is then verified—based on a
   first-come, first-served basis—and if the block gets verified, it is then added
   to the local ledger of local nodes of the federated network.
6. Once a new block is added to the ledger, the network's local nodes then train
   the data locally again for creating the next block, and a new round of communication is initiated.

Similar to the previously discussed methods, other research [8, 43] proposes serious attempts at creating privacy-friendly federated learning networks in collaboration with multiple hospitals as the network's key participants for providing EHR
records and local data training. The proposed methodology in [43] states a combination of hospitals, patients, healthcare facilities, and medical centers in order to
enhance the analytical efficiency in order to obtain better results.

## 12.4.2  FEDERATED LEARNING FOR MEDICAL IMAGING

Using centralized AI techniques for creating models which predict image datasets may require all of its participants to submit personal or sensitive images for the
purpose of training to a central server. This method poses a high risk of the data
being compromised. Thus, the introduction of FL for building medical-based image
models has proved to be significantly safer in comparison to its traditional central
AI-based schematic.

In [44], a common image space is created for the nodes of the federated network by transforming all of the images used at each node. This kind of federated model mainly focuses on solving the variation between each node. It consists of a cloud-based global classifier. A generative adversarial network is set at each local node such that it generates an artificial image dataset by transforming raw data from each node as per the aimed image space. In this way, the network eradicates the issue of variations between each node of the network and the privacy of the raw data is retained. The proposed method saw an increase in the performance of the model by 0.13% compared to its corresponding non–federated learning–based method and also achieved a great accuracy score of 97% when used for classifying images related to prostate cancer.

Another methodology proposed in [44] uses federated learning for brain tumor segmentation. Each participant (for instance, magnetic resonance imaging [MRI] scanners) in the federated network comprises a deep neural network to train the data locally. Each local node has enough power to run its component deep neural nets and even consists of sufficient resources for training the model. The local nodes then offload the calculated weights of their deep neural nets onto the federated network to be transmitted to the aggregation server. The aggregation server uses averaging techniques to make sense and create a combined result. Federated learning may be self-sufficient in preventing data leakage; however, there are always risks of data alterations at different nodes of the network. Thus, in order to prevent this from happening, noise is added to the data which is used for training. This obscures the updates and makes it difficult to make sense of any data that is compromised.

A convolutional neural net based on the SqueezeNet computer vision model is implemented in [44] for classification purposes and has shown a significant rise in accuracy while testing its classification performance on various real-world datasets. Another implementation of FL on real-world datasets is done in [45], which classifies breast density. It even sheds light on the increase in performance compared to other techniques.

When it comes to X-ray–based federated learning imaging, a proposed methodology in [46] represents an FL network that detects minor neuro-effects such as severe headaches, rendering mindlessness, and losing consciousness. The local nodes of the network, in this case being the hospitals, comprise a convolutional neural network (CNN) based on DenseNet-121. The proposed model supports the propagation of involved features and their reuse, and even allows the reduction of parameters required to train the dataset in use.

### 12.4.3 Federated Learning for COVID-19 Detection

COVID-19 has led to devastating effects worldwide. Research proposes a solution based on deep learning techniques using CNNs to diagnose COVID-19 using chest X-ray [46], while other research proposes the security concern related to the condition created due to the pandemic and states how it becomes more difficult to implement various solutions for practical use [47]. Federated learning can be an effective technique for the prevailing conditions. In order to maintain privacy, the local nodes of the federated network plane are deep learning models using various datasets consisting of images, and after training, only offload their respective necessary parameters like gradient or weight to converge at the aggregation server. There is no need to share the raw information, which could give rise to a potential threat to sensitive data which is stored at each local node.

Author [20] propose a blockchain-based federated learning architecture that consists of an enhanced classification technique. This way, the data remains secure via two means: the federated network and the blockchain architecture. The test runs of the proposed model depict a very successful result, as well as very minimal loss of data, which was proved during the transmission phase. Author [48] proposed a contact tracing scheme to detect the spread of viral infection and to predict the required resources at the time of pandemic using ensemble forecasting model is proposed by *Prasad* et al. [49]. Author [21] proposes the use of different deep learning techniques such as MobileNet/ResNet, and a third proposed a CNN for COVID-19 diagnosis which is integrated into a federated learning schematic with increased confidentiality-boosted solutions. Among the tested neural networks, ResNet provided the best results with its integration in a federated schematic. Figure 12.11 is a representation of a federated learning network that consists of local nodes training the model using GANs. Once that model is trained locally, it then uploads its parameters onto the federated network for it to have conversed at the aggregation server so that the end model updates itself and the next round of training the local nodes initiates. This keeps happening until the desired results are obtained at the end model on the aggregation server.

A variation-based approach is proposed in [22] which is based on a combinational federated learning method that consists of a time trial. Each local node trains its

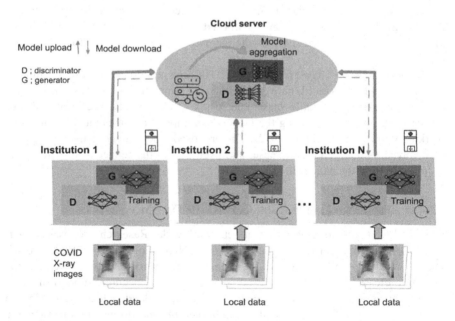

**FIGURE 12.11**   Single iteration of FL using blockchain.

model as fast as possible. The aggregation server provides a specific time limit within which all the local nodes which have finished offloading their model parameters are selected as the federated network participants for the aggregation procedure. If a local node is not able to finish within the given time interval, it is excluded from the aggregation round for that iteration of the process. Author [23] utilizes chest X-ray imaging to classify patients who are diagnosed with COVID-19 among a patch of people who may or may not have COVID-19. The local node of the federated network comprises a CNN to train its local data. All the local nodes; after training their model forward their gradient or parameters for updating the global model at the central aggregation server. The proposed methodology ensures that the data's confidentiality is maintained, which is very significant given the scenario created by the global pandemic. A similar approach is utilized in [50]. In [24], a combined learning-based is presented for the outlier effect caused in a patient's lungs by the diagnosis of COVID-19.

### 12.4.4 FEDERATED LEARNING FOR REMOTE MONITORING OF HEALTH

Due to certain diseases which require the patient to be quarantined, remote access to the patient has become a necessity in diagnosing the patient's condition and shielding from varying effects caused by the disease affecting the patient which may spread to other people. Thus, federated learning provides a promising solution to the proposed scenario. In [14], the proposed model consists of various peoples' houses as the local nodes for training the local learning models, and a central server for the purpose of aggregating the updated parameters passed by these local notes has been used. These networks have been built such that there is very minimal leakage of data; hence, preventing any sensitive data from being exposed. Each local node train sets on a CNN which then outputs a value and forms parameters based on an unaltered form of the dataset such that it deals with the issue of imbalanced and independent and identically distributed data while also improving the predictions at each local node. The proposed methodology achieved a good experimental result for both balanced and unbalanced datasets while also reducing transmission expenses. Author [15] proposes a federated learning architecture based on the principles of federated transfer learning for predicting the actions of a person remotely using their phones. Since the data is handled at the aggregation server and the phones are different in nature, the method of transfer learning has been considered. Transfer learning helps achieve a more structured training model. The proposed methodology shows an indication of an increased accuracy as compared to traditional federated learning algorithms. Another methodology proposed in [16] utilizes natural language processing with synchronous learning for monitoring obesity and the impact caused due to obesity while also keeping a lookout for other diseases.

Author [17] proposes a methodology that utilizes mobiles for creating an application that helps identify whether a person is in a proper condition or experiencing adversities such as falling or other inconveniences of such. The proposed methodology uses actual instances of the world to train local models, which use neural networks for predicting the condition and actions performed by a person. In [18], a federal dataset is being utilized from various websites for protecting diseases such as diabetes, heart-related diseases, and psychological diseases. Similar to most cases, the federated learning approach has achieved better accuracy and also provided a higher security standard to the architecture. In [19], a new methodology proposed uses the behavior with which a person uses their device keyboard for typing to predict the sentiments of a person, specifically whether the person is experiencing depression. The proposed method is called 'FedMood'. The key factors affecting the outcome of the trained model include the habits comprising a patient's keystrokes, the base of typing, specific use of words, and special characters or emoticons. The local nodes of the separated learning network train their datasets using deep neural networks and offload their relevant outputs to converge at the aggregation server. In [51], recovery of a person is examined using a federated learning approach with hospitals and healthcare centers as the local nodes of the federated learning network. The proposed methodology judges the outcome based on the patient's characteristics and the effects of the treatment on the patient.

## 12.5   EMPIRICAL FINDINGS AND DEDUCING SIGNIFICANCE OF FL BASED ON A FEW VERY RECENT USE-CASES

This section of the chapter browses through some of the relatively recent federated learning use-cases and their empirical findings in order to present empirical facts of the reliability of federated learning and its utility in security aspects. Author [52] proposes recent implementations and their corresponding architectures with validations for their corresponding empirical findings. Some of these have been discussed further in what follows.

In [53], the authors have proposed a two-phased federated natural language processing (NLP) methodology that uses phenotyping of comorbidities as means of drawing its output based on obesity. It was found that the proposed methodology not only increases the quality of data but also enhances the progressiveness of knowledge throughout the system. In the proposed system, the centralized phenotyping evidently raised the F1 score compared to the standard centralized approach with an F1 score of 0.726, which were valid due to its consistency with previously recorded values. When the federated learning approach was adopted in the phenotyping stages, its F1 score reduced slightly without having much significance of 0.03 decrement. When the centralized presentation of the system was converted to a federated learning environment, the phenotyping stage with centralized functioning displayed an F1 score of 0.715. When both the representation stage and the phenotyping stage followed the federated approach, by contrast, the F1 score increased to a result of 0.724, which was comparable to the standard centralized system; however, the federated learning approach had a higher precision of 0.753 compared to the 0.749 of the standard centralized system. This leads to the opinion that federated learning is a reliable option with enhanced privacy standards.

In [54], a novel framework known as federated topic modeling is proposed. It utilizes novel methods of Metropolis-Hastings, normalization of topics, and seamless integration. In order to determine the effectiveness of the proposed system, it was tested using its integration with an automatic speech recognizer. This way, the proposed system is also examined for its utility as a real-world application. The experiment conducted for the proposed system consisted of three parties of data, namely P1, P2, and P3. P1 consists of transcripts for 100 hours' worth of recordings, whereas P2 and P3 comprise transcripts corresponding to 50 hours of recording each. The evaluation metric used for the experiment is word error rate (WER). The lower the WER, the better the performance of the automatic sound recognition system. Automatic speech recognition (ASR) consisting of no additional capabilities showed a WER of 33.183%. The ASR consisting of topic modeling capabilities displayed a WER of 33.4%, 32.2%, and 33.0% for P1, P2, and P3, respectively. The ASR with federated topic modeling (FTM) displayed a WER of 30.0%. From the obtained results, it becomes evident that FTM is the go-to option out of these models. The proposed FTM model also solves two critical problems faced by industry-based topic modelers, which are scarcity of data and its corresponding privacy.

Author [55] proposes a federated learning approach in an attempt to achieve state-of-the-art (SOTA) performance while ensuring that the privacy of the data is retained. The proposed methodology aims at predicting hospital mortality among patients admitted to the intensive care unit (ICU). In the proposed methodology, two approaches have been taken. The first uses a linear regression algorithm, and the second using a multilayer perceptron. The evaluation metrics used for the experiment for determining the performance are AUROC (area under the receiver operator characteristic curve) and AUPRC (area under the precision recall curve). It was found that standard linear regression displayed an AUROC of 0.8152 and an AUPRC of 0.4030. The multilayer perceptron displayed an AUROC of 0.7925 and an AUPRC of 0.3900. In the federated setting, the linear regression model displayed an AUROC of 0.7890 and an AUPRC of 0.3659, whereas the multilayer perceptron in the federated setting displayed an AUROC of 0.7769 and an AUPRC of 0.3504. From this, it can be deduced that the performance was comparable to the traditional setting of the proposed system with an incremental difference in the privacy aspects of the system.

In [56], the difficulty of applying ANN in mobile networks is discussed. The proposed methodology is known as FEEL, i.e., Federated edge learning for portable devices such as mobiles is presented. In the proposed system, mobiles train parameters and offload them onto the network based on monitoring each patient. The offloaded parameters are then aggregated to build a model. Based on the results of the experiment, it was found that the traditional learning method of centralized architecture displayed a very stable and peak performance. The average F-score and accuracy were found to be 0.92 and 0.95. But in order to maintain privacy, this method cannot be implemented. Federated learning provides comparable results with an average F-score and accuracy of 0.88 and 0.91, respectively. From the results, it is evident that federated learning has fulfilled the privacy aspects of the system while maintaining comparable results. In [57], a framework for portable healthcare known as Fedhealth has been proposed. It deals with two major problems. The first problem is the existence of data in the form of isolated islands and how to tackle it. The second issue is the failure to train the model on the cloud while inserting personalized input. In order to do so, the dataset used comprised human activities such as walking, going upstairs, going downstairs, sitting, standing, and lying down. The dataset was based on 30 users, each wearing a smart gadget for their monitoring purposes. The dataset was divided into a train-test split of 0.7 and 0.3. Results were calculated for five patients based on three different learning algorithms—namely KNN (k-nearest number), SVM (support vector machine), and random forest—for comparison purposes. It was found that for an average accuracy of all five patients combined, KNN displayed accuracy of 87.2%. As for the SVM classifier, the average accuracy was 94.1%. The random forest classifier exhibits an average accuracy for five patients of 90.5%. Compared to all these methods, the proposed Fedhealth displayed a staggering average accuracy of 99.4%. Based on the results, it is safe to assume that in certain settings, federated learning is a much more promising approach.

In [58], data collected via means of a smart band for monitoring stress levels based on the behavior and activity of a patient's heart is applied using federated learning. In the proposed methodology, the authors have analyzed the training of smaller datasets using various classifiers to search SVM and neural networks. For purposes of the experiment, the proposed methodology utilizes three datasets. The proposed system was trained using all permutations of the datasets both in the traditional and federated settings. It was found that the highest accuracy found was when Dataset 1 and Dataset 2 were trained in a federated setting; they displayed an accuracy of 87.55%, whereas the traditional machine learning accuracy was found to be 82.58% for the same corresponding datasets. It was also found that compared to previously existing studies for the same types of systems, the proposed system outperforms all the previously existing ones. The proposed system utilizes the combination of federated learning and multilayer perceptron to achieve the corresponding results.

In the context of blockchain applications for federated learning in healthcare, [59] proposes a blockchain-based Deep Learning–as-a-Service (BinDaaS). It involves the integration of deep learning techniques along with blockchain technology for transferring private EHRs among different users. The proposed system works at two levels. The first level involves the authentication of users using a signature scheme based on lattice-based cryptography. The second phase involves the prediction of potential diseases based on current findings and various indicators of the patients involved. The proposed methodology has been compared to other previously existing systems in context to overall computation cost and computation cost for a final deduction of performance opinions. The system proposed by [60] displayed an overall computation cost of 505.72 ms, and a communication cost of 240 bytes for three messages exchanged. The system proposed by [61] displayed an overall computation cost of 532.43 ms, and a communication cost of 456 bytes for four messages exchanged. The system proposed by [62] displayed an overall computation cost of 26.40 ms, and a communication cost of 544 bytes for two messages exchanged. The system proposed in [63] displayed an overall computation cost of 96.64 ms, and a communication cost of 176 bytes for three messages exchanged. The system proposed by [64] displayed an overall computation cost of 5.665 ms, and a communication cost of 228 bytes for four messages exchanged. Compared to all these, BinDaaS showed an overall computation cost of 88.9 ms and a communication cost of 212 bytes for four messages exchanged. The proposed system also secures the network against various attacks such as replay attacks, side-channel attacks, distributed denial-of-service (DDoS) attacks, session-based attacks, provenance and auditability attacks, traceability attacks, signature-forgery attacks, signature verifiability attacks, quantum attacks, and known ciphertext attacks.

## 12.6    REAL-WORLD APPLICATIONS

A collaborative healthcare project [65] regarding the feasibility of federated learning in medical imaging was done by the University of Pennsylvania and various other institutions globally, for which major support was provided via Intel by leveraging the capabilities of Intel Xeon processors and Intel SGX (software guard extensions) used for running FL functions at hospitals and cloud servers. It also helps in accelerating deep learning algorithms and robust hardware tools and hereby building state-of-the-art models for the protection of sensitive data, achieving a 90% accuracy rate on image datasets.

All healthcare data utilized for model training and data communications has been connected with blockchain to allow traceability and monitoring. Nvidia Corporation took part in this initiative recently by joining a healthcare project with King's College London via Owkin platform running on NVIDIA Clara used to enable AI algorithms and trained at local hospitals to establish a platform for the UK's National Health Service (NHS) [66]. In future large-scale federated healthcare projects, NVIDIA is creating on-device AI platforms for implementing FL functionalities on smart devices to handle medical image and video processing at high data rates. Primarily focusing on data analytics of two diseases, Alzheimer's and Parkinson's, results prove that FL can improve training-based performance for improved accuracy and hence shows high applicability in medical image analytics in terms of image-related disease diagnostics.

Medical institutions based in China, Italy, and Japan participated in a real-world FL project for COVID-19 region segmentation in chest computerized tomography (CT). The multi-national database was created consisting of a total number of 1,704 scans from these three countries for setting up a framework. Evaluation is done via the experiments of semi-supervised learning of COVID-19 regions in three-dimensional (3D) CT. Better results were captured regarding ground truths and false positives; hence, FL proves to be a promising solution for collaborative projects and ensures no information leakage or hacks.

## 12.7    FUTURE SCOPE AND CHALLENGES

### 12.7.1    COMMUNICATION ISSUES IN FL-BASED SMART HEALTHCARE

Communication, an essential part of FL users, and embedded servers play essential roles in FL-supported healthcare services. Proper allocation of communication resources significantly improve learning outcomes. This is especially important if one needs to deploy a large number of IoMT devices on the aggregation server for extensive link-template updates and low-link sample deployments. In this case, the aggregation server can select an appropriate set of IoMT devices using an effective planning policy, as reported in many existing studies [67–70]. Another critical issue in terms of connectivity is the dynamic and fast change of the radio channel between the IoMT device and the aggregation server, which affects the reliability and quality of training updates. One possible solution is to consider the impact of user disturbance [71, 72] and to consider more reliable design goals such as downtime and availability of devices.

### 12.7.2 Standard Specifications for Federated Healthcare Deployment

Although there are many promising health outcomes supported by FL in the literature, there are no standard and universal results for assessing the performance of different approaches to the same issue. Several blockchain frameworks have been proposed for FL systems, for example, eliminating the need for a central server and managing local updates of IoMT devices. However, these approaches are difficult to compare because they are recommended for different status scenarios, and different network parameters/datasets are used to evaluate performance. There are also important issues related to the universality and standardization of communication protocols, device hardware, deployment scenarios, and integration methods. IEEE Std 3652.1–2020 recently provided guidance on the architectural and design perspectives of FL [73], as well as the FL rating table and the performance statistics system.

### 12.7.3 Quality of Federated Healthcare Training Data

Differences in computing power and data quality between hospitals can dramatically reduce the quality of education. A promising solution, in this case, is to develop incentives for hospitals/medical institutions to use high-quality data for education and to report reliable updates to a unified server. Game theory and the blockchain are two critical tools for designing stimulation mechanisms [31, 74, 42, 75, 40]. The FL format should be easily adaptable and adaptable for nurses, physicians, and patients by flexibly configuring learning needs (e.g., changing data types, changing learning rates, changing or regressing the classification of learning objectives). These changes may affect FL models and default learning patterns (in FL users and embedded servers) that require the development of an adaptive FL approach. AI is a promising tool because it can use historical data to improve the adaptability of FL models to future events. Therefore, deep reinforcement learning (DRL) [76] uses a traditional method to create an incentive mechanism in case of poor performance when the size of the opportunity is large enough.

### 12.7.4 Health Dataset Concerns

In some treatment scenarios, different clients may have different datasets—such as text, images, sound, and time series—and different data content, such as blood type, heart rate, face image, and body temperature. As usual, almost all FL methods in the literature are considered a single dataset with a limited number of features. For examples, [13] was tested in the diabetic retinopathy database and [4] was recommended for privacy-based FL-based healthcare but was evaluated in the EHR database. Moreover, although collaborating parties may have different models, a new heterogeneous FL approach should be developed in which a central server can explore this heterogeneity through the unique formation of the whole [77]. In this task, participants present a final strategy that allows them to use a heterogeneous set of models without having to combine data in one place.

### 12.7.5 FL-BASED HEALTHCARE INTEGRATION INTO ADVANCED NETWORKS

Even though 5G networks (the fifth-generation technology standard for broadband cellular mobile communications) are not available completely, even commercially, they do exist. Numerous research and development works for future 6G wireless systems [78]. The coming 6G Industry 5.0 provides access to many applications, such as smart healthcare, smart grid, holographic television, and personalized body area networks. In addition, many new technologies are being introduced to meet stricter 6G requirements, such as blockchain, compression probes, terahertz (THz) and visible light communications, 3D networks, quantum communications, and large-scale smart surfaces. Open-ended questions remain about how FL capabilities will be integrated into future 5G/6G medical devices and how 6G devices such as smart implants and portable devices will be used in a variety of FL-based healthcare and new healthcare services, which 6G will add for future research. For example, future e-health services will be enhanced by AI and FL capabilities to improve quality of life and reduce hospitalizations [79, 80].

### 12.7.6 FL WITH PROVABLE PRIVACY GUARANTEE

While FL has excellent potential to protect the privacy of users' data, the high sensitivity of health data presents a number of privacy issues that need to be addressed appropriately, especially in the context of smart healthcare. According to [79], federated learning privacy concerns can be classified as the final attack of the member, accidental leakage of information, and generative hostility. For example, an attacker could use the global FL template to determine if a sample of data exists in the FL health dataset. Patient information can also be obtained when a patient's device sends local model updates to central servers in hospitals and healthcare facilities. There is also an advanced encryption method for developing solutions for protecting personal information for medical FL systems and maintaining differential confidentiality. Many studies are considered to use differential confidence to continue to improve the confidentiality of the FL system [81, 13, 4, 2].

### 12.7.7 SECURITY ISSUES IN FL-BASED SMART HEALTHCARE

In a smart care system based on FL, various client participants can act as attackers, trying to send toxic model updates or misinformation to compromise model integration. An attacker could also infect data attribute information while learning local data or change local updates while transferring templates between local clients and central servers [82]. On the server side, remote attackers can use their attacks to steal information about the accumulated global pattern, which leads to sensitive privacy issues, such as information leaks. Addressing these security vulnerabilities is a real challenge for smart FL-based healthcare systems. Several solutions should be considered, such as the use of differentiated confidentiality [5] to protect the training dataset against data corruption. In addition, the development of a secure integration method [6] is a promising solution to provide a double-mask structure to protect clients from data falsification and attacks by encrypting local updates and sharing keys between the client and a central server [83, 84].

### 12.7.8 NON–IID-NESS AND DATA QUALITY IN FL-BASED SMART HEALTHCARE

In order to achieve the desired learning performance in FL-based medical systems, inconsistencies in medical datasets that can lead to learning FL in training are important issues that need to be addressed [85]. For example, a hospital may have a higher prevalence of a particular type of regional disease than another hospital in a different geographical area. In this case, it is difficult to participate in federal data education because the distribution of labels varies by the medical institution. If this does not solve the problem of inconsistency, it can degrade or even interfere with learning the data. Therefore, solutions should be developed to overcome non-IID issues, such as generating additional subsets of datasets for equitable distribution to customers, in order to shape data in FL-based smart healthcare effectively. Another promising approach is to implement the movement of characteristics between heterogeneous customers by adjusting the distribution of characteristics on the customer side using the normalization of local batches before averaging local models. Quantitative indicators are needed to assess non-IID data in the FL-based smart care sector, such as standard deviation, a curvature of label/function distribution, and accuracy and accuracy for homogeneous sections [86].

## 12.8 CONCLUSION

Federated learning is a quickly evolving field of study whose integration with IoMT can bring a significant change in the security perspective of medical data. The aim of the chapter is to understand whether federated learning (FL) is a very reliable subject in the context of increasing the confidentiality and security of data for transmission, and if it may also help achieve training a more scalable model for sensitive data. The chapter passes through some of the most important real-world applications that have been experimented with and simulated for research purposes, such as management of electronic health records, remote monitoring for the ill, and also diagnosis of diseases such as COVID-19 and their effects. The chapter also sheds light on the empirical findings of various use-cases in order to derive an understanding of whether FL is reliable and secure or not. Based on the various use-cases studied in Section 12.4, we can understand the flexibility of federated learning to adapt to most healthcare requirements while providing immense utility for data. In Section 12.5, it very evident that federated learning under most circumstances may match the traditional learning mechanism of machine learning and, in some cases, even outperform them significantly. Section 12.6 directly introduces us to some of the real-world implementations of FL for making a statement in the context of its use. To conclude the chapter, key points pertaining to the challenges faced by FL schematics and also the future scope of FL in healthcare settings have been presented. To sum up its corresponding characteristics in a short sense, it is a subject of high research potential, creating enhanced techniques related to AI in the future.

## REFERENCES

[1] Hangyu Zhu, Jinjin Xu, Shiqing Liu, and Yaochu Jin. (2021). "Federated Learning on Non-IID Data: A Survey." *Neurocomputing*, vol. 465, pp. 371–390.

[2] Raouf Kerkouche, Gergely Acs, Claude Castelluccia, and Pierre Genevès. (2021). "Privacy-Preserving and Bandwidth-Efficient Federated Learning: An Application to In-Hospital Mortality Prediction." *Proceedings of the Conference on Health, Inference, and Learning*, pp. 25–35.

[3] M. Hao, H. Li, G. Xu, Z. Liu, and Z. Chen. (2020). "Privacy-Aware and Resource-Saving Collaborative Learning for Healthcare in Cloud Computing." *ICC 2020–2020 IEEE International Conference on Communications (ICC)*, pp. 1–6.

[4] Olivia Choudhury, Aris Gkoulalas-Divanis, Theodoros Salonidis, Issa Sylla, Yoonyoung Park, Grace Hsu, and Amar Das. (2019). "Differential Privacy-Enabled Federated Learning for Sensitive Health Data." arXiv:1910.02578. https://arxiv.org/abs/1910.02578.

[5] Rui Hu, Yuanxiong Guo, Hongning Li, Qingqi Pei, and Yanmin Gong. (2020). "Personalized Federated Learning with Differential Privacy." *IEEE Internet of Things Journal*, vol. 7, no. 10, pp. 9530–9539.

[6] Hossein Fereidooni, Samuel Marchal, Markus Miettinen, Azalia Mirhoseini, Helen Möllering, Thien Duc Nguyen, Phillip Rieger, A.R. Sadeghi, T. Schneider, H. Yalame, and S. Zeitouni. (2021). "SAFELearn: Secure Aggregation for Private Federated Learning." *2021 IEEE Security and Privacy Workshops (SPW)*, pp. 56–62.

[7] Praneeth Vepakomma, Otkrist Gupta, Tristan Swedish, and Ramesh Raskar. (2018). "Split Learning for Health: Distributed Deep Learning Without Sharing Raw Patient Data." arXiv:1812.00564. https://arxiv.org/abs/1812.00564.

[8] Pavlos Papadopoulos, Will Abramson, Adam J. Hall, Nikolaos Pitropakis, and William J. Buchanan. (2021). "Privacy and Trust Redefined in Federated Machine Learning." *Machine Learning and Knowledge Extraction*, vol. 3, no. 2, pp. 333–356.

[9] Zengqiang Yan, Jeffry Wicaksana, Zhiwei Wang, Xin Yang, and Kwang-Ting Cheng. (2020). "Variation-Aware Federated Learning with Multi-Source Decentralized Medical Image Data." *IEEE Journal of Biomedical and Health Informatics*, vol. 25, no. 7, pp. 2615–2628.

[10] Wenqi Li, Fausto Milletarì, Daguang Xu, Nicola Rieke, Jonny Hancox, Wentao Zhu, and Maximilian Baust. (2019). "Privacy-Preserving Federated Brain Tumour Segmentation." In *International Workshop on Machine Learning in Medical Imaging* (pp. 133–141). Springer, Cham.

[11] Santiago Silva, Boris A. Gutman, Eduardo Romero, Paul M. Thompson, Andre Altmann, and Marco Lorenzi. (2019). "Federated Learning in Distributed Medical Databases: Meta-Analysis of Large-Scale Subcortical Brain Data." *2019 IEEE 16th International Symposium on Biomedical Imaging (ISBI 2019)*, pp. 270–274.

[12] Utkarsh Chandra Srivastava, Dhruv Upadhyay, and Vinayak Sharma. (2020). "Intracranial Hemorrhage Detection Using Neural Network Based Methods with Federated Learning." arXiv:2005.08644. https://github.com/ChanChiChoi/awesome-Federated-Learning.

[13] Mohammad Malekzadeh, Burak Hasircioglu, Nitish Mital, Kunal Katarya, Mehmet Emre Ozfatura, and Deniz Gündüz. (2021). "Dopamine: Differentially Private Federated Learning on Medical Data." arXiv:2101.11693. https://arxiv.org/abs/2101.11693.

[14] Qiong Wu, Xu Chen, Zhi Zhou, and Junshan Zhang. (2020). "Fedhome: Cloud-Edge Based Personalized Federated Learning for In-Home Health Monitoring." *IEEE Transactions on Mobile Computing*, vol. 21, no. 8, pp. 2818–2832. DOI: 10.1109/TMC.2020.3045266.

[15] Yiqiang Chen, Xin Qin, Jindong Wang, Chaohui Yu, and Wen Gao. (2020). "Fedhealth: A Federated Transfer Learning Framework for Wearable Healthcare." *IEEE Intelligent Systems*, vol. 35, no. 4, pp. 83–93.

[16] Dianbo Liu, Dmitriy Dligach, and Timothy Miller. (2019). "Two-Stage Federated Phenotyping and Patient Representation Learning." *Proceedings of the Conference: Association for Computational Linguistics. Meeting*, vol. 2019, p. 283.

[17] Gautham Krishna Gudur, and Satheesh K. Perepu. (2020). "Federated Learning with Heterogeneous Labels and Models for Mobile Activity Monitoring." arXiv:2012.02539. https://www.researchgate.net/publication/346668823_Federated_Learning_with_Heterogeneous_Labels_and_Models_for_Mobile_Activity_Monitoring.

[18] Dianbo Liu, Kathe Fox, Griffin Weber, and Tim Miller. (2019). "Confederated Machine Learning on Horizontally and Vertically Separated Medical Data for Large-Scale Health System Intelligence." arXiv:1910.02109. https://arxiv.org/abs/1910.02109.

[19] Xiaohang Xu, Hao Peng, Lichao Sun, Md Zakirul Alam Bhuiyan, Lianzhong Liu, and Lifang He. (2021). "Fedmood: Federated Learning on Mobile Health Data for Mood Detection." arXiv:2102.09342. https://arxiv.org/abs/2102.09342.

[20] Rajesh Kumar, Abdullah Aman Khan, Jay Kumar, Noorbakhsh Amiri Golilarz, Simin Zhang, Yang Ting, Chengyu Zheng, and Wenyong Wang. (2021). "Blockchain-Federated-Learning and Deep Learning Models for Covid-19 Detection Using CT Imaging." *IEEE Sensors Journal*, vol. 21, no. 14, pp. 16301–16314.

[21] Boyi Liu, Bingjie Yan, Yize Zhou, Yifan Yang, and Yixian Zhang. (2020). "Experiments of Federated Learning for Covid-19 Chest X-Ray Images." arXiv:2007.05592. https://arxiv.org/abs/2007.05592.

[22] Weishan Zhang, Tao Zhou, Qinghua Lu, Xiao Wang, Chunsheng Zhu, Haoyun Sun, Zhipeng Wang, Sin Kit Lo, and Fei-Yue Wang. (2021). "Dynamic-Fusion-Based Federated Learning for COVID-19 Detection." *IEEE Internet of Things Journal*, vol. 8, no. 21, pp. 15884–15891.

[23] Ines Feki, Sourour Ammar, Yousri Kessentini, and Khan Muhammad. (2021). "Federated Learning for COVID-19 Screening from Chest X-Ray Images." *Applied Soft Computing*, vol. 106, p. 107330.

[24] Qi Dou, Tiffany Y. So, Meirui Jiang, Quande Liu, Varut Vardhanabhuti, Georgios Kaissis, Zeju Li, W. Si, H.H. Lee, K. Yu, and Z. Feng. (2021). "Federated Deep Learning for Detecting COVID-19 Lung Abnormalities in CT: A Privacy-Preserving Multinational Validation Study." *NPJ Digital Medicine*, vol. 4, no. 1, pp. 1–11.

[25] Dong Yang, Ziyue Xu, Wenqi Li, Andriy Myronenko, Holger R. Roth, Stephanie Harmon, Sheng Xu, B. Turkbey, E. Turkbey, X. Wang, and W. Zhu. (2021). "Federated Semi-Supervised Learning for COVID Region Segmentation in Chest CT Using Multi-National Data from China, Italy, Japan." *Medical Image Analysis*, vol. 70, p. 101992.

[26] Ji-Jiang Yang, Jian-Qiang Li, and Yu Niu. (2015). "A Hybrid Solution for Privacy Preserving Medical Data Sharing in the Cloud Environment." *Future Generation Computer Systems*, vol. 43, pp. 74–86.

[27] Chang Xu, Ningning Wang, Liehuang Zhu, Kashif Sharif, and Chuan Zhang. (2019). "Achieving Searchable and Privacy-Preserving Data Sharing for Cloud-Assisted E-Healthcare System." *IEEE Internet of Things Journal*, vol. 6, no. 5, pp. 8345–8356.

[28] Maayan Frid-Adar, Idit Diamant, Eyal Klang, Michal Amitai, Jacob Goldberger, and Hayit Greenspan. (2018). "GAN-Based Synthetic Medical Image Augmentation for Increased CNN Performance in Liver Lesion Classification." *Neurocomputing*, vol. 321, pp. 321–331.

[29] Zhengping Che, Yu Cheng, Shuangfei Zhai, Zhaonan Sun, and Yan Liu. (2017). "Boosting Deep Learning Risk Prediction with Generative Adversarial Networks for Electronic Health Records." *2017 IEEE International Conference on Data Mining (ICDM)*, pp. 787–792.

[30] Yang Zhao, Jun Zhao, Linshan Jiang, Rui Tan, Dusit Niyato, Zengxiang Li, Lingjuan Lyu, and Yingbo Liu. (2020). "Privacy-Preserving Blockchain-Based Federated Learning for IoT Devices." *IEEE Internet of Things Journal*, vol. 8, no. 3, pp. 1817–1829.

[31] Latif U. Khan, Shashi Raj Pandey, Nguyen H. Tran, Walid Saad, Zhu Han, Minh NH Nguyen, and Choong Seon Hong. (2020). "Federated Learning for Edge Networks: Resource Optimization and Incentive Mechanism." *IEEE Communications Magazine*, vol. 58, no. 10, pp. 88–93.

[32] A. Verma, P. Bhattacharya, Y. Patel, K. Shah, S. Tanwar, and B. Khan. (2022). "Data Localization and Privacy-Preserving Healthcare for Big Data Applications: Architecture and Future Directions." In *Emerging Technologies for Computing, Communication and Smart Cities* (pp. 233–244). Springer, Singapore.

[33] Theodora S. Brisimi, Ruidi Chen, Theofanie Mela, Alex Olshevsky, Ioannis Ch Paschalidis, and Wei Shi. (2018). "Federated Learning of Predictive Models from Federated Electronic Health Records." *International Journal of Medical Informatics*, vol. 112, pp. 59–67.

[34] D. Saraswat, P. Bhattacharya, A. Verma, V.K. Prasad, S. Tanwar, G. Sharma, P.N. Bokoro, and R. Sharma. (2022). "Explainable AI for Healthcare 5.0: Opportunities and Challenges." *IEEE Access*, vol. 10, pp. 84486–84517. DOI: 10.1109/ACCESS. 2022.3197671.

[35] Kang Wei, Jun Li, Ming Ding, Chuan Ma, Howard H. Yang, Farhad Farokhi, Shi Jin, Tony Q.S. Quek, and H. Vincent Poor. (2020). "Federated Learning with Differential Privacy: Algorithms and Performance Analysis." *IEEE Transactions on Information Forensics and Security*, vol. 15, pp. 3454–3469.

[36] S. Banerjee, Vanga Odelu, Ashok Kumar Das, Samiran Chattopadhyay, Neeraj Kumar, Youngho Park, and Sudeep Tanwar. (2018). "Design of an Anonymity-Preserving Group Formation Based Authentication Protocol in Global Mobility Networks." *IEEE Access*, vol. 6, pp. 20673–20693. DOI: 10.1109/ACCESS.2018.2827027.

[37] Dinh C. Nguyen, Pubudu N. Pathirana, Ming Ding, and Aruna Seneviratne. (2020). "Blockchain and Edge Computing for Decentralized EMRs Sharing in Federated Healthcare." *GLOBECOM 2020–2020 IEEE Global Communications Conference*, pp. 1–6.

[38] Jiawen Kang, Zehui Xiong, Dusit Niyato, Yuze Zou, Yang Zhang, and Mohsen Guizani. (2020). "Reliable Federated Learning for Mobile Networks." *IEEE Wireless Communications*, vol. 27, no. 2, pp. 72–80.

[39] Jonathan Passerat-Palmbach, Tyler Farnan, Mike McCoy, Justin D. Harris, Sean T. Manion, Heather Leigh Flannery, and Bill Gleim. (2020). "Blockchain-Orchestrated Machine Learning for Privacy Preserving Federated Learning in Electronic Health Data." *2020 IEEE International Conference on Blockchain (Blockchain)*, pp. 550–555.

[40] A. Verma, P. Bhattacharya, M. Zuhair, S. Tanwar, and N. Kumar. (2021). "Vacochain: Blockchain-Based 5G-Assisted UAV Vaccine Distribution Scheme for Future Pandemics." *IEEE Journal of Biomedical and Health Informatics*, vol. 26, no. 5, pp. 1997–2007.

[41] A. Verma, P. Bhattacharya, D. Saraswat, S. Tanwar, N. Kumar, and R. Sharma. (2023). "SanJeeVni: Secure UAV-Envisioned Massive Vaccine Distribution for COVID-19 Underlying 6G Network." *IEEE Sensors Journal*, vol. 23, no. 2, pp. 955–968. DOI: 10.1109/JSEN.2022.3188929.

[42] Jun Li, Yumeng Shao, Kang Wei, Ming Ding, Chuan Ma, Long Shi, Zhu Han, and Vincent Poor. (2021). "Blockchain Assisted Decentralized Federated Learning (blade-fl): Performance Analysis and Resource Allocation." *IEEE Transactions on Parallel and Distributed Systems*, vol. 33, no. 10.

[43] Stephen R. Pfohl, Andrew M. Dai, and Katherine Heller. (2019). "Federated and Differentially Private Learning for Electronic Health Records." arXiv:1911.05861. https://arxiv.org/abs/1911.05861.

[44] Ferhat Ucar, and Deniz Korkmaz. (2020). "COVIDiagnosis-Net: Deep Bayes-SqueezeNet Based Diagnosis of the Coronavirus Disease 2019 (COVID-19) from X-Ray Images." *Medical Hypotheses*, vol. 140, p. 109761.

[45] Holger R. Roth, Ken Chang, Praveer Singh, Nir Neumark, Wenqi Li, Vikash Gupta, Sharut Gupta, L. Qu, A. Ihsani, B.C. Bizzo, and Y. Wen. (2020). "Federated Learning for Breast Density Classification: A Real-World Implementation." In *Domain Adaptation and Representation Transfer, and Distributed and Collaborative Learning* (pp. 181–191). Springer, Cham.

[46] Quoc-Viet Pham, Dinh C. Nguyen, Thien Huynh-The, Won-Joo Hwang, and Pubudu N. Pathirana. (2020). "Artificial Intelligence (AI) and Big Data for Coronavirus (COVID-19) Pandemic: A Survey on the State-of-the-Arts." *IEEE Access*, vol. 8, p. 130820.

[47] Mohamed Loey, Florentin Smarandache, and Nour Eldeen M. Khalifa. (2020). "Within the Lack of Chest COVID-19 X-Ray Dataset: A Novel Detection Model Based on GAN and Deep Transfer Learning." *Symmetry*, vol. 12, no. 4, p. 651.

[48] M. Zuhair, F. Patel, D. Navapara, P. Bhattacharya, and D. Saraswat. (April 2021). "BloCoV6: A Blockchain-Based 6G-Assisted UAV Contact Tracing Scheme for COVID-19 Pandemic." *2021 2nd International Conference on Intelligent Engineering and Management (ICIEM)*, pp. 271–276.

[49] V.K. Prasad, P. Bhattacharya, M. Bhavsar, A. Verma, S. Tanwar, G. Sharma, Pitshou N. Bokoro, and R. Sharma. (2022). "ABV-CoViD: An Ensemble Forecasting Model to Predict Availability of Beds and Ventilators for COVID-19 Like Pandemics." *IEEE Access*, vol. 10, pp. 74131–74151.

[50] Feng Qian, and Andrew Zhang. (2021). "The Value of Federated Learning During and Post-COVID-19." *International Journal for Quality in Health Care*, vol. 33, no. 1, p. mzab010.

[51] Xiaoqing Tan, Chung-Chou H. Chang, and Lu Tang. (2021). "A Tree-Based Federated Learning Approach for Personalized Treatment Effect Estimation from Heterogeneous Data Sources." arXiv:2103.06261. https://github.com/ChanChiChoi/awesome-Federated-Learning.

[52] Rodolfo Stoffel Antunes, Cristiano André da Costa, Arne Küderle, Imrana Abdullahi Yari, and Björn Eskofier. (2022). "Federated Learning for Healthcare: Systematic Review and Architecture Proposal." *ACM Transactions on Intelligent Systems and Technology (TIST)*, vol. 13, no. 4, pp. 1–23.

[53] Dianbo Liu, Dmitriy Dligach, and Timothy Miller. (2019). "Two-Stage Federated Phenotyping and Patient Representation Learning." *Proceedings of the Conference: Association for Computational Linguistics. Meeting*, vol. 2019, p. 283.

[54] Di Jiang, Yuanfeng Song, Yongxin Tong, Xueyang Wu, Weiwei Zhao, Qian Xu, and Qiang Yang. (2019). "Federated Topic Modeling." *Proceedings of the 28th ACM International Conference on Information and Knowledge Management*, pp. 1071–1080.

[55] Pulkit Sharma, Farah E. Shamout, and David A. Clifton. (2019). "Preserving Patient Privacy While Training a Predictive Model of In-Hospital Mortality." arXiv:1912.00354. https://arxiv.org/abs/1912.00354.

[56] Yeting Guo, Fang Liu, Zhiping Cai, Li Chen, and Nong Xiao. (2020). "Feel: A Federated Edge Learning System for Efficient and Privacy-Preserving Mobile Healthcare." *49th International Conference on Parallel Processing-ICPP*, pp. 1–11.

[57] Yiqiang Chen, Xin Qin, Jindong Wang, Chaohui Yu, and Wen Gao. (2020). "Fedhealth: A Federated Transfer Learning Framework for Wearable Healthcare." *IEEE Intelligent Systems*, vol. 35, no. 4, pp. 83–93.

[58] Yekta Said Can, and Cem Ersoy. (2021). "Privacy-Preserving Federated Deep Learning for Wearable IOT-Based Biomedical Monitoring." *ACM Transactions on Internet Technology (TOIT)*, vol. 21, no. 1, pp. 1–17.

[59] Pronaya Bhattacharya, Sudeep Tanwar, Umesh Bodkhe, Sudhanshu Tyagi, and Neeraj Kumar. (2019). "Bindaas: Blockchain-Based Deep-Learning as-a-Service in Healthcare 4.0 Applications." *IEEE Transactions on Network Science and Engineering*, vol. 8, no. 2, pp. 1242–1255.

[60] Vanga Odelu, Ashok Kumar Das, Mohammad Wazid, and Mauro Conti. (2016). "Provably Secure Authenticated Key Agreement Scheme for Smart Grid." *IEEE Transactions on Smart Grid*, vol. 9, no. 3, pp. 1900–1910.

[61] Dapeng Wu, and Chi Zhou. (2011). "Fault-Tolerant and Scalable Key Management for Smart Grid." *IEEE Transactions on Smart Grid*, vol. 2, no. 2, pp. 375–381.

[62] Hyun Jung Kim, and Hyun Sung Kim. (2011). "AUTH HOTP-HOTP Based Authentication Scheme Over Home Network Environment." In *International Conference on Computational Science and Its Applications* (pp. 622–637). Springer, Berlin, Heidelberg.

[63] Jigna J. Hathaliya, Sudeep Tanwar, Sudhanshu Tyagi, and Neeraj Kumar. (2019). "Securing Electronics Healthcare Records in Healthcare 4.0: A Biometric-Based Approach." *Computers & Electrical Engineering*, vol. 76, pp. 398–410.

[64] Gagangeet Singh Aujla, Rajat Chaudhary, Kuljeet Kaur, Sahil Garg, Neeraj Kumar, and Rajiv Ranjan. (2018). "SAFE: SDN-Assisted Framework for Edge–Cloud Interplay in Secure Healthcare Ecosystem." *IEEE Transactions on Industrial Informatics*, vol. 15, no. 1, pp. 469–480.

[65] Federated Learning for Medical Imaging. (2021). www.intel.com/content/www/us/en/artificialintelligence/posts/federated-learning-for-medical-imaging.html.

[66] Federated Learning Brings AI with Privacy to Hospitals. (2021). https://healthcare-in-europe.com/en/news/federatedlearning-brings-ai-with-privacy-to-hospitals.html.

[67] Bo Xu, Wenchao Xia, Jun Zhang, Tony Q.S. Quek, and Hongbo Zhu. (2021). "Online Client Scheduling for Fast Federated Learning." *IEEE Wireless Communications Letters*, vol. 10, no. 7, pp. 1434–1438.

[68] Wenchao Xia, Tony Q.S. Quek, Kun Guo, Wanli Wen, Howard H. Yang, and Hongbo Zhu. (2020). "Multi-Armed Bandit-Based Client Scheduling for Federated Learning." *IEEE Transactions on Wireless Communications*, vol. 19, no. 11, pp. 7108–7123.

[69] Siqi Luo, Xu Chen, Qiong Wu, Zhi Zhou, and Shuai Yu. (2020). "HFEL: Joint Edge Association and Resource Allocation for Cost-Efficient Hierarchical Federated Edge Learning." *IEEE Transactions on Wireless Communications*, vol. 19, no. 10, pp. 6535–6548.

[70] Howard H. Yang, Zuozhu Liu, Tony Q.S. Quek, and H. Vincent Poor. (2019). "Scheduling Policies for Federated Learning in Wireless Networks." *IEEE Transactions on Communications*, vol. 68, no. 1, pp. 317–333.

[71] Keith Bonawitz, Vladimir Ivanov, Ben Kreuter, Antonio Marcedone, H. Brendan McMahan, Sarvar Patel, Daniel Ramage, Aaron Segal, and Karn Seth. (2016). "Practical Secure Aggregation for Federated Learning on User-Held Data." arXiv:1611.04482. https://arxiv.org/abs/1611.04482.

[72] Jinhyun So, Başak Güler, and A. Salman Avestimehr. (2021). "Turbo-Aggregate: Breaking the Quadratic Aggregation Barrier in Secure Federated Learning." *IEEE Journal on Selected Areas in Information Theory*, vol. 2, no. 1, pp. 479–489.

[73] Fan Qiang, Tong Lixin, and Lv Richard. (2021). "IEEE Federated Machine Learning." *White Paper*, pp. 1–18.

[74] Jie Xu, Heqiang Wang, and Lixing Chen. (2021). "Bandwidth Allocation for Multiple Federated Learning Services in Wireless Edge Networks." *IEEE Transactions on Wireless Communications*. https://ieeexplore.ieee.org/document/9547778.

[75] Jiawen Kang, Zehui Xiong, Dusit Niyato, Shengli Xie, and Junshan Zhang. (2019). "Incentive Mechanism for Reliable Federated Learning: A Joint Optimization Approach

to Combining Reputation and Contract Theory." *IEEE Internet of Things Journal*, vol. 6, no. 6, pp. 10700–10714.

[76] Jie Zhao, Xinghua Zhu, Jianzong Wang, and Jing Xiao. (2021). "Efficient Client Contribution Evaluation for Horizontal Federated Learning." *ICASSP 2021–2021 IEEE International Conference on Acoustics, Speech and Signal Processing (ICASSP)*, pp. 3060–3064.

[77] Christopher A. Choquette-Choo, Natalie Dullerud, Adam Dziedzic, Yunxiang Zhang, Somesh Jha, Nicolas Papernot, and Xiao Wang. (2021). "CaPC Learning: Confidential and Private Collaborative Learning." arXiv:2102.05188. https://arxiv.org/pdf/2102.05188.pdf.

[78] Chamitha De Alwis, Anshuman Kalla, Quoc-Viet Pham, Pardeep Kumar, Kapal Dev, Won-Joo Hwang, and Madhusanka Liyanage. (2021). "Survey on 6G Frontiers: Trends, Applications, Requirements, Technologies and Future Research." *IEEE Open Journal of the Communications Society*, vol. 2, pp. 836–886.

[79] Lorenzo Mucchi, Sara Jayousi, Stefano Caputo, Elisabetta Paoletti, Paolo Zoppi, Simona Geli, and Pietro Dioniso. (2020). "How 6G Technology Can Change the Future Wireless Healthcare." *2020 2nd 6G Wireless Summit (6G SUMMIT)*, pp. 1–6.

[80] V.A. Patel, Pronaya Bhattacharya, Sudeep Tanwar, Rajesh Gupta, Gulshan Sharma, Pitshou N. Bokoro, and Ravi Sharma. (2022). "Adoption of Federated Learning for Healthcare Informatics: Emerging Applications and Future Directions." *IEEE Access*, vol. 10, pp. 90792–90826. DOI: 10.1109/ACCESS.2022.3201876.

[81] Maoqiang Wu, Dongdong Ye, Jiahao Ding, Yuanxiong Guo, Rong Yu, and Miao Pan. (2021). "Incentivizing Differentially Private Federated Learning: A Multidimensional Contract Approach." *IEEE Internet of Things Journal*, vol. 8, no. 13, pp. 10639–10651.

[82] Yunus Sarikaya, and Ozgur Ercetin. (2019). "Motivating Workers in Federated Learning: A Stackelberg Game Perspective." *IEEE Networking Letters*, vol. 2, no. 1, pp. 23–27.

[83] V.A. Patel, P. Bhattacharya, S. Tanwar, N.K. Jadav, and R. Gupta. (2022). "BFLEdge: Blockchain Based Federated Edge Learning Scheme in V2X Underlying 6G Communications." *2022 12th International Conference on Cloud Computing, Data Science & Engineering (Confluence)*, pp. 146–152. DOI: 10.1109/Confluence52989.2022.9734213.

[84] Qinbin Li, Yiqun Diao, Quan Chen, and Bingsheng He. (2021). "Federated Learning on Non-IID Data Silos: An Experimental Study." arXiv:2102.02079. https://arxiv.org/abs/2102.02079.

[85] Viraaji Mothukuri, Reza M. Parizi, Seyedamin Pouriyeh, Yan Huang, Ali Dehghantanha, and Gautam Srivastava. (2021). "A Survey on Security and Privacy of Federated Learning." *Future Generation Computer Systems*, vol. 115, pp. 619–640.

[86] J. Xu, and F. Wang. (2019). "Federated Learning for Healthcare Informatics." arXiv preprint. https://www.mdpi.com/1999-4893/15/7/243/pdf.

# 13 Blockchain for Internet of Medical Things

*Pranalini Joshi and Prasad Gokhale*

## CONTENTS

## 13.1 INTRODUCTION

Internet of Things (IoT) defines a system of interrelated physical objects (or things) which are embedded with sensors/actuators and can collect and transfer data over wireless networks without human interference via the internet. IoT provides extended internet connectivity not only to connect computers but also to connect our environmental things—including humans. Figure 13.1 shows an overall working of an IoT scheme, which is the methodology appearing in most of the works reviewed as the state of the art.

The IoT visualises a fully connected world. This domain has attracted variety of industries and many smart applications are developed and deployed in various domains like wearables, smart cities, automobile sector, smart parking, smart homes, environment, logistics, etc. IoT solutions provided in these domains are not only optimising production but also digitising industries.

### 13.1.1 OVERVIEW OF INTERNET OF MEDICAL THINGS (IoMT)

Healthcare is one of the most promising IoT applications, and Internet of Medical Things (IoMT) is the set of medical devices and medical applications which are

DOI: 10.1201/9781003303374-13

**267**

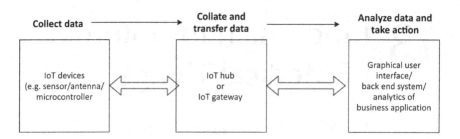

**FIGURE 13.1**   Overall working of IoT scheme.

linked to healthcare IT systems over the internet. It is an integration of software, hardware, network access, and sensors/actuators. Traditional IoMT uses cloud-based architecture. Figure 13.2 shows cloud-based architecture for an IoMT. In this architecture, end nodes like wearables, sensors, mobile phones, and smart devices scan real-time data and transfer it to the cloud via gateways. Gateways are hardware devices that facilitate communication between various IoT devices and the cloud. All stakeholders—like patients, doctors, and researchers—can access data from the cloud. Cloud-based IoMT architecture allows users to access data from anywhere and at any time. The concept of IoMT can be used in different healthcare applications like robot surgery, wireless capsule endoscopy, smart hospital information systems, remote patient monitoring, etc. However, remote health monitoring of patients with various functionality like monitoring of senior citizens, SpO$_2$ (oxygen saturation) monitoring, glucose monitoring, and depression and mood monitoring are attracting to researchers, as it increases lifespans of individuals, decreases mortality, and reduces the chances of contracting comorbid conditions [1].

Due to integration of the digital and physical worlds, medical organisations can easily monitor patients' health—even from remote locations—and can suggest immediate treatment with more accuracy, which in turn will help to improve patient health. It also makes workflow management of medical organisation more efficient [3]. With just a single click, a patient can get a proper line of treatments. Various entities use in IoMT, as shown in Figure 13.3 [3]. The patient's data is stored in centralised servers, which repels many attacks that can be handled with applying cryptographic solutions to the system such as blockchain [4, 5] and artificial intelligence (AI) in healthcare [6]. With this data and past previous history, we track [7] and can predict the use of medical resources such as beds and ventilators [8, 9].

To illustrate IoMT, Consider the scenario that results of a magnetic resonance imaging (MRI) examination is sent from the MRI centre to the patient's smartphone, or patient wears an activity tracker for sugar/blood pressure readings which is monitored by doctor or other family members by smartphone. Here, one device is communicating with others; hence, it is machine-to-machine communication. According to [10], electronic medical record (EMR) data is list of information collected and provided by hospitals right from beginning of treatment through curing of the disease. Sensor data generated from various healthcare devices and data generated through EMRs together are considered healthcare Big Data. Figure 13.4 elaborates

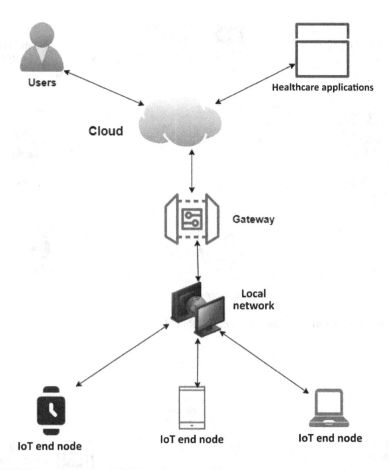

**FIGURE 13.2**   Cloud-based IoMT architecture [2].

on the concept of EMR, and Figure 13.5 shows several types of sensors. IoMT plays a significant role in the healthcare industry. By compiling these huge medical data, along with proper investigation, IoMT can provide faster diagnosis and treatment to disease, and it also increases correctness, reliability, and productivity of electronic devices.

## 13.1.2   WHY BLOCKCHAIN IN IOMT?

IoMT-enabled devices generate and transmit massive volumes of healthcare data, which is expanding at an exponential rate. According to a survey published by Stanford Medicine [11], in 2013, 153 exabytes of data were generated, and 2,314 exabytes of data was expected to be produced in 2020, which itself indicates 15% of growth. According to one survey, the annual growth rate of healthcare industries is 27.3% and it was expected that by 2022, it will reach 29.84 billion USD from 8.92 billion USD in 2017 [10].

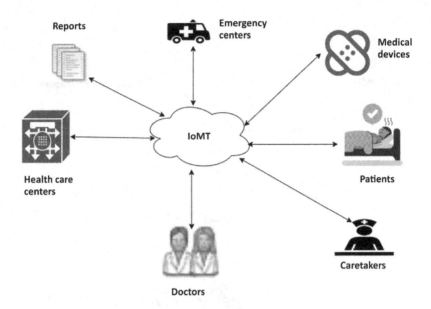

**FIGURE 13.3**    Internet of Medical Things (IoMT) [3].

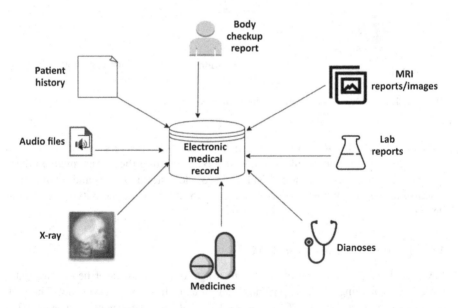

**FIGURE 13.4**    Electronic medical records [10].

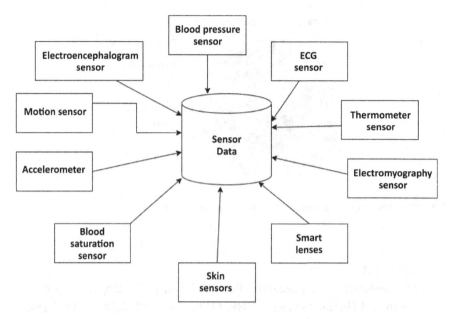

**FIGURE 13.5**   Different types of sensor data [10].

Healthcare data generates sensitive—as well as personal—information, which attracts cybercriminals. The most common attack on EHRs is ransomware attack. According [12], a survey conducted by Accenture in February 2017, around 26% of medical records had been breached in the United States, and 80 million healthcare data from a health insurance company (Anthem Blue Cross) were breached in 2015.

Hacking, unintentional data disclosure, attacks by insiders, and physical damage are main causes for such type of breaches. Figure 13.6 shows distinct types of healthcare breaches [11, 13].

According to this survey, an average of approximately 380 USD is needed to pay for each breached healthcare record. A ransomware attack occurred in 2017 at an Arkansas provider whereby 128,000 patient data were breached. Universal Health Services, Inc. faces losses of $67 million after a cyberattack in September 2020. This UHS attack was one of the most highly publicised cyber incidents in 2020. The U.S. Department of Health and Human Services (HHS) Office for Civil Rights have published statistics for U.S. healthcare data breaches occurring in 2021, which is shown in Table 13.1.

In the healthcare industry, various stockholders are patients, doctors, insurance companies, pathology laboratories, governing bodies, etc. As healthcare data is used often by all stakeholders, confidentiality and integrity of this data should be protected from unofficial access attempts from inside networks, as well as from external attackers. For example, being one of the stakeholders, insurance companies need access to patients' data to analyse it and provide services accordingly, but unfortunately, it is observed that often this data gets altered and leaked by companies [15].

**Healthcare breaches reported to HHS**

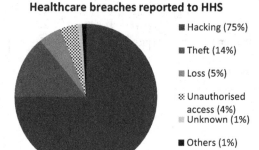

- ■ Hacking (75%)
- ■ Theft (14%)
- ■ Loss (5%)
- ※ Unauthorised access (4%)
- ▥ Unknown (1%)
- ■ Others (1%)

**FIGURE 13.6**    Different types of healthcare breaches [11].

**TABLE 13.1**

**U.S. Healthcare Data Breaches Reported to the U.S. Department of Health and Human Services (HHS) Office for Civil Rights in 2021 [14]**

| Name of Organisation and U.S. State | Number of Affected Records |
| --- | --- |
| Oregon Anesthesiology Group PC, Oregon | 750,500 |
| UF Health Central Florida, Florida | 700,981 |
| Sea Mar Community Health Centers, Washington | 688,000 |
| Wolfe Clinic, PC, Lowa | 527,378 |
| Health Net of California, California | 523,709 |

Thus, it is necessary to maintain trust during exchange of EHRs among all stakeholders. Though providing security and privacy to healthcare data is a very crucial and challenging task, it must be guaranteed. According to [16], to store and transfer data in such a way that its integrity, validity, and authenticity must be assured is called data security, and when only authorised users can access data, it is said that data privacy is maintained.

Though IoMT has the capability to connect billions of devices concurrently, due to which smart healthcare systems can deliver real-time service, developing a common security standard for these IoMT devices is quite challenging due to their heterogeneous nature. Even if IoMT has unlimited benefits, there are many issues like scalability, security, and privacy that should be taken into consideration. As we know, the traditional cloud-centric IoMT healthcare systems follow centralised client/server models and depend on the cloud to get personal health data and other medical services. In any server/client model, if the server goes down, the entire system goes down—which leads to single-point failure; also, the centralised model can be exposed to data manipulation.

Therefore, *blockchain technology* can be the solution for moving IoMT systems into distributed systems which will preserve definite trust during exchange of EHR among all stakeholders, secure data from misuse, and make this data available at a single click for emergency use which requires seamless access, transaction, and storage management.

## 13.2 OVERVIEW OF BLOCKCHAIN TECHNOLOGY: ANALYSING ITS UNIQUE FEATURES

In [17], Satoshi Nakamoto, an anonymous person, introduces a concept of distributed and decentralised ledger technology for storing financial transactions called blockchain technology. As the name suggests, blockchain represents chains of blocks and every block holds sets of transactions [18]. Some of the basic terminology that every learner should know follows.

**Node:** Every computer in network is called a node.

**Ledger:** Data exchange between nodes are called transactions; a ledger is a registry where all transactions are stored.

**Hash Function:** To prevent unauthorised access, the concept of hashing is used. Hash functions accept input (i.e., data which can be numeric, alphabetic, character-based, or media files) and convert into fixed-length output. Output generated using hash function is called as hash. Hashes can be 32-bit, 64-bit, 128-bit, or 256-bit. Various hashing algorithms are used to compute hash function; SHA256 is most popular in blockchain implementation.

Depending on which blockchain platform is being used, the number of transactions per block varies. To validate each transaction, blockchain uses the concept of distributed systems. Miners in the network verify every transaction, and then transaction gets store into distributed ledger.

Once a transaction gets stored into the blockchain ledger, it is difficult to roll back or delete a block and transaction. Each transaction is signed with a private key and then can be further verified with a public key. Every block is encrypted using cryptographic hash function. Blockchain technology further permits dispersed preservation of encrypted data [19]. Table 13.2 shows characteristics of blockchain technology, and Figure 13.7 shows structure of blockchain [20].

As per the requirements of application, blockchain can be considered as public, consortium, or private blockchain. Table 13.3 shows comparison of various kinds of blockchain based on different characteristics.

### 13.2.1 BLOCKCHAIN EVOLUTION

Blockchain generation varies from Blockchain 1.0 to Blockchain 3.0. A distributed, peer-to-peer (P2P) ledger technology which was proposed by Santoshi Nakamoto and used for financial transactions is considered Blockchain 1.0. Due to the features of blockchain, it has attracted many researchers and has been explored in many commercial applications. Newer concepts that were introduced in Blockchain 2.0 resulted in the smart contract.

**TABLE 13.2**

**Characteristics of Blockchain Technology [21]**

| Blockchain Characteristics | Description |
| --- | --- |
| **Decentralised** | Third parties do not have access to any transactions. A local copy of data is maintained on each node in the network; therefore, even if any node goes down, this does not affect the remaining network and hence ensures robustness. |
| **Secure** | All the blocks in blockchain are secured with cryptographic hash function. |
| **Immutable** | No one can roll back or delete a transaction once it is stored in the blockchain. |
| **Reliable** | Due to the decentralised nature of blockchain, failure of a node does not affect the remaining network and make the network less reliable. |
| **Efficiency** | As there is no central authority to control any transaction, less processing time is required. |

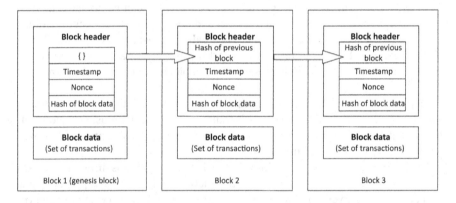

**FIGURE 13.7** Structure of blockchain. Genesis block means the first block in a blockchain. Every block in blockchain is encrypted with cryptographic hash function. Every block holds a time stamp, set of transactions and hash calculated for the prior block. As the first block does not have hash of any block prior to it, hash of previous block will be considered as null and shows as {}.

Smart contracts are just like conventional paper-based contracts. A smart contract is nothing but a computer program written using computer language and executed automatically when some conditions are met. It does not require any involvement of any third party. Smart contracts can control privileges to access data and define what type of data exchange is possible among various parties. The advantage of using smart contract is that it reduces the cost required to sign, execute, and monitor contracts. It also improves the security of transactions. Ethereum is a popular example of Blockchain 2.0. To write a smart contract, solidity language is used [22, 23].

**TABLE 13.3**

**Comparison between Types of Blockchain [21]**

| Characteristics | Public Blockchain | Consortium Blockchain | Private Blockchain |
|---|---|---|---|
| Participation | Anyone can participate | Selected multiple participants/ organisations | Only one organisation |
| Read Permission | Public | Public or restricted | Public or restricted |
| Immutability | No one can not alter it | Can be altered | Can be altered |
| Efficiency | Low | High | High |
| Centrality | No central authority is required | Partially centralised | Centralised |
| Participation | Permissionless | Permissioned | Permissioned |
| Transactions per Second | 3–20 data writes per second | 1,000 data writes per second | 1,000 data writes per second |

The advanced version of Blockchain 2.0 is called Blockchain 3.0, which places emphasis on providing solutions and services for non-financial applications.

## 13.2.2 How Does Blockchain Work?

Whenever any transaction is wished to be added into blockchain, the validity of that transaction gets checked by dissimilar nodes of networks and only valid blocks get added into blockchain. Steps to add block or transaction into blockchain are shown in Figure 13.8.

The process by which this validation is checked is called consensus mechanism. During consensus mechanism, various nodes execute algorithms to check the signature of blocks and only authenticated blocks are allowed to be added to the blockchain. Miners are nodes which participate in consensus mechanisms, with the process of execution known as mining. There are various popular consensus mechanism like proof of work (PoW), proof of stake (PoS) and practical Byzantine fault tolerance (PBFT). Table 13.4 [24] explains comparison of these mechanisms.

## 13.2.3 Blockchain Platforms

Bitcoin, Hyperledger Fabric, and Ethereum are the most popular blockchain platforms. Throughout a literature survey, it is noticed that most of the systems are designed or proposed either using Ethereum or Hyperledger Fabric as blockchain platform. Table 13.5 shows a comparison of these two popular blockchain platforms. In addition to these platforms, a few more blockchain tools are also available on the market; two of them are described in what follows.

**IOTA [26]:** It is cryptocurrency designed by IOTA foundation in Germany. Its architecture is known as IOTA tangle, which is specially designed for IoT applications. IOTA tangle is public blockchain. It does not have chain,

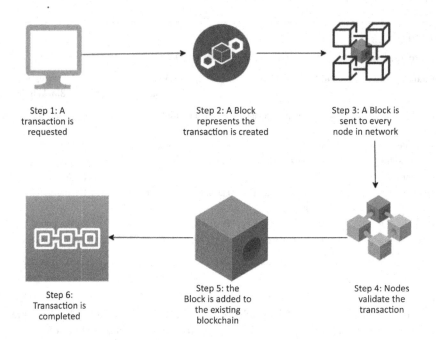

**FIGURE 13.8**  Working of blockchain.

**TABLE 13.4**

**Consensus Used in Blockchain Technology**

| Property | PoW | PoS | PBFT |
|---|---|---|---|
| **Node Management** | Open | Open | Permissioned |
| **Merits** | Provides a secure network | Energy consumption is less compared to PoW; processing of transactions is faster | Noteworthy energy usage reduction compared to PoW and PoS; transactions can be made without need for confirmation |
| **Demerits** | It is expensive as it requires high processing power; electricity consumption is very high | It is less secure than PoW | Due to large communication overhead between nodes, it works with small consensus group sizes; vulnerable to Sybil attacks |
| **Example** | Bitcoin [17] | Ethereum | Hyperledger Fabric [25] |

block, or minors; instead it uses a concept of directed acyclic graph to store
transactions. PoW is used for consensus.

**MultiChain [27]:** It is a private permissioned blockchain. It can be used as
platform to create and deploy private blockchain between different organisations. It uses API to add data. It does not support smart contract implementation [28]

## 13.3   BENEFITS OF INTEGRATING BLOCKCHAIN WITH IoMT

Integration of IoMT with blockchain may have many benefits. Some of them are explained in what follows.

Decentralisation: As mentioned above, miners in blockchain verify the transactions and check their validity and then add the transaction into a distributed ledger, and therefore, no central authority has control over the huge amount of data generated by IoT devices. The decentralised nature of blockchain reduces the cost of installation and maintenance of centralised data storage like cloud. It also eliminates centralised traffic flow, thereby avoid single points of failure associated with it.

Security: IoMT with various heterogeneous devices requires a secured network for untrusted parties, and blockchain can provide it. Hackers are required to hack additional levels of encryption to get access for stored IoMT data. It is impossible to alter the existing data [29].

Anonymity: To process the transactions, miners in network use public address. Its own identity is kept private, i.e., you will get the address of a person but cannot identify with whom who are interacting. Such an environment is suitable for most IoMT applications when user identity needs to be kept private [30, 31].

Digital Trust: The healthcare domain always attracts cybercriminal, and data generated by IoMT wearable devices contain very personal and sensitive information about an individual. According to [32], 63.0% of people use online platforms for medical emergencies; out of these, only 62.4% trust their doctors or caretakers for sharing their data. All the stockholders in the healthcare domain want trust among themselves [33]. According to [34], security, identifiability, and traceability are the factors that must be maintained to achieve digital trust. Digital trust among stakeholders can provide better analysis of data and can also resolve issues of interoperability, i.e., collaboration of data among various organisations for research and other purposes [10].

In addition to this, blockchain with IoMT provides peer-to-peer messaging and file distribution between IoT devices without central authority.

## 13.4   CHALLENGES FOR INTEGRATING BLOCKCHAIN WITH IoMT

Integration of blockchain with IoMT can have many advantages; however, blockchain technology has its own limitations and challenges. Some of them are mentioned in what follows [35, 36].

Scalability: IoMT networks contain large numbers of nodes. During blockchain implementation, every block is broadcast and verified by all miners; this leads to scalability issues, as it increases broadcast traffic and processing overhead as most of the IoT devices have limited bandwidth—this related overhead cannot be traced [37]. In addition to this, blockchain technology requires extremely high computation power which in turn requires higher consumption of electricity and it is not necessary that all stakeholders with multiple users are capable of maintaining decentralised blockchain architecture [10].

**Storage:** As mentioned earlier, IoMT devices produce mammoth amounts of data which need to be processed and stored in blockchain in such a way that integrity of this data can be maintained, which is major challenge. In blockchain technology, all nodes maintain a local copy of data which is impossible by IoMT devices due to their low computational resources and limited storage capacities [38]. Santoshi Nakamoto [17] proposed blockchain technology for financial transactions whereby the size of every transaction was small. Storing large files on-chain is expensive and increases processing speed. In addition, blockchain cannot store abstract data type data like MRI and X-ray images—and hence, scalability and storage issues of blockchain must be taken care to make blockchain more popular [39].

**Selection of Consensus Algorithms:** Selection of consensus algorithms in blockchain for IoMT is quite a challenging task, as consensus mechanisms utilise major resources of participating nodes while the majority of IoMT devices have restricted resources. Table 13.5 shows a comparative study of different consensus mechanisms [37].

**Processing:** Every IoMT device has different computing power. Some are not even able to run cryptographic algorithms at the same speed; on the other hand, processes of mining and cryptography in blockchain require more processing power and time, which can be difficult to manage by resource-constrained IoMT devices [30, 38].

**Real Time:** Most IoMT applications need immediate and real-time response, whereas creation of blocks in blockchain is a time-consuming task. Different blockchain platforms take different block creation times. for example, in Bitcoin blockchain platform [17], block size is 1 MB, and a block is created every ten minutes, whereas in Ethereum, platform expected block time is

**TABLE 13.5**

**Comparison between Ethereum and Hyperledger**

| Characteristics | Ethereum | Hyperledger |
|---|---|---|
| Governance | Ethereum Developer | Linux –Foundation |
| Type of Platform | Public, permission less | Permissioned |
| Scalability | Difficult to scale | Easy to scale |
| Consensus Algorithm | PoW, PoS | PBFT, no-consensus |
| Currency Used | Ether | No currency required |
| Programming Language to Write Smart Contract | Solidity | Go language, Java, Java Script |

10–19 minutes; therefore, selecting the proper blockchain platform is especially important—and to assemble all these data on blocks as per the real-time expectations is really a big challenge.

**Lack of Skills:** As blockchain is recent technology, very few people have enough knowledge and skill about it. In blockchain with IoMT, IoT devices are used everywhere along with blockchain; hence, implementation of this concept is possible only if people are aware about this technology or at least eager to know about it [30].

### 13.4.1 SOLUTION TO HANDLE MEDICAL BIG DATA: OFF-CHAIN STORAGE AND IPFS

**Off-Chain Storage:** IoMT generates huge volumes of data, also called Big Data. Blockchain technology was developed to handle financial transactions, which are small in size. Due to the distributed nature of blockchain, storage of large volumes of data on blockchain slows down the processing speed and initiates scalability issues [40]. In addition to this, blockchain is not able to hold abstract data types, and medical records like X-ray and MRI images cannot be stored on blockchain. Due to the immutable nature of blockchain, no one can delete transactions even if this feature is not required [41]. For example, after getting readings from wearable devices, doctors provide proper lines of treatment and patients are cured. This reading needs not to be stored perpetually, but due to blockchain's immutable nature, no one can delete this information. So, to overcome this issue, Deloitte software has proposed the concept of off-chain storage [39]. Instead of storing everything on-chain, store only standardised data on-chain and maintain the remaining data off-chain in a separate database; encrypt it with any cryptographic algorithms and links associated with that data must be store din blockchain. Advantages of using off-chain storage are as follows.

- Medical data of any size and any format can be stored.
- To achieve interoperability, it is necessary to provide access to restrict data—and this can be achieved through off-chain storage.
- Interoperable blockchain can improve data integrity and protect the digital identities of patients.

**InterPlanetary File System (IPFS) [42]:** Different authors have used various forms of off-chain storage like traditional databases, central servers, cloud, etc. Few authors have used IPFS for data storage. IPFS is designed as protocol to store and access files, various applications, and data in a distributed manner [43]. Whenever any file is stored in IPFS, it is encrypted with cryptographic hash function and can be accessed with help of hash only [44]. Advantages of IPFS over traditional centralised storage systems is that it is a distributed, P2P, content-based file system. Basic difference in centralised storage system and IPFS is that whenever any file is uploaded on centralised storage, the node which uploads file will be provider and other nodes can access that file; whereas in IPFS, all nodes will perform as content providers and even if the original provider fails,

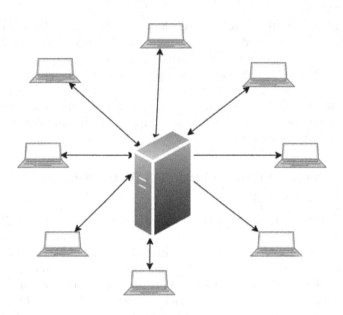

**FIGURE 13.9**   Centralised storage.

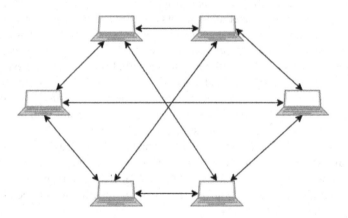

**FIGURE 13.10**   IPFS.

one can access the data. Figure 13.9 and Figure 13.10 explain the concepts of centralised storage and IPFS more clearly.

## 13.5   RELATED STUDIES: BLOCKCHAIN-BASED APPROACHES IN IoMT

Many researchers are working hard and contributing their efforts to develop a perfect blockchain-based solution for healthcare service. This section describes research that is either proposed or implemented blockchain for IoMT.

In [15], the author has used two blockchains; one blockchain is used to store data gathered due to wearable devices, and EMRs are stored in the second blockchain. Machine learning algorithms are used for analysis of collected data and a report of analysis was sent to a doctor to take immediate action. PoS consensus mechanism is used in this proposal.

In [45], authors have formed a cluster of miners, and instead of storing patients' data on each node, data will be stored in each cluster; this will help in data reduction and restrict the participation of all of miners during consensus. Also, to achieve scalability, a central server is used to store collected data and hash of it is stored on-chain. To increase security and efficiency of the network and to reduce network costs, PBFT mechanism is used for consensus.

In [28], a Hyperledger Fabric–based system is proposed for patients' remote healthcare monitoring with the use of two blockchain. The first blockchain is named as "medical device blockchain" and is used to store data produces by wearable devices—chain code is considered part of this blockchain only. The second blockchain is named as "consultation blockchain" and it is used to maintain all the history of the patients records permanently. This blockchain also helps for interoperability of records.

In [46], the author proposed an Ethereum-based architecture to monitor diabetes patients remotely. Smart contracts are used to grant access to authenticated users.

In [47, 48], the author proposed a private Ethereum-based blockchain which is used for managing medical data using smart contracts. To manage access control mechanisms among various participants, Ethereum smart contracts are used. In this system, medical records are encrypted using cryptographic hash function and stored on an external server. Hash associated with medical record is saved on blockchain.

In [49], the author has used the concept of edge nodes and blockchain to provide attribute-based access control to electronic health data. To note the genuine access events and to execute smart contracts, concepts of blockchain are used. Edge nodes are used to store electronic health data. Hyperledger Fabric composer is used as a blockchain platform. XACML polity is used in this research.

In [50], the author mentioned that integration of IoT and blockchain is possible only if scalability issues for ledger and transaction execution rate in blockchain are handled properly. To restrict the number of transactions entering blockchain, use of a local peer network is proposed. In this proposal, Hyperledger Fabric framework is used.

In [51], the author introduces the concept of a centralised manager and overlay in lightweight scalable blockchain. In this proposal, centralised manager is used to handle the blockchain and store all transactions locally. It integrates various optimisation techniques which include different algorithms which ensure that this proposal is resistant against 12 various cyber security attacks; however, how to handle issue of scalability and storage at advanced levels are not mentioned in this research.

In [52], the author proposed an optimised, lightweight blockchain-base framework with the name BIoMT. Implementation or evaluation of this proposal is not mentioned in this research, which consists of the following four levels.

**Device Layer:** This layer consists of all medical devices which are used to collect healthcare data like sensors, wearable devices, etc. Elliptic curve cryptography is used at this layer for providing data privacy.

**Facility Layer:** Facility layer is used for managing IoMT devices and the concept of bolster is used in this layer. A bolster is used as gateway which provides unique identity to devices based on their attributes.

**Cloud Layer:** This layer provides storage support. It gathers the data and forms an identical block. The user can request data by providing block number and hash of the block, which is known to authenticated users only.

**Cluster Layer:** Various medical facilities, cloud servers, and service provider are grouped together and form a cluster. Every cluster has one cluster head who communicates with other cluster heads; this will decrease the network overhead and delay, and it forms a distributed network that relates to blockchain. In this proposal, data is encrypted before storing it onto the cloud, and hash associate with it is placed on blockchain.

In [3], EMRs are uploaded by healthcare provider and data is uploaded on blockchain. PoW is used as consensus mechanism. All data is stored on-chain, and hence may face issues of scalability, which is considered as future implementation task by the authors. As everything is stored on-chain, it will increase burden to broadcast traffic and processing overhead, which are not discussed. Also, there are many disadvantages of using PoW, like energy consumption, which are not mentioned

In [53], authors have implemented an IoMT cloud-based framework which is used to monitor the progress of a neurological disorder. Wearable sensors are used to collect the data. The cloud is used as off-chain storage, and generated data is stored in encrypted format in the cloud. Ethereum smart contracts are used to share data among various parties, and a mobile application is developed to access data stored in the cloud. However, technical details regarding deployment of blockchain on Amazon Cloud was not clearly stated.

Tables 13.6 and 13.7 show the comparative studies of various existing systems.

## 13.6  RESEARCH GAPS IN INTEGRATION OF BLOCKCHAIN IN IoMT

This literature survey shows that there are significant research gaps that need to be addressed to integrate blockchain with IoMT successfully. A few prominent gaps are mentioned in what follows.

1. Not a single framework has focused on data retention [55]; i.e., how long the patient's records are stored. For example, In Australia, adults' records are maintained for at least seven years after record generation, whereas for minors, medical records are maintained until their age of 25 [56].
2. Most of the proposed models are patient-centric, which means patients have full access to and control of their data, but a limitation of such systems is that many patients are neither computer experts nor aware of what type of

**TABLE 13.6**
**Analysis of Various Existing Systems**

| Research ID | [15] | [54] | [45] | [28] |
|---|---|---|---|---|
| Access Control (Role Based/ Attribute-Based) | Patient-centric; others can view | Both | Yes, but completely patient-centric | Yes |
| Interoperability | Partial (within boundary) | Yes (using FHIR) | No | Yes |
| Integrity | Yes | Yes | Yes | Yes |
| Data Provenance | Yes | Yes | Yes | Yes |
| Scalability | Yes | Yes | Yes | Yes |
| Database Used (On-Chain or Off-chain Data) | Cloud | SQL Lite | Central server | Remote database and on-chain data |
| Consensus Mechanism | PoS | PoW (Ether is required) | PBFT | PBFT |
| Data Collection | Wearable device and EMR | EMR | Wearable devices | Manual and wearable device |

**TABLE 13.7**
**Analysis of Various Already Existing Systems**

| Paper ID | [46] | [47] | [49] |
|---|---|---|---|
| Access Control (Role-Based/Attribute-Based) | Yes | Yes | Attribute-based access control |
| Interoperability | Yes | Yes | Within institutional boundaries |
| Integrity | Yes | Yes | Yes |
| Data Provenance | Yes | Yes | Yes |
| Scalability | Yes | Yes | Yes |
| Database Used (On-Chain or Off-Chain Data) | Cloud | Local database | Edge node |
| Blockchain Platform used | Ethereum blockchain | Ethereum blockchain | Hyperledger Fabrics |
| Data Collection | Wearable devices | Manual (EHR) | Sensors are used |

information should be shared with whom and when it should be shared, which may result in inefficient healthcare services [55, 57].

3. IoT and blockchain are the leading domains. Integration of these technologies has attracted many researchers. Researchers have proposed various solutions for adopting blockchain in IoMT; however, most of the existing research do not mention technical details thoroughly [38, 59].

4. Many researchers are storing basic information of individual on-chain, which will be immutable in blockchain; however, according to Article 17 Section 2 of the European Union's General Data Protection Regulation (GDPR), individual personal information should be mutable. Therefore, there is a need to obtain consent before storing and analysing any confidential data of individuals. With proper smart contracts, this problem can be resolved, but very few authors have taken care about addressing this [10].

5. Interoperability in the healthcare domain means that healthcare data should be shared among various stakeholders for analysis and research within and across institutional boundaries, but it is challenging to attain interoperability due the complexities of data [60]. Many researchers claim that they have handled issues of interoperability; however, to what extend this data is shared is not mentioned anywhere.

## 13.7 CONCLUSION

This chapter first describes the working of cloud-based IoMT systems and focuses on their main limitation: i.e., single-point failure, security, and privacy of generated data. It then explains why there is a need for blockchain technology and elaborates basic concepts required to understand blockchain technology and features of blockchain technology that can overcome limitations of cloud-based IoMT. Further, this chapter focuses on benefits of integrating blockchain to IoMT. This chapter has provided challenges that should be addressed to achieve successful integration of blockchain with IoMT. To resolve scalability issues, on-chain and off-chain storage, along with a distributed file system (IPFS), is also discussed. In addition to this existing literature, applications have been reviewed—and after comparing and analysing, research gaps have been identified and mentioned in the chapter. During the literature survey, it is observed that security of healthcare data is the only concern that is taken into consideration by most of the researchers while adopting blockchain with IoMT. Many the researchers focus on providing privacy, integrity, and confidentiality to healthcare data. There can be various areas in the healthcare domain where IoMT—along with blockchain—can be used, but the majority of researchers have given preference only to implementing remote patient monitoring. Very few researchers have taken efforts to resolve issues of scalability and interoperability. Comparison of implemented or proposed systems with already existing systems is hardly mentioned in any research.

To summarise, this chapter gives extensive views on the current position of ongoing research, and by identifying research gaps, it provides prominent direction for integrating blockchain with IoMT.

## REFERENCES

[1] Ruby Dwivedi, Divya Mehrotra, and Shaleen Chandra. (2021). "Potential of Internet of Medical Things (IoMT) Applications in Building a Smart Healthcare System: A Systematic Review." *Journal of Oral Biology and Craniofacial Research*, vol. 12, no. 2, pp. 302–318. DOI: 10.1016/j.jobcr.2021.11.010.

[2] S.P. Amaraweera, and M.N. Halgamuge. (2019). "Internet of Things in the Healthcare Sector: Overview of Security and Privacy Issues." *Security, Privacy, and Trust in the IoT Environment*, pp. 153–179.

[3] N. Dilawar, M. Rizwan, F. Ahmad, and S. Akram. (2019). "Blockchain: Securing Internet of Medical Things (IoMT)." *International Journal of Advanced Computer Science and Applications*, vol. 10, no. 1, pp. 82–89.

[4] A. Verma, P. Bhattacharya, D. Saraswat, S. Tanwar, N. Kumar, and R. Sharma. (2023). "SanJeeVni: Secure UAV-Envisioned Massive Vaccine Distribution for COVID-19 Underlying 6G Network." *IEEE Sensors Journal*, vol. 23, no. 2, pp. 955–968. DOI: 10.1109/JSEN.2022.3188929.

[5] A. Verma, P. Bhattacharya, M. Zuhair, S. Tanwar, and N. Kumar. (2021). "Vacochain: Blockchain-Based 5G-Assisted UAV Vaccine Distribution Scheme for Future Pandemics." *IEEE Journal of Biomedical and Health Informatics*, vol. 26, no. 5, pp. 1997–2007.

[6] D. Saraswat, P. Bhattacharya, A. Verma, V.K. Prasad, S. Tanwar, G. Sharma, P.N. Bokoro, and R. Sharma. (2022). "Explainable AI for Healthcare 5.0: Opportunities and Challenges." *IEEE Access*, vol. 10, pp. 84486–84517. DOI: 10.1109/ACCESS. 2022.3197671.

[7] M. Zuhair, F. Patel, D. Navapara, P. Bhattacharya, and D. Saraswat. (April 2021). "BloCoV6: A Blockchain-Based 6G-Assisted UAV Contact Tracing Scheme for COVID-19 Pandemic." *2021 2nd International Conference on Intelligent Engineering and Management (ICIEM)*, pp. 271–276.

[8] V.K. Prasad, P. Bhattacharya, M. Bhavsar, A. Verma, S. Tanwar, G. Sharma, Pitshou N. Bokoro, and R. Sharma. (2022). "ABV-CoViD: An Ensemble Forecasting Model to Predict Availability of Beds and Ventilators for COVID-19 Like Pandemics." *IEEE Access*, vol. 10, pp. 74131–74151.

[9] A. Verma, P. Bhattacharya, Y. Patel, K. Shah, S. Tanwar, and B. Khan. (2022). "Data Localization and Privacy-Preserving Healthcare for Big Data Applications: Architecture and Future Directions." In *Emerging Technologies for Computing, Communication and Smart Cities* (pp. 233–244). Springer, Singapore.

[10] Md Mehedi Hassan Onik, Satyabrata Aich, Jinhong Yang, Chul-Soo Kim, and Hee-Cheol Kim. (2019). "Blockchain in Healthcare: Challenges and Solutions." In *Big Data Analytics for Intelligent Healthcare Management* (pp. 197–226). Academic Press, Cambridge.

[11] Harnessing the Power of Data in Health, Stanford Medicine 2017 Health Trends Report. (2017). https://med.stanford.edu/content/dam/sm/sm-news/documents/Stanford MedicineHealthTrendsWhitePaper2017.pdf.

[12] Guardian. (2018). "Top 10 Biggest Healthcare Data Breaches of All Time." https://digi talguardian.com/blog/top-10-biggest-healthcare-data-breaches-all-time.

[13] Elizabeth Snell. (2017). "41% of Health Data Breaches Stem from Unintended Disclosure." https://healthitsecurity.com/news/41-of-health-data-breaches-stem-from-unintended-disclosure.

[14] www.hipaajournal.com/december-2021-healthcare-data-breach-report/.

[15] Sabyasachi Chakraborty, Satyabrata Aich, and Hee-Cheol Kim. (February 2019). "A Secure Healthcare System Design Framework Using Blockchain Technology." *International Conference on Advanced Communications Technology (ICACT)*. http://www.wikicfp.com/cfp/servlet/event.showcfp?eventid=165772&copyownerid= 170537.

[16] Wencheng Sun, Zhiping Cai, Yangyang Li, Fang Liu, Shengqun Fang, and Guoyan Wang. (2018). "Security and Privacy in the Medical Internet of Things: A Review." *Security and Communication Networks*. DOI: 10.1155/2018/5978636.

[17] Nakamoto Satoshi. (2008). "Bitcoin: A Peer-to-Peer Electronic Cash System." *Decentralized Business Review*, p. 21260.

[18] Zibin Zheng, Shaoan Xie, Hongning Dai, Xiangping Chen, and Huaimin Wang. (2017). "An Overview of Blockchain Technology: Architecture, Consensus, and Future Trends." *2017 IEEE International Congress on Big Data (BigData Congress)*, pp. 557–564.

[19] Bhaskara S. Egala, Ashok K. Pradhan, Venkataramana Badarla, and Saraju P. Mohanty. (2021). "Fortified-Chain: A Blockchain-Based Framework for Security and Privacy-Assured Internet of Medical Things with Effective Access Control." *IEEE Internet of Things Journal*, vol. 8, no. 14, pp. 11717–11731.

[20] Tsung-Ting Kuo, Hugo Zavaleta Rojas, and Lucila Ohno-Machado. (2019). "Comparison of Blockchain Platforms: A Systematic Review and Healthcare Examples." *Journal of the American Medical Informatics Association*, vol. 26, no. 5, pp. 462–478.

[21] Pranalini Joshi, and Prasad Gokhale. (2021). "Electronic Health Record Using Blockchain and Off Chain Storage: A Systematic Review." *Information Technology in Industry*, vol. 9, no. 1, pp. 247–253.

[22] Vitalik Buterin. (2014). "A Next-Generation Smart Contract and Decentralized Application Platform." *White Paper*, vol. 3, no. 37.

[23] P. Bhattacharya, S. Tanwar, U. Bodkhe, S. Tyagi, and N. Kumar. (1 April–June 2021). "BinDaaS: Blockchain-Baseds Deep-Learning as-a-Service in Healthcare 4.0 Applications." *IEEE Transactions on Network Science and Engineering*, vol. 8, no. 2, pp. 1242–1255. DOI: 10.1109/TNSE.2019.2961932.

[24] Haider Dhia Zubaydi, Yung-Wey Chong, Kwangman Ko, Sabri M. Hanshi, and Shankar Karuppayah. (2019). "A Review on the Role of Blockchain Technology in the Healthcare Domain." *Electronics*, vol. 8, no. 6, p. 679.

[25] Elli Androulaki, Artem Barger, Vita Bortnikov, Christian Cachin, Konstantinos Christidis, Angelo De Caro, David Enyeart, C. Ferris, G. Laventman, Y. Manevich, and S. Muralidharan. (2018). "Hyperledger Fabric: A Distributed Operating System for Permissioned Blockchains." arXiv:1801.10228(1801). https://arxiv.org/pdf/1801.10228.

[26] Serguei Popov. (2017). "The Tangle." Technical Report. IOTA. https://assets.ctfassets.net/r1dr6vzfxhev/2t4uxvsIqk0EUau6g2sw0g/45eae33637ca92f85dd9f4a3a218e1ec/iota1_4_3.pdf.

[27] Gideon Greenspan. (2015). "Multichain Private Blockchain-White Paper." www.multichain.com/download/MultiChain-White-Paper. pdf.

[28] Oumaima Attia, Ines Khoufi, Anis Laouiti, and Cedric Adjih. (2019). "An IoT-Blockchain Architecture Based on Hyperledger Framework for Health Care Monitoring Application." *NTMS 2019–10th IFIP International Conference on New Technologies, Mobility and Security*, pp. 1–5. IEEE, Canary Islands, Spain.

[29] Christian Esposito, Alfredo De Santis, Genny Tortora, Henry Chang, and Kim-Kwang Raymond Choo. (2018). "Blockchain: A Panacea for Healthcare Cloud-Based Data Security and Privacy." *IEEE Cloud Computing*, vol. 5, no. 1, pp. 31–37.

[30] Hany F. Atlam, Ahmed Alenezi, Madini O. Alassafi, and Gary B. Wills. (2018). "Blockchain with Internet of Things: Benefits, Challenges, and Future Directions." *International Journal of Intelligent Systems & Applications*, vol. 10, no. 6.

[31] S. Banerjee, Vanga Odelu, Ashok Kumar Das, Samiran Chattopadhyay, Neeraj Kumar, Yongho Park, and Sudeep Tanwar. (2018). "Design of an Anonymity-Preserving Group Formation Based Authentication Protocol in Global Mobility Networks." *IEEE Access*, vol. 6, pp. 20673–20693. DOI: 10.1109/ACCESS.2018.2827027.

[32] Bradford W. Hesse, David E. Nelson, Gary L. Kreps, Robert T. Croyle, Neeraj K. Arora, Barbara K. Rimer, and Kasisomayajula Viswanath. (2005). "Trust and Sources of Health Information: The Impact of the Internet and Its Implications for Health Care Providers: Findings from the First Health Information National Trends Survey." *Archives of Internal Medicine*, vol. 165, no. 22, pp. 2618–2624.

[33] Indumathi Jayaraman, and Mokhtar Mohammed. (2020). "Secure Privacy Conserving Provable Data Possession (SPC-PDP) Framework." *Information Systems and e-Business Management*, vol. 18, no. 3, pp. 351–377.

[34] Juri Mattila. (2016). "The Blockchain Phenomenon." *Berkeley Roundtable of the International Economy*, vol. 16.

[35] Mayra Samaniego, and Ralph Deters. (2018). "Zero-Trust Hierarchical Management in IoT." *2018 IEEE International Congress on Internet of Things (ICIOT)*, pp. 88–95.

[36] Joel J.P.C. Rodrigues, Dante Borges De Rezende Segundo, Heres Arantes Junqueira, Murilo Henrique Sabino, Rafael Maciel Prince, Jalal Al-Muhtadi, and Victor Hugo C. De Albuquerque. (2018). "Enabling Technologies for the Internet of Health Things." *IEEE Access*, vol. 6, pp. 13129–13141.

[37] Scalable Blockchain for Internet of Things (IoT)—Trusted Networks Lab. https:// research.qut.edu.au/trustednetworks/projects/scalable-blockchain/.

[38] Fatma Ellouze, Ghofrane Fersi, and Mohamed Jmaiel. (2020). "Blockchain for Internet of Medical Things: A Technical Review." In *International Conference on Smart Homes and Health Telematics* (pp. 259–267). Springer, Cham.

[39] R.J. Krawiec, Dan Housman, Mark White, Mariya Filipova, Florian Quarre, Dan Barr, and Allen Nesbitt. (2016). "Blockchain: Opportunities for Health Care." *Proceedings of NIST Workshop Blockchain Healthcare*, pp. 1–16.

[40] Sahshanu Razdan, and Sachin Sharma. (2021). "Internet of Medical Things (IoMT): Overview, Emerging Technologies, and Case Studies." *IETE Technical Review*, pp. 1–14.

[41] Mahender Kumar, and Satish Chand. (2021). "MedHypChain: A Patient-Centered Interoperability Hyperledger-Based Medical Healthcare System: Regulation in COVID-19 Pandemic." *Journal of Network and Computer Applications*, vol. 179, p. 102975.

[42] Juan Benet. (2014). "IPFS-Content Addressed, Versioned, p2p File System." arXiv: 1407.3561. https://arxiv.org/pdf/1407.3561.pdf.

[43] R. Gupta, Arpit Shukla, Parimal Mehta, Pronaya Bhattacharya, Sudeep Tanwar, Sudhanshu Tyagi, and Neeraj Kumar. (2020). "VAHAK: A Blockchain-Based Outdoor Delivery Scheme Using UAV for Healthcare 4.0 Services." *IEEE INFOCOM 2020 — IEEE Conference on Computer Communications Workshops (INFOCOM WKSHPS)*, pp. 255–260. DOI: 10.1109/INFOCOMWKSHPS50562.2020.9162738.

[44] Randhir Kumar, Ningrinla Marchang, and Rakesh Tripathi. (2020). "Distributed Off-Chain Storage of Patient Diagnostic Reports in Healthcare System Using IPFS and Blockchain." *2020 International Conference on Communication Systems & Networks (COMSNETS)*, pp. 1–5.

[45] Koosha Mohammad Hossein, Mohammad Esmaeil Esmaeili, and Tooska Dargahi. (2019). "Blockchain-Based Privacy-Preserving Healthcare Architecture." *2019 IEEE Canadian Conference of Electrical and Computer Engineering (CCECE)*, pp. 1–4.

[46] M. Saravanan, R. Shubha, Achsah Mary Marks, and Vishakh Iyer. (2017). "SMEAD: A Secured Mobile Enabled Assisting Device for Diabetics Monitoring." *2017 IEEE International Conference on Advanced Networks and Telecommunications Systems (ANTS)*, pp. 1–6.

[47] Asma Khatoon. (2020). "A Blockchain-Based Smart Contract System for Healthcare Management." *Electronics*, vol. 9, no. 1, p. 94.

[48] Ayesha Shahnaz, Usman Qamar, and Ayesha Khalid. (2019). "Using Blockchain for Electronic Health Records." *IEEE Access*, vol. 7, pp. 147782–147795.

[49] Hao Guo, Wanxin Li, Mark Nejad, and Chien-Chung Shen. (2019). "Access Control for Electronic Health Records with Hybrid Blockchain-Edge Architecture." *2019 IEEE International Conference on Blockchain (Blockchain)*, pp. 44–51. IEEE, Atlanta, GA, USA.

[50] Sujit Biswas, Kashif Sharif, Fan Li, Boubakr Nour, and Yu Wang. (2018). "A Scalable Blockchain Framework for Secure Transactions in IoT." *IEEE Internet of Things Journal*, vol. 6, no. 3, pp. 4650–4659.

[51] A. Dorri, S.S. Kanhere, R. Jurdak, and P. Gauravaram. (2017). "LSB: A Lightweight Scalable Blockchain for IoT Security and Privacy." *Journal of Parallel and Distributed Computing*, vol. 134.

[52] Mohamed Seliem, and Khalid Elgazzar. (2019). "BIoMT: Blockchain for the Internet of Medical Things." *2019 IEEE International Black Sea Conference on Communications and Networking (BlackSeaCom)*, pp. 1–4.

[53] Dinh C. Nguyen, Khoa D. Nguyen, and Pubudu N. Pathirana. (2019). "A Mobile Cloud Based IOMT Framework for Automated Health Assessment and Management." *2019 41st Annual International Conference of the IEEE Engineering in Medicine and Biology Society (EMBC)*, pp. 6517–6520.

[54] Asaph Azaria, Ariel Ekblaw, Thiago Vieira, and Andrew Lippman. (2016). "Medrec: Using Blockchain for Medical Data Access and Permission Management." *2016 2nd International Conference on Open and Big Data (OBD)*, pp. 25–30.

[55] Qianyu Wang, and Shaowen Qin. (2021). "A Hyperledger Fabric-Based System Framework for Healthcare Data Management." *Applied Sciences*, vol. 11, no. 24, p. 11693.

[56] Christine M. O'Keefe, and Chris Connolly. (2011). "Regulation and Perception Concerning the Use of Health Data for Research in Australia." *Electronic Journal of Health Informatics*, vol. 6, no. 2, p. 16.

[57] Amirhossein Adavoudi Jolfaei, Seyed Farhad Aghili, and Dave Singelee. (2021). "A Survey on Blockchain-Based IoMT Systems: Towards Scalability." *IEEE Access*, vol. 9, pp. 148948–148975.

[58] https://www2.deloitte.com/ch/en/pages/innovation/articles/blockchain-accelerate-iot-adoption.html

[59] Sofia Alexaki, George Alexandris, Vasilis Katos, and Nikolaos E. Petroulakis. (2018). "Blockchain-Based Electronic Patient Records for Regulated Circular Healthcare Jurisdictions." *2018 IEEE 23rd International Workshop on Computer Aided Modeling and Design of Communication Links and Networks (CAMAD)*, pp. 1–6.

[60] Kevin Peterson, Rammohan Deeduvanu, Pradip Kanjamala, and Kelly Boles. "A Blockchain-Based Approach to Health Information Exchange Networks." https://www.healthit.gov/sites/default/files/12-55-blockchain-based-approach-final.pdf.

# Index